Taxation in Tibetan Societies

Brill's Tibetan Studies Library

Edited by

Henk Blezer (*Leiden University*)
Alex McKay (*University of London*)
Charles Ramble (*École Pratique des Hautes Études – PSL, Paris*)

VOLUME 53

The titles published in this series are listed at *brill.com/btsl*

Taxation in Tibetan Societies

Rules, Practices and Discourses

Edited by

Alice Travers
Peter Schwieger
Charles Ramble

TUTA SUB AEGIDE PALLAS · 1683 ·

BRILL

LEIDEN | BOSTON

Cover illustration: Lhasa: Woman carrying stones (Lhasa, Bundesarchiv, image 135-BB-088-09, Photo: Beger, Bruno 1938/1939)

Library of Congress Cataloging-in-Publication Data

Names: Travers, Alice, editor. | Schwieger, Peter, editor. | Ramble, Charles, editor.
Title: Taxation in Tibetan societies : rules, practices and discourses / edited by Alice Travers, Peter Schwieger, Charles Ramble.
Description: Leiden ; Boston : Brill, [2023] | Series: Brill's Tibetan studies library, 1568-6183 ; volume 53 | Includes bibliographical references and index.
Identifiers: LCCN 2022040144 (print) | LCCN 2022040145 (ebook) | ISBN 9789004518339 (hardback ; alk. paper) | ISBN 9789004529465 (ebook)
Subjects: LCSH: Taxation—China—Tibet—History.
Classification: LCC HJ2989.T39 T39 2023 (print) | LCC HJ2989.T39 (ebook) | DDC 336.200951/5—dc23/eng/20221014
LC record available at https://lccn.loc.gov/2022040144
LC ebook record available at https://lccn.loc.gov/2022040145

Typeface for the Latin, Greek, and Cyrillic scripts: "Brill". See and download: brill.com/brill-typeface.

ISSN 1568-6183
ISBN 978-90-04-51833-9 (hardback)
ISBN 978-90-04-52946-5 (e-book)

Contents

Note on the Transliteration and Transcription of Tibetan Names and Terms

Publications in the field of Tibetan Studies that are intended for a non-specialist readership commonly use simplified, roughly phonetic schemes for rendering Tibetan names and terms. While we concede that—as the dearth of publications suggests—taxation may be an esoteric field even for the specialists, it is also true that it is likely to be of interest for comparativists from outside the domain of Tibetan Studies. With this in mind, we have attempted to enhance the readability of the contributions by rendering proper nouns—the names of people, places and certain institutions—in phonetic form, generally followed, at their first appearance, by a Wylie orthographic rendering. The homogenisation of such accessible presentations of Tibetan terms has made an important advance thanks to the Simplified Phonetic Transcription of Standard Tibetan developed by David Germano, Nicolas Tournadre and the Tibetan and Himalayan Library. As helpful as this system may be, however, we have elected not to follow it rigorously, partly at least because it reproduces a relatively confined Central Tibetan pronunciation, and the cases examined in this volume encompass a vast territorial range. Furthermore, in keeping with the preference for readability over consistency we have favoured forms of names that have become well-established in English-language works (Shigatse, Tashi Lhunpo, Temisgang, Jyekundo), and in certain cases have omitted Wylie renderings when these have been deemed unnecessary or indeterminate (Lhasa, Dalai, Panchen, Leh, Mustang). In a very few cases—such as in the tables in Isabelle Henrion-Dourcy's contribution, we have retained only the orthographic form in order to avoid crowding the cells. Personal names that feature only as authors of Tibetan-language publications are likewise presented only in transliteration.

Figures and Maps

Figures

Maps

Tables

Introduction

Far from being just one particular technical and financial aspect of its administration, the fiscal structure of a country reflects the state of a society and the nature of political power. As underlined by Delalande and Spire (2010), who chose to approach taxation as an indicator of the relationship between the state and its citizens, taxation is a social fact whose history is part of a broader process that has, in the European context, accompanied the construction of the nation-state, explaining why a number of classical authors of social sciences have given taxes a prominent place:

> For Norbert Elias, the establishment of a tax monopoly constitutes an essential stage in the "sociogenesis of the state", marked by struggles against the growing demands of the central power; under the monarchy, the multiplication of taxes generated a great deal of opposition and resistance, but these in turn helped to establish state centralisation (Elias 1969). In his analysis of the mode of bureaucratic domination, Max Weber also attaches great importance to taxation: taxes are both the means by which capitalism makes bureaucracy possible, and the means by which a state can regulate its economy (Weber 1921: 230 and 368). [...] Charles Tilly has theorised the emergence of the sovereign state from war, analysed as a phenomenon that reinforces the constraint of taxation while increasing the legitimacy of the monarch (Tilly 1990). All these authors have in common that they conceive of taxes as a factor and a revealer of the relations between state and society: taxes are an institution that is inseparably political and social, which participates in power relations and shapes social relations. This postulate is corroborated by historians of the Middle Ages and the modern era, who have made it possible to understand much more precisely the social conditions in which the state managed to establish its domination through taxation (Guéry 1984; Hincker 1971). As early as the 19th century, Tocqueville had placed the tax issue at the heart of his analysis of the relationship between the Ancien Régime and the Revolution: by reaching not those most capable of paying it but those most incapable of defending themselves against it, the tax would have increased the separation between social classes and accentuated the divisions within each of them, to the point of producing a "sort of collective individualism" (Tocqueville 1856: 158).
>
> DELALANDE AND SPIRE 2010: 3, translated from French

 | DOI:10.1163/9789004529465_002

There are obvious discrepancies displayed by the cultural and historical context of Tibetan societies from the 17th to the 20th century compared to the Western context in which these considerations have been raised. To start with, before 1959 Tibetans were not citizens, but rather subjects of a variety of rulers across the areas of Tibetan culture; the majority of these were the subjects of the largest centralised political power in premodern and modern Tibet: the Ganden Phodrang (dGa' ldan pho brang; 1642–1959). However, the study of taxation in Tibet is also instrumental for understanding the history of the construction of the various Tibetan polities and the Ganden Phodrang state. In particular, the dominant role of religion in pre-modern Tibetan societies and the hierocratic nature of a number of rulers or of the summit of the government hierarchy, for the Ganden Phodrang, is likely to have weighed in a specific manner on the relationship of the Tibetan subjects to their respective rulers, and thus on the way they envisaged and lived taxation: as some chapters in this volume will illustrate, representations related to other types of prestations, such as religious donations, sometimes appear in accounts of and discourses on taxation in the Tibetan context. However, the concept of taxation was clearly expressed in the Tibetan terminology by the word *khral*, which encompassed both payments in money or in kind and corvée labour, and conveyed the idea, as in any other state, of these payments and services being imposed by the state on its subjects as a compulsory obligation.

The study of taxation, a multifaceted phenomenon, is thus fundamental in the political and social history of Tibetan societies for a better understanding of the construction of the various Tibetan polities and in particular of the Ganden Phodrang state; the nature of the power of these often religious states and of their relationships with their subjects—and thus the possible specificities of taxation in a Tibetan context; and finally, its consequences for social stratification. It was therefore integrated from the outset into the research programme of the ANR-DFG project "The Social History of Tibetan Societies, 17th–20th centuries" (SHTS, 2012–2016). Preliminary reflections on the topic were made at a conference that was held in Fontainebleau on 6–7 December 2013, entitled "'When the Taxman Cometh': Tax, Corvée and Community Obligations in Tibetan Societies", in which earlier drafts of some of the chapters contained in this volume were presented and discussed. Over the years, the initial set of studies was enriched by additional contributions, with the aim of presenting the broadest possible overview of the current state of the art on the topic of taxation in Tibetan societies.

Well before the inception of the SHTS project, this field of knowledge had been solidly established in a body of in-depth scholarship, produced mainly by three authors: Melvyn Goldstein, Wangchen Gelek Surkhang and Paljor

Tsarong (Goldstein 1968, 1971a and b, 1986; Surkhang [1966] 1984 and 1986; and Tsarong 1998a and 1998b). These works present the particularity of having primarily focused on one specific Tibetan taxation system, notably the regime that prevailed for arable land in Central Tibet within the Ganden Phodrang's territory during the first part of the 20th century. Not only do these studies outline the general principles and particular features of this rather complex system, and document its abundant terminology, but in the case of Goldstein's work also provide an exhaustive description of the set of taxes that were applied in one particular locality, within this arable farming area of Central Tibet, i.e. the village of Samada (Tib. Sa ma mda') in Gyantse district (rGyal rtse rdzong) (Goldstein 1968 and 1971a). Goldstein's work in particular clearly pointed to the fact that fiscal rules and their resulting categories of taxpayers both mirrored and produced social inequalities in Tibet.

These studies are far too detailed to be summarised here (and are considered in detail in several contributions to this volume), but a few significant features of the tax system as it existed in this particular place and time may be mentioned here: taxes (both civil and military) were for the most part, but not only, based on land (i.e. levied in exchange for the right to cultivate land) and calculated according to that land basis (*khral rten*); they were divided into outer (*phyi khral*) and inner taxes (*nang khral*) ("outer taxes" referring to taxes paid to or performed for the central government and "inner taxes" denoting taxes paid to or performed for one's immediate lord, monastic or private/aristocratic); they were "paid" to the Ganden Phodrang government either in kind—less frequently in money—(*lag 'don*) or in the form of corvée labour (*rkang 'gro*), which covered a significant variety of services; taxes were collected at the estate (*gzhis ka*) and then district level (*rdzong*), partly retained to support the local officials, and partly sent to the various treasuries and offices in Lhasa (see the two examples studied by Tsarong 1998a and 1998b), or else directly distributed to various beneficiaries. Dependent peasants (*mi ser*) owed these taxes to their landlord (either monastic, aristocratic or the government) and were divided into different categories of taxpayers, categories that were related to a variety of rights and obligations that built a specific social ladder. Taxes were calculated according to successive land settlements (*zhib gzhung*), that have been further studied in more recent publications by Kalsang Norbu Gurung (Gurung 2013 and 2017).

Because of the complexity of the topic, the technical way of calculating the taxes, the variety of the units of measurement involved, the nature of the various items taxed, as well as the large variety of tax rules, not only within the territories administered by the Ganden Phodrang government but also at its periphery, the topic of Tibetan taxation is far from exhausted. The present volume elaborates on the foundational scholarship outlined above in order to supplement our understanding of taxation in Tibetan societies and to take the analysis in new directions with the help of unexploited sources, notably archives, a Chinese government survey from the 1950s, as well as unexploited autobiographical (both oral and written) sources.

The volume examines taxation in Tibetan societies from a variety of perspectives and scales: it includes renewed attempts to present the Ganden Phodrang's taxation system based on new sources (first part); it documents in detail local systems within the Ganden Phodrang that were less well known (second part); it analyses particular types of taxes (third part); and finally, it studies taxation in Tibetan areas at the outer periphery of the Ganden Phodrang's territory (fourth part).

By documenting multiple Tibetan tax systems, the objective is not to make the "often byzantine hodgepodge of taxes" (to quote Nancy Levine, in this volume) that characterised most Tibetan fiscal contexts seem even more complex. Rather, the volume pursues two objectives. The first is to advance our understanding of the way taxation was organised from an institutional point of view and our understanding of the technical terminology related to taxation. This is made possible by a significant number of translations from Tibetan sources and also the index of Tibetan terminology at the end of the volume. The second, in line with previous endeavours of the SHTS project (Ramble, Schwieger and Travers 2013), is to put the stress on the experience of taxpayers themselves, on their representation of the tax system, and on the way they lived it and considered it.

The first chapter, by Peter Schwieger, provides a general overview of the taxation system in Central and Eastern Tibet based on surveys conducted by the Chinese authorities in the 1950s and published in 1986 in Chinese and in 1991 in Tibetan under the title *Bod ljongs spyi bshad*, a source that has so far attracted little scholarly attention and of which extended passages are here translated into English. It shows that the tax burden for the peasants and nomads in Tibet—no matter whether Central or East Tibet—was enormous, and that the greatest portion of the collected taxes was spent on clerical institutions and religious purposes.

Kalsang Norbu Gurung proposes an analysis of taxation in the 19th and 20th centuries based on the *Bod ljongs spyi bshad* as well as on the 1830 *Iron-Tiger Land Settlement* (*lCags stag zhib gzhung*) and other Tibetan archival sources. It presents the twelve "central" offices involved in the tax collecting process and aims to understand the variety of tax obligations to the Ganden Phodrang government, highlighting the difference between what was officially due and what was effectively levied as far as can be discerned from archival sources, ultimately pointing to the fact that the latter exceeded the former and also to the sheer inequality in the burden of taxes supported by the various categories of taxpayers.

The second part of the volume provides an insight into taxation in less studied areas of the Ganden Phodrang territory. Alice Travers analyses and translates parts of an autobiographical account authored by a former agent in the tax collecting process in Ngamring district (Ngam ring *rdzong*), published in 1994 in the Tibet Autonomous Region, as part of the collection entitled *Bod kyi lo rgyus rig gnas dpyad gzhi'i rgyu cha bdams bsgrigs* (lit. "Selection of Source Materials for the Study of Tibetan History and Culture"). This account has the triple advantage of furnishing new data on taxation in an area that was administratively under the semi-autonomous Tashi Lhunpo *labrang*; casting a critical eye on the tax collecting process and on the excesses of a system that gave tax collectors much opportunity for enrichment; and lastly, discussing attempts made by the Tibetan government in the 1950s to resolve this problem by reforming the tax collection system.

Nancy Levine focuses on the western province of Ngari (mNga' ris), whose taxation system has been only partly considered by Surkhang (1986). Based on interviews conducted in 1990, the chapter uses oral sources to stress, in the most exhaustive way possible, the numerous specificities of the taxation rules and their related terminology in four villages of the Western province, Ruthog (Ru thog), Tholing (mTho lding) in Guge (Gu ge), Purang (sPu hreng), and Khochar (Kho char), and to situate them in the wider economic context of the area. It highlights the significance of taxes related to trade (and the pervasiveness of forced sales by the central government) and of transportation corvée labour in the whole province. It shows striking disparities among the four villages, casting an unfavourable light on the social status of the dependent peasants of Tholing in comparison to the situation in the other three villages and in Central Tibet, and pointing to the relatively advantageous situation of taxpayers in Kochar. However, the author convincingly argues that despite a structural land (and therefore food) shortage in the whole area, the tax system precluded any actions on the part of the peasants that could have contributed to agricultural intensification and raised levels of production.

The third part of the volume proposes a shift in perspective by analysing in detail four particular types of taxes, again within the Ganden Phodrang territory. These were all provided as a service or a corvée labour, in most cases implying much more than the punctual payment of a tax in kind or cash, either because it pertained to the heaviest burden on most taxpayers, that is, the transportation corvée, or because it resulted in a kind of "professional" and lifelong specialisation (water ferry transport by fishing villages, opera performance, and the so-called "monk-tax"). Saadet Arslan's chapter sheds light on the transportation corvée by analysing it through an original angle: that of the *lam yig*, the official legal document issued by the Tibetan government to beneficiaries of the service. This allows the author not only to share her thorough investigation of the internal structure and content of such legal documents (and provide transcriptions and translations of two of them), but also to present a more general description of the wider socio-political context and of the transport and communication networks in Tibet.

From passing references in various historical accounts, we know that communities in the broader Tibetan cultural area were often required to pay taxes in conformity with the resources and circumstances of their respective ecospheres. To mention just one of many examples, Michael Aris cites the case of a local chief in Bhutan who imposed "a meat tax from the upper part of the district, a fish tax from the lower part and a road tax from the traders who travelled the roads" (Aris 1986, 37). The present volume contains several examples of commodities and services associated with a particular environmental niche, but most notably the case examined in chapter 6: the fishing village of Jun ('Jun), located in Chushur (Chu shur) county in Central Tibet, where the author, Diana Lange, conducted extensive fieldwork. Her study clearly illustrates how tax payment was adapted to a community's economic and environmental conditions, insofar as Jun paid a part of its in-kind taxes in dried fish. Although it had significantly less farmland than the surrounding villages and certainly not enough to subsist on, the inhabitants were nevertheless also required to pay a part of these taxes in the form of grain, and this they had to obtain from neighbouring farmers who were willing to barter surplus barley for dried fish. Like many other social groups whose professional activity branded them as being of low status, the fishing community provided a service that was essential to daily life in Central Tibet. In an era of few roads and bridges, watercraft were a vital part of the economy, and while the boatmen were able to generate private income by carrying people, animals and goods across rivers or downstream for travellers and merchants, they were also required to provide this service as part of their government corvée duty. The most onerous part of this provision was the return journey: the coracles (yak hide boats) could not be paddled upstream against the current and had to be carried to Jun on the boatmen's backs.

Isabelle Henrion-Dourcy offers a comprehensive analysis of the provision of a particular tax obligation, the performance of opera (*lha mo*). The author describes the troupes involved in this "performance as tax", the context in which they performed and the repertoire they presented on such occasions. Moreover, by focusing on a service that was, like a number of other types of corvée duties in Tibet (and despite descriptions by Tibetans that classify *lha mo* performance as tax-in-kind) not always restricted in time and quantity, the analysis emphasises the experience of the taxpayers, who were effectively liable to have to work on demand, occasioning a feeling of injustice and discourses of resentment against the taxation system. These conditions, among other factors, ultimately resulted in changes to the tax system at the end of the Ganden Phodrang period; notably, *lha mo* performances during the *zho ston* festival that had previously been considered as a tax started to be remunerated.

The last chapter in this part is an investigation into the well-known but little studied monk-tax (*grwa khral/btsun khral/ban khral*) by Berthe Jansen. The author examines the concept, the history and the occurrences of monk-tax in Tibetan Buddhist regions before the 1950s. Since the monk-tax was not common in general and even highly uncommon in large successful monasteries, she puts forward the hypothesis that the documented presence of this tax at a given monastery could be seen as an indicator of the unstable socio-economic circumstances of that particular institution and its networks at a certain point in time. The author also discusses two other meanings of the word *grwa khral* (alternatively *btsun khral*) as "chores" and "sustenance payments made to monks", definitions that are not attested in dictionaries.

The fourth part of this volume encompasses Tibetan territories at the external periphery of the Ganden Phodrang, both in Eastern Tibet and in the Western Himalayas, areas that have rarely received attention as far as taxation is concerned. The first two chapters involve the Ganden Phodrang and show how taxation could play a central role in the domain of external politics. Based on local narratives authored by lama-historians, read in comparison to Central Tibetan accounts, secondary literature presenting some Manchu and Mandarin records and rare reports by Western travellers, Maria Turek investigates the tax system of the Nangchen (Nang chen) kingdom in Kham (Khams) between the 17th and the 20th centuries. Following the various political shifts experienced in this area, she shows how they affected the taxation system and in particular monastic obligations in Nangchen. She analyses the escalating 20th-century dispute over taxation between the Zurmang (Zur mang) estate and the Ganden (dGa' ldan) convent as intertwined with the larger conflict opposing Tibet and China.

The next three chapters take the reader to the West. John Bray focuses on the crucial role taxes (in particular labour obligations) played in sustaining the wider economic and diplomatic relationships between Ladakh and the Ganden Phodrang state between the 17th and the 20th century, relationships that were largely based on trade and shaped by the Treaty of Temisgang (gTing mo sgang) that had been signed in 1684. This trade itself relied on a burdensome transportation corvée on both the Tibetan and Ladakh sides of the border for the support of the Ladakhi government Lopchak and the Tibetan government

Zhungtsong missions. The chapter shows that the 17th-century "ancient engagements" benefitted the Ladakhi court and the Ganden Phodrang at an institutional level and provided a source of profit to individual government officials and traders who were able to make use of corvée labour and forced sales for their own enrichment. At the other end, the farmers and nomads had to provide the labour and buy and sell at non-market prices in both Ladakh and Tibet.

The last two chapters take us to Tibetan areas that are disconnected from the orbit of the Ganden Phodrang. Isabelle Riaboff's article was originally presented as a paper at the Eighth Seminar of the International Association for Tibetan Studies in Bloomington in 1998, and since there were no proceedings of that seminar, the article has remained unpublished until now. The research was based on almost two years of doctoral fieldwork carried out by the author in the 1990s, and reflects the fiscal situation that prevailed in Zangskar at this time. Until its annexation by the Dogras in 1830 Zangskar had comprised two kingdoms, Padum and the much smaller Zangla, whose ruling family retained its royal privileges until 1950. The article considers the taxes paid to Zangla's king prior to this time, and also to the monasteries of Zangskar as a whole at the time of the author's fieldwork. Households in Zangskar are grouped into three categories, one of which consists of freeholders, an unknown class in Central Tibet. All taxes in kind were paid by the second category, the *khral pa*, though all three categories were liable for the provision of corvée services. In addition to "ordinary" taxes (paid in barley) to the lay and clerical landlords, there were also "allocated" taxes that householders paid directly, in the form of flour, to finance dedicated ceremonies. As Riaboff shows, the fiscal base of the monasteries was geographically complex: while the parishes of the monasteries were clustered in their immediate vicinity, not all these villages paid them taxes, while those in which they did have revenue-yielding land were often situated in the parishes of other monasteries.

In the final chapter, Charles Ramble examines the types of taxes that non-Hindu religious institutions in Mustang, a culturally Tibetan area of Nepal, were liable to pay during the Rana era (1846–1951). The institutions in question included Buddhist monasteries and convents, as well as families and communities of Buddhist and Bönpo tantric householder-priests. While these priestly clusters occupied a privileged fiscal position under the traditional local rulers—the king of Lo and the Buddhist aristocracy—the privileges they enjoyed were eroded under a contractual scheme of tax collection introduced by the Ranas. In the case of one priestly community, a group of better-off households adopted an existing financial mechanism to ease what they considered to be an unjust tax burden on their fellow-villagers. Ceremonies in the community are mostly financed with the interest raised from capital investments, and these households established precisely such a dedicated endowment fund that generated interest exactly equal to the annual tax debt. Surprisingly, this fund was maintained and continued to generate income for the community for several decades after the fall of the Rana government and the abolition of the tax for which it had been created.

This volume sheds light on a multitude of facets of the social history of taxes in Tibetan areas. From an institutional point of view, it shows the multiplicity of actors involved in tax collection at the local and central level; it highlights the administrative organisation, rules and documents that framed the tax collecting process and makes it possible to identify beneficiaries of the system; it shows that, if the Ganden Phodrang could manage to rely on a relatively small number of central offices and officials dedicated to taxation, it was mainly because a large part of the taxes were directly distributed from the taxpayers to the benefactors instead of being first centralised and then distributed; it documents rare modifications made by the Tibetan state of the land settlements on which the tax collection was based (when taxpayers faced excessive tax burdens that resulted in increasing abandonment of landholdings) as well as some late attempts, at the end of the period, to reform the system in order to reduce its excesses and to mitigate the inappropriate behaviour of its own agents. The various chapters also enable us to understand better the general organisation of labour in Tibet at the local and state level (when taxes were provided in the form of corvée) and to document the diversity of local production across the Tibetan territories (when taxes were levied in kind).

Finally, the volume provides insights into the experience of taxpayers themselves, shedding light on the possible specific relationship towards a state largely based on Buddhist ideology, displayed by subjects through their experiences and discourses on taxation. The difficulties faced in trying to fulfil their obligations, their subsequent impoverishment and even flight in extreme cases, their often-critical representations of the tax system, to a certain extent undermine an image of Tibet in which a bodhisattva-led state was likely to arouse "natural consent" to taxpaying; but to a certain extent only, because, if testimonies clearly express resentment towards a number of aspects of the system (the overall burden of taxes preventing a majority of taxpayers from improving their economic and social status, the fact that the tax system often resulted in taxpayers being liable to work on demand, the practice of forced sales which seemed so common in the Western provinces and the corruption of some tax collectors) and thus clearly indicate tensions between the state and its subjects, it seems that the criticism was directed against the agents of the state who were perceived as either taking advantage of the system or as plainly corrupt, rather than voiced in condemnation of the Tibetan state itself.

References

Aris, M.V. 1986. *Sources for the History of Bhutan*. Wien: Arbeitskreis für Tibetische und Buddhistische Studien Universität Wien.

Delalande, N. and A. Spire. 2010. *Histoire sociale de l'impôt*. Paris: La Découverte.

Elias, N. [1969] 1991. *La dynamique de l'Occident*. Paris: Calmann-Lévy.

Goldstein, M.C. 1968. An Anthropological Study of the Tibetan Political System. Ph.D. thesis, University of Washington.

Goldstein, M.C. 1971a. Taxation and the structure of a Tibetan village. *Central Asiatic Journal* 15(1), 1–27.

Goldstein, M.C. 1971b. Serfdom and mobility: an examination of the institution of "human lease" in Traditional Tibetan Society. *The Journal of Asian Studies* 30(3), 521–34.

Goldstein, M.C. 1986. Reexamining choice, dependency and command in the Tibetan social system: "tax appendages" and other landless serfs. *The Tibet Journal* 11(4), 79–113.

Guéry, A. 1984. Le roi dépensier. Le don, la contrainte et l'origine du système financier de la monarchie française d'Ancien Régime. *Annales ESC* 39(6), 1241–69.

Gurung, Kalsang Norbu. 2013. The role of the Ambans in the Dalai Lama government according to the *Ten-Point Edict*. *In* C. Ramble, P. Schwieger and A. Travers (eds) *Tibetans who Escaped the Historian's Net. Studies in the Social History of Tibetan Societies*. Kathmandu: Vajra Books, 27–39.

Gurung, Kalsang Norbu. 2017. Different copies of *Iron-Tiger Land Settlement* and their historical value as taxation manuals. *In* J. Bischoff and S. Mullard (eds) *Social Regulation. Case Studies from Tibetan History*. Leiden: Brill, 209–30.

Hincker, F. 1971. *Les Français devant l'impôt sous l'Ancien Régime*. Paris: Flammarion.

Ramble, C., P. Schwieger and A. Travers (eds). 2013. *Tibetans who Escaped the Historian's Net. Studies in the Social History of Tibetan Societies*. Kathmandu: Vajra Books.

Surkhang, Wangchen Gelek. [1966] 1984. Tax measurement and lag 'don tax in Tibet. *The Tibet Journal* 9(1), 20–30.

Surkhang, Wangchen Gelek. 1986. Government, monastic and private taxation in Tibet. *The Tibet Journal* 11(1), 21–40.

Thupten Sangyay. 1986. Glossary of the "Government, monastic and private taxation in Tibet" (translated by Tsepag Rigzin). *The Tibet Journal* 11(1), 41–47.

Tilly, C. 1990. *Coercion, Capital and European States, AD 990–1990*. Cambridge: Blackwell.

Tsarong, Paljor. 1998a. Economics of a Tibetan state treasury: the barley supply office. *The Tibet Journal* 23(2), 3–10.

Tsarong, Paljor. 1998b. Tseja: structure and economy of a Tibetan state treasury. *The Tibet Journal* 23(3), 23–33.

Weber, M. [1921] 1971. *Économie et société*. Paris: Plon.

CHAPTER 1

The Tax System in Central and Far East Tibet Towards the End of the Ganden Phodrang Reign: An Outline of Its Structure and Terminology

Peter Schwieger

1 Introduction

Like any other government, the Ganden Phodrang (dGa' ldan pho brang) had to meet regular financial obligations. Among these, contrary to what one would expect, paying salaries to its officials was not an issue to be reckoned with. In Tibet, government officials were recruited from the aristocracy and their service was regarded as a recompense for usufruct of their aristocratic estates. Nevertheless, the Tibetan government did levy various taxes, at the central as well as at the district level. A small portion was consumed by the bureaucracy. Some of the revenues were used for paying the salaries of the Tibetan army. Money or material goods were also provided for the expenditures incurred by constructing and restoring government buildings.[1] The greatest portion, however, was spent on religious institutions and purposes. In particular, it was used to contribute to the financial support of Gelukpa (dGe lugs pa) monasteries. Salaries were paid to monks for the regular performance of religious rituals for the common welfare, and financial support was given to cover the costs of the great religious festivals. The use of the revenues for religious purposes was legitimised by the principle of *chos srid zung 'brel*, the union of religion and politics. According to this principle, the monks guaranteed the welfare of Tibet and its people through their prayers and religious services, and the government prepared the ground for the good practice of religion and promoted an environment for the populace to tread the path to salvation.

During the time of the Ganden Phodrang there were several major modifications of the Tibetan tax system. These were all responses to perceived inefficiencies. It seems to have been a general feature of the Tibetan tax system that it did not react flexibly enough to fluctuations in the income and agricultural productivity of the taxpayers. All too often, this resulted in the impoverishment of peasants and their abandonment of their holdings. That

1 For an example see the document described in Schuh 1981a: no. 15.

 | DOI:10.1163/9789004529465_003

in turn led to dwindling government tax revenues. For the most part, taxation in Tibet entailed taxation of agricultural land. Thus, taxation and its successive modifications were based on surveys of landholdings, their size and their fertility. These surveys resulted in official settlements called *zhib gzhung*. Surkhang mentions a first such land settlement for the year 1740, the so-called *Iron-Monkey Land Settlement* (*lCags spre zhib gzhung*) (Surkhang 1966: 15). Towards the end of the 18th century, impoverishment of the peasants and depopulation had increased especially in those rural areas which had suffered from the military invasions of Tibet by the Gorkhas of Nepal between 1788 and 1792. In 1794, after the Qing government in Beijing had successfully expelled the Gorkhas from Tibet, pursuing them with a large military force to the very gates of Kathmandu, the Emperor sent a new Amban to Lhasa as his representative: Song-Yun (1752–1835). In spring of the following year, this experienced official undertook an inspection tour through Central Tibet. He was struck by the poverty of the rural population and ascribed this to indiscriminate and excessive taxation and labour obligations. A few months later he proclaimed reforms in the Tibetan tax system (Dabringhaus 1994: 169–83). The reforms are fixed in the so-called *Ten-Article Edict*.[2] On the initiative of the Ambans stationed in Lhasa twenty-five years later, another reform of the Tibetan tax system was carried out. For that purpose, on 5 November 1830 an investigatory committee was established under the leadership of the Cabinet Minister Shedra Döndrub Dorje (bShad sgra Don grub rdo rje, died 1840). The other members were the monk official in charge of the religious utensils of the Dalai Lama (*sku bcar mchod dpon mkhan po*), the head of the Revenue Office (*rtsis dpon*) Phalhawa (Pha lha ba) and his assistant Kesang Ngawang (bsKal bzang ngag dbang; Bod rang skyong ljongs lo rgyus yig tshags khang [ed.] 1989: 2, 8).[3] The result was the so-called *Iron-Tiger Land Settlement* (of the Iron-Tiger Year) or *lCags stag zhib gzhung* (Bod rang skyong ljongs lo rgyus yig tshags khang [ed.] 1989). So far this is the only land settlement which has been handed down to us.[4] In 1831 some corrections were made and included in the settlement, known as the *Notes of the Iron Hare to the Settlement* (*lCags yos zhib gzhung gi mchan*, abridged as *lCags yos zhib mchan*) (Surkhang 1966: 20f). Thirty years later, the excessive tax burden and an increasing abandonment of landholdings again demanded a modification of the land settlement. It was completed

2 See Gurung 2013. English translations of its Chinese and Tibetan versions will be jointly published by K.N. Gurung and Liu Yuxuan.

3 The date was calculated in accordance with the information provided by Petech 1973: 163. On Shedra Döndrub Dorje see *ibid.*: 161–64.

4 See Gurung 2017 and Gurung in this volume.

in 1864 and is thus known as the *Wood-Mouse Land Settlement* (*Shing byi zhib gzhung*). The distinctive feature of this settlement was that it put neighbouring lords of aristocratic or monastic estates in charge of government taxpayers. In case the government taxpayers supervised by them fled the land, the neighbouring non-government lord was held liable. This regulation was called "the calf is fastened to the neck of the bull" (*glang ske be'u 'dogs*), the bull being the aristocratic or monastic lord and the calf being the government taxpayers. This scheme was introduced to only three districts: to Gyantse (rGyal rtse) as a model for a larger district, to Nam (rNam) as a model for a district of medium size, and to Wangden (dBang ldan) as a model for smaller districts. Though the implementation seems to have been effective, political unrest prevented an application to all districts under the jurisdiction of the Ganden Phodrang government.[5]

2 Taxes in the Farmland Areas

Peasant households that held such land on a hereditary basis were the taxpayers, called *khral pa*. Taxes were paid in money, in kind or in corvée labour. Thus, the terms "pay" and "payment" are here not to be understood as being restricted to the payment of money, but may refer to the transfer of any valuable items or to the performance of services in order to meet tax obligations. The taxpayers bore not the total, but the main tax burden in Tibet. In the village studied by Goldstein the taxpayers were the smallest group (Goldstein 1971). Most of the villagers belonged to *dud chung* families, households of landless peasants. By contrast, a Chinese publication on Tibet's social history states that for the entirety of Tibet the taxpayers accounted for between 60 and 70 per cent of all the *mi ser*, the serfs (The Cultural Palace of Nationalities 1991: 45). The peasants were bound to an estate, either a governmental one, or an aristocratic one or a monastic one. They cultivated and lived on their land in exchange for services and duties to be delivered to the estate holder. They were not entitled to sell the land they cultivated. Their land was called *khral rten*, "base for the tax."

According to Surkhang and Goldstein, the agricultural land of governmental estates was measured in *rkang*, while the land of the aristocracy and the

5 On the land settlement of 1864 see Surkhang 1966: 21f. Goldstein (1971: 5f, 25f) further mentions a settlement of 1847, the so-called *Fire-sheep settlement* (*Me lug zhib gzhung*). Surkhang does not mention a land settlement in the corresponding year. The content of the 1847 settlement seems to be more or less the same as the 1864 settlement listed by Surkhang. The settlement of 1847 is probably just a preliminary version of the later one. According to Goldstein (1971: 25f), the settlement of 1847 already applied the concept of *glang ske be'u 'dogs*.

monasteries was measured in *'don*, which would be equivalent to two *rkang* (Surkhang 1966: 15; Goldstein 2001: 580). Dung dkar explains both terms on one and the same scale that came into use during the Yuan Dynasty (Dung dkar 2002: 200). According to him, the size of the *'don* could vary in relation to the unit *rkang* (*ibid.*: 1154). One *'don* could correspond to two *rkang*, but in some cases up to four *rkang*. A large *'don* would be an area on which more than hundred bushels, *khal*, of seed could be sowed. Small *'don* could sometimes only absorb 20 to 30 *khal*. Specifications for the *khal* vary in Western literature from 28 pounds to 50 pounds of barley.[6]

The studies of Goldstein and Surkhang deal only with *khral pa* who were bound to governmental estates. These *khral pa* therefore belonged to the so-called *gzhung rgyugs pa* (sometimes also written *gzhung rgyug pa*), a term denoting all taxpayer serfs bound to governmental estates.[7] In the documented cases, the taxes in kind or cash were directly collected by the District Commissioner and his staff (Surkhang 1966: 18).

Some of the aristocratic estates were exempted from taxes, while others were taxed. In cases of tax exemption the landlord could keep all the revenues for himself. When taxed, the dues from the estate were collected either by specially selected and trustworthy peasants or by the headman of the valley or the official of the subdistrict, called *sde pa*. The local official could keep a portion of the taxes for himself (Carrasco 1959: 102–104).

Following Carrasco (*ibid.*: 104f), monastic estates in the realm of the Ganden Phodrang were generally exempted from taxation. Though widely applicable, this statement is not true as a general rule. As Tibetan legal documents can prove, monasteries under the Ganden Phodrang, including those of the Gelukpa, could be taxed by the government, and the tax obligations could also include the demand for labour services.[8] Nevertheless, complete tax exemptions and even the granting of privileges to collect dues themselves, for example from passing traders, were widely practised—explicitly justified by the monks' duty to perform regular rituals for the common welfare.[9] Under the Thirteenth Dalai Lama new dues were also collected from the aristocracy as well as from the monasteries as a means to strengthen the Tibetan army (Tshe ring don grub *et al.* 1991, I: 596).

6 See Carrasco 1959: 240f n. 89. According to Winnington (2008: 230) 1 *khal* was equal to about 13 kg of grain.

7 On this term see also Dung dkar 2002: 342.

8 See for example Schuh 1981b: nos. XIII, XX, XXV, XXVI; see also Tshe ring don grub *et al.* 1991, I: 596.

9 See for example Schuh 1981b: no. XXVIII.

What we know so far about the tax system under the Ganden Phodrang we owe for the most part to three articles and a book chapter published by Surkhang and by Goldstein.[10] While the two articles of Surkhang, the first published in 1966 and the second posthumously in 1986, contain brief overviews based on the author's personal memory of his own service in the Tibetan government, Goldstein presented as part of his dissertation in 1968 as well as in a later article in 1971 a case study of a village in Tsang (gTsang) province. By contrast, Chinese-Tibetan studies, which give quite comprehensive information on the Tibetan tax system, have attracted little scholarly attention. After the Chinese occupation of Tibet in 1951 and especially after the Tibetan revolt of 1959, the Communist cadres had undertaken detailed analyses of Tibet's society (Winnington 2008: 243 n. 1). Results of these surveys were published in the 1980s and 1990s. They present general outlines of Tibet's society and tax system as it was in operation at the end of the Ganden Phodrang period in Tibet. Though of course ideologically framed and published to serve the legitimisation of Chinese Communist rule in Tibet, they nevertheless offer an approach to the structure and terminology of the Tibetan tax system. Like no other studies, they inform us about the regional varieties in the system and about different terms that were used—some of them designating more-or-less similar phenomena. Thus, these studies supplement the well-known publications in Western languages, especially those of Goldstein and Surkhang.

To make available the results of the above-mentioned Chinese-Tibetan surveys with regard to taxation in Tibet, this chapter presents a translation of one relevant Tibetan publication, together with a discussion of the terminology and supplementary notes. The work in question consists of several sections of a two-volume encyclopaedia on Tibet, published first 1986 in Chinese, and then in 1991 in Lhasa also in Tibetan under the title *Bod ljongs spyi bshad* and edited by Tshe ring don grub and O rgyan chos 'phel.[11] It is a description of Tibetan society within the territories immediately under the jurisdiction of the Ganden Phodrang. Here, I am relying on the Tibetan edition which enables us to collect the Tibetan terminology:[12]

10 Surkhang 1966, 1986; Goldstein 1968, 1971.

11 Tshe ring don grub *et al.* 1991, I. The title of the first Chinese edition is given in *ibid.* (5), as *Xizang zizhiqu gaikuang* 西藏自治区概况.

12 *Ibid.*, chapter 5.3.4 (595–615). Unless they enclose transliterations of original Tibetan terms, round brackets are part of the Tibetan original. Square brackets enclose supplements added by me for a better understanding. The use of three types of numbering (one), (1), and 1., follows the original.

Fourth chapter: Taxes and Corvée Labour

The term Tibetan tax (*bod kyi khral*) is a general name for various taxes including a wide range of meanings like corvée labour (*'u lag*), taxes [in the narrower sense] (*dpya khral*) and fee for leasing fields (*sa bogs*). The various taxes may be divided into two major kinds: (1) *rkang 'gro* [rendering of services]; that is, a category of tax such as the provision of riding horses and transport animals (*rta'u dos khal*),[13] corvée labour and messenger service (*bang chen*). (2) *lag 'don* [tax paid in kind or in cash], a category of tax where one pays money or goods. Based on the research carried out at the time of the democratic reforms, labour obligations (*las khral*) amounted to about 60 per cent, while taxes paid in kind or cash represented about 40 per cent within the Tibetan taxes and corvée labour. The so-called *sa khral* [tax on land holdings] was mainly the imposition of labour obligations. Although the terms for the Tibetan taxes [in the narrower sense], the corvée labour and the land tax, these three, were distinguished in some areas, they appeared in other cases as synonyms. For instance, as the type *sa zhing dpya khral* [field tax] does not apply to taxpayers of the military field units (*dmag rkang*) or to the estates held by some aristocrats and monasteries, it is [in the present study] represented as a separate category. Based on that, taxes [in the narrower sense], corvée labour and fee for leasing fields are [here] altogether called *khral 'u lag* [taxes in kind and taxes in corvée labour].

First: About field tax (*sa zhing gi dpya khral*)

(One) Based on the bushels (*khal*) of seed [required] for the arable field, the government taxpayers (*gzhung rgyug khral pa*) of [the land] separated as government estates (district estates administered by the local government [of the Dalai Lama])[14] had to pay every year for land [with a capacity] of 1 *khal* [of seed], a field tax of 1 *khal* or 10 *bre* grain. That is the field tax. However, the land tax was not a main type of tax to be paid by the agricultural serfs (*zhing bran*). Moreover, they had to pay numerous other *khral 'ul* [taxes in kind and taxes in corvée labour].

(Two) The collecting of taxes [consisting] of detailed leases (*bogs zhib*) and fees (*zhib 'bab*) from the various aristocratic families and monasteries

13 The text erroneously has *rta 'u dos khal*. Later in the text (p. 650) the correct spelling *rta'u dos khal* is used.

14 Note that the term "local government" (*sa gnas srid gzhung*) used throughout this chapter for the Ganden Phodrang Government in Tibet is an external denomination introduced by the Chinese government in Beijing.

by the local government [i.e. the Ganden Phodrang Government]: when the eminent Thirteenth Dalai Lama expanded the army, he determined that in order to meet military expenses, except those for the fields of the salary estates (*thab rten sa zhing*)[15] belonging to the aristocrats and the monasteries, for each of [their] remaining fields, each land [having the capacity] of 1 *khal* of seed, 1 *khal* of grain had to be collected for the military. This was a tax to be collected on the basis of the arable fields. However, the various aristocratic families and monasteries found ways to shift that tax onto the agricultural serfs.
(Three) Tax for cultivating new land (*sa stong gsar sbol gyi khral*): (one tenth) [*bcu zur*] In the year 1906 the assistant Amban, stationed in Tibet, Krang dbyin thang [Zhang Yintang 張蔭棠, 1866–1937],[16] established a so-called Agricultural Office (*so nam las khungs*) in Tibet.[17] When serfs (*mi ser*) cultivated new land, it was determined that after four years they had to pay a tax of one tenth of their yield to the Agricultural Office. Based on an investigation carried out in the year 1956, every year there was an income of about 27,000 *khal* from the territory under the Dalai Lama.
(Four) Tax supplement (*khral gsab*): Brag g.yab was subordinate to the *qutuqtu* Loden Sherab (Blo ldan shes rab). The taxpayers of this area had to pay every year for the land [having the capacity] of 1 *khal* [seed], 1 *khal* [of the yield's grain] as lease. This was called the "great tax" (*khral chen*). After the local government of Tibet had seized possession of the area of Chamdo (Chab mdo) in 1918, it was determined that in Dragyab (Brag g.yab) district, for example, for every unit of land having the capacity of 6 *khal* of seed, an additional lease of 1 *khal* of grain had to be paid. This was called the "tax supplement" (*khral gsab*).

What has been explained above is one way in which leases had to be paid in grain.

---

15 The term is explained by Goldstein (2001: 488) as "an estate held by a government official as a source of income."

16 Zhang Yintang arrived in autumn 1906 as the newly-appointed High Commissioner for Tibet, to strengthen Chinese control over Tibet and to reduce the British influence. Nevertheless, Charles Bell described his official and personal relations with him as excellent. See Bell 1924: 88–91. For details on his life see Ding (1943: 129–34) and Wu *et al.* (1988: 262–74).

17 According to Dung dkar (2002: 2062f) this office was also called *mi so'i las khungs*. He explains *mi so* as an abbreviation for *mi rtsa dang so nam skor do dam byed pa*. Dung dkar states that originally in 1907 it was intended to establish this office as one of altogether nine new offices. But due to the journey of the Thirteenth Dalai Lama to Mongolia this office, together with two others, could only be established in 1913.

Second: Special taxes and lease [paid] from tax fields.
(One) Tax [paid] in cash for the Mönlam (sMon lam) [festival].
(Two) Price for [fire]wood for the Mönlam [festival] (*smon lam shing rin*).
(Three) Tax [paid] in grain for the Ambans stationed in Tibet.
(Four) Tax [paid] in charcoal for the Ambans stationed in Tibet.
(Five) Substitute for the horse corvée tax (*rta 'ul khral dod*), substitute for the messenger horses (*bang chen rta dod*) of the Ambans stationed in Tibet.

Concerning the above-mentioned taxes, the local Tibetan government had given special arable fields to be used as a base for the tax. They were cultivated by the taxpayers of the various estates. Every year, they had to pay taxes either in grain or cash to the concerned office of the local government. After the revolution of the Iron-Pig Year 1911 took place, the Manchu or Qing Dynasty brought down and the Guomindang established, the office of the Ambans stationed in Tibet during the rule of that dynasty was abolished. However, in some areas those taxes were nevertheless still collected as before. For example, on the estates of Namseling (rNam sras gling), head of the Revenue Office,[18] leases continued to be collected from the tax fields of the Ambans previously stationed in Tibet until the year 1958.

Third: Special taxes in corvée labour and in kind [paid] from tax fields.
The main special taxes in corvée labour and in kind [paid] from tax fields were associated with arable fields, [defined as] military tax units (*dmag rkang sa zhing*), and to tax fields of the postal relay stations (*sa tshigs kyi khral zhing*). The arable fields [defined as] military tax units were special tax fields for the Gyajong (rGya sbyong) military regiment,[19] established in the year 1792 on the basis of the [29] articles for the course of action in Tibetan affairs.[20] At that time 3,000 military [tax field] units were determined for the 3,000 Gyajong soldiers throughout Tibet. In addition, [for

18 On his appointment see Goldstein 1989: 370.

19 Gyajong refers to the 3,000 soldiers "trained by the Chinese" (Travers 2015: 257).

20 This apparently refers to the 29-Article Decree issued by the Qianlong Emperor after the first Gorkha war. In 1791 General Fu Kang'an had justified to the Qianlong Emperor in a memorandum the requirement for a standing Tibetan army consisting of 3,000 soldiers. In 1793 the Emperor picked up this idea in Article Four of his famous 29-Article Decree. Concerning the financing of the troops, nothing is said in Fu Kang'an's memorandum or in the decree itself, at least in the versions known so far. However, after the Gorkha crisis a certain number of field units of governmental estates in Central Tibet were calculated to finance the supply of the soldiers. See Dabringhaus 1994: 186f; Schwieger 2015: 186–92.

each individual case] the government demanded that the arable land of one military [tax field] unit be cultivated. And it was determined that from that [land], one soldier had to be supplied by assuming responsibility for his provisions. There were two different ways in which the fields [defined as] military tax units were cultivated:
(One) When one taxpayer household cultivated a field [defined as] a military tax unit, that [household] therefore had to pay the military tax (*dmag khral*). And if that taxpayer household became defunct or was no longer able to pay the tax, that land had to be given to another taxpayer household.
(Two) The arable land [defined as] the military tax unit was distributed among individual taxpayer households. In addition, the number of tax fields was first analysed, then the military tax imposed.

By enlarging the army, the local government of Tibet had, in the year 1912, established the bodyguard regiment (*sku srung dmag*).[21] Therefore, the burden on the taxpayer households of the military field units also became heavier. At that time it was determined that, for each soldier, an additional man had now to be sent, by recruiting the soldiers from military field units that were being established in the area of Dokham (mDo khams): from every military field unit one-and-a half soldiers had to be supplied; from every military field unit in the area of dBus gTsang one-and-a-quarter soldiers had to be supplied.

In the year 1921 the local government of Tibet established the *'don dmag* (*'don zhing gi dmag khral*, military tax from fields [measured in] *'don*).[22] It was determined that from every eight *rkang* of the government taxpayers and from the tax land of every [four][23] *'don* which was owned by the monasteries and the aristocratic families, one man had to be both supplied and fed as military tax.[24] This [tax] is therefore called *rkang 'don brgyad bzhi* (eight *rkang* and four *'don*). From the year 1949 onwards, there was a change insofar as from every twelve tax-*rkang* of the government taxpayers, and from the tax land of every six tax-*'don* owned by the monasteries and the aristocratic families, one man had to be supplied and fed as military tax. This was called *bcu gnyis drug sna* (the twelve-six-kind).

21 According to Goldstein (1989: 66f), it was in 1913 and 1914 that the Thirteenth Dalai Lama ordered an increase of the army by a thousand soldiers.

22 On the terms *rkang* and *'don*, see above.

23 No number of *'don* is mentioned here. This is obviously a mistake, because—as evident from the next sentence—the tax as a whole is called *rkang 'don brgyad bzhi*.

24 See also Goldstein 1989: 95, 120f.

In the year 1957 the military tax unit fields in the area of the government serfs amounted to a total of 3076 *rkang*.

The taxpayers who cultivated the arable land [defined as] military tax units had in the main to ensure the provisions linked to paying the military tax. The degree of exploitation of those taxpayers amounted in general to about 60 per cent of the income from the arable land.

Tax for the postal relay stations (*sa tshigs khral*): the so-called tax fields of the postal relay stations (*sa tshigs kyi khral zhing*) were [also] called tax unit fields, cultivated by the taxpayers, who specifically had to pay a tax for the postal relay stations to the local Tibetan government. In the past, those tax fields were mainly located along various important travel routes.

Fourth: Taxes in kind and in corvée labour (*khral 'ul*) for the local government.

There are two different *khral 'ul*, the *khral 'ul* [paid] from the various government estates directly administered by the local government, and the *khral 'ul* [paid] from the private estates of the various aristocratic families and monasteries and of the religious estates (*mchod gzhis*).[25] From the point of view of the taxpayers of the monasteries and the aristocratic families, the latter is called external tax (*phyi khral*). Beside the special taxes and corvée duties mentioned above, there were several [other] taxes and corvée obligations to be provided for the local government. They are explained below:

(One) Whenever a travel document (*lam yig*) of the local government was presented, people and loads had to be carried without charge for horses, pack animals and people.

(Two) Itinerant chiefs, government officials out on official business and Tibetan troops had to be received wherever they stopped for a meal or lodged overnight.

(Three) Construction work had to be carried out for the local government as tax (*ar khral rgyug pa*).

(Four) Various taxes had to be paid in cash or kind (*lag 'don*) to the local government.

The main external taxes (*phyi khral*) for the local government are explained below:

25 Apparently the text differentiates between estates being the economic base of the monasteries and the *mchod gzhis*. It seems that the latter were estates which were specially determined to finance religious offerings.

'u lag: *'u lag* is a corrupted word from the Drugu (Gru gu) language.[26] During the Yuan Dynasty, it was a kind of tax by which horses and pack animals were provided for chiefs, messengers and transport travelling between Tibet and Xining (Zi ling). Later it became a general name for all tax in the [form of] labour for the local government. If one analyses that tax in detail, [it consisted of the following obligations]:
1. construction work as tax, 2. repairing dams, 3. cutting wood, 4. transporting wood, 5. mowing hay, 6. cleaning irrigation channels, 7. providing horse corvée, resting place and lodging overnight for travelling chiefs and Tibetan troops, 8. welcoming and seeing off government post-riders.

FIGURE 1.1 Lhasa: woman carrying stones , Lhasa, 1938/1939. Photo by Bruno Beger
BUNDESARCHIV, IMAGE 135-BB-088-09

26 According to Zhang Yisun *et al.* (1998: 401) the name refers to an ancient kingdom in the north of Tibet, near the Kokonor. The language was Turkic. In Mongolian the service for the postal relay stations was called *ulaγa* (Petech 1990: 50).

By using various terms, the varieties of corvée labour were differentiated in some areas into sets of ten:[27]

Taxes [consisting] of transporting loads from one corvée station to the next (*sa rim dos skyel gyi khral rigs*): this meant mainly the transportation of goods required by the local government, for example grain, tea, butter, meat of cattle and sheep and rice. If the taxes [consisting] of transporting loads from one corvée station to the next are [further] differentiated, [there were]:

1. *sa tshigs kyi khral*, which referred to short-distance transportation between a half and a full day.
2. *rdzong skyel* referred to transportation over slightly longer distances, from one district to the next.[28]
3. Various forms of corvée labour for the great Mönlam [festival].
4. Taxes [consisting] of the demand for various duties in the sphere of religion, for example: when religious ceremonies were performed, the district government demanded horses and people and asked for monks to be welcomed and appropriately sent off.
5. Various minor other taxes.

Taxes [paid in the form] of goods: taxes [paid in the form] of various goods required by the local feudal[29] government were mainly grain, butter, meat of cattle and sheep, and so forth. The taxes [paid in the form] of goods from the various district estates were classified into numerous different kinds, based on the local resources, for instance, in Tshona (mTsho sna) district tax [took the form] of medicinal ingredients, a dye tax, tiger skin tax, fruit tax; in Thetrog (Thad krog) district there was a paper tax; in Gongkar (Gong dkar) district a wool tax; in Chonggye ('Phyongs rgyas) district a meat tax; in the various districts of the nomads' area there were animal tail, felt, salt, leather, sack and soda taxes, amongst others. Accordingly, in places of gold deposits a gold tax was imposed, a jade bowl tax was imposed in places where jade bowls were produced, a whetstone tax where whetstones were produced, earthenware pottery,

27 What is actually meant by "sets of ten" is not explained by an example in the following.

28 Surkhang (1986: 24f) explains the meaning of the terms *sa tshigs* tax and *rdzong skyel* tax slightly differently: the *sa tshigs* tax was limited to providing fewer than ten horses for riding and fifteen mules, and the horses were exchanged after comparatively short intervals. *rDzong skyel* was the term for the provision of a larger number of horses and mules. Also, the horses had to go for longer distances since there was no opportunity to change them along the way.

29 The term is *bkas bkod rgyud 'dzin*, a modern neologism.

charcoal, whitewash and red ochre taxes were all imposed in their respective places of production, and so on in this fashion.

The various taxes paid to the local Tibetan government were very numerous. In addition, the taxes added by the various local [authorities] were even more numerous. Therefore, very many agricultural serfs had to suffer ruthless exploitation. One point has to be made clear here: although there were only just over ten main kinds of taxes imposed by the local government of Tibet, the additional taxes imposed by the various local lords were very numerous. Among the taxes for the jurisdictions of individual chiefs, there were various other light and heavy ones, for example: the taxpayers under Medro Gungkar (Mal gro gung dkar) district had to pay around eighteen different taxes [in the form] of goods:

(1) *sa khral*: for a field on which 1 *khal* of seed could be sown (*sa zhing son khal gcig*), 10 *bre* of grain tax had to be paid.[30]

(2) *pad kha'i khral*: from the output of 6 *khal* of rapeseed (*pad kha*), 1 *khal* had to be delivered as tax.

(3) *lci khral*: based on the number of cattle, for every head of the large kind of cattle, eleven human loads of dung [had to be delivered].

(4) *phyugs khral*: for five sheep one *zho*,[31] for every ox (*ba glang*) one *zho* and for every pig three *zho* [had to be paid.] For horses and mules no money had to be given, but the horse corvée tax had to be provided instead.

(5) *sgong khral*: for a every piece of farmland [equal to] 15 *khal* [of seed], five eggs [had to be delivered].

(6) *rtswa khral*: for grazing sheep and cattle, a grass tax had to be paid to the District Commissioner.

(7) *chu khral*: the serfs of Gungkar village of the district of the same name had to pay the district a price for water.

(8) *ri khral*: a tax on the fuel gathered on the mountains by the people.

(9) *'jag khral*: every year five thousand brooms made of *cogon* grass had to be collected from the whole district. They had to be manufactured by the 260 taxpayer households under the Gung dkar estate. Every year the larger taxpayer households had to manufacture 240 brooms, and the smaller ones twenty-four brooms [each].

(10) *bul khral*: three households had to provide 30 *khal* of soda annually.

(11) *'breng khral*: thirteen households had to manufacture leather straps from fifteen entire hides every year.

30 One *khal* was equal to 20 *bre*.

31 Less than one ounce; 10 *skar* = 1 *zho*, 10 *zho* = 1 *srang*.

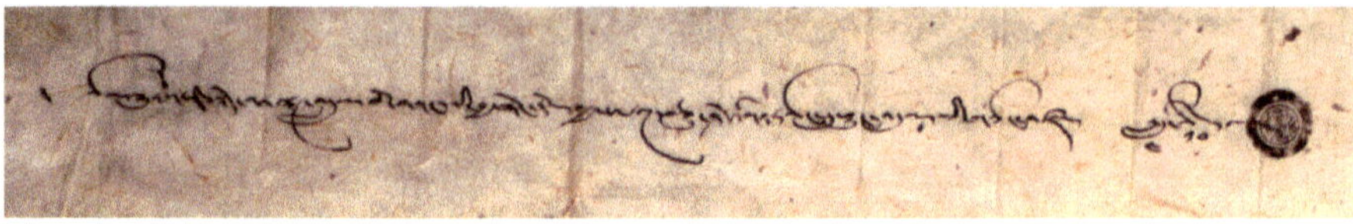

FIGURE 1.2 "Receipt that for the Iron-Dragon Year the 150 eggs [which have to be delivered] by the steward of Tshaggur (Tshag sgur) estate every other year, have been received in the lower storehouse, 4th month, 10th day. [seal imprint]"
DTAB: ID 1588
Note: *tshag sgur gzhis sdod nas lcags 'brug lo gnangs kyi bya sgong rdog brgya dang lnga bcu shod gnyer tshang du byung 'dug pa'i gtsang 'dzin/ zla 4 tshes 10*. Preserved in the Kündeling (Kun bde gling) archives are a few more receipts for 150 eggs provided by the Tshaggur estate (also abbreviated as Tshagzhi [Tshag gzhis]). In the other receipts the eggs are merely mentioned as the egg tax (*sgong khral*) of the Fire-Tiger Year, the Wood-Dog Year or the Earth-Dragon Year (DTAB: ID 1613, 1615, 1566); only in the receipt depicted above it is explicitly stated that this tax had to be paid every other year. However, the years provided by the few documented examples are all in agreement with this pattern.

(12) *lha 'bebs khral*: fifteen oracles had to pay 10 silver coins (*ṭam dkar*).
(13) *btsag khral*: the Labtön (bSlab ston) estate had to deliver 300 *khal* ochre annually.
(14) *me tog khog ma'i khral*: two estates had to provide five hundred flowerpots every year.
(15) *zhabs rim khral*: when the district asked the monastery to perform a large religious ceremony, every other year, all subjects of the districts had to pay a tax.
(16) The District Commissioner had to see the Dalai Lama once a year. Therefore, an audience tax (*mjal khral*) had to be paid [by the taxpayers].
(17) *mar khral*: the Terdrom (gTer sgrom) estate had to deliver ten skin-bags of butter every year.
(18) *bshas khral*: each butcher household had to deliver a butcher tax of two and a half sheep and one goat annually. In addition, they had to do corvée labour for the district.

If you ask how much the tax revenue for each *khal* of seed with regard to the tax fields was approximately, and if you analyse the taxes which were paid to the local [Tibetan] government by the seven taxpayer households of the Tsangtog (gTsang rtogs) estate belonging to the Tagtse (sTag rtse) district, and since those taxpayer households also cultivated eight *rkang* of agricultural land, (for each *rkang* of agricultural land 7 *khal,* 5 *bre* and 2 *phul* of seed [was needed]) they had to pay the local [Tibetan] government approximately as much corvée tax (*rkang 'gro*) and tax in cash or kind (*lag 'don*) as follows:

(1) For each *rkang* of agricultural land, 1 *khal* and 3 *bre* of barley and 1 *khal* and 3 *bre* of legumes had to be paid.

(2) For the great Mönlam [festival] in Lhasa, kitchen servants had to be sent. And for each *rkang* of agricultural land, 9 silver *srang* had to be delivered.

(3) As payment for the whitewashing of the Potala and the painting in ochre and yellow [colour], for every *rkang* of agricultural land 60 silver *srang* had to be delivered.

(4) Whenever flowerpots were transported to the Nor bu gling ka, for every *rkang* of agricultural land, 58 silver *srang* had to be delivered as salary for the transport.

(5) From every *rkang* of agricultural land, 11 *bre* of grain had to be paid as a coracle fee for the transport of grain destined for the government. If one converts this into cash, it was [equivalent to] 33 silver *srang*.

(6) For every *rkang* of agricultural land, 45 silver *srang* had to be paid for public expenditures in Lhasa.

(7) Whenever firewood for the great Mönlam festival in Lhasa was transported, for every *rkang* of agricultural land, 30 silver *srang* had to be paid.

(8) For every *rkang* of agricultural land, 160 silver *srang* had to be paid for the transport of construction wood for the government.

(9) For every *rkang* of agricultural land, 48 sixty silver *srang* had to be paid for the transport of furniture for the government.

(10) For every *rkang* of agricultural land, 80 silver *srang* had to be paid for the transport of butter for the government.

(11) At the time of the periodic offerings to Ganden (dGa' ldan) monastery, the district collected five loads of dung for every *rkang* of agricultural land, and [in addition], two people had to be sent on a five-day hike to fetch water for the monks. Similarly, four loads of hay and four horses [had to be provided], and [moreover], for every *rkang* of agricultural land 116 silver *srang* had to be paid.

(12) For every *rkang* of agricultural land, 10 silver *srang* had to be paid to ensure that the chiefs came to the harvest festival (*'ong skor*).

(13) Every year four monks had to go to the Ramoche (Ra mo che) [temple in Lhasa] to recite religious scriptures. From every *rkang* of agricultural land, 54 silver *srang* had to be paid for expenditures incurred.

(14) Every year the district invited four monks of the Namgyel (rNam rgyal) *grwa tshang* [of the Potala] to perform the summoning of the fertility of the soil and [the summoning of] prosperity. For that purpose, for every *rkang* of agricultural land, one horse corvée tax had to be performed and two water bearers had to be sent for.

If the different types of taxes mentioned above are averaged, for the farmland of each and every *khal* [of seed] 137 Tibetan silver *srang*, 3 *khal* of grain, twenty labourers and fourteen and a half horses and transport animals had to be provided. Therefore, based on the then yield of grain, the degree of exploitation amounted to 68 per cent [of the total yield].[32]

The determination of how much tax had to be paid in compulsory labour and in cash or kind for each *rkang* of agricultural land was not uniform across the country. Therefore, the weighting of taxes was also not equal. Likewise, there were fluctuations at different times with regard to taxes and corvée labour. Between areas which touched major roads, and remote areas, the taxes [paid] in compulsory labour and in cash or kind were also not uniform. The closer places were to roads, the more severe the taxes in cash or kind were. If one analyses Gyantse, Panam (Pa snam) and Medro Gungkar, taxes [paid] in cash or kind were very numerous. If one converts those taxes [paid] in cash or kind into grain as a value, then for every *rkang* of agricultural land, between 20 and 25 *khal* of grain had to be paid. Furthermore, taxes [paid] in compulsory labour were added. The overall degree of exploitation in terms of a tax burden amounted to more than 65 per cent of the yield for each *rkang* of agricultural land.

nang khral: the taxes paid in compulsory labour and in cash or kind by taxpayers [living] on the estates of monasteries and aristocrats were called internal taxes (*nang khral*).[33] The corvée labour belonging to the

32 For comparison: Alan Winnington (2008: 230f), a British Journalist and Communist, who had worked in China since 1948 and visited Tibet in 1955 and 1959, encountered a Tibetan serf whom he regarded as a typical representative of his class. Winnington compared his income with his outgoings, including those for seed and the interests of his debts. He calculated that overall 74 per cent of his family's labour was consumed by government expenses.

33 This explanation of the term *nang khral* as an obligation of peasants towards an aristocratic or monastic landlord is in accordance with other modern Tibetan publications like Zhang Yisun *et al.* (1998: 1502) and Dung dkar (2002: 1198). It is also confirmed by the information gathered by Nancy Levine (1992: 330) during field research in summer 1990 in Tholing village in West Tibet. However, the term was also applied to the taxpayers classified as *gzhung rgyugs pa* (see above). In their case, *nang khral* referred to the tax paid to the district as their immediate lord (Goldstein 1971: 10).

FIGURE 1.3 Shigatse: ploughing with yaks, 1938/1939. Photo by Ernst Schäfer
BUNDESARCHIV, IMAGE 135-S-14-19-12

internal tax differed depending on the local conditions. Therefore, the way in which the corvée labour was imposed was also not uniform. In general, the taxes paid as corvée labour can be divided into two main types: first, corvée labour, including ploughing and planting the fields of the estate, constructing buildings for the estate, repairing the agricultural implements, carding wool, fetching water, splitting firewood, grazing cattle, roasting grain, grinding roasted barley, softening leather, pressing oil and weaving sacks. Secondly, there was transport for the estate and messenger trips to both nearby and more distant areas, as required.

The taxes [paid] in kind consisted mainly of grain. In addition, they were fixed in accordance with the resources of the individual estate. In brief: everything the serf owner needed for his livelihood and production was demanded and paid in the form of tax. If one examines how taxes and leases were paid, the taxes carried out as compulsory labour were heavier than those paid in kind on estates having many fields and in areas adjacent to major roads. On estates with fewer fields and [located] in remote areas, the taxes paid in kind were slightly heavier. For example, if we consider the corvée labour tax of all of Tibet, in areas which were slightly more remote, cash was paid as a substitute for the [corvée labour] tax. On the estates of the monasteries and aristocrats, the proportion of corvée labour was slightly larger. Since the proportion of arable land was larger on the estates of the monasteries and the aristocrats, most of the internal tax had to be undertaken in the form of corvée labour.

How much arable land the agricultural serfs (*zhing bran*) were allowed to cultivate, and how much corvée labour they were forced to do, all depended on what the stewards of the estates said. Beside this requirement, there was no [other] clear regulation. In terms of the individual estates, the degree of exploitation experienced by the agricultural serfs [thus] also varied. The Tsangtog (gTsang rtogs) estate in Tagtse (sTag rtse) district was a religious estate of Ganden monastery. On this estate there were seven taxpayer households. They had to undertake internal [corvée labour] tax for the monastery. It has been said that, nominally, they only had seven *rkang* of internal tax fields (*nang khral sa zhing*). In actual fact, they had no more than [the land for] 107 *khal* of seed. (The categories of corvée labour are shown in Table 1.1 below.)

For all seven households, the time [spent] for [the payment of] the above-mentioned taxes took up 65 per cent of the work day.

The categories of corvée labour which had to be performed by these households throughout the year are shown below:

TABLE 1.1 Annual corvée labour performed by households of Tsangtog estate

Number of *'u lag*	Tibetan months	Number of days for each household	Number of days for providing riding horses and pack animals for each household	Total number of days [for the 7 households]	Total number of horses and pack animals	Additional remarks
Cultivation of the fields	6 months 1st–6th month	360		2,520		
Transport of grain	3 months 7th–9th month	240	240	720	720	had to be done by 3 households
Autumn labour		135		945	49	
Roasting and grinding	3 months 10th–12th month	25	1	175		

TABLE 1.1 Annual corvée labour performed by households of Tsangtog estate (*cont.*)

Number of *'u lag*	Tibetan months	Number of days for each household	Number of days for providing riding horses and pack animals for each household	Total number of days [for the 7 households]	Total number of horses and pack animals	Additional remarks
Transport of loads		24		168		
Occasional work		116		812		
Transport of grain granted as loan		2	32	14	124	
Weeding		286		2,001 [*sic*, 2,002]		
Transport of dung		81	108	72 [*sic*, 324]	432	Had to be done by 4 households
Grain transport for the Mönlam festival		1	1	7	7	
Total		1207	388	7,433 [*sic*, 7,687]	1332	

The Taglung Jang (sTag lung byang) estate was an estate of the Tagdrag (sTag brag) *qutuqtu*. It was directly administered by his lama household (*bla brang*). To tot up all [the farmland] on the entire estate, there was enough arable land for 1,445 *khal* [of seed]. From that [land], there was enough arable land for about 1,200 *khal* [of seed] to be planted for the estate. The ten households of agricultural serfs who took part in the internal [corvée labour] tax, only had enough arable land for 255 *khal* [of seed that they farmed for their own needs]. On the estate were a total of 98 rooms [in houses] (40 rooms were given over to the taxpayers as a housing fee. To the seven households who had no tax fields, twelve rooms were given) as well as 106 horses, donkeys and domestic animals (*sgo phyugs*), and 300 goats and sheep. The agricultural serfs had to do internal [corvée labour] tax for the religious estate, and they also had to do external [corvée labour] tax for the government. Both the internal and external taxes were large and numerous. For the land of the tax fields [being able to take] 7 *khal* and 5 *bre* [of seed], the taxpayers had to send, on all 360 days of a given year,[34] one [person to do] corvée labour, established as an internal corvée tax, and [in addition] on 270 days of a year, one [person to do] corvée labour in the form of an external tax. For one [lodging] room, eight days of internal [corvée labour] tax and five days of external [corvée labour] tax had to be undertaken as a fee for the housing. Over the course of the whole year, internal [corvée labour] tax had to be done on the estate for 11,826 days, and external [corvée labour] tax on 9,440 days, altogether giving a total of 21,266 days of external and internal tax. Based on the number of inhabitants, 67.3 people had to undertake corvée labour all year long. On this particular estate there were no more than a total of 81 individuals who were capable of working. Therefore, about 82 per cent of the agricultural serfs of the entire estate were occupied solely with paying external and internal [corvée labour] tax.

As we can see from the above-mentioned examples, the fees paid to the serf owner for leasing fields and the corvée labour taxes were very significant. Although the agricultural serfs had in general small [owned] fields or leased fields, most of the work of a household had, therefore, to be done in the form of corvée labour for the landlord. Obviously, it was very difficult for the agricultural serfs to cultivate their own fields adequately.

Fifth: Commercial tax

The commercial tax of Tibet was mainly a taxation on merchandise. During the Qing Dynasty the local Tibetan government issued general ordinances (*rtsa tshig*) concerning tax matters. Two [types of traditional taxes] had been established in Tibet: toll (*sho khral*) and trading tax (*tshugs khral*).[35] Together they are referred to as *sho tshong dpya khral*. *Sho khral* was the term used for a tax which had to be paid upon the merchandise's arrival in each region (*sa gnas*), and *tshugs sho*[36] for the tax for buying and selling on the market. Before the [so-called] liberation, the local Tibetan government had established wool, salt and tea tolls, among

34 The Tibetan calendar is a lunisolar calendar consisting of twelve lunar months of thirty days each. The difference between the lunar and solar year is compensated by the occasional intercalation of leap months. For details see Schuh 1973: 107–17, 135–41.

35 The term *tshugs* actually denotes the stations or stopover places. Apparently, these stations were also the marketplaces where goods were sold and bought.

36 Apparently *tshugs sho* is used as a synonym for *tshugs khral*.

others, in Gar Yarsa, Lhatse, Phari, Nyanang[37] and so on, and were able to cash (from local products illustrated here by salt, tea and wool) a tax yield of about 140,000 Chinese silver dollars from travelling merchants each year. What is more, in Nagchu, Lhari and Drigung,[38] from the tea toll alone, 859 bamboo baskets containing tea bricks and 532 bamboo baskets containing tea balls were collected every year as tax yield. On the pastureland of Yardrong Lhakhang (Yar grong lha khang) in Tshona district, *tshugs sho* was established. In Dromo (Gro mo) and Nyanang, custom offices (*sho pa*) were also set up. The local [Tibetan] government established thirty-six customs offices across Tibet. The taxes for merchandise in Tibet were collected after the amount had been checked when the merchandise both arrived and was taken away. Goods were mainly collected for *sho khral*. Barely a hundred years from the dawning of the modern age, the signing of deeply unfair treaties was enforced through the aggression and power of imperialism. Based on that, the [yield from] duties on imported goods was very small because there was no way that the local Tibetan government could set up a customs office for travelling foreign merchants. From 1950 onwards, it was fixed that in various regions, for example Gro mo—regardless of the number of goods—for each pack animal's load, 3 *srang* should be collected as customs duty. The local Tibetan government gave various special permits for business enterprises to the monasteries and greater noble families. Therefore, from the entire financial income of the Tibetan government, there were no more than about 400,000 Chinese silver dollars coming in from customs duties. Proportionally, that is very low. In Tibet there were various kinds of customs duties. For some of them, the system of taking complete responsibility [on the district level] was implemented and, based on a fixed [amount], the tax revenue was then paid to the government annually. How much tax the government really collected cannot be investigated. The responsibility for collecting customs duties was leased from the office [in charge] of tea and salt [taxes] by persons of influence. The money for the lease was paid to the government in accordance with a fixed amount. Afterwards the customs duties were collected. There were also some remote districts which collected the customs duties on their own initiative. They not only did not have to transmit [reports and tax revenues] through the office [in charge] of tea and salt [taxes], but the income from the tax was also not transferred to the above, instead being

37 sGar dbyar sa, lHa rtse, Pha ri, gNya' nang.
38 Nag chu, lHa ri, 'Bri gung.

taken by the District Commissioner. Or indeed, other than a negligible amount, nothing was paid at all. For example: when someone leased the responsibility to collect the toll and trading tax of mTsho sna district, he paid 450 Chinese silver dollars to the District Commissioner annually as lease money for having assumed the responsibility to collect the taxes. Thereafter, he set up customs offices in the areas of Legpo (Legs po) and Yardrong [within Tshona district] and was allowed to collect the taxes.

3 Taxes in Nomadic Areas[39]

All the tribes of the nomadic areas were subordinated either to the local [Tibetan] government, the monasteries or the aristocrats. For ease of management, a portion of those which were subordinated to the local [Tibetan] government was left to be picked up by single monasteries and aristocrats. All tribes had to undertake a corvée labour tax for the local [Tibetan] government. [However], the nomadic serfs not only had to perform various corvée duties for the local [Tibetan] government, they also had to pay taxes in the form of meat, butter, hides, wool, cash, and so on. Taxes and corvée labour in the nomadic areas differed somewhat from the taxes and corvée labour of the farmland areas. In most nomadic areas the taxes were collected on the basis of quantity of cattle. Because taxes mainly in the form of nomadic products had to be paid, the demand for corvée labour was small. At set times or at irregular intervals the local [Tibetan] government, the monasteries and the aristocrats counted the cattle, took notes of the various domestic animals, divided the different kinds of taxes and collected them.

(One) In the past the unit for levying the taxes in the various districts of the thirty-nine groups [of nomads] was called *hram pa*. According to tradition, it was established at the time of Gushri Qan. At that time a field [with a capacity] of 11 *khal* and 4 *bre* of seed, or else four horses or seventy-five goats or sheep or thirty head of cattle, whichever was appropriate, was fixed as the standard for one *hram pa*. However, the way to calculate this [*hram pa*] was not the same in each district. For example, with regard to a nomadic household in the sTeng chen district, six horses or thirteen head of cattle or twenty-five goats or sheep, whichever was appropriate, was calculated as one *hram pa*. Whereas for a nomadic household in the Ser tsha district, five horses or ten head of cattle or thirty goats or sheep, whichever was appropriate, was calculated as one *hram*

39 This chapter is a translation of Tshe ring don grub *et al.* 1991, I, chapter 5.7.4 (646–53).

FIGURE 1.4 Lhasa, New Year: bringing dried sheep and cattle carcasses for the festival, 1938/1939. Photo by Ernst Schäfer
BUNDESARCHIV, IMAGE 135-S-12-06-30

pa. For a nomadic household in lower A mdo, five head of cattle or two horses or fifty sheep or a hundred goats, whichever was appropriate, was calculated as one *hram pa*, and up to half a *hram pa* was imposed as tax.

The different taxes which had to be paid for one *hram pa* in lower A mdo:

1. Commodities (*dngos rdzas*): 1 *khal* and 5 *nyag* of butter, 2 *khal* of wool (1 *khal* is about 7 *rgya ma*),[40] one sheepskin and 50 silver *srang*.
2. Corvée labour (*'u lag*): transport of loads (Here a differentiation was made between short and long distances. The long journeys were called *rdzong skyel*. Those were transports from one district to another. The short ones were called *sa tshigs* and were transports between single transport stations.).
3. Taxes to be paid to the District Commissioner: for one *hram pa* he received one sheep and 2.5 *khal* of butter.

Moreover, based on the number of cattle, that particular district [in A mdo] collected one tenth as interest for leasing the animals (*she skyed*).

Every year one uncut hide and one load of dung were also collected from each household.

The taxes to be paid for one *hram pa* in Tengchen (sTeng chen) district:

(1) Corvée labour for transporting goods (*dos skyel 'u lag*): with regard to one pack animal, for one *hram pa* corvée labour for the transportation of goods had to be done thirty times per year. (One tax for human [lease] (*mi khral*)[41] and one pack animal were interchangeable.)
(2) Payment in lieu of sending a soldier (*dmag dod*).
(3) Kitchen servant (*thab g.yog*): "kitchen servant" was the name for the tax [consisting] of making fire, fetching water, arranging the encampment for short stopovers or overnight stays, and so on, for when government officials, Tibetan troops, messengers, et cetera, travelled across the country.

(Two) In the areas of Nagchu, Sangzhung and Damzhung,[42] the taxes also had to be paid on the basis of the number of cattle. The units for paying the tax were *dmag rkang* and *rta mgo*. For the nomadic serfs in Damzhung district, one horse or else five head of cattle or twenty sheep

---

40 Although synonymous with the unit of measurement for volume, the *khal* mentioned here is a unit for weight. It is also called *'degs khal* and divided into 20 *nyag* or *nya ga*. Charles Bell has given as the equivalent of the weight unit *khal* "about 6 or 7 lb." (Bell 1928: 303), which would be a weight between 2.72 and 3.17 kg. As stated here and confirmed by Zhang Yisun *et al.* (1998: 227), it equals about seven *rgya ma*. One *rgya ma* equals half a kilogram or 1.1023 pounds (Goldstein 2001: 254).

41 According to Goldstein (2001: 793) the term *mi khral* is synonymous with *mi 'bogs*, "'human lease' (the annual fee paid by a serf to his lord or owner for exemption from having to live on the estate and provide corvée labor)".

42 Nag chu, gSang gzhung, 'Dam gzhung.

or fifty goats, whatever was appropriate, was fixed as one *rta mgo* unit for the payment of the taxes. Fifty *rta mgo* were fixed as one *dmag rkang*. (The meaning of the *dmag rkang* which we are concerned with here, and of the *dmag rkang* in the farmland areas is in fact the same.) When external taxes were provided in the Sangzhung area, six head of cattle were fixed as one *rta mgo*, and 30 *rta mgo* were fixed as one *dmag rkang*. In Nagchu district, one-and-a-half horses belonging to the nomadic serfs or else six head of cattle or thirth-six sheep or seventy-two goats, whichever was appropriate, was fixed as one *rta mgo*, and thirty *rta mgo* were fixed as one *dmag rkang*.

The number of external taxes in Damzhung district:

1. The method for paying the *spyi rim khral gzhung* (This tax was one that was demanded by Gushri Qan in the past, when military exercises were presented for inspection in Damzhung. But since the obligation to present military exercises for inspection was later no longer important, [this tax] was converted into a tax for the performance of public religious ceremonies [to eliminate obstacles].): every year, one nomadic household in possession of five *rta mgo* had to pay two and a half *rgya ma* of butter, 4 *bre* of roasted barley flour, 1 *bre* of cheese, 1 *bre* of grain, one tenth of a *bre* of salt or soda (one *bre* [corresponded] to about 1 *rgya ma* and 4 *srang*).
2. Provision of riding horses and transport animals (*rta'u dos khal*).
3. Local military tax (*sa gnas kyi dmag khral*).
4. Tax for food expenses for prisoners (*btson pa'i zas gron gyi khral*).
5. Taxes to [cover] the expenses for the reception of the officials who counted the cattle.

Apart from that, the taxes collected on the basis of the *dmag rkang* [unit] included tax in the [form of] butter, cash, wood and wool.

Nomadic households which could not reach one *rta mgo* had to pay an annual tax (*lo khral*). In this respect, there existed no standardised way to measure the tax for the individual nomadic groups. For some nomadic groups it was fixed that they had to pay, for one head of cattle, 1 *srang* of butter and 1 silver *srang*. [However], for some [other] nomadic groups it was fixed that they had to pay, for one head of cattle, 2 *srang* of butter, 1 silver *srang* and three sacks of dung.

A nomadic household which possessed neither cattle nor sheep had to pay 1 silver *srang* (similar to the human lease) every year.

The corvée labour and the military taxes had to be undertaken by the different households as an annual tax. At the same time as [working] to pay taxes, the nomadic groups were [also] collecting and paying proportionately for their cost of living and wages (*gla cha*) on the basis of the *rta mgo* [unit].

If we ask how much the tax on one head of cattle might be according to the detailed calculation of the taxes above, let us take for example the fact that, in the year 1958 in the A pa tribe, one head of cattle had to yield [as taxes] 2 *khal* and 5 *nyag* of butter over the course of the year. A female milk yak produces no more than about four or four and a half *khal* of butter per year. Therefore, the degree of exploitation by the three great feudal lords [government, monasteries and the aristocracy] amounted to more or less 60 per cent.

(Three) The method of tax collection in the area of Palgön (dPal mgon) district: five sheep or six goats or one head of cattle were interchangeable. Eighty head of cattle constituted one meat unit (*sha rkang*). The number of taxes which were collected for each *sha rkang* were as follows:

To the various monasteries every year [altogether] were sent 8 *khal* of butter, eight sheep, twelve lamb skins, eight sacks of salt (each salt sack usually contained about 100 *rgya ma*), one entire hide, one [new] sack, forty *khre tse*[43] of material woven from yak hair (*re lde*), as a substitute for dung and dung pellets [of sheep and goats] two sheep, [as well as] both a thick and a thin rope made of [yak] hair, five loads of twisted wool (*bal sgor*) and six barrels of soda (each barrel [contained] between eight and ten *rgya ma*). Moreover, every year one pack yak had to be provided.

A household owning more than five head of cattle had, in the course of the year, to pay [i.e. *'bri, g.yag* or *mdzo*] 24 silver *srang* for each head of cattle. A household owning up to five head of cattle had to pay 1 silver *srang* for each head of cattle during the course of the year.

With regard to the taxes which had to be paid by the various tribes to the local [Tibetan] government, 250 silver *srang* had to be paid every year to the office in charge of military affairs (*dmag spyi khang*) and [in addition], every year 400 silver *srang*, 1 *khal* of butter, 4 *bre* of cheese and five yaks to be slaughtered for meat (*tshags po*) were all sent to the various authorities by the local [Tibetan] government. Likewise, every year five goats also had to be given to the messenger of the district. Moreover, as an annual grass tax thirty sheep, 180 *'degs khal*[44] of wool and half a load (*rgyab*) of tea had to be paid.

43 According to Goldstein (2001: 149) *khre rtse* is a linear measure equal to 0.32 metres.

44 See above note 40.

(Four) The authorities of Lhathog (lHa thog) in the Chamdo (Chab mdo) area mainly collected butter as tax from the nomads' area under their control. The rate for collecting the taxes was calculated based on two thirds of the amount of the adult cattle for each household. For all the nomads belonging to the authorities of Lhathog in possession of one head of cattle or else four sheep or eight goats, whichever was appropriate, this was without exception fixed as one *sgur ru*. For one *sgur ru* 1 *khal* of butter had to be paid every year. Furthermore, the taxes were levied proportionately, based on the amount of *sgur ru*.

(Five) Brag g.yab district collected the taxes by treating the butter tax on leased cattle (*she khral*), the [normal government] tax (*dpya khral*) and the lease fee (*bogs ma*) as one and the same. The lama household (*bla brang*) of Brag g.yab[45] had specified that every year, for one female yak, eight *rgya ma* of butter and for 100 sheep one carcass of meat had to be paid.

(Six) In the Pashö (dPa' shod) district of the Chamdo area, the lama household of Kündeling (Kun bde gling) which united religious and secular rule [in that area],[46] had specified that, for ninety head of cattle and 129 goats or sheep, the nomads had to pay 160 *rgya ma* butter, 212 *rgya ma* of wool and 52 silver *srang*.

For the nomadic tribes in the area of Lhokha (lHo kha) the landlords had divided the grazing land into tax units (*khral rkang*) similar to the agricultural land, and then given it back to the single nomadic households. Without regard for the number of cattle, the taxes were demanded according to the number of [these] pasture units owned. Another method was to fix the tax income of the entire nomadic grassland and then leave the pastures to the taxpayers collectively. Based on the actual number of cattle the taxes were then collected proportionally.

45 On the administration of Dragyab see Dagyab 1980.

46 Originally, the seat of the Tatshag (rTa tshag) *rje drung rin po che* was in Pashö, and after Kündeling monastery near Lhasa had been built as his new seat, he still remained the owner of the estates located in Pashö. For details see Schwieger 2015: 25, 81, 113, 255 n50.

4 Derge (sDe dge)

For comparison let us now look at the taxation system in the East Tibetan kingdom of Derge. Three studies in some way make reference to the Derge tax system.

First, there are a very few sentences in Surkhang's article published in 1986 dealing with taxation in sDe dge: "Under this kingdom are 25 *rZong*.[47] To the north of 'Bri-chu, there are 37 *tsho-khang* of nomads. To the south there are 5 *tsho-khang* of nomads. They also have no custom of *rKang* and *'Don*. The taxation is done by the sDe-dge king. The king will pay 250 *srang* of Chinese silver known as *Khral-phud* and 400 *srang* of silver to sPar-khang as *bogs-ma*.[48] All the grain taxes will be collected by the king who must provide for the many monasteries in his kingdom. He must give to the government[49] 500 *khal* of grain as *thog phud* every year" (Surkhang 1986: 29).

Second, a few remarks on taxation in Derge are scattered through Rinzin Thargyal's book *Nomads of Eastern Tibet* (Thargyal 2007: 37, 49f, 67, 206): in the same way as in the territory directly administered by the Ganden Phodrang all land theoretically belonged to the Dalai Lama, so in Derge the king was the owner of all the land. The territory of the whole kingdom was divided into twenty-five districts. Eight ministers, given the titles of *gnyer pa* or *gnyer chen*, one or two treasurers (*phyag mdzod*) and the officials were appointed from among a group of about 30 aristocratic families called *mdun skor*. Four of the ministers were appointed as external, and four were internal. The external ones were stationed outside the centre and were especially responsible for the defence of the country. Below the upper strata of the aristocracy there were two lower classes of leading families, called *dpon cha* and *hor 'dra*. While there were only a few *dpon cha* families, there were about eighty *hor 'dra* families. According to Thargyal they were not regarded as nobles, but had opportunities to climb the social ladder. These groups of people provided administrative services on a more limited local level. Still below these people were the taxpayers, here also called *khral pa*. Thargyal states that the taxpayers had on the one hand to pay heavy taxes, but on the other had no great burden of corvée service (*ibid.*: 67). Finally, there was the group of landless people who offered their labour force to the estates of their lord. Unlike in Central Tibet, this latter group was not named *dud chung*. Thargyal calls these people *'khor pa*.

---

47 In Surkhang's article the spelling *rz* corresponds to the more usual form *rdz*.

48 According to Thupten Sangyay (1986: 45) *bogs ma* "is the amount of yield given by tenants to the owner of the land for cultivation." Goldstein gives "leasing, renting".

49 This refers to the Ganden Phodrang Government.

Thirdly, there is a Tibetan book, published in 1990, in a series edited by the political council of Kandze (dKar mdzes) Autonomous Tibetan Prefecture (Srid gros dkar mdzes bod rigs rang skyong khul u yon lhan khang 1990). Regarding social strata, as well as duties of taxpayers and landless peasants, this study is by far the most detailed and differentiated. The description and appellation of the different strata differ in part from Thargyal's study. It is said that the seventh king Phüntsok Tenpa (Phun tshogs bstan pa) already ruled over 25 districts (*rdzong*) and 43 nomad tribes (*sde shog*) (*ibid.*: 145). According to Kolmaš, this king belonged to the forty-first generation of the royal genealogy and in 1738 had followed his father as abbot of the family monastery Lhündrub Teng (lHun grub steng), and also as the secular ruler (Kolmaš 1968: 40, 50). The year of his death is unknown. The basic social and administrative structure of the kingdom should be even older. Beginning with the first king, Jampa Phüntsok (Byams pa phun tshogs), who had benefited greatly from his cooperation with Gushri Qan (*ibid.*: 33, 49), four political administrators called *gnyer chen* and two treasurers (*phyag mdzod*) were placed immediately under the king. In each greater district, that is to say those with up to 300 households, a governor, called *rdzong dpon*, was stationed. In the smaller districts, starting from 200 households downwards, there were so-called *gzhis gnyer*, "estate stewards". Every village, said to contain several dozen households, received a chief, the *gtso bo*. For some households, living in remote areas, so-called "chiefs of ten", *bcu dpon*, were appointed. The above-mentioned four *gnyer chen* not only had internal duties, but were additionally responsible for the defence of the kingdom's border. Each of them was in charge of one border: the Sershul (Ser shul) *dpon* for the Sershul border, the Lhari *dpon* for the Yilhung (Yid lhungs) border, the Drangba ('Brang pa) *dpon* for the Joda ('Jo mda') border and the Gaje (sGa rje) *dpon* for the Pelyul (dPal yul) border. Thus, according to this study there were only four ministers or *gnyer chen*, but each with both internal and external duties.

Up to the fourteenth and last king, there were always between forty and fifty leading noble families who could provide the District Commissioners. From among the District Commissioners, the *gnyer chen* and *phyag mdzod* could then be selected. The study lists the names and places of 49 families whose members had functioned as leading officials over the course of Derge's history. Only nine of them had provided people for the office of a *gnyer chen*. Beside the District Commissioners, the king had further sent so-called *hor 'dra* to the various districts. According to Goldstein, *hor 'dra* was a name for petty officials (Goldstein 2001: 1175). This meaning also applies to the situation in Derge. They collected the tax and proclaimed the king's edicts. They were also responsible for arresting criminals. Under the king there were altogether eighty *hor 'dra* households. Their status was hereditary. If the king considered a member of this group trustworthy, he could promote him to the position of *gzhis gnyer*, estate steward. All these leaders (*dpon*)[50] were in control of their own farmland and subjects. A *gnyer chen* as well as a *rdzong dpon* could each have between ten and 200 households working on his estates. A *hor 'dra* only had between two and four households working for him.

Below these families of the upper stratum were the taxpayers, the *khral pa*. Unlike Thargyal, the study published by the council of Kandze Autonomous Tibetan Prefecture does not state that the taxpayers were more or less exempt from corvée. By contrast it is explained in detail that they were obliged to perform various kinds of compulsory labour. The following is a translation of the chapters on corvée labour and taxes to be paid in kind:[51]

> 1. About corvée labour (*'u lag*)
> In general, all the taxpayers (*khral pa*) and the farmworkers (*khol pa*)[52] had to perform corvée labour.
>
> Among the taxpayers, some had to pay taxes by [providing] a person [as a servant] (*mi khral*), some taxes by [providing] a pack animal (*khal khral*) and some taxes by [providing] a horse (*rta khral*).[53] And there were even those who had to pay two types of [such] corvée labour. For example, there were those who had to pay a tax [burden] of one pack

50 I assume that the term of leader (*dpon*) was used by the authors of the book in retrospect of the described historical situation and does not reflect the self-description of the historical social order.

51 Srid gros dkar mdzes bod rigs rang skyong khul u yon lhan khang 1990: 165–82. Quotation marks are part of the Tibetan original. Square brackets enclose supplements added by me for a better understanding.

52 The term *khol pa* derives from the verb *'khol*, "to make somebody serve, to put someone into service, to bind someone as a servant". The *khol pa* seem to be equal to the *'khor pa* not mentioned in this study, but occurring in Thargyal's monograph. Carrasco (1959: 65f, 145f) identified a group of people in Derge called *khol po*, meaning "servant" or "slave". According to Carrasco these people worked as servants for the taxpayers or for the king himself and received in exchange some land on lease. However, according to the survey published by the council of Kandze Autonomous Tibetan Prefecture, the term *khol pa* did not denote agricultural labourers who had to work as servants for the *khral pa* or the king. Instead, exactly as stated by Goldstein with regard to the tied *dud chung* (Goldstein 1971: 5), *khol pa* also denotes farmworkers without heritable land, who were bound for the most part to the private estates of the monasteries and the leading noble families.

53 These three classes of taxpayer households primarily represented three different levels of wealth. As will be seen below, the names given to the different classes thus do not imply that only the workforce specified by the name had to be provided, but that those designated as belonging to a superior class had to provide more labourers or a higher quality workforce.

animal corvée tax and one horse corvée tax, and those who had to pay a tax [burden] of one horse corvée tax and two pack animal corvée taxes. In terms of the basic tax burden, one could be placed in a superior category, but not downgraded. For example, when the economic situation of a household that had to provide a person as tax (*mi khral dud tshang*) improved, the king quickly classified that *mi khral dud tshang* as a household that had to provide a pack animal as tax (*khal khral dud tshang*). But a *khal khral dud tshang* could not be downgraded to a *mi khral dud tshang*. When some taxpayers were impoverished and were therefore really unable to pay the tax, they were totally downgraded [i.e. they lost their taxpayer status].

One person of a *mi khral dud tshang* had to perform corvée labour for the king throughout the entire year: cultivating fields, grazing cattle, collecting wood, making tea, collecting grass, fetching water, grinding roasted barley, running errands, and leading horses. When doing the corvée labour tax, the provisions had to be carried by the incumbent himself, who was required to carry out whatever duties were specified by the king or the steward. Even when corvée labourers were free from working in the fields, they were unable to rest. As a consequence, many taxpayers died of sheer exhaustion.

The *khal khral dud tshang* constantly had to keep one person and one [pack] animal in readiness. They had to hold themselves ready to be sent [somewhere] by the king. At the king's or the steward's command, they had to leave immediately. The time taken for paying the pack animal corvée tax was about one half to two thirds of a year. For those in the group who had to undertake corvée labour, some had to cultivate the private estates of the king, some had to fetch various pieces of merchandise, some had to welcome and send off government officials, and so on.

One person and one horse from a household which had to provide a horse corvée tax (*rta khral dud tshang*) had to carry out horse corvée tax for the king. The position of those who paid the tax was for the most part similar to the ones who paid the [pack] animal tax. About six to nine months were needed to complete the yearly corvée labour tax. Furthermore, sometimes corvée labour over long distances to Lhasa or other places had to be carried out. When undertaking this corvée labour tax, the taxpayers had to carry the provisions and the fodder for the horses themselves. For each long distance corvée labour trip undertaken, inevitably some pack animals were lost.

The royal household had a list of names of the taxpayers for the entire territory. And there were various people who were specially appointed to supervise the affairs pertaining to the corvée labour. The chiefs of each and every village had to personally bear the responsibility. If the number of those who worked the tax was incomplete, then they absolutely had to fill in, otherwise they were punished heavily.

The taxpayers had to bear the responsibility to cultivate all the 666 *mu'u*[54] of the king's "private estates"[55] without salary. The yield of the private estates had to be given in total to the king. The king determined that one portion had to be given to himself and one portion was handed over to the monastery. By directly commissioning an individual, the royal household allowed him to supervise the "private estates". The person who supervised the "private estates" was called the foreman (*thog dpon*). This individual was generally a reliable servant of the king's household. It was also possible that a *hor 'dra* took on the responsibility, and occasionally one of the taxpayers was promoted to this position. In terms of the prerequisites, these were individuals who had been kind and sincere towards the king. Their responsibility was to supervise the taxpayers' work on the "private estates". Once every three years the *thog dpon* had to be changed. In the exceptional case that he was someone who had been very sincere towards the king, he was allowed to continue to hold the responsibility. When they acted as work supervisors, these men were allowed to eat and drink whatever they liked, and were allowed to cover all expenses from the king's stores of barley. To strengthen their own position, every year the work supervisors delivered one sheep or one quarter of one head of cattle to each of the king's four *gnyer chen*. The king sent not only the *thog dpon* to Pelyul, Denkhog ('Dan khog) and Thangphug (Thang phug), places far away from the king's residence, but the government officials (*gzhung dpon*) of that area also had to take on the duties of managing the "private estates".

For the most part the "private estates" were fertile lands. Concerning the tillage, the taxpayers of each surrounding area had in turn to carry out the tasks of planting seed, weeding, harvesting and threshing. If a taxpayer could not work, it was acceptable to hire a substitute worker. It was also permissible that money was given directly to the work supervisor and that he then employed a substitute worker. In the [village] Dzepa (mDzes pa) *grong* of Gönche (dGon ched) *shang*[56] was a "private estate"

54 Chinese area measurement, *mu* 亩, equal to about 1/6 acre or 1/15 hectare.

55 Note that here and in the following the inverted commas are present in the original.

56 *shang* (Chin. *xiang* 乡) is a rural administrative unit consisting of several villages (Goldstein 2001: 1093).

of the king totalling sixty *mu'u*. It had to be cultivated by the 190 taxpayer households of one *shang*. Planting seed had to be done by the taxpayers of [the villages] of Bame (Ba smad) *grong* and Dzepa (mDzes pa) *grong*. Some taxpayers from amongst the villagers who planted seed also had to assume the responsibility of weeding. The taxpayers of [the village] Baring Nangdrong (Ba ring nang grong) had to assume the responsibility of ploughing. For the harvesting the taxpayers of the three [villages] Jama Shipa, Beda and Ngülphu Nangdrong[57] had to do the work. Threshing the barley had to be done by the taxpayers of the three [villages] Hyame, Phushi and Naphu *grong*.[58] Annually, at the opportune moment, the king sent the "*thog dpon*" to make the taxpayers start planting seed. Upon the "*thog dpon*"'s arrival, the taxpayers had to immediately abandon their own fieldwork, regardless of how busy they were. The sixty *mu'u* of the "private estate" were located next to the fields of the chief (*'go pa*) and the fields which were apportioned to the taxpayers. Therefore, after one field had been cultivated, the next one had to be cultivated.

When the taxpayers performed their jobs as tax on the "private estates", they had to bring the *mdzo* for ploughing, the tools and the provisions themselves. Except for the seed, the king supplied nothing. When ploughing the fields, two *mi khral dud tshang* had to provide two persons and one *mdzo*, a *zog khral dud tshang* had to provide one person and one *mdzo*, and a *rta khral dud tshang* had to provide one person and two *mdzo*. The fodder for the *mdzo*, they had also to provide themselves. If [the *mdzo*] ate the grass on the boundaries of the "private estates" of the royal household, a fine was paid. It was common that the taxpayers worked on the "private estates". The *thog dpon* distributed the work. His word was law. In general, those whose capacity to work was weaker led the *mdzo*, and those who more capable of heavy labour did the ploughing work. All taxpayers had to live near the "private estates". Every day, they had to start working before sunrise, and they stopped working at nightfall. The ploughing on the "private estates" had to be done carefully. On each *sgro ba*[59] of the field, twenty baskets of manure had to be dumped. (One basket of dung contained between forty and sixty *rgya ma*.[60])

---

57 mJa' ma gshis pa, Bad mda', dNgul phu nang grong.

58 Hya smad, Phu gshis, rNa phu grong.

59 Here the term *sgro ba* is obviously a surface measure (*zhing sgro ba gang rer ...*). Below it is used as a measure for the seed that could be sown on a piece of land. The meaning is not documented in the dictionaries. But apparently its usage is similar to that of the Central Tibetan term *khal*.

60 See above note 40.

The taxpayers had to provide [the dung]. The weeds had to be removed twice [a year]. After each harvest, the fields that in turn should remain fallow for the year, and those to be cultivated had to be ploughed over. After the taxpayers had threshed the barley well, dried it, and separated the grain from the chaff, it was loaded onto the pack animals and sent to the king's household to be stored in the storehouse. When working on the "private estates" of the king, the taxpayers had to perform their work under the supervision of the *thog dpon*. The *thog dpon* came to the fields every day, brandishing a whip. On a whim he beat the taxpayers and rebuked them harshly. [As far as he was concerned,] it was perfectly acceptable to embezzle valuables. Therefore, when the taxpayers were only a little behind with their work, they were beaten and rebuked, and whosoever's family member's labour force was weaker, [that family] was ordered to exchange the person [in question]. If [the taxpayers] were not able to break the clumps of earth very finely, they were whipped. For fear of being beaten or rebuked, the taxpayers gave butter, beef and roasted barley flour. Since the taxpayers had no interest in this kind of work, the yield of the "private estates" was mostly low, and amounted to no more than about four or five times of the seed that had been sown.

For the farmworkers it was usually sufficient that they pay corvée labour tax for single masters (chiefs and monasteries). The farmworkers of the monasteries were taken care of by the monasteries, and the farmworkers of the chiefs (*'go pa*) were taken care of by the chiefs.

Because the monasteries to which [the farmworkers] belonged were different, the amount of time for the corvée labour to be performed by the taxpayers, as well as their [individual] burdens, were also different. The four farmworker households of the [village] Dzepa (mDzes pa) *grong* of Gönchen (dGon chen) monastery had to give half in commodities (*dngos rdzas*) and half as a lease fee (*sa bogs*). Moreover, with regard to their duties of [paying] labour tax (*las khral*) and tax in the form of goods (*sho khral*),[61] each year they had three days to reap the barley for the monastery, and each [household] also had to give four loads of wood and four loads of grass. The labour tax of the farmworkers of Pelpung (dPal spungs) monastery was a very heavy duty. They had to provide various labour taxes for the monastery. They were required to perform tasks such

61 In general *sho khral* is understood as a kind of toll or customs duty (Goldstein 2001: 1104). As evident from the specifications given below, the term is here used as a tax on local products and paid in form of local products, for example wood and grass. See also the chapter below on *dngos rdzas kyi sho khral*.

FIGURE 1.5 Dotra (rDo bkra): women spinning, 1938/1939. Photo by Ernst Schäfer
BUNDESARCHIV, IMAGE 135-S-04-18-26

as transporting goods, constructing new monastic buildings, chopping wood, fetching water and making tea. Some had to do corvée labour tax (*khral 'u lag*) for the monastery all year long, by [earmarking] the whole person [for that duty alone]. Some had between six and nine months to provide corvée labour tax every year.

The amount of time which the farmworkers had to do corvée labour tax for [secular] chiefs was longer [than that done for the monasteries]. There were those in particular who paid their tax by permanently living in the chief's house. There were also those who were at the beck and call of their masters, without various specially appointed people having to be sent. Especially during the busy farming period, more or less all members of the farmworker household had to do corvée labour tax for the chief. The main corvée labour tax of the farmworkers was the duty to cultivate the private fields of the chief. Their field work ran the gamut, from ploughing to harvesting. In terms of the work of the nomads, the grazing of cattle and the processing of the livestock products had to be done. For example, they had to milk, churn butter and soften leather. With regard to handicraft work done in the house and incidental work, spinning wool, weaving woollen cloth, manufacturing agricultural tools and packsaddles had to be done. [Moreover,] minor tasks for the general sustenance of the chief had to be done. For example, wood had to be chopped, water had to be fetched, tea had to be made, roasted barley had to be ground, and houses had to be repaired. On the estates of the great chief Jamyang Chödrön ('Jam dbyangs chos sgron) of [the village] Lhaphu (lHa phu grong) in Gönchen (dGon chen) *shang*[62] the sixteen farmworker households had altogether 66 people, and there were 45 hired labourers. (This included all full and part time workers.[63]) However, during the busy period in farm work there were sixty labourers on the private estate. Thus, on average, every household provided 3.7 hired labourers.[64] Also during periods without fieldwork, at least twenty *khral pa*[65] had to do various minor labours on the estate of the chief. Thus on average, at that time every *farmworker* household [still] had to provide 1.25 hired labourers.

While the farmworkers had to toil on the chief's fields for nothing, the chief took seed, *mdzo* for ploughing and agricultural tools. The entire grain yield had to be given over to the chief. Great chiefs sent a representative and let him directly supervise the private fields. The supervisor of the private fields was called the foreman (*thog dpon*). Such individuals were usually servants whom the chief could trust. If they were very sincere towards the chief and the chief trusted them, they were allowed to assume continual responsibility. Their main responsibility was to supervise the work of the farmworkers on the private fields.

When the farmworkers carried out corvée labour on the private fields of the chief, everything was collective work. At the time of ploughing, all the farmworkers had to work [together] on one piece of land, and after finishing one area, they had to work on another. The chief had determined: the fields had to be ploughed and turned three times. In this way, the land had to be ploughed once after the grass grew, after some days the soil had to be turned over again, and when sowing, ploughing had to be done for the third time. The earth had to be ploughed deep. Weeds had to be pulled out two or three times. The stones had to be removed from the field. On each piece of land, on which one *sgro ba*[66] of seed

62 On the term *shang* see above note 56.

63 The term used here for full time worker is *las gson* and the one for part time worker *las phyed*.

64 Sixteen hired labourers divided by sixty households, 3.75.

65 Here *khral pa* is obviously a mistake for *khol pa*.

66 See above note 59.

was to be be sown, 60 baskets of dung had to be dumped. All the dung had to be provided by the farmworkers. When the farmworkers worked on the field, the *thog dpon* acted as work supervisor (*las dpon*). The work started at dawn, and could not cease until after dark. The work supervisor carried a whip and went everywhere on inspection. During work, rest periods were not permitted. Even when going to defecate, one had to ask the work supervisor for permission. When drinking tea, one had to drink it secretly. Sometimes the chief [himself] came to inspect the fields.

The sixty *mu'u* agricultural land of the great chief Lunglha Tshang (Lung lha tshang) were located in [the village] of Dzepa *grong*. It had to be cultivated by the farmworker households. Among them seven households lived in [the village] Bame *grong*. When doing the spring planting and the harvest work, they stayed in Dzepa *grong*, and they were only allowed to return [home] after the fieldwork was completed. Likewise, three farmworker households of Dzepa *grong* had to go to Bame *grong* for work. Even when the private fields of the chief were scattered over various locations, the farmworkers had to do their work jointly, for the sake of an easier supervision. If hired labourers were needed somewhere, the farmworkers had to go to that place to work.

When the farmworkers carried out corvée labour for the great chief, the chief gave each farmworker no more than two bowls of inferior barley per day. Therefore, they were not inclined to hard labour. When the work supervisor's back was turned, they did their work in a slipshod way or lost agricultural implements. And they also regularly pulled up fresh sprouts by the root while weeding.

The taxpayers and the farmworkers did not only carry out the above [mentioned] corvée labours. In addition, all the great and small monasteries of the entire area solicited them, in the name of the gods, to do corvée labour for their own individual purposes, without feeling obligated to provide any payment to the taxpayers and farmworkers. For example, they were made to do work like transporting goods, constructing monasteries, bringing firewood and fodder, fetching water and making tea. The amount of time for that kind of corvée labour was not fixed. Whenever they were summoned [for corvée labour], they had to go immediately.

2. On collecting *sho khral* for commodities (*dngos rdzas*)

The king, the chiefs and the monasteries, all forced the taxpayers and the farmworkers to do corvée labour. This was the main kind of exploitation. However, at the same time it also was determined for the taxpayers and the farmworkers that they had to give numerous *sho khral*[67] of commodities. The *sho khral* of commodities were not only ordered agricultural products. The taxpayers had to pay *sho khral* to the king, and the farmworkers had to pay a lease fee [in the form] of commodities and various taxes to their lords (*bdag po*). On top of the different tax duties which the taxpayers had to pay, they paid *sho khral* of commodities.

rkang khral: barley of one quarter of the sown seed had to be paid to the king as *sho khral*. Barley of half of the sown seed was calculated as grain for the [Tibetan] government and had to be given to the government [in Lhasa].[68] With regard to barley, of one eighth of the sown seed, religious ceremonies had to be performed by giving it to the monastery.

khal khral: One bundle (*do pa*) of grain had to be paid to the king as *sho khral*, half a bundle of grain had to be given to the monastery for [covering] expenses [incurred for] the recitation [of prayers], and two bundles of grain had to be given to the [Tibetan] government.

rta khral: About one or two bundles of grain had to be paid to the king as *sho khral*, one bundle of grain had to be given to the monastery for [covering] expenses [caused by] the recitation [of prayers], and three bundles of government grain had to be given to the [Tibetan] government.

The taxpayers had no choice but to give the various *sho khral* of the above [mentioned] commodities. In addition, a great many other kinds of taxes still had to be paid. For example, there were duties for marriages and funeral rites in the household of the king and the great chiefs. On New Year and at festival time, all the taxpayer households had to deliver presents. Moreover, they had to deliver gifts to the reincarnations and grand lamas of the monastery. Therefore, except for a small yield of their work the taxpayers were not able to keep anything by at the end of the year. Given the very low income of the households, it was impossible to have any quality of life. Each year, most of the taxpayers were between three and six months short of grain. They regularly had to try to satisfy their hunger with wild plants growing on the mountains.

Among the farmworkers of the monasteries, some were [so-called] *phyed ma len mkhan* ("those who take the half") of the monastery. That was a kind of unstable lease fee. Afterwards, at the time of the autumn

---

67 See above note 61.

68 After the end of the Nyarong (Nyag rong) war in 1865 Derge was subordinated to the Ganden Phodrang and the subjects of the Derge king had also to pay taxes in kind and labour to the Tibetan government (Srid gros dkar mdzes bod rigs rang skyong khul u yon lhan khang 1990: 101f).

harvest the government grain had been subtracted from the barley and wheat yield of the fields, the monasteries and the taxpayers (*sic*)[69] of the monasteries were allowed to divide it equally. However, seed grain was not subtracted from that [quantity left after deductions], whereas half of what the farmworkers of the monasteries had received [pre-tax] was subtracted as seed grain. In fact, there was not even one half [left over for the farmworkers afterwards]; [instead] the monastery received two thirds and the farmworkers of the monastery received only one third [of what was left over after 25 per cent government tax had already been subtracted beforehand]. Thus, the degree of exploitation reached about 70 per cent. At the time of the autumn harvest, the monastery sent the steward to the fields in person[70] for inspection. They made sure that the farmworkers did not receive the better quality[71] grain. The taxpayers had furthermore to prepare roasted barley flour, butter and beef for the steward of the monastery. When the harvest began, the steward went in person on an inspection tour of the fields of the "*phyed ma* [*len mkhan*]". He supervised whether the barley on the field was reaped completely or not and whether the barley was threshed clean or not. In case it was not threshed clean, it had to be threshed again. If at the time of harvesting and threshing the barley, there were not enough hired hands among the farmworkers, it was permitted to hire wage labourers. [Covering] the salary for the wage labourers was the responsibility of both parties, the lord and the farmworkers. The salary for the wage labourers was subtracted from the yield of the various grains. Afterwards the grain was divided equally.

The farmworkers mainly undertook corvée labour tax for the chiefs and the monasteries. And they paid lease fees [in the form] of commodities. In addition, for New Year and festivals, or when there were duties for marriage or funeral ceremonies in the household of their lord, they were obliged to deliver presents. And they were also obliged to deliver tokens to the great reincarnations and the grand lamas of the monastery. Among the farmworkers there were only very few who had cattle. If this was the case, then the chiefs and monasteries told them that they were obliged to give butter, beef and mutton regularly. Therefore, farmworkers often

69 Again, here taxpayer (*khral pa*) is obviously a mistake for *khol pa*. Cf. note 52.

70 The wording *sko ngo ma* is a mistake for *sku ngo ma*. The latter also occurs in a parallel construction a few lines below.

71 The lexeme *ya lhag* is not documented in the dictionaries. The meaning was inferred from the context.

> had to take high-interest loans. But it was not easy for the taxpayers to take loans. The lord considered that the farmworkers would not be able to repay a loan at the high interest rates. Thus, he insisted on the farmworker finding someone to act as guarantor [for them]. However, wealthy people did not want to act as guarantors for the farmworkers. The livelihood of the farmworkers was very miserable. Every year they had a deficit of between six and nine months of foodgrain.

5 Conclusion

Without having access to the sources on which the surveys were based, it is of course not possible to verify in detail the data handed down to us through the Chinese-Tibetan surveys. Only the possibility of such a critical verification would put them on a reliable basis. However, even if the description of the Tibetan taxation system and its effects on the people presented here might be exaggerated in one way or another, there is no reason to question its general outline.

The surveys confirm that the peasant households holding land on a hereditary basis were the main taxpayers in Tibetan society. Commercial tax was of less importance for the government revenues. It was a taxation on merchandise and consisted of toll and trading tax. The toll was paid upon the merchandise's arrival in each region, and the trading tax was paid for buying and selling goods on the market. The peasants' tax obligations consisted of the transfer of any valuable items and the performance of labour. Believing the surveys, toward the end of the Ganden Phodrang period labour obligations amounted to about 60 per cent and taxes paid in kind or cash to about 40 per cent. However, there was no uniform regulation of how much arable land the agricultural serfs were allowed to cultivate, and how much corvée labour they were obliged to do. The main tax was the so-called field tax which was calculated in accordance with the amount of seed required for the arable fields. Moreover, the peasants had to pay numerous other taxes in kind and taxes in corvée labour. Special taxes included tax paid in cash or services to be rendered during the Mönlam festival, for the Ambans stationed in Tibet, for the military, and for the postal relay stations. The Tibetan government had given special arable fields to be used as a base for this kind of tax.

In principle, there were two different types of taxes paid to the government: those paid from the various estates directly administered by the Tibetan government, and those paid from the private estates of the various aristocratic families and monasteries. From the point of view of the taxpayers belonging to the latter category, the tax paid to the government was called external tax (*phyi khral*). By contrast, the tax paid in compulsory labour and in cash or kind by taxpayers living on the estates of monasteries and aristocrats and benefiting the monastic or aristocratic landlord was called internal taxes (*nang khral*).

Taxes in the nomadic areas differed somewhat from the taxes of the farmland areas. In most nomadic areas the taxes were calculated on the base of the amount of the cattle. The taxes had to be paid mainly in the form of nomadic products. In contrast to the peasants, the cattle breeders had little obligation to perform corvée labour.

Without doubt the tax burden for the peasants and nomads in Tibet—no matter whether Central or East Tibet—was enormous, making it hard for them to provide for their own daily subsistence and very difficult to amass any surplus as security in times of need. It nevertheless did not result in a great tax income for the government, because the people had hardly any incentive to exert themselves for their labour. Moreover, they could not see that the taxes were used to improve their living conditions, except for the vague hope that the massive support provided for the clergy would somehow result in their having a better lot in the next life.

References

Bell, C.A. 1924. *Tibet. Past and Present*. Oxford: The Clarendon Press.

Bell, C.A. 1928. *The People of Tibet*. Oxford: The Clarendon Press.

Bod rang skyong ljongs lo rgyus yig tshags khang (ed.). 1989. *lCags stag zhib gzhung: dGa' ldan pho brang ba'i chab 'bangs dbus gtsang dwags kong rong khag bcas kyi lcags stag zhib gzhung dam 'byar ma'i zhal bshus dge*. Beijing: Krung go bod kyi shes rig dpe skrun khang (Zhongguo Zangxue chubanshe 中国藏学出版社).

Carrasco, P. 1959. *Land and Polity in Tibet*. Seattle: University of Washington Press.

Dabringhaus, S. 1994. *Das Qing-Imperium als Vision und Wirklichkeit. Tibet in Laufbahn und Schriften des Song Yun (1752–1835)*. Stuttgart: Franz Steiner Verlag.

Dagyab, L.S. 1980. Die Verwaltung des Bezirkes Brag-g.yab (= Dagyab, Osttibet) durch die Brag g.yab skyabs-mgon. *In* H. Franke and W. Heissig (eds) *Heilen und Schenken. Festschrift für Günther Klinge zum 70. Geburtstag*. Wiesbaden: Otto Harrassowitz, 12–21.

Ding, Shicun 丁實存. 1943. *Qingdai zhuzang dachen kao* 清代駐藏大臣考. Taipei: Mengzang weiyuanhui yinxing (Published by the Committee for Mongolian and Tibetan Affairs).

Dung dkar Blo bzang 'phrin las. 2002. *Dung dkar tshig mdzod chen mo (mKhas dbang dung dkar blo bzang 'phrin las mchog gis mdzad pa'i bod rig pa'i tshig mdzod chen mo shes bya rab gsal)*. Beijing: Krung go'i bod rig pa dpe skrun khang (Zhongguo Zangxue chubanshe 中国藏学出版社).

Goldstein, M.C. 1968. An Anthroplogical Study of the Tibetan Political System. Ph.D. thesis, University of Washington.

Goldstein, M.C. 1971. Taxation and the structure of a Tibetan village. *Central Asiatic Journal* 15(1), 1–27.

Goldstein, M.C. 1989. *A History of Modern Tibet, Volume 1: The Demise of the Lamaist State (1913–1951)*. Berkeley: University of California Press.

Goldstein, M.C. (ed.). 2001. *The New Tibetan-English Dictionary of Modern Tibetan*. Assistant Editors: T.N. Snelling and J.T. Surkhang. Berkeley, Los Angeles: University of California Press.

Gurung, Kalsang Norbu. 2013. The role of the Ambans in the Dalai Lama government according to the *Ten-Point Edict*. *In* C. Ramble, P. Schwieger and A. Travers (eds) *Tibetans who Escaped the Historian's Net. Studies in the Social History of Tibetan Societies*. Kathmandu: Vajra Books, 27–39.

Gurung, Kalsang Norbu. 2017. Different copies of the Iron-Tiger land settlement and their historical value as taxation manuals. *In* J. Bischoff and S. Mullard (eds) *Social Regulation. Case Studies from Tibetan History*. Leiden: Brill, 209–30.

Kolmaš, J. 1968. *A Genealogy of the Kings of Derge (Sde-dge'i rgyal-rabs)*. Prague: Academia.

Levine, N. 1992. Traditional taxation system in Western Tibet (中国藏学). *China Tibetology* 1, 322–45.

Petech, L. 1973. *Aristocracy and Government in Tibet, 1728–1959*. Rome: Istituto Italiano per il Medio ed Estremo Oriente (Serie Orientale Roma 45).

Petech, L. 1990. *Central Tibet and the Mongols. The Yüan-Sa-skya Period of Tibetan History*. Rome: Istituto Italiano per il Medio ed Estremo Oriente (Serie Orientale Roma 65).

Schuh, D. 1973. *Untersuchungen zur Geschichte der ribetischen Kalenderrechnung*. Wiesbaden: Steiner Verlag GmbH (VOHD, Supplementband 16).

Schuh, D. 1981a. *Tibetische Handschriften und Blockdrucke. Teil 8. Sammlung Wadell der Staatsbibliothek Preußischer Kulturbesitz Berlin*. Wiesbaden: Franz Steiner Verlag GmbH (VOHD XI, 8).

Schuh, D. 1981b. *Grundlagen tibetischer Siegelkunde. Eine Untersuchung über tibetische Siegelaufschriften in 'Phags-pa-Schrift*. Sankt Augustin: VGH Wissenschaftsverlag (Monumenta Tibetica Historica III/5).

Schwieger, P. 2015. *The Dalai Lama and the Emperor of China: A Political History of the Tibetan Institution of Reincarnation*. New York: Columbia University Press.

Srid gros dkar mdzes bod rigs rang skyong khul u yon lhan khang. 1990. *Rig gnas lo rgyus kyi dpyad gzhi'i yig rigs. deb bzhi pa*. Kangding: Zhengxie sichuan sheng ganzi zangzu zizhizhou zhengzhi xieshanghui 政协四川省甘孜藏族自治州政治协商会.

Surkhang, Wangchen Gelek. 1966. Tax measurement and *Lag 'don* tax. *Bulletin of Tibetology* 3(1), 15–28. Namgyal Institute of Tibetology, Sikkim.

Surkhang, Wangchen Gelek. 1986. Government, monastic and private taxation in Tibet. *The Tibet Journal* 11(1), 21–40.

Thargyal, Rinzin. 2007. *Nomads of Eastern Tibet: Social Organization and Economy of a Pastoral Estate in the Kingdom of Dege*. Edited by T. Huber. Leiden: Brill.

The Cultural Palace of Nationalities (ed.). 1991. *Social History of Tibet, China. Documented and Illustrated*. Beijing: The Photograph Publishing House.

Thupten Sangyay. 1986. Glossary of "Government, monastic and private taxation in Tibet." *The Tibet Journal* 11(1), 41–47.

Travers, A. 2015. The Tibetan army of the Ganden Phodrang in various legal documents (17th–20th centuries). *In* D. Schuh (ed.) *Secular Law and Order in the Tibetan Highland: Contributions to a workshop organized by the Tibet Institute in Andiast (Switzerland)*. Andiast: IITBS GmbH, 249–65.

Tshe ring don grub, O rgyan chos 'phel (eds). 1991. *Bod ljongs spyi bshad*. 2 vols. Lhasa: Bod ljongs mi dmangs dpe skrun khang (Xizang renmin chubanshe 西藏人民出版社).

Winnington, A. 2008. *Tibet: Die wahre Geschichte*. Berlin: Das Neue Berlin.

Wu, Fengpei 吴丰培 and Zeng, Guoqing 曾国庆. 1988. *Qingdai zhuzang dachen zhuanlüe* 清代駐藏大臣傳略. Lhasa: Xizang renmin chubanshe 西藏人民出版社.

Zhang Yisun 张怡荪 *et al.* 1998. *Bod rgya tshig mdzod chen mo. Zang han da cidian* 葬漢辭典. Beijing: Mi rigs dpe skrun khang (Minzu chubanshe 民族出版社).

Internet Sources

DTAB: *Digital Tibetan Archives Bonn*: (https://dtab.crossasia.org).

CHAPTER 2

A Perspective on the Ganden Phodrang's Administration of Taxation in the 19th and 20th Centuries Based on Archival Sources

Kalsang Norbu Gurung

1 Introduction

Tibet has a history of more than a millennium regarding tax payments to its ruler or the government, but the taxation system in Tibet seems to have been very complex, and, for the external observer, sometimes looks unsystematically structured and inconsistent.[1] One might wonder if this characteristic could be, at least partially, explained by the fact that taxation in Tibet was partly administered by representatives of the Tibetan government on a local level (i.e. estate holders and District Commissioners), and the fact that some of the concerned officials were sometimes corrupt increased the complexity of the taxation system. Through a handful of highly valuable pioneering publications on Tibetan taxation (Surkhang 1966, 1986; Goldstein 1968, 1971; Levine in this volume), we know about a number of issues concerning the types of tax obligation and different classes of taxpayers and estates, and how the Tibetan government administered various tax obligations. However, these publications are mostly based on the information gathered from village tax experts and former government employees, and to lesser extent on the archival material. Apart from the extensive chapter about the administration of lands, estates and taxation in Tibet in the first volume of *Bod ljongs spyi bshad* (see Ngag dbang 1991), not much is known about Tibetan taxation on the basis of archival material.[2]

This paper will therefore present a perspective of the Ganden Phodrang (dGa' ldan pho brang) government's administration of taxation according to archival material from the 19th and 20th century. This study aims, in particular,

1 According to *Bod longs spyi bshad*, the tax system was introduced in 13th century during Yuan dynasty (Ngag dbang 1991: 519).

2 The two-volume publication *Bod ljongs spyi bshad* is a collection of research publications translated into Tibetan from originals apparently written in Chinese. It is a very informative and extremely valuable source for the study of Tibetan social, political and economic history. However, this publication lacks essential details regarding references for its sources, from which many valuable conclusions are drawn.

 | DOI:10.1163/9789004529465_004

at understanding the variety of tax obligations to the Ganden Phodrang government and at calculating the basic tax obligation in accordance with the list of lands recorded in the *Iron-Tiger Land Settlement* of 1830 (*lCags stag zhib gzhung*). I will begin my discussion with a description of the responsible offices involved in collecting and managing the central government taxes in Lhasa, followed by an explanation of the types of government taxpayers; I will then explain the units on which tax was calculated in relation to land; this will be followed by the variety of taxes mentioned in documents, in comparison to the secondary sources, and finally, I will discuss the question of the proportion in government tax obligations in Central Tibet during the 19th and 20th centuries. For this, I will use some scattered information from the secondary publications besides the primary sources like *lCags stag zhib gzhung* and two documents belonging to the Documents of Kündeling monastery in Tibet,[3] namely an edict issued in 1830 (see *bKa' rgya*) and a travel document from 1894 (see *Lam yig*). The latter two documents have been transcribed and translated at the end of this paper. It has to be borne in mind that, since we do not have access to the entire archive of materials related to Tibetan taxation, the investigation carried out here will be far from conclusive, but is intended as a preliminary step towards a better understanding of the Ganden Phodrang tax system. For the sake of brevity and consistency, this article will focus particularly on agricultural land.

2 The Tax Administration Offices of the Ganden Phodrang

According to the information collected so far from the secondary publications, we could name at least twelve different offices which directly or indirectly administered the government tax regulations and registered under the administration of the Ganden Phodrang government. I will list these offices with relevant details in order of the year of their establishment.

1. The Bla brang phyag mdzod (abbreviated as *bla phyag*) was established in 1642 as the main administrative body to manage the expenses of the three main Gelukpa monasteries (Sera, Drepung and Ganden)[4] and several neighbouring ones. This office also collected all kinds of tax to

---

3 In this paper, I have used abbreviation DTAB/DKMT to refer to Documents of Kündeling Monastery in Tibet, and DTAB/TDL to refer to the Tibetan Historical Documents and Letters published online as the Digital Tibetan Archives Bonn (DTAB).

4 Se ra, dGa' ldan, 'Bras spungs.

meet those expenses (*Bod kyi srid 'dzin sgrig gzhi*: 34–42, *Dung dkar tshig mdzod*: 1508–1509).

2. The *rtsam bzhes las khungs* was barley supply office responsible for collecting *rtsam pa* and oil for the *smon lam* prayer festival and other religious festivities (*Bod kyi srid 'dzin sgrig gzhi*: 67–69, *Dung dkar tshig mdzod*: 1674, Tsarong 1998a: 9, fn. 12). Dung dkar Blo bzang 'phrin las (*Dung dkar tshig mdzod*: 1674) writes that this office was also responsible for transporting taxed products by requisitioning all-round corvée labour (*gar dgos 'u lag*). According to Paljor Tsarong (1998a: 6), this office was one of the oldest offices established soon after the formation of the dGa' ldang pho brang government in 1642.[5]
3. The Zhol office was established in 1675 to deal primarily with legal administration, punishment and rewards for the inhabitants of Zhol areas and its 18 neighbouring estates, but it also collected taxes (*Bod kyi srid 'dzin sgrig gzhi*: 60–62, *Dung dkar tshig mdzod*: 1783).
4. The *rtse phyag las khungs* (abbreviation of *rtse phyag mdzod las khungs*), also known as *rtse 'phral bde las khungs* was one of the major state treasuries of the Potala palace established already during the Fifth Dalai Lama by *sde srid* Sangs rgyas rgya mtsho (1653–1705) in 1680 (Tsarong 1998b: 24). Its responsibilities were to keep the gifts and offerings presented to the Dalai Lama and the Prime Minister (*srid skyong*) of Tibet, to manage the expenses and to handle the rules of the Potala and Norbulingka palaces, and to deal with the merchants who were engaged in trade for the government (*Bod kyi srid 'dzin sgrig gzhi*: 29–31, *Dung dkar tshig mdzod*: 1679; Tsarong 1998b: 23). According to a former Ganden Phodrang official Surkhang Wangchen Gelek (1910–1977), the office collected gold and other items for trade (Surkhang 1986: 28), and according to Tsarong (1998b: 23, 26) this office collected agricultural and nomadic goods, woollen fabrics, minerals, tea and paper.[6]
5. The *rtsis khang las khungs* (formal name *rtsis khang phun tshogs bkod pa*) was a finance office initially founded in 1646, but officially registered from 1699 and it was one of the main offices of the Ganden Phodrang government. This office prepared, administered and kept tax-related

5 I shall refer to the excellent study by Paljor Tsarong (Tsarong 1998a) for those who are interested to know further details regarding the administration and economic responsibilities of this office.

6 See Paljor Tsarong (1998a) for more details about this office.

documents such as land settlements (*Bod kyi srid 'dzin sgrig gzhi*: 43–47, *Dung dkar tshig mdzod*: 1675–76, *gZhung yig tha snyad*: 161–63).[7]

6. The *rtse gnyer tshang* was a store house in Potala palace responsible for the supply of barley, *rtsam pa*, meat, butter, tea, rice, salt, baking soda and oil for the religious ceremonies at the Potala palace; it had been established during the time of *sde srid* Sangs rgyas rgya mtsho (1653–1705). The office collected *rtsam pa* as the *smon brngod* tax (*Bod kyi srid 'dzin sgrig gzhi*: 32–33, *Dung dkar tshig mdzod*: 1679).
7. The *rtswa gnyer las khungs* was the office to manage fodders for the government transportation animals, and it was responsible for collecting grass (*Bod kyi srid 'dzin sgrig gzhi*: 66–67, *Dung dkar tshig mdzod*: 1685). Although not exactly known, this office seems to be active already since the Ten-Point edict (*rTsa tshig don mtshan bcu*) was issued in 1795.
8. The *shing gnyer las khungs* was the office that managed firewoods used in the government offices and during official ceremonies. This office collected firewood (*Bod kyi srid 'dzin sgrig gzhi*: 69, *Dung dkar tshig mdzod*: 1993). This office seems to be active also since 1795 when the *rTsa tshig don mtshan bcu* was issued.
9. The *so nam las khungs* in Lhasa established in 1913 was the agriculture office responsible for the welfare of people who had wandered from other places or estates, settled in Central Tibet and worked on government estates (*Bod kyi srid 'dzin sgrig gzhi*: 57–58, *Dung dkar tshig mdzod*: 2062–63, *gZhung yig tha snyad*: 189). According to Surkhang (1986: 23), these resettled *mi ser* paid an annual poll tax (for example, one *srang* per man and five *zho* per woman)[8] to the agriculture office, as they did not officially belong to the class of taxpayer *mi ser*.
10. The *ja tshwa las khungs* was an office established in 1915 and it was responsible for collecting tax revenue from trade (*Bod kyi srid 'dzin sgrig gzhi*: 58–59, *Dung dkar tshig mdzod*: 870–71, *Gzhung yig tha snyad*: 116–17). According to Surkhang (1986: 32), this office was established in about 1906 and had collected tax for importing or exporting commercial goods such as tea, salt, wool, yak tails, leather and hides, *gya 'gro* (cf. *rgya gro*, "Chinese wheat" or *rgya gro ma*, "potato"), *bad smug* (unidentified) and caterpillar fungus.

---

7 Dung dkar Blo bzang 'phrin las (*Dung dkar tshig mdzod*: 1675) believed that this office was established during the Seventh Dalai Lama (1708–1757), however, Gling dbon Pad ma skal bzang (*gZhung yig tha snyad*: 162) has dismissed this possibility.

8 *srang* and *zho* were coins used in Tibet. For more on these coins, see Rhodes 1980, Bertsch 2002 and Gurung 2018.

11. The *rtse rnam sras gan 'dzom* (aka *rtse rnam gan dngul skyed do dam*) office had been active since 1919 (*Bod kyi srid 'dzin sgrig gzhi*: 33, *Dung dkar tshig mdzod*: 1679), and Surkhang (1986: 36) writes that this office collected a sort of house or property tax in Lhasa.
12. The *'bab zhib las khungs* was established in 1920 as the investigation commission to investigate and register any new land cultivated after the *lCags stag zhib gzhung* of 1830 was recorded, as well as the new lands owned by some individuals under aristocratic and monastic estates but pretended to be the old ones to hide tax duty (*Bod kyi srid 'dzin sgrig gzhi*: 64–65, Surkhang (1986: 32). This office collected revenue from those newly registered lands known as *'bab*.

3 Taxpayers of the Ganden Phodrang

As is generally agreed (cf. Surkhang 1986: 21, Goldstein 1971: 4), there were basically three types of taxpayers. The first group consisted of the *mi ser* who paid taxes either directly to the government or indirectly through the government-owned estates in its various districts (*rdzong gzhis*). These *mi ser* were known as government *mi ser* and they were obliged to pay tax only to the government.[9] The other two groups were the monastic *mi ser* and aristocratic *mi ser*, who paid their taxes to their respective landlords, the monastic estate holders or the aristocrats, as well as to the government. In summary, as mentioned in the *Bod ljongs spyi bshad* (Ngag dbang 1991: 591), the *mi ser* under aristocratic estates were required to pay a two-part tax.[10] One part, called the outer tax (*phyi khral*), was paid to the government and the other, known as the inner tax (*nang khral*), was paid to their immediate lords, the aristocrats. Although such a system was implemented, the tax obligation in the monastic and aristocratic estates actually sometimes seems to have been applied differently. As indicated in the *Bod ljongs spyi bshad* (Ngag dbang 1991: 591), not every single taxpayer paid the government tax. Some lords among the monastic and aristocratic estates divided their farmlands into two categories: land for *phyi khral* and land for *nang khral*. They demanded that their *mi ser*, who were cultivating the land for *phyi khral*, pay the outer tax to the government and those who cultivated the land for *nang khral* pay the inner tax to the estate. As Surkhang (1986: 26) suggests, the same system apparently applied for tax obligations or

9 Ngag dbang 1991: 591, "*zhung rgyug khral pa tshos gzhung gi khral rigs las de min gyi khral rigs gzhan 'jal mi dgos.*"

10 *Ibid.*: 591 "[*sger gzhis*] *khral pa tshos gzhung phyogs la phyi khral dang gzhis kar nang khral rgyugs dgos.*"

corvée: the *mi ser* were divided into two groups, one only working the field and paying the land tax only to their estate, while the other group provided corvée labour only to the government.

Apart from these three groups of taxpayers, another was called *dud chung*, "small family". The *mi ser* in this group were formally not classified as taxpayers (cf. Goldstein 1971: 4–5, 23), but they also paid a substantial tax, though only to their land-leasing lords, who were largely rich *mi ser* or estate holders, as a return for the land they leased on temporary contract. As shown here, not every *mi ser* in Tibet was formally considered as a taxpayer (*khral pa*). How, then, was one classified as a taxpayer? Looking at the basic status of the three main taxpayer groups outlined above, we can assume that a family had to be a member of one of the three groups or affiliated formally with the three types of estates (government, aristocratic or monastic) in order to qualify as a taxpayer. In addition, a family accountable for paying tax encompassed members between the age range of thirteen and sixty. This is to say that every member in a family was liable for taxation except for those over sixty years old and children under thirteen (Surkhang 1986: 21, 23) whether or not they were formally considered as taxpayers.

Before moving to the next section, I wish to mention here briefly how the Ganden Phodrang government administered its estates in terms of taxation. According to the *Bod ljongs spyi bshad* (Ngag dbang 1991: 583–84), the government estates were administered in four ways. First, the larger government estates were kept under direct control through the governmental appointment of an estate manager (*gzhis sdod*). Secondly, the medium estates and its sub-estates were leased to ordinary aristocrats, to monasteries and to government officials, who were obliged to pay a small leasing fee as well as any other tax that was required by the government. The leasing fee estimated here is about one *khal* of barley (22 lb) from the land having the growing capacity of one *khal* of seed. Thirdly, some government estates were awarded to higher aristocrats as compensation for their service and thus these aristocrats owned and managed these estates. Fourthly, apart from a few exceptional cases such as military fields and *sa tshigs* transportation labour, all the estates under the control of aristocrats and monasteries were obliged to pay a definitive tax to the government.

4 The Units of Tax Calculation

The taxation system calculated payments in relation to the amount of land, which was itself calculated in terms of two units, *rkang* and *'don*. These *rkang* and *'don* units were applied only for the measurement of land capacity in tax-related documents, and their usage was therefore limited. The *rkang* is a traditional unit that was used to measure arable land by the volume of seed grain that could be sown within a delimited area. In the documents, we find various types of *rkang*, namely *phyi rkang* (external unit), *nang rkang* (internal unit),[11] *dmag rkang* (the unit to measure military land), *'brog rkang* (the unit to measure land in nomadic areas),[12] and *g.yog rkang* (possibly the unit to measure the lands given to a servant (*g.yog zhing*) as compensation (Gurung 2017: 219). The criterion of a standard *rkang* measurement varies according to particular estates, area (e.g. agricultural or nomadic), potential fertility of the soil[13] and the overall climatic conditions of the area. This means that this traditional Tibetan unit of land measurement could actually refer to various areas of land, due to the quality and location of arable fields from district to district, and also between agricultural land and pastoral land. It is apparently due to the criteria mentioned above that one finds at least four different views about the *rkang* measurement as calculated by the number of *khal* or Tibetan bushels. The Tibetan bushel or *khal* is a unit of volume, and the weight of its content differs depending on the product, such as crops, flour, meat, butter, wool and so on. In this calculation, I will estimate the weight of barley per Tibetan bushel as 27 lb (12.25 kg).[14] In the following, I will list four different views in regard to how many Tibetan bushels of seed can fill the size of one *rkang* of land.

1. According to the *rTsa tshig don mtshan bcu* (the Ten-Point Edict) of 1795, a field of one *rkang* has a seed capacity of 13 Tibetan bushels of barley.[15]

---

11 In the case of the government taxation, *phyi rkang* is used and on the village or internal estate, *nang rkang* measurement is applied (Goldstein 1971: 7).

12 Surkhang (1986: 21) provides two different examples of calculating *'brog rkang*. In the pasture used for grazing their cattle, one *'brog rkang* is equal to the area with a planting capacity of 120 Tibetan bushels of seed grains. In nomadic regions, it is based on livestock, for example twenty-five yaks are equal to one *'brog rkang*. He also reports that six sheep and twelve goats equal to one yak, and that means approximately 150 sheep and 300 goats makes one *'brog rkang*).

13 It should be noted that soil fertility normally deteriorates year by year, and therefore the seed capacity for a field of the same size also changes by year.

14 Surkhang (1966: 18) has estimated the weight of one Tibetan bushel as being equal to 27 lb without specifying the type of grain, while Ryavec (2001: 355) has adopted 28 lb for one Tibetan bushel. In his earlier publication, Goldstein (1968: 62, 64) has converted the weight of wheat per Tibetan bushel as 27 lb and the weight of barley per Tibetan bushel as 22 lb, but in his later publication (Goldstein 1971: 9) he has approximated the weight of barley per Tibetan bushel as 27 lb.

15 See "[line 61] *son 'bru khal bcu gsum re 'gro ba'i sa zhing la rkang gcig yin*" in the *rTsa tshig don mtshan bcu* of 1795 (see Gurung 2013 for a summary of this document). This *rTsa tshig don mtshan bcu* was issued about thirty-five years before the *lCags stag zhib gzhung*

This suggests that a total of about 351 lb or 159.21 kg of barley could be sown on one *rkang* of arable land.

2. According to research published in the *Bod ljongs spyi bshad* (Ngag dbang 1991: 606), about 7 *khal*, 5 *bre* and 2 *phul* of seed are required for one *rkang* of agricultural land in the sTag rtse district. This suggests that the unit of one *rkang* is equal to 7 ¼ Tibetan bushels of barley which is approximately 195.75 lb or 88.79 kg.
3. According to Surkhang, the *rkang* is equal to an area of land with a seed capacity of about 60 to 80 Tibetan bushels of barley (Surkhang 1966: 19), and would be equal to an area with a capacity of 120 Tibetan bushels in pastoral land. Following Surkhang, we can estimate that one *rkang* of land is equal to the size of a field with a seed capacity of 1,620 lb (734.81 kg) to 2,169 lb (979.75 kg) of barley in agricultural areas and 3,240 lb of barley in pastoral land.
4. Following Sir Charles Bell (1928: 301), Ryavec (2001: 354–55) has estimated that one *rkang* is equal to 40 Tibetan bushels of barley. The corresponding weight of 40 Tibetan bushels of barley would be 1,080 lb (of barley. Using a specific calculation method combining Tibetan and a standard land measurement in China today, Ryavec converted the size of one *rkang* of agricultural land into roughly 2.49 hectares (his formula: 1 *rkang* × 40 *khal* × 28 lb ÷ 30 lb/mu × 0.0667 mu/ha = 2.49 ha).

As shown here by these different calculations, there is no single method to measure the unit *rkang*. The views above reveal a huge difference between the smallest, about 195 lb according to the *Bod ljongs spyi bshad*, and the largest about 2160 lb of barley in agricultural areas according to Surkhang.

The size of a *'don*, however, may be easily estimated as it is generally agreed that two *rkang* is equal to one *'don*. Although it is not possible to convert the unit of *rkang* or *'don* accurately into any modern unit of measurement such as acre, hectare, square feet or metre, I will present the approximate size of the *rkang* unit in acres by converting the required number of Tibetan bushels of seed per *rkang* and applying the conversion of Tibetan bushels into acres following Goldstein and the specific formula used by Ryavec in their publications. For clarity, I have labelled these methods "Goldstein's method" and "Ryavec's

issued in 1830. This *zhib gzhung* is said to be a result of the resolution about tax regulation passed in 1796 (see Gurung 2017) and it is also significantly related to the purpose of the *rTsa tshig don mtshan bcu* of 1795. Like the *rTsa tshig don mtshan bcu* was issued to reduce the impoverishment of taxpayers, the *lCags stag zhib gzhung* was to resolve inequality in tax obligations that had caused financial instability for both the government and its taxpayer.

TABLE 2.1 Conversion of *rkang* into acres

	Tibetan bushel per *rkang*	Acre per *rkang*	
		Goldstein's method[a]	Ryavec's method[b]
rTsa tshig don mtshan bcu of 1795	13 Tibetan bushels	4.60–2.92 ac	1.92 ac[c]
Bod ljongs spyi bshad	7.25 Tibetan bushels (7 *khal* 5 *bre* 2 *phul*)	2.57–1.63 ac	1.06 ac[d]
	60 Tibetan bushels	21.27–13.51 ac	8.89 ac[e]
Surkhang	80 Tibetan bushels	28.36–18 ac	11.86 ac[f]
Ryavec (cf. Bell)	40 Tibetan bushels	14.18–9 ac	5.93 ac[g]

a Goldstein (1971: 9) informs us that an average of 1.59–2.5 US bushels of barley is sown per acre (of irrigated land) in the US and one US bushel of barley weighs 48 lb. Since one Tibetan bushel of barley weighs 27 lb, we can estimate one US bushel equals to 1.777 Tibetan bushels. This helps us to understand that 2.82–4.44 Tibetan bushels of barley can be sown on one acre of land. So, when we divide the number of Tibetan bushels per *rkang*.

b An adjustment of 27 lb per one Tibetan bushel from his 28 lb per one Tibetan bushel is made here to calculate Ryavec's method. So, the formula is 1 *rkang* × 40 *khal* × 27 lb ÷ 30 lb/mu × 0.0667 mu/ha = total hectare (= acre). by the number of Tibetan bushels of barley sown per acre, we will find out the approximate number of acre per one *rkang*.

c 1 *rkang* × 13 *khal* × 27 lb ÷ 30 lb/mu × 0.0667 mu/ha = 0.78 ha (= 1.92 ac).

d 1 *rkang* × 7.25 *khal* × 27 lb ÷ 30 lb/mu × 0.0667 mu/ha = 0.43 ha (= 1.06 ac).

e 1 *rkang* × 80 *khal* × 27 lb ÷ 30 lb/mu × 0.0667 mu/ha = 4.80 ha (= 11.86 ac).

f 1 *rkang* × 60 *khal* × 27 lb ÷ 30 lb/mu × 0.0667 mu/ha = 3.60 ha (= 8.89 ac).

g 1 *rkang* × 40 *khal* × 27 lb ÷ 30 lb/mu × 0.0667 mu/ha = 2.40 ha (= 5.93 ac).

method" in Table 2.1 above, however, the calculation is solely mine and thus any misinterpretation found in this calculation is my responsibility.

5 The Government Tax Obligation and the Question of Its Proportion

5.1 *According to Surkhang and the Bod ljongs spyi bshad*

As I have not yet found any standard manual explaining the complete range of tax obligations, it is difficult to confirm how many different types of taxes a *mi ser* had to pay in Central Tibet. Nonetheless, we do know that *mi ser* paid many varieties of tax, as Surkhang Wangchen Gelek has outlined in his excellent papers on taxation (1966 and 1986) and also as mentioned in the volume of the *Bod ljongs spyi bshad*. Surkhang's publications provide valuable first-hand information as he was a high-ranking official with the title of Cabinet Minister (*zhabs pad*) in the Ganden Phodrang government. For that reason, I will summarise some of the tax obligations related to my discussion from his research. According to Surkhang (1986: 21), the basic tax paid to the government included corvée labour (*rkang 'gro*), tax in kind and money (*lag 'don*), military tax (*dmag khral*),[16] customs duty paid at the border (*'gag sgo*) and customs duty paid inland (*sho khral*).[17] The two duties on goods for commercial purposes are designated in *Bod ljongs spyi bshad* as *sho khral* and *tshugs khral*[18] (Ngag dbang 1991: 613–15).

Surkhang (1986: 24) suggests that there were four types of corvée or labour tax (*rkang 'gro*): two kinds of manual labour and two kinds of transportation duty. The two categories of manual labour comprised reaping grass in swamps (*'dam 'ul*) and construction labour (*ar 'ul*). Reaping swamp grass was obligatory only in areas such as gTsang, lHo kha and Phen po, while construction labour was carried out in all districts of Central Tibet. In general, one person had to be provided per *rkang* of land that they owned. However, when the days were short during the autumn and there was much work to be done, the demand was doubled to two people per *rkang*. When the government required labour for construction projects about every three to five years, one more person per *rkang* had to be sent. This means one to two people per *rkang* and, every three to five years, one additional person per *rkang* for construction work. As sufficient food and salary for these labourers were not provided by the government, the taxpayer was required to provide all the food and clothes for the swamp labourers and also a part of the expenses for the construction workers.[19] The two transportation duties were *sa tshig*[20] or transportation across short

16 As for the military tax, the government *mi ser* were to supply one soldier per *rkang*, and the same number of soldiers per *'don* would be supplied by the monastic and aristocratic estates (Surkhang 1986: 30).

17 Some examples of these taxes are provided in Surkhang (*ibid.*: 32–33) as follows: one Indian rupee (worth 5 Tibetan *srang*) for each maund (82 lbs) of wool exported to India and one box of tea from every 20 boxes imported in Phari, 100 *tram dkar* for each sheep for sale to India or Nepal in Western Tibet, and 5 ½ *zho* for every load of salt in Central Tibet were collected.

18 Peter Schwieger has translated *sho khral* toll tax and *tshugs khral* as "trading tax" in his contribution in this volume.

19 The partial expenses that the government covered are listed as: 3 *khal* 6 *bre* and 4 *phul* of *rtsam pa*, 1 Tibetan bushel of beer grain, 6 *nyag* of butter, half a *spor* of tea, 1 *bre* of salt, 1 *phul* of soda, 1 head of sheep, 1 *bre* of oil for lamps per month and 1 *zho* as a daily wage.

20 According to Levine (in this volume), it was known as *rta zam* or *rta tshig*, and labourers were obliged to travel three stations in Western Tibet.

distances between one station and another, and *rdzong skyel* or transportation across longer distances from district to district.[21]

According to Surkhang, not every district was subject to these obligations, but only areas around Lhasa, gTsang and on the route to eastern Tibet. In regard to tax in kind and money, or *lag 'don*, Surkhang (1966: 24–25, 1986: 24) describes four types of taxes to be paid to the government; these are allowances and services for Chinese officials in Lhasa (*rgya gsos/bsos*),[22] wood tax (*shing khral*), *rtsam pa* tax (*smon brngod*) for the *smon lam* prayer festival and a tax paid to the government during the Tibetan New Year (*rgyal po lo khral*) (Goldstein 2001).

In the chapter on Tibetan taxes in the *Bod ljongs spyi bshad*, the author also writes that in general all tax obligations could be divided into corvée or labour tax (*rkang 'gro*) and tax in kind and money (*lag 'don*) (Ngag dbang 1991: 595). An investigation carried out during the democratic reform era reveals that the corvée or labour tax (*rkang 'gro*) comprised 60% percent and the latter 40% of the total tax. However, as no testimonial reference is provided to support how the author reached such a conclusion, it remains open for further investigation. Nevertheless, the author has explained in detail the various types of taxes throughout five sub-chapters in the *Bod ljongs spyi bshad*, which in fact covers much more than the two categories of obligation mentioned above.[23] Of the five sub-chapters I wish to summarise here the fourth (*sa gnas srid gzhung gi khral 'u lag*), which provides a detailed account of most of the *rkang 'gro* and *lag 'don* tax obligations to the government (*ibid.*: 601–13):

There are various taxes and corvée labour obligations to the government and some include transportation labour, receiving and providing accommodation for government officials and the army en route, construction labour and tax in kind and money (*lag 'don*). Further tax obligations—here classified as

---

21 According to the *Bod ljongs spyi bshad* (Ngag dbang 1991: 602), *sa tshigs* transportation could be covered within a day. Surkhang (1986: 24) interprets this obligation by the number of animals required for transportation. He suggests approximately up to ten horses and fifteen mules were required for *sa tshigs* transportation, whereas the *rdzong skyel* was a longer transportation duty covering more than a day and requiring more animals.

22 According to Tibetan dictionaries (Zhang 1996: 538–39, *Dung dkar tshig mdzod*: 647) *rgya gsos* was a tax in the form of mainly grain or its value in cash, initially collected to pay for the Lhasa Amban and other Chinese officials until the end of the Qing dynasty. Although the administration of the Ambans in Lhasa was discontinued soon after the collapse of the dynasty in 1912, *rgya gsos* tax collection still continued as a source of income for the reception of government guests.

23 For an English translation of the chapter on Tibetan taxation from this book, see Schwieger in this volume.

phyi khral and apparently demanded from monastic and aristocratic estates—in particular are:

a) eight different types of corvée labour (i.e. construction labour, repairing dams, wood cutting, wood transport, reaping grass, cleaning canals, providing horses and accommodation for travelling officials and soldiers, receiving and escorting the government messenger);
b) two types of transportation labour, *sa tshigs* or *rdzong skyel* (for transporting the government's grain, tea, butter, meat, rice, etc.);
c) transporting monks and goods for *smon lam* and other prayer festivals;
d) about twenty-one different types of tax in kind on the basis of local products from specific areas such as raw medicines, dye, tiger skins, fruit, paper, woollen cloth, meat, tail, felt made of wool or yak hair, salt, leather, sacking, soda, gold, nephrite cups, whetstone, clay goods, charcoal, whitewash and red ochre.[24]

As illustrated here by Surkhang and the *Bod ljongs spyi bshad*, there were many different types of taxes collected by the government. It is obviously due to the characteristics of the various administrations in individual estates and districts that the obligations could not be applied equally to all, and not every *mi ser* had to pay the same types and number of taxes to the government.

5.2 *According to Tibetan Archival Documents*

As the core of my discussion in this paper focuses on the administration of taxation in the Ganden Phodrang according to the archival materials, I will explore the tax obligation specified in a few documents. To begin with, according to the opening section of the *lCags stag zhib gzhung* issued in 1830,[25] the tax obligations are grouped either into two general categories: *rkang 'gro* and *lag 'don*, or into five particular types: *sa tshigs, rdzong skyel, rgya gsos, shing dngul* and *smong brngod* (see Table 2.2). The phrases *rkang 'gro lag 'don* and *'don* are not found in the *rTsa tshig don mtshan bcu* of 1795. However, phrases such as *lam thog* (elsewhere *lam thog sa tshigs*),*'u lag*, and *rta khal* do correspond with *rkang 'gro* and *rgya bsos/gsos, shing khral, shing dngul* with *lag 'don* tax. The first of the two general categories, *rkang 'gro*, is associated with the two types of transportation labour, i.e. *sa tshigs* and *rdzong skyel*. The second category, *lag 'don*, is explained principally by the three obligations: allowance and service for Chinese officials in Lhasa (*rgya gsos*), fire-wood tax or its value in cash (*shing dngul*), and roasted-barley flour for the *smon lam* prayer festival (*smon brngod*). These three types of tax are abbreviated as *rgya shing brngod*

24 These tax obligations are not specified in figures.
25 I have translated the opening section of the *lCags stag zhib gzhung* in Gurung 2017: 221–24.

gsum in many archival documents (see for example, *lCags stag zhib gzhung*, *sNyan zhus*, *Kun gling chos gzhis bsnyel tho*).[26]

Another related document that I have recently discovered in the archives is a copy of an edict issued in 1830 (see *bKa' rgya* in Appendix 1). This edict also highlights the above-mentioned category of tax obligations. It was issued on 13 April in 1830, which is about two months before the first document of the well-known *Iron-Tiger Land Settlement* issued on 24 June in 1830. This document not only presents the summary of a decision taken prior to the *lCags stag zhib gzhung* regarding the obligations of taxation in Central Tibet, but also reflects the background of the administrative part of the process of writing the land settlement (see Appendix 1). It is evident that this edict is of equally great important as the land settlement in terms of understanding government taxation. For this reason, I have chosen to present here a brief summary of the tax obligations recorded in this document.

As this edict reveals, the Tibetan and Chinese members of the council had passed a resolution to carry out a survey of the size of the fields owned by the government, aristocrats and monasteries in Central Tibet in 1829, a year before the *lCags stag zhib gzhung* was issued. After this investigation, the following decisions were made. All government taxpayers in Central Tibet (dBus and gTsang), except from those whose lands were calculated as *'don bsgril* or merged *'don*,[27] had to pay their *rkang 'gro* and *lag 'don* taxes by the *rkang*, unless their income came from the leased land or if they had received a tax reduction on the basis of their having insufficient grain and if they had lost their harvest due to flooding. Government *mi ser* who were exceptional cases and *mi ser* under aristocratic and monastic estates also had to fulfil their *sa tshigs* obligation on the basis of *rkang*. However, they fulfilled their *rdzong skyel* obligation and the three taxes in kind (*rgya gsos*, wood tax and *smon lam* festival tax) according to a system termed *nyis sna zhe gcig*.

26 Tsarong (1998a: 9, fn. 12) also confirms that the first among the three, the *rgya gsos*, was a barley grain tax collected to pay the Chinese; however, his interpretation of that tax as a revenue collected "in order to repay a debt to the Chinese" is not known. Furthermore, Thupten Sangyay (1986: 43) interpreted it as the tax levied for supplying fodder to the horses used for postal services. It must be noted that supplying fodder was actually a part of corvée transportation labour.

27 This term *'don sgril* seems to be a very important taxation terminology, but it is not defined in any known Tibetan dictionary. Fortunately, Goldstein has defined this term as "merging a *'don* tax unit of land to another *'don* tax unit" in his Tibetan-English dictionary (Goldstein 2001: 580). As it is a merging of two *'don* into one *'don*, it is a sort of tax reduction policy (cf. Gurung 2017: 223, fn. 23).

In order to avoid confusion in this discussion, the meaning of *nyis sna'i 'don* and *nyis sna zhe gcig* must be explained. In the *Bod rgya tshig mdzod* (Zhang 1996), the phrase *nyis sna'i 'don* is described as a tax unit of land equal to two *rkang* (see also Goldstein 2001: 418). Except for its specification as a tax unit, this phrase is defined similarly to the term *'don*, which as mentioned above is a unit of land equal to two *rkang*. However, according to archival documents (see *lCags stag zhib gzhung*), *nyis sna'i 'don* is applied differently from the term *'don*. For example, phrases like "*rkang gnyis la* ***nyis sna'i 'don*** *gcig sgrub*" cannot be translated in the same way as "*rkang gnyis la sgrub* ***'don*** *gcig*". Both phrases can be found in the same document close to each other, but indicate different contexts. According to my understanding from reading the documents, the phrase *nyis sna'i 'don* should not be defined like *'don* as a unit of land equal to two *rkang*. The exact meaning of this phrase is still open to discussion and further research on archival materials is important for its correct definition. For the time being, I will define here the phrase *nyis sna'i 'don* or *nyis sna zhe gcig* speculatively on the basis of my reading of relevant passages from the archives. This phrase is used in a special context for a tax unit, which indicates that the obligation is less than in the case of a standard *'don* tax unit. To be more specific, if, for example, the standard tax rate is one *'don* of barley for one *'don* of seed sown, the obligatory standard tax would be 80 Tibetan bushels of barley (that is, two 40 Tibetan bushels of barley following Ryavec's calculation). However, in the case of *nyis sna'i 'don* or *nyis sna zhe gcig*, the tax payment of 80 Tibetan bushels of barley (normally for one standard *'don*) can equal the tax obligation for two *'don* (2 × 80 Tibetan bushels) of seed sown. In other words, the tax obligation of half a *'don* of barley would be sufficient for one *'don* of seed sown in this special case, which suggests only about 50 percent of the total obligation. This speculative calculation is also supported by the fact that the *mi ser* on monastic and aristocratic estates as well as the *mi ser* on less fertile land were obliged to pay one half to the government and the other half to their monastic estate or their aristocratic lords or estate.

Returning to tax obligations, as mentioned in the opening section of the *lCags stag zhib gzhung* and the Edict of 1830, a part of the total tax obligation, the *sa tshigs* transportation labour, was supplied equally by all *mi ser* under the three types of estates, and a part of that was calculated based on the specific type of estate (see Table 2.2). For example, the government estate *mi ser* had to supply *rdzong skyel* transportation labour and to pay the three *lag 'don* taxes (*rgya shing brngod*) by the *rkang*, unless he owned land consisting of merged *'don* (*'don bsgril*). All *mi ser* under the monastic and aristocratic estates were allowed to fulfil *rdzong skyel* and the three *lag 'don* taxes by *nyi sna zhe gcig*.

Based on this *nyis sna zhe gcig* system, I speculate that the tax obligation standardised by the government through the *lCags stag zhib gzhung* was that the *mi ser* under monastic and aristocratic estates pay 50 per cent of the total tax to the government, whereas they paid the other 50 per cent to their lords. The government *mi ser*, except from those who were granted *'don bsgril* concession, paid full tax to the government as they did not fall under this *nyis sna zhe gcig* taxation policy.

At the end of the lists of recorded land throughout chapters in the *lCags stag zhib gzhung*, we can find phrases like, "[*xyz*] *nas sgrub rkang gcig*", "[*xyz*] *nas rkang gnyis la sgrub 'don gcig*" or "[*xyz*] *nas rkang gnyis la nyis sna'i 'don gcig sgrub*". These three phrases clearly explain the basic tax obligation in proportion in *rkang* or *'don* according to the size of the land. The first example "[*xyz*] *nas sgrub rkang gcig*" suggests that one *rkang* must be fulfilled as the tax obligation in proportion per *rkang*. The second examples "[*xyz*] *nas rkang gnyis la sgrub 'don gcig*" shows one *'don* for two *rkang*, which is the same proportion as the first example but expressed in a different way since two *rkang* equal one *'don*. The third example "[*xyz*] *nas rkang gnyis la nyis sna'i 'don gcig sgrub*" suggests that one *nyis sna'i 'don* must be fulfilled for two *rkang*, which can be interpreted as half of the two *rkang* to be fulfilled per two *rkang* of land.

However, these lines do not provide particular details of the tax obligations in various other categories such as the two corvée labours and the three taxes in kind and in money. I would therefore like to explore further the proportion of these categories as given in other sources. This investigation will also illustrate how the obligations described in the archival documents differ from the collection of various taxes in practice. The exact number of obligations for the two types of corvée or labour (*rkang 'gro*) tax by *rkang* or *'don* cannot be clearly specified, as it depends upon the number of people and animals actually required and provided for transportation (see Table 2.3). As mandated in the *rTsa tshig don mtshan bcu* of 1795, the required number of animals for *sa tshigs* or *rdzong skyel* corvée transportation may be supplied by a taxpayer as written in a travel document. I have found one such travel document issued in 1894 (see *Lam yig* in Appendix 2), which contains an example of corvée transportation labour demanded from the *mi ser* residing along the route between Lhasa and Sho mdo (aka Shopado is situated to the northeast of Lhasa on the route to Chab mdo). With this travel document, the travelling official demanded up to five horses, eight pack animals and ten private riding horses for his services, as well as animal fodder,[28] firewood and the necessary expenses to cross by boat and bridge.

Let us put this information in perspective with a detailed explanation regarding the number of animals for *sa tshigs* and *rdzong skyel* transportation to be found in Surkhang (1986: 24–26). As Surkhang writes, the number of animals required for one trip of *sa tshigs* transportation was limited to ten riding horses and fifteen mules including the accommodation, while the animals required for *rdzong skyel* transportation exceeded these numbers. The total number of animals supplied for transportation was counted each year, and the tax proportion per *rkang* for all *mi ser* liable for this tax obligation was calculated and fulfilled accordingly. This clearly shows that the proportion of corvée transportation labour per *rkang* would be different every year.

According to the archival materials, many different kinds of tax in kind or of equivalent value in cash were paid to the government as *lag 'don* tax. Nevertheless, the three *lag 'don* taxes (*rgya gsos, shing dngul* and *brngod smon*) are described in *lCags stag zhib gzhung* as the main obligations to be paid per *rkang* or *'don* to the government. In order to illustrate the proportion of these three main obligations, I wish to compare the regulated tax proportion in 1795 according to the *rTsa tshig don mtshan bcu* of 1795 and its actual collection as described in the secondary sources (see Table 2.3). The proportion of *rgya gsos* tax is not specified in this *rTsa tshig don mtshan bcu*. For wood tax or *shing dngul*, 8 silver *zho* for each *rkang* of land must be paid annually. Elsewhere in the same document, it is written that 8 Tibetan bushels of barley and 10 Tibetan bushels of *rtsam pa* must be paid annually for each *rkang*. This obligation could be considered for *smon brngod* and/or *rgyal po lo khral*.[29]

In order to fulfil the missing part and to estimate an average tax proportion, I will compare the above ratio with Surkhang's description, because it is the only one I have come across so far that clearly refers to the three *lag 'don* taxes. Surkhang's description of the proportion is most likely based on his knowledge of the tax obligation during the first half of the 20th century when

28 According to the *rTsa tshig don mtshan bcu* of 1795, one must pay 5 *zho* of *tram kha* per *rkang* annually for animal fodder, which is approximately 2 ½ Tibetan bushels of beans converted back from the conversion rate per Tibetan bushel. According to Surkhang (1966: 27, fn. 10), *tram kha* or *tram dkar* was a coin first minted in Tibet in 1782 and was equal to 4 *srang*.

29 Some more taxes in kind, apparently from nomad families, recorded in this *rTsa tshig don mtshan bcu* are: one yak or 7 ½ *skar*, ten sheep or 1 *tram kha*, twenty goats or 1 *tram kha* every two years; people from Kongpo were to pay one pig of every twenty pigs annually. Furthermore, some paid meat, butter and oil taxes which are not proportioned in the *rTsa tshig don mtshan bcu*.

he was a government official. According to Surkhang (1986: 24), a government *mi ser* must pay one *srang* for the *rgya gsos* tax,[30] 5 *zho* and 15 *'degs rgya* for the wood tax,[31] one Tibetan bushel of *rtsam pa* for the *smon lam* festival tax and 3 Tibetan bushels of barley for *rgyal po lo khral* per *rkang* of land.[32] Apart from Surkhang, the author of *Bod ljongs spyi bshad* wrote that each family from Tsangtog (gTsang rtogs) estate in Tagtse (sTag rtse) district had to supply one kitchen helper and 9 silver *srang* per *rkang* for the *smon lam* festival (Ngag dbang 1991: 606–608).[33] The entire taxes in proportion described above were apparently collected from the government *mi ser*, because the taxes were calculated per *rkang*. As mentioned earlier, *mi ser* under monastic and aristocratic estates as well as some government *mi ser* were obliged to pay only half the amount per *rkang* calculated for the majority of government *mi ser*.

TABLE 2.2 Five basic government tax obligations

	***sa tshigs* per**	***rdzong skyel* per**	***rgya gsos* per**	***shing dngul* per**	***smon brngod* per**
Govt. *mi ser*	*rkang*	*rkang*	*rkang*	*rkang*	*rkang*
Govt. *mi ser*, exceptional cases	*rkang*	*nyi sna'i 'don*	*nyi sna'i 'don*	*nyi sna'i 'don*	*nyi sna'i 'don*
Monastic *mi ser*	*rkang*	*nyi sna'i 'don*	*nyi sna'i 'don*	*nyi sna'i 'don*	*nyi sna'i 'don*
Aristocratic *mi ser*	*rkang*	*nyi sna'i'don*	*nyi sna'i 'don*	*nyi sna'i 'don*	*nyi sna'i 'don*

30 In an earlier publication, Surkhang (1966: 25) wrote that the tax proportion for the same purpose was 7 ½ *skar* per *rkang*.

31 According to Surkhang (1966: 25), it is 2 *zho* and 5 *skar* per *rkang*.

32 Surkhang (1966: 24–25) states that *brngod smon* tax was a part of the *rgyal po lo khral* tax, which in total is one Tibetan bushel of barley per *son khal*, one quarter of which was to be paid in *rtsam pa*. More tax obligations such as 20 *rgyab* of hay and one Tibetan bushel of butter were collected per *rkang*, probably in proportion to the area of grazing land.

33 Goldstein has reported that the total annual payment to the Central government for the *rgya shing brngod gsum* tax in Samada village was 3 *zho* per *rkang* (Goldstein 1968: 67; 1971: 13).

TABLE 2.3 Tax obligations in proportion to the government

	Government *mi ser* (according to the sources)	**Govt. *mi ser* (exceptional cases) and the other *mi ser***
sa tshigs	No limit	No limit
rdzong skyel	No limit	No limit
rgya gsos	per *rkang* – 1 *srang* (in 20th c.)	
shing dngul	per *rkang* – 8 silver *zho* (in 1795) – 5 *zho* and 15 *'degs rgya* (in 20th c.)	These three taxes were collected by *nyi sna'i 'don*, and were thus half the amount owed by government *mi ser* (*estimated hypothetically*).
smon brngod	per *rkang* – 8 Tibetan bushels of barley and 10 Tibetan bushels of *rtsam pa* (in 1795) – 1 Tibetan bushel of *rtsam pa* (in 20th c.) – 1 kitchen helper and 9 silver *srang* (date unknown)	

6 Conclusion

Most previous studies on Tibetan taxation were carried out in the absence of archival documents, which left a potentially wide gap between what was announced as tax obligations in the official tax documents and what was actually collected in proportion from the people of Tibet. Tax obligation and its proportion in Tibet cannot be understood conclusively and accurately without studying the archival material. This paper has attempted to present a perspective of the Ganden Phodrang's administration of taxation based mainly on some archival material, and has also tried to clarify the types of tax a Tibetan taxpayer were required to pay the government, and how these were proportioned. To conclude this discussion, I will summarise my findings.

The administration of taxation was carried out through at least twelve offices under the government. These offices would collect taxes from three basic groups of taxpayers: government *mi ser*, *mi ser* under monastic estates, and those under aristocratic estates. The government *mi ser* had a tax obligation only to the government, but the other two groups also owed taxes to their estates and to individual landlords. This study has shown that many varieties of tax were paid to the government by these three taxpayer groups; however, it is difficult to determine exactly how many different types of tax an individual family was actually obliged to provide. As indicated in previous studies, the archival documents also suggest that the basic category of tax obligation to the government was divided into two categories: *rkang 'gro* (corvée labour) and *lag 'don* (tax in kind and money). However, the sources contradict each other concerning the further divisions of the two obligations. For instance, according to the archival documents (cf. *lCags stag zhib gzhung* and *bKa' rgya*), corvée labour includes essentially the two transportation duties of *sa tshigs* and *rdzong skyel*, while Surkhang mentions four types of corvée labour. As for the *lag 'don* tax owed to the government, three principal obligations are found in the archival documents, namely *rgya gsos* or allowance and service for Chinese officials, *shing dngul* or firewood tax or its value in cash and *smon brngod* or tax for the *smon lam* prayer festival. By contrast, Surkhang mentions four types of tax in kind. According to *Bod ljongs spyi bshad*, more than ten different types of corvée labour and many more taxes in kinds were paid to the government. This clearly shows that in reality there was no specific limit on tax obligations to the government, leading us to conclude that the actual tax collection by the government was much greater than the obligation officially announced in the tax-related documents.

The archival documents also suggest that not every taxpayer fulfilled the obligation to the government equally. As said, one part of the corvée labour was fulfilled equally by all taxpayers, but the other obligations of corvée labour and taxes in kind were calculated according to the individual taxpayer's affiliation to estates or landlords. In this case, if the full obligation in proportion to the government is one *rkang* per each *rkang* of land as announced in *lCags stag zhib gzhung*, then the taxpayers, who comprised mostly the monastic and aristocratic *mi ser*, were obliged to fulfil half of the total obligation of the government *mi ser*. It should not be understood that the obligation of government *mi ser* was heavier than that of others, because the government *mi ser* were obliged to pay tax only to the government, while the *mi ser* under monastic and aristocratic estates were obliged to pay taxes both to the government and also to their estates and landlords. In brief, although the government tax obligation and its proportion were systematically balanced among all taxpayers according to tax-related documents like the *rTsa tshig don mtshan bcu* of 1795 and the land settlements issued in 1830, secondary literature reveals that actual tax collection seems to have been carried out differently.

This discussion on the administration of taxation is still far from conclusive at its current stage, as many more archival documents still remain to be studied. Nonetheless, I hope this perspective of the Ganden Phodrang government's administration of taxation based on archival documents will shed some light on the history of Tibetan taxation.

Appendices

Preface

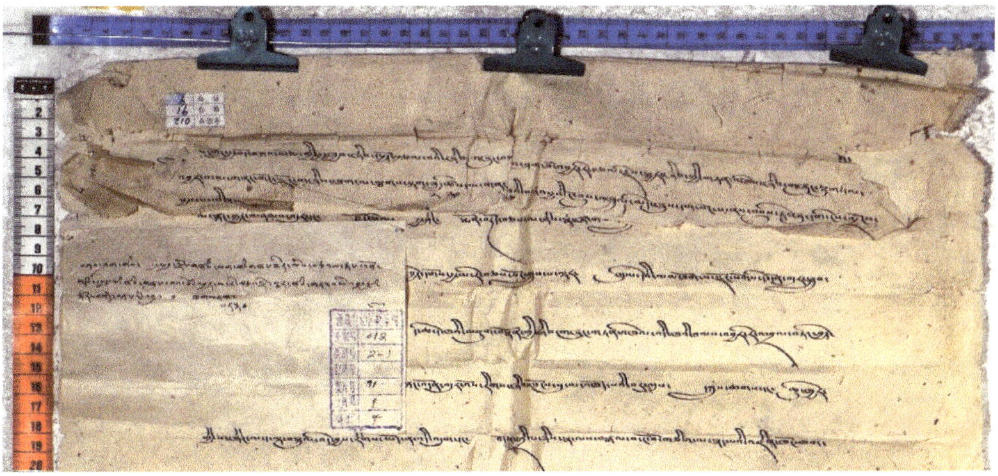

The Edict

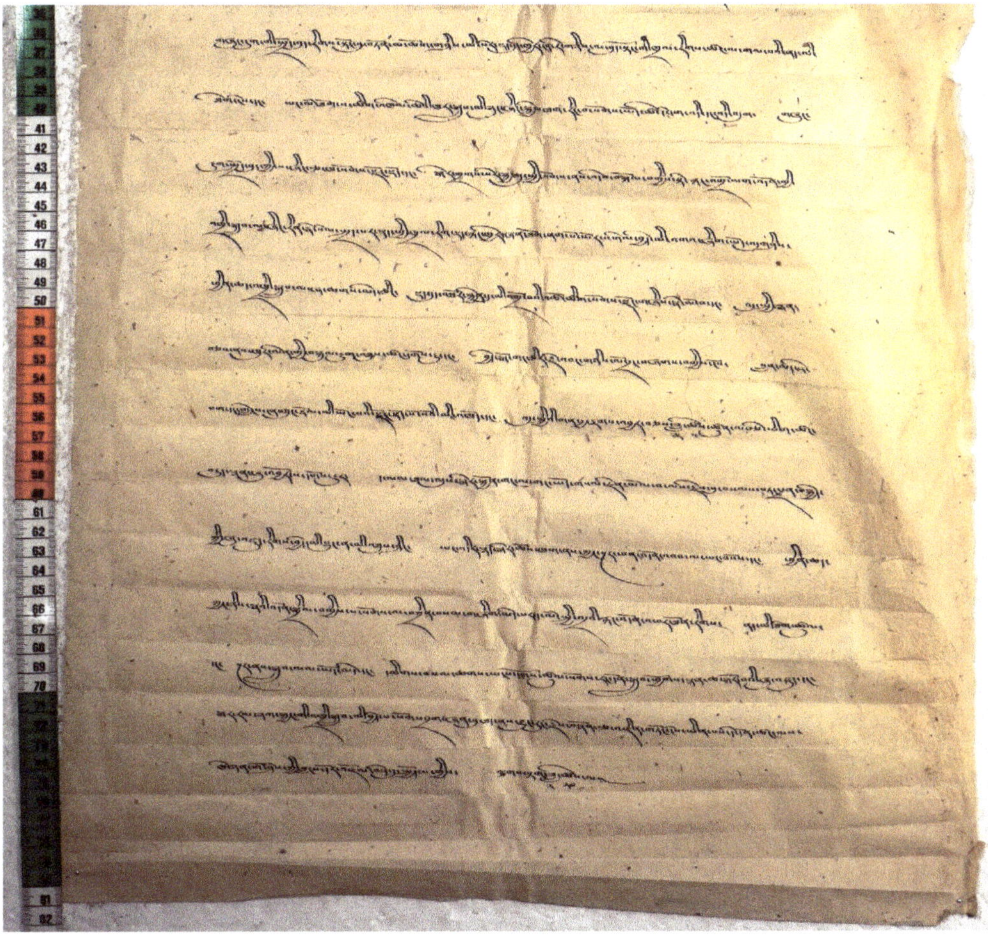

FIGURE 2.1 *Bka' rgya. Bka' rgya'i ngo shus 'khrul med* (The genuine copy of an edict issued in 1830) DTAB/ DKMT: 012 2-1/#/91/9/4

1 *Transliteration*

Preface

1. sa glang rgya bod bka' mol gyi rgya khyab zhib dpyod stsal ba'i zhib gzhung bka' shag tham 'byar re stsal rjes skyar zhib kyi gtan 'bebs zhib gzhung sbug dam
2. 'byar ba ma gnang gong rdzong gzhis khag la lcags stag zla 2 tshes 20 la gnang ba'i bka' rgya'i ngo shus 'khrul med zhus dag song pa nas bshus te zhu dag nges 'drongs
3. byas pa yin /

The Edict

1. § tho don/ snga lo rgya bod bka' mol steng nas mnga' khul gzhung sger chos gsum tshang ma'i rkang 'don la zhib dpyod byed bcug thog/ shes sleb
2. dkrus chag/ chu khyer sogs phud pa'i dbus gtsang bying sngar rgyun rkang rkyang dang/ sger chos dang gzhung rgyug 'don sgril yod rigs rnams kyang sa tshig
3. la rkang rkyang mnyams 'dur dang/ rdzong skyel/ rgya shing/ smon brngod bcas la nyis sna zhe gcig sgrub blangs dgos pa rgyal bcad song ba'i don bzhin
4. gyi zhib gzhung bka' shag gi tham 'byar dang/ byed dgos rgya ma re bcas song grub pa ltar/ khul de'i lam thog sa rdzong sogs de don 'dur sgrub
5. bskul rgyug byed gi yod pa gzhir bcas shing/ da cha de kha'i mjug bsnon gyi zhib gzhung gtan 'khel 'di kha'i thams 'byar re 'phral btang byed
6. rgyur/ zhib gzhung sngon btang nang gsal la rkang 'don 'dur 'os rigs zhib khongs su ma 'khod pa'i bar lus/ dkrus chags dang/ chu khyer
7. gyi sa zhing la da lta bskul bde byas rigs yod na 'di 'dug dang / 'don sgril nyis sna las brgal ba ngo bo gcig la snyad pa'i 'dzin khong khag
8. mang la nges chag thal ba/ rkang 'don la nor 'khrul dang/ nyis 'khor/ bud rnying shes sleb 'bud tshems sogs byung yod tshe ngo 'dzin zol
9. 'jogs dang nye skyor phyogs lhung spang pa'i khongs so sor 'di dang 'di 'dug gi gnas tshul dngos gnas dag dkrus 'pher pa bsring dgos rgyur/ lhag don
10. gzhung rgyug gi sprod bud rigs stong su bton ma chog gshis mi ser sdad dud khyer ngan re gnyis la bud stong gi khral rigs tshang ma gal ba'i nad mi
11. theg nges dang/ yang lam thog sa tshig 'khel che'i khar sgrub mi nyung zhing skyel thag ring ba sogs yod tshe de dag 'di dang 'di 'dug/ gzhung
12. rgyug sprod bud kyi sa zhing rtsa kha sogs rdzong sdod dang/ sger grags ser skya 'du spyi sogs nas 'deb bskol bgyis ste rkang 'gro lag 'don gyi
13. 'khri sgrub la zhing rin sne sel sprad par snyad phyi khral rig sdad rkang khyer zhan thog nag po yor 'gel byed mi 'ga' zhig yod 'dug shis
14. phyin chad 'khri sgrub la zha chags med cing/ sdad dud 'thor skyen du mi 'gro ba'i 'tsho tshig sogs rdzong gzhis sne mo ba dang/'du spyi rgan
15. bcas nas khur len gyi bskul rgyug 'thus tshang dgos rgyu dang/ byed sgo gang cir rje 'bang gnyis lo drang bzhags bgyis ngos/ slan chad he
16. bag dang glengs ngan khung rdol mi yong ba'i rdzong sdod so so'i ming 'khod dang/ 'du spyi'i gan rgya rtags 'byar bcas zla 3 tshes 5 tshun la rtse yig tshang
17. brgyud snyan zhu 'byor pa dgos rgyur/ da lam thal lus sger skyon gang la gang yod gsal rjen mol ba las rjes su bsams btang dran bskyed
18. kyi zhu 'dzud rigs byed mi byung na mi 'thus shing/ yang 'dir snyad sger chos khag nas kyang sngar phan 'don 'bab la yang bsos dang/ phyin chad
19. kyang nyis sna'i 'don sgril bgyis pa sogs la bka' drin bsam gzhig med par da lam spyi 'dra'i rkang 'don 'phar thon rigs/ nad mi theg tshul
20. dang/ sngar nas sgrub lam yod med dang/ dmigs bsal chags yangs dgos tshul sogs rang don sgrub phyogs snyan cha skor ba'i zhu 'dzud dang

21. sgar ral nyag skyang gi 'khri sgrub mi byed pa sogs drag zhan su thad nas byung rung rjes bsnon rtsa 'dzin gtong nges yin pas de don tshang mas
22. khe nyan go shes kyi blangs dor 'dzol med du spyod pa gyis/ lcags stag zla 2 tshes 20 la /

2 *English Translation*

Preface

In the year of the Earth Ox (1829), a land settlement under-stamped by the *bka' shag* was issued as a result of an investigation carried out according to a resolution passed by [the council of] Tibetan and Chinese. Thereafter, an edict was issued to all districts on the 20th of the 2nd month in the year of the Iron Tiger (13 April 1830) before the revised land settlement with the seal (of the Dalai Lama) was issued. This [document] was copied from a genuine and corrected copy of that edict and corrected thoroughly [again].

The Edict

The content [of the edict].

Following the resolution [passed by the council of] Tibetan and Chinese in the previous year (i.e. 1829), an order was sent to investigate the size of *rkang* and *'don* [of the lands] in the area (Central Tibet) belonging to the government, aristocrats and monasteries. The decision has been made as follows. Unless one has income from the leased land (*shes sleb* or *shas slebs*), or has acquired tax reduction due to insufficient grain[34] or [the crops were] swept away by flood, all taxpayers in Ü (dBus) and Tsang (gTsang) must fulfil their tax obligation by *rkang*. The *mi ser* under aristocratic and monastic estates, and those government *mi ser* who have acquired "merged *'don*" must pay their tax obligation by *rkang* for the *sa tshigs* transportation duty. In the case of *rdzong skyel* transportation duty, *rgya* [*bsos*], wood tax and *rtsam pa* for the *smon lam* festival, they must pay by *nyis sna zhe gcig*. Following the decision, a land settlement was stamped by the *bka' shag* and sent together with a required *rgya ma*[35] [to the districts].

Assuming that the transportation labour such as *sa* [*tshigs*] and *rdzong* [*skyel*] are taking place accordingly in all districts, the land settlement with an additional update has now been prepared and will be stamped and sent forward immediately.

If there is any missing record of *rkang* and *'don* in the previously issued land settlement, or if [the situation regarding] insufficient grain and damaged crops has improved and become easier to fulfil, then notification of these must be given. If there is any record exceeding the number of *'don sgril* or *nyis sna*, or if any extra reduction given

34 *dkrus chag* alternatively spelled as *bkrus chag*, a tax concession based on a sworn oath that one does not have enough grain (Goldstein 2001).

35 This possibly refers to a seal or a stamp, which may be used afterwards by the district officials for tax matters. Cf. *bka' yig rgya ma*, which means "a sealed edict" (Zhang 1996: 534).

is based on falsely claimed *ngo bo*,[36] if there is any error or repetition in the record of *rkang* and *'don*, if any field is deserted for long time, any income from leased land, or any missing record of the field that belonged to expelled *mi ser*, [all such details] must be identified without letting it go unnoticed and biased. Each district must submit a true and clean account of any situation in the district.

Moreover, since the deserted lands belonging to government *mi ser* cannot be erased [from the record], a few impoverished *mi ser* will definitely be unable to carry a burden of tax obligation in full due to their deserted fields. Furthermore, it must also be reported if there are fewer labourers, but the distances [to cover] are longer in the heavy *sa tshigs* transportation duty (*lam thog sa tshig*). There are some District Commissioners and representatives of monks and laypeople[37] from aristocratic estates who have cultivated the lands and grassland belonging to the government, or have hired others to cultivate these for them. As they made the excuse of paying a nominal price for the field [they cultivated], they shifted [their burden of] outer tax obligation for the government of both the *rkang 'gro* and *lag 'don* unjustly onto the destitute *mi ser*. Henceforth, there will be no exception to fulfilling their tax obligation. To protect the existing family of taxpayer from being scattered, the district officials and the representatives must take responsibility for their means of survival and must employ [the family] appropriately. All activities must be carried out honestly between the lord and subjects.

To avoid discrepancy and bad rumours in the future, all District Commissioners must submit a letter with their signatures and stamp for agreement by all representatives to the palace office (rTse yig tshang) by the 5th of the 3rd month. Any personal complaints remaining must be clearly stated [in the letter] at this time. No letter containing any fabricated complaints influenced by more thoughts will be accepted in the future. Also, if any aristocratic and monastic [estates] ignore the favour in which [the government] resumed the previous *'don* calculation and merged the lands into *'don*, or [complain] about the updated number of *rkang* and *'don* with the excuse of not being able to meet the tax burden, or if anyone submits a fabricated [letter] stating that the system did not exist previously, if anyone demands special exemption in order to fulfil his own wishes, and if anyone does not fulfil the tax obligation with the excuse that he had a broken saddle,[38] all culprits, regardless of upper or lower [social status], will be

36 Cf. *ngo chag*. This tax reduction was allowed when a family had a member serving as a government official (Goldstein 2001: 304).

37 *'du spyi* was an association of representatives from various places under the jurisdiction of a particular district (Goldstein 2001: 574).

38 This phrase *sgar ral nyag rkyang* is an interesting expression comparable to a "wrecked ship", as it seems to suggest a situation in which there is no possibility for transportation due to the saddle (*sga*) being broken.

severely punished with the whip (*rtsa 'dzin*). Thus, all must know the benefits or dangers and act accordingly without confusing what to take and what to leave.

Issued on the 20th day of the 2nd month in Iron-Tiger Year (13 April 1830).

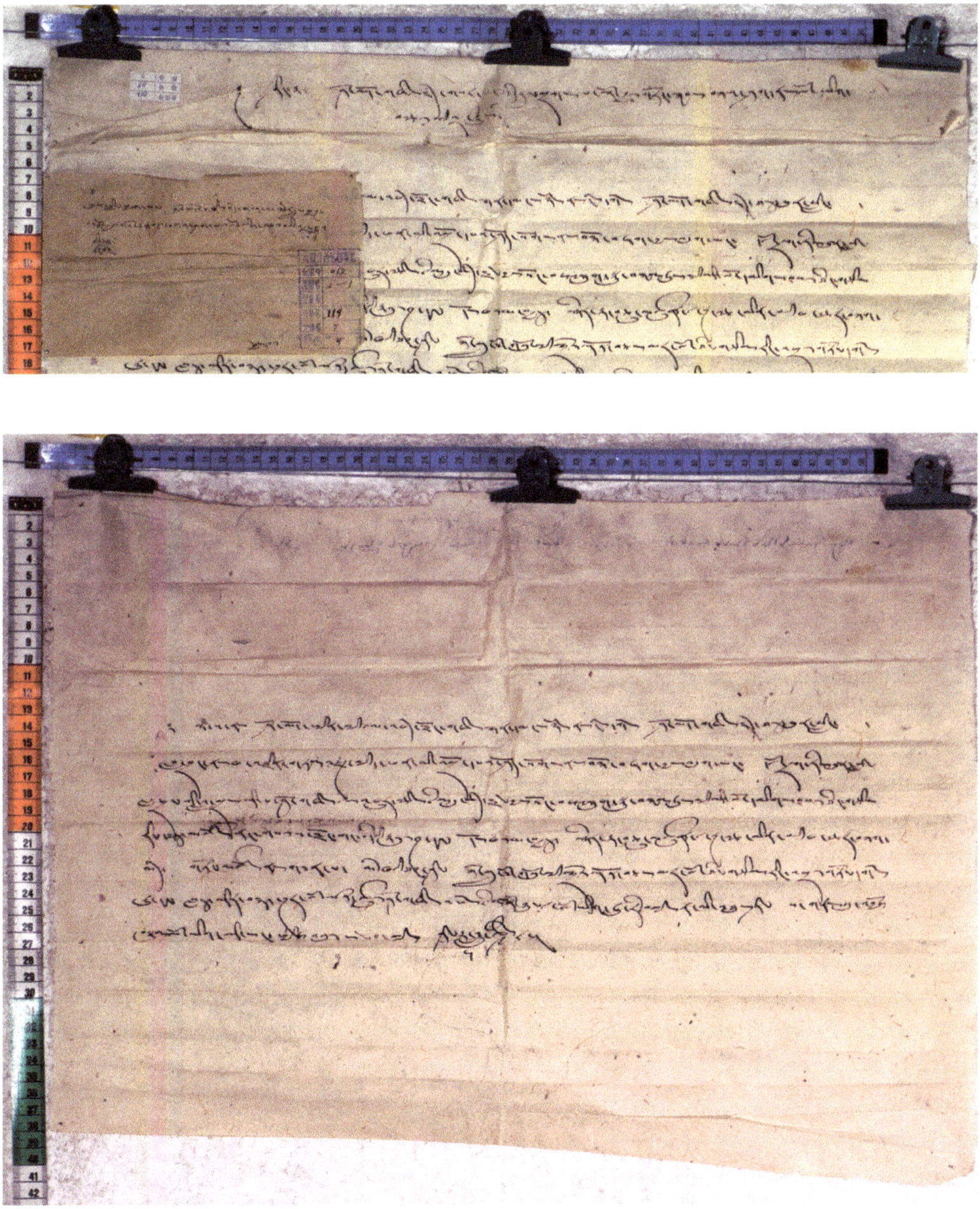

FIGURE 2.2 *Lam yig* (a travel document issued by *bka' shag* in 1894)
DTAB/DKMT: 012 2-1/#/119/7/4

1 *Transliteration*

§ shing rta/ sho mdo gzhis sdod gsar pa rtse drung grags pa rnam rgyal gtong skabs bka' shag nas lam yig bstsal ba'i 'dra shus/

1. § lha sa nas sho mdo phyin gyi lam 'khod rdzong gzhis rgan dmangs rnams nas nges dgos/ sho mdo gzhis sdod thad kun gling
2. bla brang nas kha 'dzin gtan 'jags kyi da phan mi 'gro dpa' shod sogs nas bsko bzhag byas 'dug yang/ da lam drag res kun gling
3. bla brang gi zla gras 'di pa sho gzhis las 'khur rtsis len du ched rdzong byas song bar 7 sbug tu bsnyan zhus kyi 'di lo dmigs bsal theng gcig
4. ring dpyad mtshams nang gsal sa rdzong gang bde'i rta 'ul lnga dang/ dos khal ma brgyad/ sger rta bcu mtshun la rnga rtsa min pa'i kha rtsar bkag
5. med/ gtong mtshams nas gzan pa/ me kha'i thab shing/ ko gru zam gsum gyi sgron 'don bcas mar lam theng gcig ring 'phral gtong dgos
6. rgyu dang/ slad 'dir bsnyad sngar lam yin tshul sho gzhis 'phos len nam byung la lam yig zhu re bgyis na mi 'thus shing / sa gnas su 'byor
7. bstun lam yig 'di yang phyir 'bul yong ba gyis/ shing rta zla 5 tshes 9 la /

2 *English Translation*

Wood-Horse Year (1894). A copy of the travel document issued by *bka' shag* to escort the new estate manager of Shodo (Sho mdo), *rtse drung* Grags pa rnam rgyal.

All the headsmen and the people of the district and estates on the route between Lhasa and Sho mdo must be aware of [this letter]. As the *bla brang* of Kündeling (Kun bde gling) has the permanent right of ownership (*kha 'dzin gtan 'jags*), a person for the post of estate manager of Shodo district has so far been appointed from Pasho and others. But this time, an aristocrat has especially sent a servant (*zla gras*) of Kündeling *bla brang* to take responsibility of the Shodo estate and requested [a travel document] from the inner office (*sbug*).[39] Exceptionally for one occasion this year, five horses and eight pack animals must be delivered for *sa tshigs* or *rdzong skyel* transportation as listed in the verdict, and there should be no limitation on grass supply, except the harvested grass,[40] [to feed] up to ten private horses. The labour provider must also take care of the animal fodder, wood for fire and the expenses to cross bridges and boats for one occasion on the way to [Shodo]. If anyone considers this [permission] as an excuse to be a regular custom, and asks for a travel document in the future at any point during the replacement of the Shodo estate manager, it will not be accepted. As soon

39 I assume this refers to the private office of the Dalai Lama (cf. *mdzod sbug*), as there was a possibility of issuing travel document with the personal seal of the Dalai Lama known as *sbug dam lam yig* (*Dung dkar tshig mdzod*: 1577).

40 The *rnga rtsa* means "harvested grass" and *kha rtsa* means "grass on the open meadow", which were supplied as part of the tax to feed the animals used during transportation.

as [the estate manager] reaches the place of destination, this travel document must be returned [to the government].

Issued on the 9th day of the 5th month in the Wood-Horse Year (12 June 1894).

References

Bell, C.A. 1928. *The People of Tibet*. Oxford: Clarendon Press. [Reprint: Motilal Banarsidass, Delhi 2000].

Bertsch, W. 2002. *The Currency of Tibet. A Sourcebook for the Study of Tibetan Coins, Paper Money and other Forms of Currency*. Dharamsala: Library of Tibetan Works and Archives.

Bka' rgya. Bka' rgya'i ngo shus 'khrul med [the genuine copy of an edict issued in 1830]. DTAB/DKMT: 012 2-1/#/91/9/4.

Bod kyi srid 'dzin sgrig gzhi. 1991. *Bod kyi lo rgyus rig gnas dpyad gzhi'i rgyu cha bdams bsgrigs* Vol. 4 (general series 13). Edited by Padma skal bzang and Blo bzang tshe brtan. Beijing: Mi rigs dpe skrun khang.

Bod ljongs spyi bshad. 1991 edition. Edited by Tshe ring don grub and O rgyan chos 'phel. 2 volumes. Lhasa: Bod ljongs mi dmangs dpe skrun khang.

Dung dkar tshig mdzod. Dung dkar Blo bzang 'phrin las. 2002. *mKhas dbang dung dkar blo bzang 'phrin las mchog gis mdzad pa'i bod rig pa'i tshig mdzod chen mo shes bya rab gsal zhes bya ba bzhugs so*. Beijing: Krung go'i bod rig pa dpe skrun khang.

Goldstein, M.C. 2001. *The New Tibetan-English Dictionary of Modern Tibetan*. Edited with T.N. Shelling and J.T. Surkhang. Berkeley and Los Angeles: University of California Press.

Goldstein, M.C. 1971. Taxation and the structure of a Tibetan village. *Central Asiatic Journal* 15(1), 1–27.

Goldstein, M.C. 1968. An Anthropological Study of the Tibetan Political System. Ph.D. thesis, University of Washington.

Gurung, Kalsang Norbu. 2018. The value of Tibetan money: a study of the use of Srang in late 19th century Tibet. *In* A. Travers and J. Bischoff (eds) *Commerce and Communities—Social Status and the Exchange of Goods in Tibetan Societies (the mid-17th–the mid-20th Centuries)*. Berlin: Bonner Asienstudien, EB-Verlag, 223–70.

Gurung, Kalsang Norbu. 2017. Different copies of the *Iron-Tiger Land Settlement* and their historical value as taxation manuals. *In* J. Bischoff and S. Mullard (eds) *Social Regulation: Case Studies from Tibetan History*. Leiden: Brill, 209–30.

Gurung, Kalsang Norbu. 2013. The role of Ambans in the Dalai Lama government according to the Ten-Point Edict of 1795. *In* C. Ramble, P. Schwieger, and A. Travers (eds) *Tibetans Who Escaped The Historian's Net*. Kathmandu: Vajra Books, 27–39.

Gzhung yig tha snyad. Gling dbon Padma skal bzang. 2011. *De snga'i bod sa gnas srid gzhung gi gzhung yig thog gi tha snyad spyod srol dang 'brel yod phyogs bsdus gsal 'grel.* Beijing: Mi rigs dpe skrun khang.

Kun gling chos gzhis bsnyel tho. Bka' dgongs bla brang chos gzhis khag gi rgya 'bab sgrub rnam gan sger 'bul dang dmag dang bka' chag skor gyi bsnyel tho (Kundeling estate records and tax exemption notes). DTAB/DKMT: 012 2-1/#/7/7/4).

Lam yig. Shing rta: Sho mdo gzhis sdod gsar pa rtse drung grags pa rnam rgyal gtong skabs bka' shag nas lam yig bstsal ba'i 'dra shus. DTAB/DKMT: 012 2-1/#/119/7/4.

lCags stag zhib gzhung. 1989 edition. *Dga' ldan pho brang ba'i chab 'bangs dbus gtsang dwags kong rong khag bcas kyi lcags stag zhib gzhung dam 'byar ma'i zhal bshus dge.* Edited by Bod rang skyong ljongs lo rgyus yig tshags khang. Beijing: Krung go bod kyi shes rig dpe skrun khang.

Ngag dbang (Tr.). 1991. *Bod kyi bkas bkod rgyud 'dzin zhing bran lam lugs. In* Tshe ring don grub and O rgyan chos 'phel (eds) *Bod ljongs spyi bshad* vol. 1, 515–662. Lhasa: Bod ljongs mi dmangs dpe skrun khang.

Rhodes, N.G. 1980. The development of currency in Tibet. *In* M. Aris and Aung San Suu Kyi (eds) *Tibetan Studies in Honour of Hugh Richardson: Proceedings of the International Seminar on Tibetan Studies, Oxford, 1979.* Warminster: Aris and Phillips, 261–68.

rTsa tshig don mtshan bcu. rTsa tshig don mtshan bcu pa'i zin bris (The Ten-Point Edict). Issued in 1795. DTAB/DKMT: 012 1-1/#/3/1/4.

Ryavec, K.E. 2001. Land use/cover change in Central Tibet, c. 1830–1990: Devising a GIS methodology to study a historical Tibetan land decree. *The Geographical Journal* 167 (4 December), 342–57.

Snyan zhus. Gus 'bangs ding ri sdod mda'i ngo tshab dang shel rdzong zung nas 'bul ba'i rnyan zhus (Letter from Ding ri representative and Shel dkar district commissioner). DTAD/TDL: SBB6752.

Surkhang, Wangchen Gelek. 1986. Government, monastic and private taxation in Tibet. *The Tibet Journal* 11(1), 21–40.

Surkhang, Wangchen Gelek. 1966. Tax measurement and *lag 'don* tax. *Bulletin of Tibetology* 3(1), 15–28. Namgyal Institute of Tibetology, Sikkim.

Thupten Sangyay. 1986. Glossary of the government, monastic and private taxation in Tibet. Translated from Tibetan into English by Tsepag Rigzin. *The Tibet Journal* 11(1), 41–47.

Tsarong, Paljor. 1998a. Economics of a Tibetan state treasury: the barley supply office. *The Tibet Journal* 23(2), 3–10.

Tsarong, Paljor. 1998b. Tseja: structure and economy of a Tibetan state treasury. *The Tibet Journal* 23(3), 23–33.

Zhang Yi Sun *et al.* (eds). 1996 edition. *Bod rgya tshig mdzod chen mo.* Beijing: Mi rigs dpe skrun khang.

CHAPTER 3

"When You Count, Everything Is There, and When Everything Is There, Everything Vanishes": A Criticism of Tax Collecting in Ngamring District (*rdzong*) during the First Half of the 20th Century

Alice Travers

1 Introduction

The variety and complexity of the tax systems that existed concurrently in the Tibetan territories administered by the Ganden Phodrang (dGa' ldan pho brang) government before 1959 renders any attempt to produce a general picture of taxation quite a delicate enterprise. The multitude of variations in the tax systems across the Ganden Phodrang territories can be linked to a number of factors: first, taxes depended on which of the three types of land they were levied on, i.e. land occupied by farmers (*zhing pa*), nomads (*'brog pa*) or semi-nomadic farmers (*sa ma 'brog*); second, they depended on which of the three different types of landlords these lands belonged to, and thus whether it was a monastic estate (*chos gzhis*), a lay aristocratic (*sger gzhis*) one, or an estate directly administered by the government (*gzhung gzhis*); third, they depended on the specific natural resources of this territory, as well as on its manufactured production; and last, but not least, on its local history.

In this context, authors of works in Western languages have so far chosen to highlight the main principles or "general frame" of just one specific type of tax system at a time, mainly that which was applied to arable land in Central Tibet (see Surkhang [1966] 1984 and 1986 and Goldstein 1968 and 1971a), and/or to document the system that prevailed in one particular locality, here again in the arable farming area of Central Tibet, as seen in the thorough work of Melvyn Goldstein on the village of Samada (Tib. Sa ma mda') in the Gyantse district (rGyal rtse rdzong) located in the Tsang (gTsang) province (Goldstein 1968 and 1971a).[1] Following that lead, the present paper will document yet another

1 In his [1966] 1984 paper, Surkhang's description focuses on "Central Tibet" in the sense that it includes only the arable land of Ü (dBus), Tsang, Kongpo (Kong po), Dakpo (Dwags po), and a few districts of Tö Ngari (sTod mNga' ris). Surkhang's 1986 paper documents the diversity of

 | DOI:10.1163/9789004529465_005

particular local tax system, that of Ngamring district (Ngam ring rdzong), based on a twelve-page, eyewitness account authored by Trentsa Tamdrin Gyelpo (Phran rtsa rta mgrin rgyal po), entitled "A brief description of Ngamring district's history and of several District Commissioners' behaviour when I was myself a District Clerk there" ("Ngam ring rdzong gi lo rgyus dang bar skabs rdzong sdod 'ga' zhig gi byed phyogs rang nyid las drung byed skabs bcas skor rags bsdus").[2] Published in 1994 (and hereafter referred to as Phran rtsa rta mgrin rgyal po 1994), this account covers the period of the 1930s to the 1950s. It belongs to a thirty-volume collection of autobiographical and biographical accounts entitled *Bod kyi lo rgyus rig gnas dpyad gzhi'i rgyu cha bdams bsgrigs* (lit. "Selection of Source Materials for the Study of Tibetan History and Culture"; in short *Materials for the History and Culture of Tibet*, hereafter MHCT) published in the Tibet Autonomous Region between 1981 and 2014.[3]

This account is a particularly interesting source for the study of the history of taxes in Tibet for two reasons. First, it provides a description of the accounting and tax collection process at the district (*rdzong*)[4] level—districts representing the basic territorial administrative units of the Tibetan government and the largest units for land settlements and tax collection[5]—and thus offers an additional understanding of the tax collection system as a link between

---

various tax systems across the Ganden Phodrang territories, with a few passages dedicated to the specificities of the tax systems of nomadic land (1986: 27–28) and the areas under the Ganden Phodrang that were not in Central Tibet, mainly Western Tibet, Southern Tibet and Eastern Tibet. Only a few particular specificities of each of these areas or systems are mentioned. Therefore, the tax systems operating in other Ganden Phodrang territories in the northern nomadic areas, in Western, Eastern and Southern Tibet still need further research, as well as tax systems operating in territories that were not under the direct administration of the Ganden Phodrang. The most detailed local examples of tax systems in nomadic and in these other areas are to be found in the *Bod ljongs spyi bshad*, a Tibeto-Chinese survey of "traditional Tibet". The work contains a section on taxes that is translated and discussed in Peter Schwieger's contribution to this volume, and is also referred to in Kalsang Norbu Gurung's chapter.

2 The same Trentsa Tamdrin Gyelpo was also the author of an earlier account in this collection, recounting a dispute that took place between the aristocrat Rutokpa (Ru thog pa), whose estate was in Ngamring district, and the subjects of Ngamring (Phran rtsa rta mgrin rgyal po 1985).

3 For a presentation and analysis of the collection MHCT as a whole, and its main characteristics as a historical source, see Travers 2020a.

4 The Tibetan term "*rdzong*" designates both the district as an administrative unit in its entirety and a district's headquarters as the centre of management for this administrative unit.

5 There were around 170 districts and government estates on the Ganden Phodrang territories. Only 58 districts are listed in the *Iron-Tiger Land Settlement* (on this source, see explanations in the following section of this paper), and 120 districts are given in Goldstein (1968: 32–37); for an updated list of 166 districts and government estates on the Ganden Phodrang's

the lower village and estate levels, which are particularly well documented in Goldstein's work, at one end of the chain, and the level of the State treasuries and offices in the capital of Lhasa at the other end.[6] Second, Trentsa Tamdrin Gyelpo's account stands out because Ngamring district,[7] located in the Shigatse (gZhis ka rtse) area, was originally under the Tashi Lhunpo semi-autonomous administration (bKra shis lhun po *bla brang*)[8] before passing, in December 1923, under the direct control of the Lhasa government after the flight of the Ninth Panchen Lama (Thub bstan chos kyi nyi ma, 1883–1937);[9] the Tashi Lhunpo tax system[10] has so far been less well documented than other areas of Central Tibet which were under the direct jurisdiction of the Ganden Phodrang government in Lhasa.

---

territory between 1830 and 1959 based on the two later sources as well as on research with other primary sources, see Travers 2020b.

6 See Tsarong 1998a and 1998b for instance on the barley supply office (*rtsam bzhes las khungs*) and the Potala treasury (*rtse phyag*).

7 Alternatively known as Chang Ngamring (Byang Ngam ring), it is located on the northwestern edge of Tsang, along the northern bank of the Yarlung Tsangpo river. According to another account in the *MHCT* collection dedicated to the history of Ngamring, the name of Ngamring district itself is derived from a long ravine (*ngam grog ring mo*) at the entrance to the district's territory. The district is said to be alternatively, though less frequently, known as Ngang ring because of a big lake called Kyemtsho (sKyem mtsho) in which the sound of the wild geese (*ngang pa*) reverberates endlessly (gZhis rtse sa gnas srid gros lo rgyus rtsom 'bri tshogs chung nas 2005: 52).

8 A *bla brang* "refers to the residence of an incarnate lama. It often is a large land holding unit and in this sense is considered, along with monasteries, as a religious estate" (Surkhang [1966] 1984: 29). Tashi Lhunpo monastery enjoyed a semi-autonomous status, as did Sakya (Sa skya) monastery. As such, these two, along with the Lhasa government, were often referred to as "*gzhung bla sa gsum*" (lit. "the [Lhasa government], the [Tashi Lhunpo] *bla brang* and Sakya [monastery]"). For a presentation of the administration of Tashi Lhunpo see Sle zur 'Jigs med dbang phyug and bDe zur Rin chen dbang 'dus 1991 and Jagou 2011: 249–56. On Sakya and its administration see Cassinelli and Ekvall 1969; lCam grwa nor bzang and Kun dga' chos bzang 1991. The estate of the Lhagyari (lHa rgya ri) lineage was also considered an additional semi-autonomous entity; see Karsten 1979. See also Goldstein 1971b for a detailed explanation of the balance between the autonomy of these sub-entities and the centralisation of the Ganden Phodrang government and its authority over them, which explains why it is referred to as the Tibetan "Central Government".

9 On this event and its consequences, see Jagou 2011.

10 A note of explanation of the use of "tax system" in the present article: in Tibet, as elsewhere, the "tax system" was mostly composed of patchy elements, resulting more from historical sedimentation and juxtaposition than of any abstract theorisation produced at a higher administrative level and resulting in a logical combination of levies on this territory. Therefore, in this paper, the idea of "tax system" simply refers to the ensemble of taxes in kind and cash and of corvées and obligations levied on a given territory.

Tibetan tax systems reflect significant aspects of a given territory's social history: the nature and quantity of the production of the territory, the local networks that the circuits of taxes drew—indeed, if taxes were partly sent to the capital in Lhasa, they were very often also directly delivered to more nearby locations in order to provide other communities—monastic ones in the example documented in the present article—with their subsidies. Lastly, in the case of Trentsa Tamdrin Gyelpo's account, the description of the tax collection process also reflects the hierarchy and status of individuals involved in the local administration of the village and the district.

Thus, focusing on Trentsa Tamdrin Gyelpo's account, and drawing together additional information available in a few other sources (other accounts from the *MHCT*, oral interviews with former Tibetan government officials, and archival sources), this article intends to contribute further to our understanding of the Ganden Phodrang tax system before 1959, in particular of its collection process, by providing another local example from a district under the Tashi Lhunpo administration. After recalling a few basic principles linked to the tax system as it is already known from previous studies of arable farming areas in Central Tibet, which will set a comparative frame for Trentsa Tamdrin Gyelpo's account, this article will introduce the particular tax system of Ngamring district as described in the abovementioned source; finally, it will focus on the accounting process at the district headquarters and on the opportunities for enrichment that the system offered to people involved in tax collection.

2 The Tax System in Agricultural Areas of Central Tibet as Described in Secondary Western-Language Literature

2.1 *Land Units of Tax Calculation:* rkang *and* 'don

The tax system that existed on agricultural land in Central Tibet is without any doubt the best documented, thanks to the work of Surkhang Wangchen Gelek and Melvyn Goldstein. The system there was more uniform in the sense that a few principles were common to most districts. Indeed, before 1959, in all but three districts in Central Tibet[11] where the *Wood-Mouse Land Settlement* (*Shing byi zhib gzhung*) dated 1864 was in effect,[12] taxes were levied according

11 Gyantse (rGyal rtse), Nam (rNam) and Wangden (dBang ldan) districts (Surkhang [1966] 1984: 25).

12 For the distinctive regulation (*glang ske be'u 'dogs*) applied to this later land settlement, see Peter Schwieger, in this volume.

to the land registered in the previous *Iron-Tiger Land Settlement* (*lCags stag zhib gzhung*) of 1830 and its later amendments.[13]

With the exception of the nomads of Central Tibet, taxation was based on the number of *rkang* or *'don* (1 *'don* = 2 *rkang*) of land cultivated by dependent peasants (*mi ser*)[14] belonging to the three types of landlord, i.e. the government, monastic and aristocratic landlords, where *rkang* and *'don* are the basic units of land measurement calculated by the planting capacity of the land. The estimates given for that capacity in Tibet vary, but according to Thupten Sangyay, the seed capacity of 1 *rkang* in Ü was 30 *khal*[15] of seed, and 50 *khal* of seed in Tsang (Thupten Sangyay 1986: 41). A related piece of information is then the productivity of the land: according to Surkhang ([1966] 1984: 22–23), 1 *rkang* usually yielded about 80 *khal* of grain, but it could vary from as low as 60 to as high as 120 *khal*. The taxes of government estates were based on the number of *rkang*, whereas the taxes of monastic and aristocratic estates were based on the number of *'don*.[16] Government *mi ser* paid taxes only to the

13 On the *Iron-Tiger Land Settlement* in particular, see Gurung 2016 and Ryavec 2002. For a discussion of the historical background of land settlements in general see Surkhang 1986, Gurung 2016: 209–10, as well as the contributions by Schwieger and Gurung in this volume. The *Iron-Tiger Land Settlement* did not comprise all districts under the Ganden Phodrang, but as Surkhang puts it, only those "from Shelkar to Kongpo" (Surkhang 1986: 28), and excluded a number of districts located in Northern, Southern and Western Tibet (see *ibid.* for the list of districts of Western Tibet which are not included in the *Iron-Tiger Land Settlement*).

14 There has been ongoing debate regarding the adequate English translation of this term and the question of whether the term "serf" was appropriate. For a presentation and discussion of the debate, see Travers 2009: 97–104. In using the translation "dependent peasant" here, we follow Bischoff's choice (see Bischoff 2017: 152), informed by what represents the most up-to-date analysis of the legal and social status of *mi ser*, based on previous secondary literature as well as new research on archival sources.

15 The *khal* was the basic measure for volumes. One *khal* is equal to 20 *bre*, and 1 *bre* is equal to 6 *phul*. It was standardised and was the only volume measure accepted by the Tibetan government for the calculation of taxes. The *khal* was calculated through the use of a wooden box called *'bo*, and the standardised box used for government purposes was called *gtan tshigs mkhar ru* or *mkhar ru* (for more explanations on this term see Schwieger 2021). Thus, one also finds the term *mkhar khal*, an abbreviation for *mkhar ru'i khal*, itself similar to a *mkhar ru*, which is a "standard government volume measure" (Goldstein 2001: 154). For barley, if converted into weight, 1 *khal* equalled about 27 pounds (Surkhang [1966] 1984: 22–23) or about 27–33 pounds (Goldstein 2001: 154). It should be noted that there was another type of *khal* that designated a weight measure (as opposed to a volumetric measure for grain) that was used for non-dry products such as butter; see footnote 83.

16 Surkhang [1966] 1984: 20. This author could substantiate the use of the *rkang* to measure land from 1740 onwards, though he thinks it most probable that this unit was used prior to this date.

government while *mi ser* belonging to monastic and aristocratic estates paid taxes to the government and worked on their landlord's land (Surkhang 1986: 223).[17] Most taxes were based on land holdings (and related to the size of the land) but some other taxes were not—and just had to be collectively taken care of (Surkhang 1984: 26).

2.2 Basic Categorisations of Taxes: Outer and Inner Taxes, Taxes in Kind and Corvée Labour

Taxes based on land holdings can be first divided into outer (*phyi khral*) and inner taxes (*nang khral*). "Outer taxes" refers to taxes paid to or performed for the Tibetan Central Government (i.e. the Ganden Phodrang in Lhasa) and "inner taxes" denotes taxes paid to or performed for one's immediate lord—monastic or private/aristocratic—from whom the land which formed the tax basis (*khral rten*) was obtained (Goldstein 1968: 65). In the case of government *mi ser*, "inner taxes" meant the taxes paid to or performed for the district of which they were a part (Goldstein 1971a: 10).

"Outer taxes" and "inner taxes" can be both further divided into two main categories: the *lag 'don* (tax in kind or money) and the *rkang 'gro* (corvée labour). The nature of the taxes included in those two categories depended on whether the *mi ser* belonged to governmental, monastic or aristocratic estates. As tax in kind (*lag 'don*), in most agricultural parts of Central Tibet[18] government *mi ser* had to pay four main different types of taxes (their quantity being determined for each *rkang* of land): the *rgyal po khral* (lit. "tax of the king") was the most important, usually an amount of grain (*'bru*) and a generic term which would be delivered either in barley (*nas*), peas (*sran ma*) or wheat (*gro*) and measured in *khal*, but this could also sometimes be replaced by a local product such as oil, paper, or butter;[19] the *smon brngod* or tax for the Great Prayer (*smon lam*) in Lhasa, paid in roasted barley flour (*rtsam pa*) and also measured in *khal*; the *rgya bsos* tax,[20] paid in money and the *shing dngul* (lit. "wood money") tax,

17 However, in practice, the landlord did collect taxes from its government *mi ser* and then paid them to the government (*ibid.*: 27).

18 This excludes Western Tibet, where other types of taxes were paid (Surkhang 1986: 28).

19 The amount and kind of product or money that a district had to pay as tax was written on a document called a *'bab gzhung* (Surkhang [1966] 1984: 27).

20 The *rgya bsos* tax is not translated literally by Surkhang but defined as a tax "collected by the District Commissioner and turned over to whoever is *rgya bsos dbu re* of that year. This is not much money and most of it is used to pay salaries of the sweepers in Lhasa, and part of the wages of the giant prayer wheel turners in Central Tibet. Whatever is left over is stored in the Rtse rnam sras gan mdzod" (*ibid.*: 27). This probably reflects the new use of this tax in post-1911 Tibet (i.e. after the end of Manchu suzerainty) since *rgya bsos* literally means "compensation for the Chinese". It seems that the tax was formerly meant to "support the Amban" if we follow Kalsang Norbu Gurung's translation of it in the opening section of the 1830 *Iron-Tiger Land Settlement* (Gurung 2016: 224). As for this

formerly paid in wood but later converted to cash (Surkhang ([1966] 1984: 27; Goldstein 1968: 71). These taxes were delivered to the barley supply office in Lhasa (Tsarong 1998a: 6). The last three taxes were usually referred to as *rgya shing brngod gsum* and were considered an old tax (*ibid.*).[21]

Surkhang states that the corvée labour (*rkang 'gro*) consisted largely of *'u lag*, which meant sending one or two persons per *rkang* (depending on the season) to take part in different works such as the reaping of swamp grass (*'dam 'ul*), government construction projects (*ar 'ul*), or lastly and mainly the transportation of goods and government officials and their families (on which see also Saadet Arslan's contribution in this volume), which was itself divided into two types: *sa tshig* and *rdzong skyel* (when it involved providing more than ten riding horses and fifteen mules), as well as provisions for military troops (Surkhang 1986: 24).[22]

In addition to the *lag 'don* (tax in kind or money) and the *rkang 'gro* (corvée labour), Surkhang adds three other categories of taxes paid in proportion to the size of the land: the military tax (*dmag khral*)—which is treated by Goldstein as a further category of the corvée labour tax type (*rkang 'gro*) (Goldstein 1968: 72); the *sga 'go*, described as being "most probably [...] a small sum of money for owning transportation animals"; and the *sho khral*, described with a certain degree of uncertainty as a "taxation on imported goods" (Surkhang 1986: 21 and 32–33) or a "tax levied on domestic commodities such as salt, wool, and tea" (Thupten Sangyay 1986: 41).[23]

---

new, post-1911 usage, another description is alternatively provided by Thupten Sangyay in his Glossary, as a "tax levied on subjects for supplying fodder to the horses used for postal services" (Thupten Sangyay 1986: 43).

21 Tsarong (1998a: 9) provides a slightly different definition of the three taxes: "rGya, is a barley grain tax which was collected in order to repay a debt to the Chinese. Shing is the tax for fire-wood, which was collected by the *smon lam shing sgrub pa*, for the *smon lam* ceremonies. brNgos, is the roasted barley flour tax paid to the barley supply office". These three taxes are mentioned in the opening section of the 1830 *Iron-Tiger Land Settlement* (see Gurung 2016: 222) with the alternative spelling *dngos* instead of the usual *brngos/ brngod* (past and future tenses of *rngod*, to roast).

22 There were also two other important taxes. On new fields, after three years of tax exemption, a *mi ser* had to pay the *bcu bogs* (one tenth of the yield after deducting the seed needed for the next planting), a tax directly paid to the government and not to the district (Surkhang 1986: 25–26). The second were the taxes on cattle, which comprised two systems of calculating taxes: first, the *skye med 'chi med* system for government cattle (the income from male yaks went to the herder, and for each female yak the herder had to submit 1 *khal* of butter to the *she dpon*, the man in charge of government cattle); second, the *skye yod 'chi yod* system (which is "the annual animal tax equivalent to one *Khal* and ten *Nyag* of butter collected from the subjects on the basis of the actual number of cattle surviving and dead", see Thupten Sangyay 1986: 46), mostly for monastic and aristocratic cattle.

23 According to Goldstein (1968: 72), the "military tax" and the *sa tshig* transportation corvée were the two main "outer taxes".

Surkhang underlines a difference between government *mi ser* (*gzhung rgyug*), on the one hand, and monastic and aristocratic *mi ser* on the other hand (again in Central Tibetan areas under the direct administration of the Ganden Phodrang), namely that government *mi ser* did not pay a heavy tax in kind or money (the four above-mentioned taxes), but that their corvée labour was more difficult (Surkhang 1986: 24 and 26); monastic and aristocratic landlords owed the government only three out of the four above-mentioned *lag 'don* types (*rgya shing brngod gsum*),[24] plus the military tax and the transportation corvée (*ibid.*: 26).[25]

Even in exclusively arable areas of Central Tibet, the system was not entirely uniform, because of geographical factors. As Surkhang underlines, there were "particular taxation practices due to particular products of the *rdzong*" (*ibid.*: 29). A few examples are given, such as blue and green dye in Nyemo (sNye mo), white lime from Yangchen (dByangs can), construction wood from districts in Kongpo (*ibid.*), oil from Nedong (sNe gdong) and Rinpung (Rin spungs), paper from Tshona (mTsho sna), Gyantse and Sangngakchö (gSang sngags chos) (Surkhang [1966] 1984: 30). More generally, the comparison between Goldstein and Surkhang's descriptions enables us to have a preliminary understanding of the disparities in terms of tax systems even among agrarian territories under the direct administration of the Lhasa government. Goldstein's description of the Samada's *phyi khral* for instance resembles what Surkhang describes, but they obviously have other types of *lag 'don* and *rkang 'gro* taxes as *nang khral* (i.e. for their landlord) (see Goldstein 1968: 72).[26]

2.3 *People Involved in the Tax Collection Process*

Having established the framework, we may now turn our attention to a particularly significant aspect of taxation in pre-1959 Tibet: the actual process of tax collection and the people responsible for it. The District Commissioners (*rdzong sdod* or *rdzong dpon*)[27] were usually one or two lay or monk government officials (*gzhung zhabs*) holding the seventh to the fifth rank—depending on the size and significance of the district—and usually served a term of three years.

---

24 Only government estates had to pay the *rgyal po khral*.

25 However, if a monastic or aristocratic landlord was given an additional estate to manage by the government, then the taxation would be due as on government land. As explained by Surkhang (1986: 26), "the profit for the owners from such specially granted land is similar to the profit a *rdzong dpon* makes from administering a particular *rdzong*".

26 Also, to give another example, the monastic tax (*btsun khral* or *grwa khral*) described by Goldstein (1968: 80) for Samada is not mentioned by Surkhang. On this monastic tax, see Berthe Jansen's contribution in this volume.

27 The official designation of *rdzong dpon* was *rdzong sdod*, which is the only term used in Trentsa Tamdrin Gyelpo's account.

Thanks to Goldstein's work, the District Commissioners' work as tax collector operating at the highest territorial level of the district, among their other duties, has been well described. The various responsibilities of the District Commissioner can be summarised as follows: "(1) to collect taxes; (2) to act as clearing house for all commands and orders descending from the centre and for all petitions and the like coming up from the residents of the district; (3) to adjudicate disputes and try and punish criminals" (*ibid.*: 20).

Tax collection entailed considerable work, because of the great number and complexity of taxes and corvées, some recurrent and others non-recurrent. In most (but not all) districts of Central Tibet, District Commissioners were helped by other government officials[28] called "tax collectors" (*yong bsdus*) sent by the Tibetan Central Government when the taxes were due to be paid (*ibid.*: 21).

District Commissioners were also assisted in the tax collection process at the district level by local agents, whose status and titles were not entirely uniform across districts and whose number depended on the district's size. These lower ranking actors in the tax collection process have received less attention, except for the village of Samada studied by Goldstein (*ibid.*). As this author has underlined, the majority of the actual work of tax collection was carried out not by the District Commissioner himself but by the lower ranking local employees under his orders. Among them, the most important position was that of the District Clerks (*las drung*), who were part of the category of government employees called *nang gzan*, ranking below the category of government officials (*ibid.*: 27).[29] *Las drung* played the role of secretary-*cum*-intendant in the district's headquarters, assisting the District Commissioner or his representative in his various tasks. As Goldstein explains: "Their actual duties included such things as writing communiques for distribution in the district or submission to Lhasa, supervising the measurement of taxes, and making arrangements for religious leaders and government officials who officially visited the district" (*ibid.*: 28). They were *mi ser* and their position was most of the time, but not always, hereditary.[30] Because they were stable members of the district headquarters' staff, unlike the District Commissioner who was replaced every few years, their knowledge of the district and especially of its

28 Those working for the Ganden Phodrang government who enjoyed the rank of government officials (*gzhung zhabs*) were either lay officials (*drung 'khor*) or monk officials (*rste drung*), and ranked from the 7th to 3rd rank. See Goldstein's work (1968) and Travers 2009 for more explanation on the general organisation of the Ganden Phodrang.

29 The *nang gzan* referred to here are different from the *nang zan* who were household servants, as described by Okawa (2016).

30 For one instance of such hereditary transmission of the position, see bDud 'dul chos dbyings 1984: 173.

tax affairs was highly valuable (*ibid.*). In Samada, *las drung* received a "tax-free estate as a salary" (*phogs thob*) (*ibid.*: 27). It is known from other sources that there were usually between two and four *las drung* in each district.

In the large Gyantse district described by Goldstein, in addition to the two District Commissioners who held the fifth rank, among those working for the districts and bearing responsibilities in the administration and taxation of the district were four District Clerks (*las drung*), five *glang* managing the taxes in kind that the government *mi ser* had to pay, six *tsho dpon* responsible for organising and doing the accounting for the corvée animal transportation taxes at the *tsho* level,[31] four *rgan chen* ("senior headmen"), and one *khang gnyer*, translated as "District messenger" (Goldstein's description does not make any distinction between the staff working in the district headquarters and those in charge at the village level) (*ibid.*: 28–31). In other places, according to secondary and primary sources, people holding other titles were appointed at the village level to positions related to the village organisation, including the tax collection process. There was always the headman or *rgan po* (lit. "elder") chosen from among the *mi ser*, whose charge might or might not be hereditary, and who was responsible at the lowest level of judicial and tax affairs (Surkhang [1966] 1984: 21). We also find *spyi mi* (a people's delegate or representative), *gtso drag* (a position that is certainly close to the above-mentioned *tsho dpon*) and appointed among the estate holders, aristocrat or larger *mi ser* families (*ibid.*); and sometimes also *lding dpon* and *bcu dpon*.[32]

Just as a point of comparison, let us consider the composition of the staff of one smaller district, Dakpo kunam (Dwags po sku rnam), documented in the *MHCT* collection and described by its own District Commissioner between 1953 and 1957. For this district, in which the agricultural land of all three landlords totalled 280 *'don*, and which consisted of 2,000 households (*them*) of *mi ser*, the district administration comprised: a single District Commissioner holding the sixth rank, one *las drung*, three *gtso drag*, three *lding dpon*, one *spyi mi*, and one *rgan po* per "locality" (*lung tshan*) of which there were fourteen (Chos 'byor dar rgyas 2005: 206). Now that the main principles and context of the tax systems and tax collection in Central Tibetan have been established, let us turn to the particular case of Ngamring district.

31 The *tsho* was a small territorial unit directly linked to the system of *sa tshig*.

32 It should be emphasised that the significance of these terms is different from their better-known usage in a military context to denote certain officer ranks. In Nyemo (sNye mo) district for instance, there were three *gtso drag* and three *bcu dpon* who assisted the District Commissioner in his administrative work (Anonymous interview, Lhasa, 2012).

3 The Tax System in Ngamring District According to the MHCT

3.1 *Status and Possible Use of This Type of Source*

Several new sources are now available that allow us to continue documenting the tax system and the process of tax collection at the local level in other areas of Central Tibet. One of them is the MHCT, in which we find several accounts written by former District Clerks (*las drung*), among them the testimony of Trentsa Tamdrin Gyelpo, which is the focus of this article (Phran rtsa rta mgrin rgyal po 1994). The primary aim of this account is to describe in detail how a few people working in Ngamring in the 1920s and 1930s exploited and mistreated the *mi ser* of the district, abusing their official position to enrich themselves.

It is important to situate this account in the political context in which the MHCT was compiled, and more generally of post-1950 Tibetan communist society, in order to fully appreciate its content. The autobiographical accounts published in this collection, like the whole enterprise of *Wenshi ziliao* in the People's Republic of China (PRC), are related to the compulsory practice of recounting one's life, in an oral or written form, during the most radical years of the Mao era. At that time, these life accounts could be divided in two types, depending on the social origin of their author: either the expression of bitterness (Ch. *suku*), in which exploited classes in the old society expressed their resentment toward their former oppressor; or a confession (Ch. *zhaogong*), in which oppressors would repent for their social and political crimes and would show that they had changed their way of thinking for the better (Henrion-Dourcy 2013: 3). They have also been associated with the category of denunciation (Ch. *qianze*).[33]

Trentsa Tamdrin Gyelpo's account belongs primarily to the "denunciation" category, with the addition of a limited dimension of confession (more a rhetorical one), a combination that might be linked to the ambiguous social status of the author, in the context of the so-called "class struggle" introduced to Central Tibet by the Chinese authorities: indeed, Trentsa Tamdrin Gyelpo, though of humble social extraction, was himself a *las drung* and took part in the process of tax collection. This lends him the legitimacy to denounce the actions of his colleagues, as a first-hand witness to what is being condemned there in relation to the general exactions of the "class of feudal lords" (*mnga'*

33 The exile Tibetan essayist and intellectual Jamyang Norbu has also remarked on this collection: "Although serving an ancillary academic purpose, they are not entirely unrelated to 'confession' (*zhaogong*) and 'denunciation' (*qianze*) writing, from an earlier period" (Jamyang Norbu 2008).

bdag gral rim), as it was designated in post-1959 Tibetan society; at the same time, he is himself a member of another class enemy group, i.e. the social intermediate elite then labelled the "class of representatives/steward of feudal lords" (*mnga' tshab gral rim*),[34] and as such he needs to confess his own crimes, as can be seen in the concluding part of his account, which opens with his rhetorical apologies:

> As far as I am concerned, despite the fact that I held at this time the rank of senior District Clerk (*las drung khri pa*), I was expert in taking only small opportunities in the context of this bad system and, for this reason, all *mi ser* held me in a little higher respect. However, because greater exploitation than that has also occurred, it is appropriate that I apologise to the people of this region.
>
> PHRAN RTSA RTA MGRIN RGYAL PO 1994: 77[35]

As for the denunciation of pre-1959 Tibetan society and that political system, the author repeatedly describes the tax system and tax collection as being "feudal" (*bkas bkod rgyud 'dzin lam lugs gtong*, see *ibid.*: 69) or "bad" (*lam lugs ngan pa*, see *ibid.*: 76 and 77) and singles out the corruption of some of the elites. To give an example, he describes one administrator as follows:

> These people, when they first arrive in the district, have their saddle bags empty and later [when they return], they have become reputedly very rich. Under this bad system, those above the heads of the *mi ser* are experts in exploiting the latter; they differ from each other only by their degree of greediness, but there is none who does not exploit [the *mi ser*]. However, after the Iron-Rabbit year (1951), when all estates and districts of Tashi Lhunpo *labrang* were seized by the government,[36] there was no such excessive corruption (*za bed 'phar brdabs*). For instance, when the monk official sMon skyid pa was personally put in charge of Ngamring

34 This terminology (*mnga' bdag gral rim* and *mnga' tshab gral rim*) was one used in the general context of post-1950 society, but it is not used by the author in this account. On the place of the *las drung* within the "middle class" of Tibet and their occasional intermarrying with aristocratic *sger pa* families, see Travers 2009 and 2013.

35 *nga rang la ltos na skabs der las drung khri pa zer ba'i go ming yod kyang lam lugs ngan pa de'i thog bya thabs cung zad mkhas pa'i stabs kyis mi ser yongs nas brtsi bkur che tsam yod tsang de bas bshu gzhog kyang che ba byung yod pas khul de'i mang tshogs la dgongs dag thugs bden zhu 'os pa zhig yin/* (Phran rtsa rta mgrin rgyal po 1994: 77).

36 We will return in greater detail to the subject of the administrative changes that took place in the 1950s at the end of this paper.

> district, because the way he took care of the *mi ser* was rather good, they nicknamed him "Lama Mañjuśrī". In this system, for each District Clerk (*las drung*) also, it is as in the proverb "On big mountains there is a lot of snow and on small mountains only a little": they exploit [the *mi ser*] depending on their qualities.
>
> *ibid.*: 76–77[37]

Despite the fact that it is common knowledge that there were indeed corrupt officials in the Ganden Phodrang and Tashi Lhunpo governments, as well as honest ones, one has to remember that criticism of the whole system was certainly a requirement for producing any account of the "old society" in the *MHCT* collection. In any case, an accusation or rumour of corruption can always be purely slanderous and historians are in no capacity to judge the veracity of the behaviours denounced or praised therein.

Yet another limitation of such a source has to be underlined, one relevant to any source of the "oral history" type, even when, as in this account, it has been edited and printed in book form. The description of the tax system in this district was published in 1994, thirty-five years after the end of the system it describes,[38] which is a significant amount of time when it comes to remembering precise figures, as is the case in this recollection and explanation of the tax collection and accounting processes. On occasion Trentsa Tamdrin Gyelpo himself underlines that he does not clearly remember this or that particular quantity, measure, etc. For this reason, the list of taxes is not (and cannot be) exhaustive and does not allow the reader, in the end, to draw a complete and precise list of incomes and expenses, or to compare their balance. Thus, all figures given by the witness and quoted in the present paper must be understood only as examples of the way the system worked, but it is not possible to draw any quantified conclusion from them.

---

37 *kho pa tsho ni dang thog rta sgro stong pa zhig las khyer rgyu med pa nas rjes su skad grags ldan pa'i 'byor phyugs tu gyur cing/ lam lugs ngan pa'i 'og mi ser gyi 'go la sdod mkhan zhig yin phyin bshu gzhog gtong mkhas lod dang za rngam che chung tsam ma gtogs rtsa ba'i cha nas bshu gzhogs mi gtong mkhan med / 'on kyang lcags yos* (1951) *lor bkras lhun bla brang gi rdzong gzhis tshang ma gzhung 'dzin byas rjes za bed 'phar brdabs che rigs byung med / dper na ngam rdzong rtse las tshan smon skyid pa 'go khrid ngo las skabs mi ser 'tsho skyong cung legs pa byung tsang khong la mi ser gyis bla ma 'jam dpal dbyangs zhes 'bod kyi yod pa red / lam lugs de'i nang las drung so sor yang ri che chung la kha ba che chung gi dpe ltar mi so so'i 'jon thang byed phyogs la gzhigs pa'i za bed che chung yod /* (*ibid.*: 76–77).

38 The date of collection of this particular oral account is not given and it could have happened at a slightly earlier date, but this would not change the consideration expressed here.

This being said, even if the primary aim of Trentsa Tamdrin Gyelpo's account is political and even if it cannot serve as a source for a thorough description of Ngamring's tax system,[39] it is still of great interest to historians: while shedding light on the precise way administrators managed to profit personally from tax collection during their time in office, it also explains specific aspects of the territorial and tax organisation in this territory of the pre-1959 Tashi Lhunpo *labrang*, including the way this particular district was administered, the various people in charge of its administration and the different types of taxes that they collected. Lastly, whatever the limitations this type of source may have, it still has the undeniable advantage in revealing a topic—accounting creativity, tax evasion, fraud and corruption—that the types of official sources that are otherwise available (land settlements, lists of taxes, decisions on tax exemption, etc.) usually do not permit historians to study.

3.2 *Introductory Remarks on the System of Taxes, Corvées and Obligations in Ngamring District*

As the tax system of districts belonging to the Tashi Lhunpo *labrang* has not been studied so far,[40] Trentsa Tamdrin Gyelpo's account allows a first understanding of it and, to a certain degree, a comparison with the tax systems prevailing on territories directly administered by the Ganden Phodrang.[41] The first remark is that taxes in Ngamring district, broadly speaking, followed the same basic principles explained in the first part of this paper: taxes based on the number of *rkang*, fixed in land settlements, with, as we will see, the mention of an "inner tax",[42] of taxes paid both in kind and money and corvée obligations by *mi ser* belonging to the three types of landlord. Taxes in kind and money and corvée labour resemble in nature and content those described by Surkhang for districts under the direct administration of Lhasa, including payment in wool, grain, butter, oil, meat, wool, and cloth. The author goes into great detail regarding a number of specific *lag 'don* taxes, such as those related

39 Contrary to Goldstein's Ph.D., for instance, with Samada.

40 There is only a brief mention in Surkhang (1986: 37), according to which Tashi Lhunpo *labrang* was an exception as it did not pay taxes to the Lhasa government on its roughly 2,000 *rkang* of land; this estimate of land is based on the information provided in the *Iron-Tiger Land Settlement* (*lCags stag zhib gzhung*).

41 The other account in the *MHCT* collection on Ngamring history (gZhis rtse sa gnas srid gros lo rgyus rtsom 'bri tshogs chung nas 2005: 52–65) contains much less detailed information on the taxation system of the district; however, whatever additional explanations are available there have been included in this paper.

42 There is, however, no mention of "outer tax" (*phyi khral*) in the account and we do not know whether this term used to refer to taxes due to the Tashi Lhunpo *labrang* (following the model of districts under the Ganden Phodrang government).

to local manufactured products, for instance a paper tax paid with the local production of the district, as we will examine in more detail in the next part.

However, except for the units of measurement for volume and weight, which are quite similar, the names of taxes clearly differed from those observed in territories under the direct administration of Lhasa, whether in Ü or in Tsang (Surkhang [1966] 1984 and 1986, and, for Samada, Goldstein 1968 and 1971a). For instance, there is no *rgyal po khral* or *rgya shing brngod gsum*,[43] and more generally, almost none of the taxes presented in the above-mentioned works appears in this description of Ngamring taxes. Two different reasons might account for this: first, Ngamring district was located in the area of Tö (sTod), or more precisely at the frontier between Tsang and Tö, or eastern Tö,[44] and as Surkhang has underlined, the taxation system and terminology differed in the western parts of Tibet, even for districts directly under the Ganden Phodrang; second, although this is not yet ascertained, the tax system under Tashi Lhunpo *labrang* might also have differed in more fundamental ways from those under the Ganden Phodrang.

The semi-autonomous status of the Tashi Lhunpo *labrang* on territory that included districts in Tsang and Tö started in the early 18th century, when the Manchu Emperor Yongzhen (1722–1735) first offered the Panchen Lama the two districts of Phüntsokling (Phun tshogs gling) and Lhatse (lHa rtse) (Goldstein 2009: 266). At some point, the Panchen Lama was also given six other districts or estates, including Ngamring, on which he had full tax exemption vis-à-vis the Ganden Phodrang.[45] Despite the fact that the Tashi Lhunpo *labrang*

43 It seems to have been a typical tax due to districts under the Lhasa government, and thus did not exist in districts under the Tashi Lhunpo *labrang*. The only *lag 'don* tax found in this account with a designation found in descriptions by Surkhang and Goldstein could be the livestock tax called *rgyab dod* (Surkhang [1966] 1984: 28), a sum of money collected for each male yak and an amount of butter for each female yak. However, in the case of Ngamring, the word appears in the larger context of a livestock tax collected for the so-called "treaty yaks". This tax was used to pay money to Nepal, and the term might therefore be understood more generally as a "monetary substitute for a payment in kind" (see below; Phran rtsa rta mgrin rgyal po 1994: 71–72).

44 Eastern Tö is usually considered part of Central Tibet while Tö Ngari designates Western Tibet (Goldstein 1968: 11). Trentsa Tamdrin Gyelpo's account mentions only Tö to define the location of Ngamring district, while Goldstein places it in "West Tibet" (list of districts in *ibid.*: 36).

45 The list of nine districts (*rdzong*) and estates (*gzhis ka*) under the direct administration of the Tashi Lhunpo *labrang* until 1923 is given by Goldstein (*ibid.*: 32–37) as: in Tsang, Tanak Rintse (rTa nag rin rtse), Phüntsokling (Phun tshogs gling), Lhenlhün Rapzhi (lHan lhun rab gzhis), Chiblung (lCib lung), Gampa (Gam pa), Zhetong Mönzhi (bZhad mthong smon gzhis), Dam Lama ('Dam bla ma); and in "West Tibet", Lhatse (lHa rtse) and Ngamring. We were not able to find the exact date when these particular estates were

enjoyed the greatest degree of autonomy compared with the two other such sub-entities, Sakya (Sa skya) and Lhagyari (lHa rgya ri), the Ganden Phodrang government kept the right to impose new rules over its sub-entities.

In this context, the Thirteenth Dalai Lama's government asked Tashi Lhunpo in 1913 to participate in financing the growing needs of the new Tibetan standing army by paying one fourth of the expenses incurred during the two Tibet-British wars (1888 and 1904) and the Chinese war (1912–1913) (Goldstein 1968: 237–38, Goldstein 1971b: 179, Goldstein 1989: 110–13). The Panchen Lama refused and paid only a small portion of the sum. Relationships between the two hierarchs further deteriorated when, in 1917, the Thirteenth Dalai Lama issued the *Fire-Snake Year Order* by which he imposed a new transportation tax on the *mi ser* of Tashi Lhunpo in Gyantse district, and with the *Water-Pig Year Ordinance* (*Chu phag bka' rtsa*), in 1923, the Ganden Phodrang extended this transportation tax to all *mi ser* of the Tashi Lhunpo districts.[46] The Ninth Panchen Lama refused and fled to China in December 1923.[47] This resulted in the transfer of power of all Tashi Lhunpo districts to the Ganden Phodrang government, with the districts being placed under the supervision of a Lhasa-appointed administrator termed *dza sag bla ma*.[48] Lhasa officials (*gzhung zhabs*) were henceforth sent as District Commissioners (*rdzong sdod*) instead of Labrang officials (*bla zhabs*) (Phran rtsa rta mgrin rgyal po 1994: 67).

Trentsa Tamdrin Gyelpo's account, which starts in 1932, covers the period *after* the Tashi Lhunpo *labrang* districts had been transferred to Lhasa in 1923, and we do not know whether this administrative change affected the prior nature, organisation and distribution of the taxes locally (and not only their final destination), and if so to what extent. It is therefore not easy to assess whether or to what extent Trentsa Tamdrin Gyelpo's account reflects a possible specific "Tashi Lhunpo *labrang* tax system". In the present state of knowledge,

---

given to the Panchen Lama. Some of these territories seem to have been given earlier on in the 17th century by the Fifth Dalai Lama (see the list of monasteries and territories given at that time to the Panchen Lama in Jagou 2011: 11–12), however, Ngamring is not part of them.

46 They were to "pay one-seventh of the horse and carrying-animal corvée tax on levies of over 100 horses and 300 carrying animals" (Goldstein [1989] 1993: 112). Even prior to 1924, in the three sub-entities enjoying a certain degree of autonomy (Tashi Lhunpo *labrang*, Sakya and Lhagyari), the transportation corvée had always been a tax due directly to the Central Government in Lhasa (see Goldstein 1968: 234).

47 On this event, its historical causes and consequences, see Jagou 2011. His successor, the Tenth Panchen Lama, would come back to his seat only twenty-nine years later in 1952 (Goldstein 2009: 395–96).

48 Goldstein [1989] 1993: 115.

we only know that it reflects the way taxes were collected during his own period in office as District Clerk; and given the seeming antiquity of a number of taxes he describes, we can suppose that at least part of the taxes and their organisation had existed earlier, and that, if passing to the Ganden Phodrang did affect the system, it did so only partially.

Trentsa Tamdrin Gyelpo describes Ngamring district as being divided into six[49] smaller administrative units called *brgya tsho*,[50] with over 360 *rkang* of land in total,[51] belonging to the three usual types of landlords—government, monastic or aristocratic (*gzhung sger chos gsum*) (*ibid.*: 68). Very interestingly, he mentions as the source for this figure the *Iron-Monkey Land Settlement* (*lCags sprel zhib gzhung*), which is dated 1740,[52] rather than the more recent *Iron-Tiger Land Settlement* (*lCags stag zhib gzhung*) of 1830. The obvious reason is that the *Iron-Tiger Land Settlement* does not include any of the districts that had been given to the Tashi Lhunpo *labrang*, while the 1740 *Land Settlement*,

---

49 The names of the six *brgya tsho* of Ngamring district are not precisely listed in Trentsa Tamdrin Gyelpo's account. The author mentions only the "four villages of the lower part" (*smad kha brgya tsho bzhi*) of which only one, Chungpa, is later named (*mnga' khul smad rgya bzhi nas gcung pa rgya tsho* [*sic*]); and also "the two villages of the upper part, at the limit with gTsang" (*stod kha gtsang zur rgya tsho gnyis*), which could be also interpreted as "the two villages of Tökha (sTod kha) and Tsangzur (gTsang zur)". A list of only five *brgya tsho* is given in another source for Ngamring, among which none bears any resemblance to the above-mentioned names: Khangnam Gyatso, Cirwa Gyatso, Dorong Gyatso, Tshokhor Gyatso, Tsangzo Gyatso (Khang rnam brgya tsho, gCir ba brgya tsho, mDo rong brgya tsho, mTsho 'khor brgya tsho, gTsang bzo brgya tsho; gZhis rtse sa gnas srid gros lo rgyus rtsom 'bri tshogs chung nas 2005: 56). Interestingly, a list of the six *brgya tsho* of Ngamring, yet again with different names, appears in the archival document DTAB ID 2677 (signatory in archives 0056_SBB6679; I am indebted to Kalsang Norbu Gurung for sharing this information with me): Khatö Gyatso, Gyabar, Dramnyi Sönjung, Gya Serpo Sum, Bongshö, and Chu[druk] Gyatso (Kha stod rgya tsho, rGya bar, Gram nyi son byung, rGya ser po gsum, Bong shod, and Chu [drug] rgya tsho). No explanation could be found for such discrepancies in these various sources regarding the toponomy.

50 Translated in this paper as county, following Goldstein 1971a: 1. This larger administrative unit that comprised either one hundred villages or one hundred households (Goldstein 2001: 289) was relevant in terms of corvée transportation taxes (Goldstein 1968: 42), and in Ngamring in terms of other forms of corvée labour, as we will see later, like cleaning drainpipes, repainting the walls of the district headquarters, etc. Note that in the second volume of his history (Goldstein 2009), Goldstein translates *rdzong* by "county" instead of "district". In the present paper, *rdzong* remains consistently translated as "district", and *brgya tsho* as "county".

51 gZhis rtse sa gnas srid gros lo rgyus rtsom 'bri tshogs chung nas gives a different figure of 331.6 *rkang* (2005: 58).

52 This land settlement was the first of its kind (see Surkhang [1966] 1984 for a brief discussion of it and the later ones dated 1830 and 1864).

which had been composed before Ngamring was given to the Panchen Lama, apparently did.[53] We thus arrive at a fuller picture to the effect that the administration of most districts in Central Tibet under the direct authority of the Ganden Phodrang was based on the 1830 *Iron-Tiger Land Settlement* and three districts on the later 1864 *Wood-Mouse Settlement* (*Shing byi zhib gzhung*), while some others, like Ngamring, were still based on the 1740 *Iron-Monkey Land Settlement*.[54]

The environment is described by Trentsa Tamdrin Gyelpo as comprising 60 per cent cultivators, then semi-nomadic farmers (*sa ma 'brog*), and only a very small percentage of nomads. The *mi ser* under Ngamring district had the responsibility of paying (*'khri sgrub*) between forty and fifty different taxes in money and kind (*lag 'don khral rigs*) with only very little difference between the *lag 'don* payments made by the *mi ser* of aristocratic and monastic landlords (*sger chos khongs khri'i dbye ba phran bu yod pa*) (*ibid.*: 68). Corvée labour taxes (*rkang 'gro*), including the usual transportation service (*sa tshig* and *rdzong skyel*), were shouldered by *mi ser* of the four lower counties (*smad rgya*).[55]

53 There is unfortunately no possibility of obtaining access to any version of the *Iron-Monkey Land Settlement* (Surkhang mentions having read about it in a handwritten introduction to a copy of the *Iron-Tiger Land Settlement* in Tibet), that has not yet surfaced (see Gurung 2016: 210), and thus to check the information on Ngamring district there. Note that Ngamring district interestingly also appears in another text, described as a land settlement, dated to an undetermined Iron-Sheep Year, the *lCags lug zhib gzhung*, an excerpt from which is published in Schneider 2012: 311–12 (document Hs.or.6898).

54 According to Goldstein (1968: 28, 59 and 1971a: 6), the Samada taxation system was based on land recorded in yet another land settlement, the "*Fire-Sheep Land Settlement* (*Me lug zhib gzhung*)" dated 1847. Goldstein (1968: 38 footnote 6, and 102 footnote 3; 1971a: 6 footnote 8) quotes Surkhang (1966) as a source for a description of all land settlements. However, Surkhang does not mention this particular 1847 land settlement in either the first version of his paper (1966) or its later reprint (1984), and since Samada was part of Gyantse district, Surkhang's work rather suggests that it should have followed the later 1864 *Land Settlement* (*Shing byi zhib gzhung*). Schwieger (in this volume) considers that this *Me lug zhib gzhung* was probably only a preliminary version of the 1864 settlement.

55 *rdzong der mnga' khul mi ser brgya tsho drug gi khongs su rkang gzhung rtsa 'dzin lcags sprel zhib gzhung zer bar byed kyi yod cing / der gsal gzhung sger chos gsum rkang gsum brgya drug cu lhag tsam yod/ de dag chags yul brgya cha drug cu tsam phu chu dang chu mig la brten dgos pa'i zhing khul dang / sa ma 'brog /'brog pa'i sa khul nyung shas bcas yin/ khong tshor lag 'don khral rigs sna tshogs rnam grangs ha lam bzhi bcu nas lnga bcu skor 'khri sgrub dgos pa nas sger chos khongs 'khri dang mi 'khri'i dbye ba phran bu yod pa las mang che ba 'khri sgrub byed dgos pa dang / rkang 'gro sa tshigs so sos ga sel dang rdzong skyel rta khal mi gsum 'khri yul smad rgya bzhi'i khongs chag chod [yod?] phud rta 'khri rkang zer ba rkang nyis brgya lnga bcu lhag tsam yin/* (Phran rtsa rta mgrin rgyal po 1994: 68).

3.3 *People Responsible for Tax Collection at the District Level in Ngamring*

Trentsa Tamdrin Gyelpo starts his account by giving a brief historical introduction to the district and its officials. Ngamring was said in ancient times to have been the palace of Jangdak Trashi Topgyel (Byang bdag bKra shis stobs rgyal),[56] and the headquarters of Ngamring district were called Khyungdzong Karpo (Khyung rdzong dkar po), because of the Garuda-shaped hill on which it was built (*ibid.*: 67).[57]

Before the flight of the Ninth Panchen Lama to China in December 1923, the district officers (*rdzong sdod*) of the three districts of Lhatse, Ngamring, and Phüntsokling were chosen among monk and lay officials of the Tashi Lhunpo *labrang* ("*bkras bla*" in the account) and called *bla zhabs* (i.e. the equivalent of *gzhung zhabs* for the Ganden Phodrang Central Government) (*ibid.*: 67, 77). After 1923, only officials of the Ganden Phodrang government were selected and appointed as District Commissioners in Ngamring as in all the territory formerly under the Panchen Lama; in 1934, discussions took place between representatives of the Tashi Lhunpo *labrang* and the Lhasa government, who again approved sending Tashi Lhunpo officials as District Commissioners to these districts. After 1951, a new rule made it compulsory to have one monk and one lay *labrang* official appointed as District Commissioners in Ngamring (*ibid.*: 77–78).

At the beginning of the period covered by this account, in 1932, the author had reached eighteen years of age and had become a District Clerk (*las drung*) after his request for the position had been granted by the Lhasa representative *dza sag bla ma*, and by a Lhasa aristocratic lay official named Tshogo (mTsho sgo), who then occupied the top post of the Ngamring local administrative hierarchy as District Commissioner (*ibid.*: 67).[58]

---

56 Probably the famous Nyingma master Changdak Trashi Tobgyel (Byang bdag bKra shis stobs rgyal, 1540/50–1603), a holder of the *byang gter* tradition and son of the king of Chang (Byang). See his biography by Samten Chhosphel in the *Treasury of Lives* (https://treasuryoflives.org/biographies/view/bkra-shis-stobs-rgyal/9052, last consulted on 19 June 2020).

57 Another explanation is given in an account in the MHCT collection about the history of Ngamring: since the name is given only as "Khyungdzong", the author of this account thinks it could be related to Dorje Khyunglungma (rDo rje khyung lung ma), who is one of the twelve protective deities of Tibet as well as the birth divinity of Changdak Sengge (Byang bdag seng ge; gZhis rtse sa gnas srid gros lo rgyus rtsom 'bri tshogs chung nas 2005: 54).

58 The personal name of this District Commissioner from the Tshogo aristocratic family (a family from Western Tsang) is not given in the account. He might be one official later known as Tshogo Zurpa Ngödrup Dorje (mTsho sgo zur pa dNgos grub rdo rje, 1904–1972).

Several local staff members are described as working in the district headquarters under this District Commissioner: three District Clerks (*las drung*), one person in charge of measures (*bre kha ba*), and one house intendant (*khang gnyer*);[59] there were also two persons in charge of the storehouse (*bkar khang*), called the *bkar rgya*.[60] A "tax collector" (*yong bsdus pa*) is also mentioned twice, as we will see, but he was probably the official sent by Lhasa only for the time when the district taxes were collected, as was the case for districts under Lhasa administration in general, rather than a member of the local district personnel.[61]

According to Petech, he entered government service in 1924 and was in charge of "Snam gling rdzong" (*sic*) from about 1926 to 1936 (Petech 1973: 140). Petech here uses as sources information given to him by Hugh Richardson and most probably based on the various *Who's Who* available to the latter. Indeed, there this Tibetan official is said to have been District Commissioner of "Namling Dzong" in Northern Tibet until 1936 (*Who's Who 1948*: 140). There was indeed a district with such a name but spelled "rNam gling rdzong", that was under Ganden Phodrang administration. However, British representatives seem to have sometimes confused the two districts of rNam gling and Ngam ring, as is evident in other British archival sources: see for instance the quote from British archives dated 1933 reproduced in Goldstein (1989: 258) where "Namling" is (wrongly) listed as one of the districts formerly belonging to the Tashi Lhunpo *labrang* and then claimed back by the Panchen Lama, and a few lines later in the same quote it is (still wrongly) referred to as "Namring" instead of Ngamring. On this District Commissioner's identity, it should also be noted that there is a divergence between Petech, who gives Tshogo Ngödrup Dorje as the younger brother of Tshogo Sonam Wangdü (mTsho sgo bSod nams dbang 'dus, born 1891), and another *Who's Who* that records him as the latter's adoptive son (*Who's Who 1937*: 76).

59 It is not specified whether this *khang gnyer* acted, as in Samada, as district messenger as well. In Goldstein's (1968: 67 and 1971a: 12) description of Samada organisation, the *khang gnyer* were villagers provided as a corvée tax; there were thirteen in total, working as district messengers and also responsible for the upkeep of the district heaquarters (each of the thirteen being responsible for the upkeep of one section of the building) with their salary paid by the village. In Ngamring, it seems that there was only one such person and that his salary was taken in charge by the district.

60 According to another source (gZhis rtse sa gnas srid gros lo rgyus rtsom 'bri tshogs chung nas 2005: 55), all these local positions in Ngamring district's headquarters were held hereditarily.

61 As for the local representatives involved in the tax collection system at the village level, the description by Trentsa Tamdrin Gyelpo mentions a *tsho dpon*, as we will see later. We know from another source (*ibid.*: 56), that each *brgya tsho* in Ngamring was headed by a *tsho dpon*, and that each *brgya tsho* also had one *rgan chen* and one *rgan chung*.

4 The Economy of the District and the Enrichment of People Involved in the Tax Collection Process in Ngamring

The author explains how the district managed its income and expenses. He starts by explaining that in Ngamring there were twelve estates "governed by the district" (*rdzong skyong gzhis ka*), eight large and four small, and that government *mi ser* performed the corvée of the "inner tax" (i.e. the tax that was due to the district) (*nang khral gzhis g.yog 'khri yul gzhung rgyugs* [*sic*] *mi ser yin*).[62] The author states that these twelve estates governed by Ngamring district required annually a total of 1,400 *khal* of grain to be sown (*son 'bor*) and produced an average yearly harvest (*ston 'bras*) of 7,000 *khal*.[63] The yield ratio here indicated of five times the seed seems consistent with what is known, for instance, for the village of Samada, for which Goldstein gives a yield ratio of six times the amount of seed as being considered a good harvest (Goldstein 1968: 120). It is likely that these 1,400 *khal* of grain correspond only to what was sown on lands whose entire production went to the district as *nang khral*.[64]

4.1 *Expenses of the District*

These 1,400 *khal* of "sowing grain" (*son 'bru*) needed to be kept on the side (*zur 'jug*) in the district headquarters for the next sowing, as well as other quantities needed for the district headquarters' expenses, both regular and extraordinary (*'char 'phar*) which, if we try to summarise, could be divided into three different types.

First, there was a fixed amount of taxes in kind to be redistributed to particular monasteries of the district: according to land tenure documents (*lag 'dzin*

62 *rdzong der rdzong skyong gzhis ka che ba brgyad dang /le lag gzhis chung bzhi bcas yod cing / de dag gi nang khral gzhis g.yog 'khri yul gzhung rgyugs mi ser yin/* (Phran rtsa rta mgrin rgyal po 1994: 68). Goldstein explains the "*gzhis g.yog 'u lag*" as "the basic inner tax to one's lord" (Goldstein 1968: 122).

63 *gong gsal gzhis ka bcu gnyis kyi son 'bor bsdoms khal chig stong bzhi brgya skor 'gro zhing / lo re'i ston 'bras 'bring la cha gzhag na cha snyom khal bdun stong skor thon gyi yod/ de thog nas son 'bru zur 'jug* (Phran rtsa rta mgrin rgyal po 1994: 68).

64 They do not count toward the global surface of the land under the district, including private and monastic land that was given in the beginning of the account, i.e. 360 *rkang*. Indeed, if we follow Surkhang's information according to which 1 *rkang* equals an average 80 *khal* of sowing grain, we would reach a total of 28,200 *khal* of sowing grain for the entire territory under Ngamring. The fact that the author mentions only the production of the land worked by the government *mi ser* seems to indicate that the district was responsible only for collecting that portion, which would be consistent with the affirmation that districts were responsible for collecting only the taxes due on government estates (*gzhung gzhis*) (Surkhang [1966] 1984: 28).

nang gsal) 500 *khal* of grain were given on the one hand as allowances (*gtong sgo*) to Ngamring *chos sde* and Samga (bSam dga') *dgon pa* (the two main monasteries of the district) during their two teaching sessions in summer and winter; and, on the other hand, as offerings and salaries, etc. (*mchod phogs sogs*) to the twenty-one big and small monasteries of the district,[65] conveyed in the form of grain, butter, meat, tsampa, oil (the author gives here the corresponding sum of 500 *khal* of grain as an equivalent to simplify the accounting).[66] In addition, the district had to give monks from the two monasteries of Lhatse (lHa rtse) *chos sde* and Tashi Lhunpo an "appropriate"—unspecified—amount of meat, tsampa, tea, butter and other commodities when they came on tour (Phran rtsa rta mgrin rgyal po 1994: 69).

Second, when "chiefs" (*dpon rigs*; i.e. officials and representatives) of the Tashi Lhunpo *labrang* and Lhasa governments travelled in the Tö area, the district had to provide them with whatever additional food and cooking equipment (*bzo chas*) they needed (*ibid.*), according to specific orders delivered by the Tashi Lhunpo *labrang*.

Third, the functioning of the district headquarters incurred particular expenses, which included 1) providing tea to the District Commissioner, his family and servants, to the office that took care of horses (*rta gsos las khungs*), and for the New year; 2) paying an annual salary (*phogs*) to the district headquarters staff, i.e. the three District Clerks (*las drung*), the person in charge of measures (*bre kha ba*), the housekeeper/building superintendent (*khang gnyer*), that consisted of 180 *khal* of grain, forty meat carcasses (*sha khog*), and "forty copper *bre* measures of oil" (*snum zangs bre bzhi chu*);[67] 3) giving to the two caretakers of the Dükhor (Dus 'khor) and Trepel (bKras dpal) temples (*lha khang*, probably located inside or just near the district headquarters, since they are listed separately and not along with the expenses for other district monasteries) an annual salary (*phogs*) of 48 *khal* of grain, meat and oil; 4) providing the tax collector (*yong bsdus pa*) and the storehouse manager (*bkar rgya ba*) with articles and tools (*bzo chas*) and whatever they needed (*ibid.*).

The account then explains the way the district managed to meet these expenses, and it seems that the District Commissioner and his associates needed to exhibit a certain amount of creativity in terms of producing revenues.

65 For a full list of all monasteries in Ngamring with estimates of their monastic population, see gZhis rtse sa gnas srid gros lo rgyus rtsom 'bri tshogs chung nas 2005: 62.

66 No such equivalent is given in the rest of the author's explanation, which hinders any attempt to draw up a chart showing precisely the district incomes and expenses.

67 It is not mentioned in this account whether *las drung* in Ngamring received a tax-free estate as a salary, as was the case in Samada.

4.2 *The Management of the District's Income: The District Commissioner and His Associates as "Revenue Contractors"*

The personal enrichment of agents involved in tax collection is a well-known fact in pre-1959 Tibet. The particular position of District Commissioner in pre-1959 Tibet has been described by external observers as one of a "revenue contractor" (Richardson 1998 [1945]: 94),[68] who tried to maximise profits during their tenure.[69] The way administrators could make a profit from their estates and districts has been described by various authors (Bell [1928] 1992, Richardson 1998 [1945], Surkhang [1966] 1984 and 1986, Goldstein 1968: 24), the most detailed being that of Goldstein:

> In general, government officials perceived the position of District Commissioner as a source of income rather than as a source for increasing their power and influence and as a result of this in many instances did not bother to actually leave Lhasa, sending in their place a reliable household servant-official. Before 1954 the salaries that the District Commissioners formally were paid were insignificant. Although the amount of tax collected from villagers was fixed and a District Commissioner could not unilaterally increase it, nevertheless he could do a number of things to augment his nominal salary income. One of these hinged on the fact that the District Commissioner (along with the tax collector) had to send only a specified amount of the collected taxes to Lhasa and specified monasteries. Whatever remainder there was went into the pockets of those two officials. Another way was through the manipulation of the quality of taxes paid. A District Commissioner might insist that taxes be paid in good quality meats and grains but then sell these and send poor quality goods to Lhasa, keeping the difference. Another method was by manipulating the weighing and measuring of taxes. One of the largest sources of income was gifts received from disputants involved in disputes pending adjudication. A less common, though effective method was for the District Commissioner to buy items from the villagers monopolistically at low prices and then resell them in other areas at a large profit. Other means for the extraction of private income existed but the above

68 See Travers 2009 and 2013 on the position of District Commissioner between 1895 and 1959 among lay aristocrats.

69 According to Goldstein, in all districts land was divided in two parts: the land conceded to *mi ser* of government, monastic or aristocratic estates, which produced revenues for them, and the land cultivated for the district itself, which produced grain from which a fixed amount was stored as revenue for the district and the remaining parts went to the District Commissioner as his own profit (Goldstein 1968).

> enumeration suffices to illustrate the usual means the District Commissioner used to make his stay in the provinces lucrative. One should not, however, conclude that peasants were helpless in the face of ruthless, avaricious officials since they could, as mentioned above, appeal to the government for aid.
>
> *ibid.*

In any case, one understands why there are reports of District Commissioners who refused to hand over their charge to their successor, as they did not want to forgo the profit obtained through district administration and tax collection.[70]

A number of these means of enrichment were linked to their role in tax collection, and the enrichment concerned not only the highest level of the tax collection process (i.e. the District Commissioner) but also the lower levels (his subordinates). This is documented in sources like the *MHCT*, in the clear context of social criticism,[71] but also in other examples published in exile, which genuinely acknowledge the enrichment of their forefathers through such positions.[72] In this particular account of Ngamring district, Trentsa Tamdrin Gyelpo underlines the process by which the district and its related officials and workers could make a profit and keep it for themselves—he invariably uses the term "*za*", lit. "to eat", which is usually used to express the action of "taking bribes"—quantities of goods and money. The author explains:

70 *Letter of the British trade agent, Gartok, dated 3rd/9th August 1931* (IOR/L/P&S/12/4163/P7900).

71 For another example of the acknowledgement that the position of District Clerk for instance was a source of enrichment, see for instance in the same *MHCT* collection the account of bDud 'dul chos dbyings who states: "Thanks to the authority I had in becoming a *las drung* when I was twenty-two years old, the prosperity of our family increased a lot" (*nga lo 22 thog rdzong gi las drung byas pa'i dbang char brten nas khyim gyi dpal 'byor yang gang 'tshams gong 'phel phyin yod*) (bDud 'dul chos dbyings 1984: 173).

72 It is also documented and acknowledged in sources produced in exile. One example is to be found in the autobiography of Kanying Lobzang Dekyi (bKa' rnying Blo bzang bde skyid) regarding her father Kanying Phüntsok Khangsar Lobzang Zöpa (bKa' rnying Phun tshogs khang gsar Blo bzang bzod pa). Born in 1895 and after having been ordained as a monk in Drepung ('Bras spungs) monastery, he served in different positions, first as administrator (*gnyer pa*) and representative of the aristocratic family Dompo (Dom po) as District Commissioner in Tö Tsareng (sTod rTsa hreng), and then as administrator or storekeeper (*bkar rgya*) in different estates and districts, among those in Ngamring district (he is mentioned as such in the present account by Trentsa Tamdrin Gyelpo). According to his daughter: "When he returned from Tö Tsareng district to Ngamring district, it is said that he had accumulated much wealth, which included silver coin money and Indian paper money and goods of high value transported on several hundred horses and mules" (bKa' rnying Blo bzang bde skyid 2002: 2).

> In any case, when one needed to calculate the total production of the district,[73] the district's total yield or harvest (*thon 'bab*) needed to reach the officially fixed (*gtan 'bebs*) amount of 10,000 *khal*;[74] after deduction of the quantity of grain necessary for the next field sowing (*son 'bor*), and whatever was needed for its diverse regular and extraordinary (*'char 'phar*) expenses, there was a quantity between 1,400 and 1,600 *khal* of grain—depending on whether or not there had been an annual increase in expenses (*gtong 'phar*)—known as *yang snying gtong lhag*, that was set aside (*bkar 'jug*) and was clearly stipulated on the official list of collected tax bearing seals that had to be given by the Tax collector to the storekeeper.[75]

Thus, here we understand that despite the fact that the expected production of the district as fixed by the government (i.e. 10,000 *khal*) exceeded the average real outcome of the district (which was, after all, only 7,000 *khal*), the district still succeeded in keeping in the storehouse an excess quantity (*gtong lhag*) of 1,400 and 1,600 *khal* for its usage. The author therefore proceeds by raising an interesting question:

> Since the yield (*lag 'bab*) was in reality less than the required official amount [lit. "the measure of the *bcu 'bo*" (*bcu 'bor* [*sic*] *gyi grangs tshad*), the *bcu 'bo* being a wooden box used to measure a quantity of half a *'bo*, i.e. 10 *bre* of grain] fixed in written documents, thus, those who knew might wonder where still so much as this [above-mentioned] surplus (*gtong lhag*) came from?[76]

---

73 This is how we understand the phrase: *rdzong skyong gzhis khag rnams kyi bcu 'bor 'bab*: lit. "what falls in the *bcu 'bo* [a *bcu 'bo* being the wooden box used to measure a quantity of half a *'bo*, i.e. 10 *bre* of grain, cf. *Bod rgya*] coming from the estates governed by the district".

74 The author does not explain the reason behind the difference between the 7,000 *khal* collected from the district and the 10,000 *khal* officially expected by the government.

75 *gang ltar rdzong skyong gzhis khag rnams kyi bcu 'bor 'bab ngam ring yongs bsdus par rtsis rgyag dgos par thon 'bab gtan 'bebs khal chig khri skor dgos pa nas/ gong gsal son 'bor dang / 'char 'phar sna tshogs bza' 'then gyi yang snying gtong lhag ces pa lo rer gtong 'phar yod med kyi bka'* [*bkar*] *'jug 'bru khal chig stong bzhi brgya nas chig stong drug brgya skor re dgos pa yong bsdus pas bsdu tho tham 'byar bkar rgya bar sprad gsal 'bru 'bab rdzong nas bkar rgya bar sprod dgos kyi 'dug/* (Phran rtsa rta mgrin rgyal po 1994: 69).

76 *gtan 'jags yig thog tu gsal ba'i bcu 'bor gyi grangs tshad las lag 'bab dngos nyung ba yod bzhin par mkhyen ldan rnams kyis da dung gtong lhag de tsam yong don gang yin nam dgongs srid kyi red/* (*ibid.*). Surkhang describes each district has having to maintain a certain officially fixed (depending on the size of the district) level of grain called *gzhis 'bru bkar 'jig* (sic = *'jug*) in its storeroom, and to hand it over to the next District Commissioner

The next few pages comprise a detailed explanation of the methods by which the district managed to increase its income by making a profit on every tax collected, which thus also reveal very interesting details on the actual taxes collected and the tax system in Ngamring. The first method was to take advantage of a system in which the tax collection agent was also the redistributing agent, by cheating on the quality and value of the taxes the district was supposed to transmit directly to local beneficiaries:

> And as per the feudal system (*bkas bkod rgyud 'dzin lam lugs*), there was this habit called "the seventh handful of grain" (*'bru sbar bdun ma*) according to which, for the allowance in grain given to the various district monasteries, only a little quantity of grain would be mixed with a majority of grass and other things. As for the meat, tsampa, salt and oil, they would be converted into only nominal cash[77] which would be then sent as offering and salaries.[78]

Two proverbs are used to describe the various tricks: "when you count, everything's there, and when everything's there, everything has vanished" (*rtsis dus tshang zhing tshang dus yal*), a sentence that might refer to the fact that tax collectors managed to make a part of what was actually collected disappear in their hands. Another proverb, "it's in the mouth but not in the hands" (*kha yod lag med*), is quoted to comment on the fact that despite the surplus of grain officially given to the district storehouse manager, the District Commissioner would manage to keep privately for himself an annual surplus of between 400 and 500 *khal* of grain.[79]

The second means relates to the seemingly pervasive custom of collecting from the *mi ser* higher quantities than officially fixed by the government, either

([1966] 1984: 29 and 1986: 22). Whether the *yang snying gtong lhag* mentioned here is an equivalent of this *gzhis 'bru bkar 'jug* remains unclear.

77 It is not specified here if the nominal value of the cash resulted from a unilateral decision on the part of the tax collection agent or because of a more general situation where old conversion rates were used when converting taxes from kind to cash. On the problems resulting from the combination of growing monetarisation of taxes in the 1940s and rapid inflation (if paid according to old conversion rates, the value of taxes paid in money was far inferior to its initial equivalent in kind), see Tsarong 1998a: 6–7.

78 *de ni bkas bkod rgyud 'dzin lam lugs skabs ngam ring rdzong khongs dgon sde khag la gtong sgo gzhis 'bru sbar bdun ma zer ba 'bru phran bu yod pa las mang che ba rtswa sogs bsres nas sprod srol dang / sha / rtsam/ tshwa/ snum sogs dngul bsgyur sne sel las med pas dgon sde khag la mchod phogs kyis mtshon gtong* (Phran rtsa rta mgrin rgyal po 1994: 69).

79 *gong gsal gtong lhag 'bru 'bab bkar rgya bar sprad rung / da dung rdzong sdod so sor lo re 'brul khal bzhi brgya nas lnga brgya'i bar re za rgyu yod la* (*ibid.*: 70).

in the form of a "customary gift" or through other means. In the following tax, additional presents from the *mi ser* were customarily requested:

> The district would also perceive from the government *mi ser* a sum called the "Capital and interest of the Water-Dragon year" (*chu 'brug ma skyed*), according to which for each *rkang*, the district would collect 1 *khal* and 4 *bre* of grain, and for every 100 *khal* of grain from this interest and capital, they had to offer on the side (*zur sprod*) to the storehouse keeper a little more than 100 *khal* of grain, which would be kept by the district.[80]

The district could thus "help itself" when collecting taxes in kind that it was supposed to redistribute to other entities like monasteries or to send to the government through various offices, because it collected more than what was actually needed for redistribution. The author gives a number of examples:

> From the *mi ser* of all three types of estates (*gzhung sger chos gsum*) a tax called "quality butter" (*spus mar*) would be collected, according to which for each *rkang*, butter in a quantity of 1 *khal* and 10 *nyag*[81] of the standard steelyard measure (*mkhar nyag*);[82] from the government *mi ser*, the tax called "the butter to be stored" (*bkar mar*) was collected, according to which for each *rkang* around 5 *mkhar nyag*[83] of butter would be

80 *da dung rdzong sdod so sor lo re 'brul khal bzhi brgya nas lnga brgya'i bar re za rgyu yod la gzhung rgyugs* [*sic*] *mi ser rnams nas chu 'brug ma skyed zer ba rkang re nas 'bru khal gcig bre bzhi re bsdu rgyu yod pa de khongs nas ma skyed bkar 'jug ces lo rer khal brgya re bkar rgya bar zur sprod dgos pa phud 'bru khal brgya lhag tsam yang rdzong la za rgyu 'dug/* (*ibid.*).

81 The *khal* mentioned here designates the weight measure (and not the *khal* as a volume measure when used for grain). One *khal* of the weight measure unit equals 20 *nyag*, and 1 *nyag* equals 4 *spor*. In secondary literature, the unit of weight measurement for products such as butter, wool, cheese, yak tail, meat, etc., is usually described, for the Lhasa area, as being the *rgya ma* (which, like the weight *khal*, is divided into 20 *nyag*, see Surkhang [1966] 1984: 30). The *rgya ma* is not used in Trentsa Tamdrin Gyelpo's account.

82 A *mkhar nyag* is described by Goldstein as "a unit of weight which is 1/20 of a *mkhar rgya*", itself defined as a "traditional weighing unit (equal to about four kilograms)" (Goldstein 2001: 154). However, in the present context the expression *mkhar nyag* should be read as the abbreviation for *mkhar gyi nya ga* and understood as the "(government) standard steelyard measure", in the same way as the *mkhar khal* designates the volumetric *khal* as measured by the *mkhar ru* or government standard *'bo* (the wooden box used to measure grain volumes), on which see also footnote 17. Thus, the phrase "*mar mkhar nyag gi khal gcig nyag bcu*" is translated here as "1 *khal* and 10 *nyag* as weighed by the standard steelyard measure for butter".

83 Here and below, the *mkhar nyag* has to be understood as a *nyag* weighed with the standard steelyard measure.

collected, and every year the treasurer of Tashi Lhunpo had to be offered (by the district) a little more than 100 *khal* of butter, as well as the usual tea and additional things. Moreover, from the 42 *rkang* from nomads (*'brog rigs rkang*),[84] for each *rkang* 15 fathoms/measures (*rgyug 'dom*) of fabric (*re lde*) woven from yak wool (*rtsid pa*), 6 fathoms of fabric woven from sheep wool (*bal*), and 4 fathoms of fabric woven from goat hair (*ra spu*) were collected; from this collected wool, in the same way, the treasurer of Tashi Lhunpo had to be given the so-called *sgrigs 'bul* (lit. "arranged/fixed present", designating taxes in kind)[85] of a little more than 800 fathoms of all three types of wool fabric. In both cases, for the butter and wool, some remnants of these portions would be kept by the district (*phud de 'phros kyang rdzong la 'bab*).

From two counties in Tö and Tsang and nomadic areas, every year the so-called "quality sheep" (*spus lug*) tax was paid in the form of 130 sheep, and they were given to the six families of butchers of Ngamring called "Ngam zhol lcags pa" (lit. "the iron-workers of the lower area [of] the district headquarters") to be slaughtered, a small part being sent away, and the biggest part of it kept by the district.

84 In Surkhang's earliest paper, the basis of the nomadic *rkang* (*'brog rkang*), was said to be the amount of pasture a group (*shog ka* or *'tsho shog*) held, but without further information on their size (Surkhang [1966] 1984: 26). In 1986: 21, Surkhang has gathered more details and he established that: "In determining the *rkang* in the nomadic regions, 6 sheeps and 12 goats equal one yak. 25 yaks are considered equal to one *rkang*"; he also gives information on the northern nomadic areas (*ibid.*: 27).

85 The term *sgrigs 'bul* designates here the taxes in money and kind to be given by the districts under Tashi Lhunpo *labrang* to the treasurer of Tashi Lhunpo (*bkras lhun bla brang phyag mdzod*) mentioned further on in this passage, as explained in another account on Ngamring in the MHCT collection: "*lo star rdzong sgrig 'bul zhes dngul dngos sna tshogs bla brang phyag mdzod du deb gsal ltar 'bul sgrub bya dgos*" (gZhis rtse sa gnas srid gros lo rgyus rtsom 'bri tshogs chung nas 2005: 59). When used in the Lhasa taxation system context, *sgrigs 'bul* denotes the dues in kind (and sometimes in money) to be given by the district and estates of Central Tibet to the *bla phyag las khungs* in Lhasa, cf. personal communication with Peter Schwieger, quoting the description of the Lhasa *bla phyag las khungs* in Shedra, Chabtsom and Sekshing (Bshad sgra, Chab tshom, Sreg shing; 1991: 39), as well as one of the Waddell documents described by Schuh in VOHD XI,8: no 13 (= Wadd 135a), line 15. Note that the term *sgrigs 'bul* is translated only as "tribute" in Goldstein's dictionary (2001: 285), a translation that is usually used for gifts accompanying political and diplomatic interstate relationships, and thus could not apply here. Other Tibetan terms corresponding to "tribute" (like *sba yer, legs 'bul, 'bul rten*) are documented in Schwieger 2018. A definition of *sgrigs 'bul* closer to the meaning of tax that we find here is to be found in Surkhang (1986: 28), though designating only a tax in money (and not in kind) that every district had to give the Tibetan government.

The same system was applied to the paper tax.[86] For the raw material used for government documents (*las shog rgyu cha*), the government *mi ser* were taxed, for each *rkang*, 12 *mkhar nyag* of dried bark of daphne plant (? *shog shing gad ma skam seng*), 4 *mkhar nyag* of crushed "poisonous mineral" (? *dug thal*), and 8 *dngul srang*[87] for the transportation fees (*'ul gla*). In addition, every year in summer, from the first day of the fifth month onwards, twenty corvée workers from the general taxpayers of the lower quarter of Ngamring district headquarters (*'ul mi ngam zhol khral spyi nas*) had to come and would be given, as salary (*gla cha*), innards of mutton and some nominal quantity of tsampa and oil, and would start working under the supervision of the person in charge of measures (*bre kha ba*) for a period of two months. They would produce a little more than 100 bundles of 10 paper sheets (*bcu sdems*)[88] of large size paper (*shog bu yug chen*), as well as around 500 bundles of middle size (*yug 'bring*) "tax-in-kind paper" (*sgrigs shog*, explained by Trentsa Tamdrin Gyelpo himself as *sgrigs 'bul gyi shog bu*, "paper for the tax in kind", i.e. same terminology as for the above mentioned woollen fabric that also had to be given to the Tashi Lhunpo treasurer) and around 200 bundles of small size paper. From this, the Tashi Lhunpo treasurer had to be given 170 bundles of the middle size "tax-in-kind paper", and thirty bundles of the small size paper. Then the district tax collector and the storehouse manager were each given around 200 bundles of small and large size papers. A certain amount went for the government documents used or for government work in the district's headquarters, but the remainder was kept as personal property by the District Commissioner.

There were somewhat more than 300 yaks, males and females, distributed in two groups of nomads (*ru ba*) that were given to the successive Panchen Lamas as a "faith offering" (*dad 'bul*) by the Tö area and that had been given on loan (*rtsis 'khri*) to Ngamring district. To the two teams of dairy men/nomad workers (*she ma*), a salary of 30 *khal* each had to be given in grain. For the annual *she mar* [butter tax], [the nomads paid]:

86 A full list of manufacturing skills that Ngamring was famous for, independently of the tax system, is given in gZhis rtse sa gnas srid gros lo rgyus rtsom 'bri tshogs chung nas (2005: 62–63), starting with an old tradition of manufacturing porcelain cups and including copper- and iron-smithing, pottery, sculpture, sewing, tangka painting, carpet weaving, blanket weaving, paper making, arrow making, engraving printblocks, metal casting and masonry.

87 For a detailed presentation of the money used in Tibet in the late 19th century, and in particular of the *srang*, see Gurung 2018.

88 Not in the dictionaries but based on *sdem*, meaning "to tie".

1 *mkhar khal*[89] and 10 *nyag* of butter for each [newborn] *'bri* calf, and 1 *mkhar khal* of butter for each calf in its second year [*yar mar* = *ya ru mar*]; for each of the remaining animals (*sems can ngo rer*), they paid 2 *spor*,[90] which was known as "after/back butter" (*rgyab mar*). From this butter, around 80 *mkhar khal* had to be given to the Tashi Lhunpo treasurer, while the rest would be kept as a property of the district.[91]

The next four taxes collected in money and kind are linked to historical events in this particular area. They again presented opportunities for the district to help itself in the process of tax collection. The first one was a tax related to a former indemnity (*chings dngul*) paid to the Gorkhas since the end of the

89 Here the *mkhar khal* has to be understood a *khal* weighed with the standard steelyard measure.

90 One *spor* equals 1/4th of a *nyag ga*, itself 1/20th of a *khal*; see footnote 83 on the *khal* weight measurement unit.

91 *gzhung sger chos gsum mi ser yongs nas spus mar zhes rkang re nas mar mkhar nyag gi khal gcig nyag bcu re dang / gzhung rgyugs* [*sic*] *khong nas bkar mar zhes rkang re nas mkhar nyag lnga skor re bsdu rgyu yod khongs nas lo re bkras lhun bla brang phyag mdzod du mar khal brgya lhag tsam 'bul dgos phud de 'phros rgyun ja dang 'char 'phar gtong dmigs red/ phyogs mtshungs 'brog rigs rkang bzhi bcu zhe gnyis skor nas rkang rer rtsid pa'i re lde rgyug 'dom bco lnga re dang / bal gyi re lde rgyug 'dom drug re/ ra spu'i re sde rgyug 'dom bzhi re bcas bsdu rgyu yod khongs nas gong bzhin bla brang phyag mdzod du sgrigs 'bul zer ba rtsid bal ra gsum gyi re lde bsdoms rgyug 'dom brgyad brgya lhag tsam re 'bul dgos phud de 'phros kyang rdzong la 'bab cing / stod kha gtsang zur rgya tsho gnyis dang 'brog rigs khongs nas lo re spus lug zer ba lug grangs brgya dang sum cu skor bsdu rgyu yod pa de ngam zhol lcags pa zer ba bshas pa them grangs drug yod par bshas su bcug pa de thog nas gtong sha mngon mdog phran bu las mang che ba rdzong la za rgyu yod/ las shog rgyu cha gzhung rgyugs* [*sic*] *mi ser rkang re nas shog shing gad ma skam seng mkhar nyag bcu gnyis dang / dug thal snur ba mkhar nyag bzhi re/ 'ul gla dngul srang brgyad re bcas bsdu rgyu yod pa de dag lo ltar dbyar zla lnga pa'i tshes gcig nas 'go btsugs te 'ul mi ngam zhol khral spyi nas yong dgos mi grangs nyi shu skor la gla cha lug gi nang cha dang / rtsam snum sne sel re sprod pa dang / 'go pa rdzong gi bre kha bas byed srol gyis las yun zla gnyis tsam 'gor gyi yod/ shog bu yug chen bcu sdems brgya lhag tsam dang sgrigs shog* (*sgrigs 'bul gyi shog bu*) *yug 'bring bcu sdems lnga brgya skor yug chung bcu sdems nyis brgya skor bcas thon pa nas bla brang phyag mdzod du lo rer sgrigs 'bul yug 'bring bcu sdems brgya dang bdun cu dang / yug chung bcu sdems sum cu/ yong sdud pa dang bkar rgya ba gnyis la las shog yug che chung bcu sdems grangs nyi shu skor re sprod dgos shing / rdzong gi las shog tu gang 'tshams 'gro ba las de byings rdzong sdod sger la bdag gi yod/ kun gzigs paN chen sku thog rim par stod khul nas dad 'bul 'bri g.yag gang byung ngam rdzong la rtsis 'khrir gnang ba'i ru ba khag gnyis la sems can pho mo ngo grangs sum brgya lhag tsam yod cing / she ma khag gnyis la gla cha 'brur phab so sor khal sum cu re sprod dgos/ she mar lo re 'bri bi'u mar mkhar khal gcig nyag bcu re dang / yar mar mkhar khal gcig re/ de byings la rgyab mar zer ba sems can ngo rer mkhar nyag gi spor do re bcas 'bab pa de thog nas bla brang rtse phyag mdzod du lo ltar mar khal brgyad cu skor re 'bul dgos pa'i 'phros rdzong rang la bdag gi yod/* (Phran rtsa rta mgrin rgyal po 1994: 70–71).

18th century and called *gor shugs* (lit. "power of the Gorkhas"): according to the treaty made after the end of the Gorkha wars, Ngamring district had to pay an instalment of 1,200 *gortam* (*gor ṭam*, i.e. the Tam of the Gorkhas; at this time, a Tam = half a rupee) every year to Nepal through the General of Dingri (Ding ri).[92] The district arranged a system of investing capital money in yaks (therefore) called "treaty yaks" (*chings g.yag*). In collecting interests on them, it managed to raise 1,600 *gortam* instead, of which they would keep (*za*) 400 for the district (Phran rtsa rta mgrin rgyal po 1994: 71–72).

The second and third "historical taxes" were linked to the 1904 British invasion and subsequent presence of their representatives, military escort, and school on the lCang lo estate in Gyantse, which the Tibetan government had to furnish with animal fodder, called the "customs duty office's hay bales" (? *'gag sgo'i rtsa* [*rtswa*] *shag*),[93] as well as with firewood, mutton, short and long hair of cattle (*khul rtsid*), which was actually given to them by means of a tax levied on the neighbouring estates of the Tashi Lhunpo *labrang*. Then, a sum of money (*dod dngul*; i.e. given in place of, as substitute for the corvée labour) that was called the "*rgyal phag las g.yor*" (lit. the "borrowed labour force [from the districts of] rGyal [rtse and] Phag [gru]") had to be presented (*'bul*), seemingly again to the British Agent through [a particular office called] the "Office that calculates the units of land" (*rkang rtsis las khungs*)[94] (*ibid.*: 72). Therefore, 4 *dngul srang* were levied annually on each *rkang* of the estates under the authority of the district, and after 450 *dngul srang* had been given to the Office that calculates the units of land, 400 *dngul srang* were kept by the district (*ibid.*).

The historical reason behind the last of these taxes is unfortunately not clearly explained. It was called "the yak tax of Xining" (*zi ling g.yag khral*) and

---

92 This is one of the few explicitly named taxes in the other account on Ngamring district in the *MHCT* collection (gZhis rtse sa gnas srid gros lo rgyus rtsom 'bri tshogs chung nas 2005: 52–65), and it is there also designated as "*gor shugs chings dngul*" (lit. "treaty money [for the] Gorkha power") (*ibid.*: 59).

93 *'gag sgo*: "the custom duty office at the borders that collects custom duty from those traders going to trade outside Tibet" (Thupten Sangyay 1986: 41). The question remains whether the *sga 'go*, a tax described by Surkhang as being "most probably" "a sum of money for owning transportation animals" on which he does not seem to have any other information and which is not documented anywhere else, could actually be related in nature to this customs duty.

94 This office is most probably the abbreviated name of the "*rkang rtsis sgang ngam 'tsho zhib las khungs*", an office of the Tashi Lhunpo *labrang* described in the latter administration's description in the *MHCT* collection (Sle zur 'Jigs med dbang phyug dang bDe zur Rin chen dbang 'dus 1991: 139). According to this account, it was founded in 1923 by the above-mentioned *Ordinance of the Water-Pig Year* (*Chu phag bka' rtsa*).

was linked to a "former Grand-lord of Xining" (*de snga zi ling dpon chen*). It amounted to 1 *dngul srang* and 8 *zho* per *rkang* of the 42 *rkang* inhabited by nomadic hearths (*'brog dud*, lit. "nomadic smokes"),[95] and 9 *zho* for every *rkang* of cultivators (*zhing pa*). It was levied and given to the Office that calculates the units of land (*rkang rtsis las khungs*), and a small remaining part of what had been collected was again kept by the district (*ibid.*).

Last, the drainpipes of the district headquarters had to be cleaned every year, and the walls whitewashed. Therefore, among the four lower counties (*smad kha brgya tsho*), two counties would take turns in performing the task. But the burden of the task was actually borne by all *mi ser* under the district's authority since a sum of 7 *dngul srang* would be collected on each *rkang* for the corvée of whitewashing (*dkar rtsi 'ul*) and 3 *dngul srang* and 2 *zho* for the corvée of cleaning the drainpipes, and then used to pay the corvée workers living in the *zhol* area of the Ngamring district headquarters (*'ul mi ngam zhol*, i.e. the abovementioned "lower counties"). Through the process of paying the workers less than the money actually collected for the task, the district would manage to keep a surplus of 700 *dngul srang* (*ibid.*: 72–73).

The author then explains that, besides the above-mentioned means (i.e. helping oneself in the process of tax collection after collecting more than necessary), there were numerous other ways such as extorting from the *mi ser* small amounts through bribery (*za bed*).[96] He proceeds with giving a number of examples. A few relate to the imposition of fines (*chad pa*) of various kinds. The first fine was imposed on the owners of animals that had eaten sections of fields, for which the District Commissioner and his representatives made inspection tours in summer (called the *sngo skor*) before the harvest took place. They would make a list of such incidents, and then would collect the fine in autumn (*ston bsdu*, later called *ston bzhes*) from the *mi ser* concerned by making them pay five times (*lnga skor*) the amount of seed needed to plant the land (*son 'gro*) on the surface that had been eaten (it should be recalled that this corresponded to the average yield ratio indicated for this territory, which meant that they had to repay the entirety of what would have grown on that surface had it not been eaten by animals). If it had not been possible to ascertain the exact field area that had been lost, they would check for the

95 In the description given here of the nomadic *rkang* within Ngamring district, no mention is made of the nomadic population unit of a *shog kha*, which comprised several hundred families, on nomadic land directly under the Ganden Phodrang (Surkhang 1986: 22), but the reason could also be that this source refers only to smaller population units (the nomadic hearth).

96 Goldstein gives as definition for *za bed*: "sm. *sa bsnyad*" (Goldstein 2001: 954), which itself is defined as "causing difficulties in order to get a bribe" (*ibid.*: 953).

prints of animals' hoofs in the field and collect one *bre* of grain per hoofprint (the fine was accordingly termed *rmig bre*, "hoof bushel"). These two tours took place in three of the four lower counties (*smad rgya*) of the district, while the fourth lower county and the two upper counties (*stod rgya*) received another type of "visit", once a year in winter,[97] when ordinary *mi ser* and better-off families (*grong drag ming chen rnams*) had to present themselves to the District Commissioner and his representatives with meat, butter and money (*ibid.*: 73).[98]

Other means of enrichment did not directly relate to the tax collection process, but either first to the role of the district staff to locally administer justice in the name of the Tibetan government, such as in the case of fines imposed through legal punishment (*khrims chad nyes dngul*) that in the present case would be kept by the district (Phran rtsa rta mgrin rgyal po 1994: 74),[99] or second to the role of the district staff in enacting governmental regulative actions regarding trade. The greediness of the successive District Commissioners and their staff is described as being variable, and the author gives as an extreme example a situation that had started just before his arrival and continued after he was in post and that he says he himself directly witnessed:

> Among the greediest individuals (*rgyu rnams za bed che shos*) were a man called *tsho dpon* [county chief] Püngyel (Phun rgyal), a servant of the District commissioner Tshogo who acted for three years as his representative, and a man from among the Tashi Lhunpo *labrang* officials working

---

97 The three "tours" and their names—in summer (*dbyar sngo skor*), autumn (*ston 'ong bzhes*) and winter (*dgun mar bsdud*)—made in villages by the representatives of the district in relation to taxation are confirmed in gZhis rtse sa gnas srid gros lo rgyus rtsom 'bri tshogs chung nas 2005: 59).

98 *rdzong skyong gzhis khag rnams kyi sa zhing ston 'bras brtsas ma rnga ma ran tsam la sngo skor zhes lo ltar rdzong ngo g.yog dang las drung re 'gro srol thog sa zhing dud 'gros zas rnyog byung rigs la chad pa son 'gro 'di la 'di 'gro zhes 'ol tshod son 'gro tho bkod rjes ston bsdur rdzong ngo g.yog 'gro skabs tho bkod nang gsal la lnga skor dang / rig bzos la son 'bor tho gsal ngo bo de rang bcas gzhis g.yog rgyugs [sic] mkhan mi ser spyi nas len gyi yod/ dper na/ son 'gro skor stangs ni dud 'gro'i bzas rnyog smos ci dgos/ ston 'bras zas shul sngo thogs pa med rung / sems can gyi rmig pa'i shul zhig yod na rmig bre zhes rmig rjes rer chad pa 'bru bre gang re 'gel rkyang byed kyi yod/ mnga' khul smad rgya bzhi nas gcung pa rgya tsho'i khongs su rdzong skyong gzhis ka med pa phud/ smad rgya gsum khul rdzong sdod ngo g.yog dang las drung re bcas lo ltar sngo skor dang / ston bzhes zer ba'i dbyar ston thengs gnyis re dang / stod rgya gtsang zur gnyis dang / gcung rgya bcas par lo re mar bsdus ces [zhes] dgun dus thengs re khral bsdur bskyod skabs mi ser spyi nas sa mjal dang / grong drag ming chen rnams nas sger mjal sha /mar / dngul sogs 'bul srol len* (Phran rtsa rta mgrin rgyal po 1994: 73).

99 Such legal fines were to be, in principle, sent to the government.

as copyists (*bla zhabs e pa*) named Mebar Yeshe (Me 'bar ye shes) who later became a Grand-secretary (*drung che*) of Sakya and who then acted as representative of one District Clerk (*las drung*).[100] Because the *labrang* copyist seemed so efficient to the Lhasa lay official Tshogo, he was granted leave from the local authority, and, together with the representative of Tshogo and with a third man named Karnying Söpa (bKar rnying bzod pa) who was a servant of *mkhan che* (*a monk official's honourific title*) Dompo (Dom po) and who worked as the storekeeper (*bkar rgya ba*) of Ngamring district for quite a number of years, they harassed the *mi ser* so excessively in order to get bribes (*za bed 'phar brdabs*), that the *mi ser* came to "have no choice but to depart from their patient acceptance". Around 1929, the "local government" [i.e. the Ganden Phodrang] having appointed and authorised Pomdatshang (sPom mda' tshang) as the official collector and purchaser (*sgrub bsdu dam*) of products like wool, tail and skins, when Karnying Söpa was acting as representative of the merchant Chöden (Chos ldan) on the territory of Ngamring, a final decision was reached according to which it was strictly forbidden to sell to anyone else than him, and for a nominal price, whatever product did not have to be sold to Pomdatshang. Although for wool, tail and skins the value based on local price was clearly stated in the permit (*lag khyer*), he [Karnying Söpa], out of tyrannic greediness (*rgyu rngam dbang shed kyis*), would not give more than a nominal price called "the price of the eyes" (*ring gong mig rin*) [i.e. a token price] and in addition also engaged in some illegal commerce. Also, when people who did not know or had not heard about it [the new regulations] carried on commerce in the many products that were not clearly stated on the permit like musk, etc., and medical products, he would immediately seize both the seller and the buyer, confiscate (*gzhung len*) the products, impose a fine greater than their value (*ma las bu che ba*), and on top of that in some cases whip the men as punishment. Thus, for the unfortunate *mi ser*, there was extreme hardship as if their own property had turned against them as their enemies. At that time, this was of public notoriety in this area, but I myself also witnessed that verses describing in detail and protesting against these actions of serious oppression were pasted on the walls of the Nechu (gNas bcu) temple in the lower part of the district headquarters (*ngam zhol*).[101]

---

100 The system of sending representatives was not limited to the position of District Commissoner (i.e. to government officials' positions), but also to lower positions. We learn here that *las drung* could also use representatives (*ngo tshab*) instead of doing the work themselves.

101 *rgyu rngams za bed che shos kyi gras te dper na/ rdzong sdod thog mar mtsho sgo ba'i g.yog gras tsho dpon phun rgyal zer ba lo gsum tsam ring ngo tshab tu bzhag pa dang gcig /bla*

Moreover, in the process of the district personnel's self-enrichment, a very lucrative custom is mentioned several times in Trentsa Tamdrin Gyelpo's account: the collection of "support gifts" (*zhu rten* and *skyabs rten*)[102] offered on various occasions, either by people who brought legal cases (*khrims gtugs byed mkhan*)[103] to the District Commissioner (*ibid.*: 74), or whenever someone sought a favour in contexts that were more directly linked to the collection of taxes. This was the case in the example the author provides regarding the new military tax levied in 1931 in Ngamring for the new elite regiment (*grong drag dmag sgar*) raised by the Thirteenth Dalai Lama's favourite Kunphela (Kun 'phel lags, 1905–1963).[104] The author recounts that in 1931, when the Copyist Grand-secretary (*e drung*, i.e. *e pa drung che*) Me 'bar ye shes was the District Commissioner's representative in Ngamring, sons from better-off families (*grong drag*) who had reached an age between eighteen and thirty-five had to be enrolled in the army. In the area of Ngamring, at this time, the District Commissioner of Phünling (Phun gling) was a monk official named Gendün Damchö (dGe 'dun dam chos). He established a list of sons from relatively wealthy families who had reached the age and sent this list of names to the

---

zhabs e pa'i mi khongs me 'bar ye shes (rjes su sa skya'i drung che yin) zer ba rdzong las drung gi tshab gcig yod pa de dag shod drung mtsho sgo ba'i mig lam du 'jug po byung gshis bla zhabs e pa'i sa nas 'khrol 'dzin blangs te rdzong sdod mtsho sgo ba'i ngo tshab tu bzhag pa dang gnyis/ mkhan che dom po pa'i g.yog khongs bkar rnying bzod pa zer bas ngam ring bkar rgya ba lo rgyun gang 'tshams byas pa de dang gsum bcas nas mi ser thog bza' [*za*] *bed 'phar brdabs chen po byung tsang mi ser rnams 'u thug bzod bral gyi gnas su gyar zhing sa sbrul* (1929) *lo tsam la sa gnas srid gzhung gis bal rnga pags rigs nyo sgrub bsdu dam spom mda' tshang la lag khyer dang sbrags bsko bzhag byas pa nas gtsang khul gyi bsdu dam spom tshong chos ldan gyi ngam khul ngo tshab bkar rnying bzod pas byed skabs bal rnga pags rigs ji yod kho par tshong dgos pa las gzhan la sne rtags tsam btsong mi chog pa'i mtha' 'doms 'gan len byas shing / bal rnga pags rigs la lag khyer nang rin gong yul thang gzhir bzhag sprod dgos lugs gsal tshod kyang kho pas rgyu rngams dbang shed kyis rin gong mig rin zhes sne sel tsam las mi sprod khar phran bu lkog tshong byed mkhan dang / tha na lag khyer du ma gsal ba'i gla rtsi sogs sman rigs nyo tshong byed mi shes thos byung 'phral nyo tshong byed po do bdag gnyis ka ngo 'gug thog dngos rigs gzhung len dang 'brel nyes dngul ma las bu che ba 'gel len byas pas mi tshad da dung 'ga' rer rta lcag gi* [*gis*] *mtshon nyes brdung yang btang ba bcas mi ser nyam thag la rang rgyu dgrar lang lta bu'i brdabs bsigs ha cang chen po byung yod pa red/ skabs der tshabs che'i brdabs mnar byed po de dag gi bya ngan zhib phra dang der ngo rgol byed pa'i tshigs bcad ka phreng zhig ngam zhol gnas bcu lha khang gi gyang ldebs su sbyar ba de bzhin khul der yongs grags su gyur pa ma zad rang nyid nas kyang dngos su mthong byung* (Phran rtsa rta mgrin rgyal po 1994: 74–75).

102 For a discussion of such gifts to officials in the context of their governmental work, see Travers 2009 and Gurung 2021.

103 Cüppers indicated the use of *khrims gtugs* to mean "legal case" ("Gerichtsfall" in German) in the phrase "*khrims sar gtugs sbyangs*" (Cüppers 2004: 34) while Goldstein translates *khrims khang la btugs bzhag* as "this case has been brought to court" (Goldstein 2001: 451).

104 About him and the foundation of this regiment, see Goldstein 1989: 148 and following pages.

Cabinet of Ministers in Lhasa. The Cabinet selected thirty-five names from the list and sent back to the area of Ngamring the order to dispatch these conscripts to the district headquarters in due course. At this time, many families requested not to have their sons enlisted in the army by offering large quantities of money, goods and animals as supports for their request (*zhu rten*). Not everyone seems to have been treated in the same way: some who had already given gifts to support their request (*skyabs rten*) were told that permission for them would be sought but that permission could be denied, and if so they would have to be enrolled. The author himself explains that he too was concerned by the obligation; the monk official Gendün Damchö agreed to support his request but firmly refused his gifts (*ibid.*: 75–76).

Elsewhere (Travers 2009 and 2012) I have discussed how these District Commissioner's charges were considered by officials as "units of economic maximisation" in a context where the Tibetan state not only tolerated them within certain limits but also officially considered the post of District Commissioner as an official avenue of enrichment for its holder, a way of making up for the official's lack of salary in certain cases, or even making good for a previous position in which the official concerned would have had to underwrite government expenses with his own private finances; the Tibetan government gave the administration of estates or districts to some lay officials in lieu of salary, and the administration of some of the estates or districts was specifically linked to the occupation of particular positions in the Tibetan administration. Some districts were reputedly very good at yielding profits and were coveted by officials.[105] Certain means of enrichment were accepted ways of generating income through work, while others were clearly considered by all as corrupt. These were criticised as such by the *mi ser*, who would for instance publicly complain and denounce the culprit by putting notices on walls, as described in the present account of the Ngamring district, or complain directly to the Tibetan Central Government in Lhasa; it quite often happened that the District Commissioner would be punished.

One question remains regarding the overall apparent deficit between the income and expenses of Ngamring district. Indeed, Trentsa Tamdrin Gyelpo quotes the 1740 *Iron-Monkey Land Settlement* as the source for establishing the number of *rkang* under the district's administration, and thus used as the basis for the taxation system. However, as explained by Surkhang, the 1740 *Iron-Monkey Land Settlement* "became inadequate mainly due to the rapid increase in new farm land which was put under cultivation" and "since taxes had been fixed according to the amount of land, i.e. *rkang* or *'don* a

105 On this phenomenon, see Goldstein 1968: 19, Tsarong 1998a and Travers 2012.

family worked in 1740, the government was losing a tremendous amount of income".[106] It would thus seem quite remarkable if the amount of arable land in Ngamring district had not expanded as well between 1740 and 1932, in the almost two centuries between the *Iron-Monkey Land Settlement* and Trentsa Tamdrin Gyelpo's taking of office as District Clerk. Therefore, if taxes in the 1940s were still levied in Ngamring based on the 1740 calculation of land, this should be a foremost explanation as to why it was possible in the first place to make a seemingly huge profit from the tax collection process in Ngamring district. However, this is strangely neither discussed nor implicitly apparent in Trentsa Tamdrin Gyelpo's account. It is very much possible, working with the hypothesis that arable land did actually increase in the district, that later addenda were made to the 1740 *Iron-Monkey Land Settlement* that allowed a certain degree of adaptation.

4.3 *The Wood-Horse Reform (1954), an Attempt at Modernising District Administration and Tax Collection in Particular*

In the aftermath of the signature of the Seventeen-Point Agreement with the People's Republic of China in 1951 and before the end of the Ganden Phodrang government in Tibet in 1959, reforms were initiated by the Tibetan government, which aimed at modernising Tibet on several levels. The elaboration of these modernising reforms was launched by convening the "reform assembly" (*legs bcos tshogs 'du*) in 1952 and followed by the work of a standing committee known by the name of the Reform Office (*legs bcos las khungs*) (Goldstein 2009: 456). There was debate regarding the opportunity to proceed with a thorough land reform but this option was rejected in 1952, and instead it engaged in "less radical reforms" (*ibid.*: 455) directed at improving the welfare of Tibet's dependent peasants.

Thus, the first decree promulgated by the Cabinet of Ministers in 1953 aimed at decreasing interest rates and at solving the problems of accumulated loans for poor and middle-level *mi ser*. A second reform was enforced, establishing

106 Gurung has shown (2016: 211) that another reason for the enforcement of a new land settlement was mentioned in the introduction of the *Iron-Tiger Land Settlement*: land previously belonging to the government was given to aristocratic and monastic landlords, and thus made the corvée and tax burden too heavy on the remaining government taxpayers in these districts; Gurung concludes more generally on the reason behind the issuance of the *Iron-Tiger Land Settlement*: "It was issued not only to revise the older tax system and to balance the inequality of tax obligations among its taxpayers, but also to protect people from the injurious tax system that had developed to support political and social interests of the estates holders. It was also issued to stabilize the government's tax income. It was intended to improve the government's finances so that it could maintain the important offices and sponsor important religious ceremonies" (*ibid.*: 220).

that a fee should be paid to *mi ser* for transportation service and reducing the number of people allowed to use this service, to alleviate the overall burden this corvée created for *mi ser*. A third reform, imposed in 1954 by a *Five-Point Proclamation*, focused on the administration of the districts and the tax collection process. According to Goldstein:

> Counties [i.e. districts/*rdzong*] generally provided lucrative income for their heads, since they were required to transmit only a specified amount of grain and other taxes to Lhasa. Anything they collected over the required amount they kept for themselves. [...] The Reform Office, therefore, set about to end this form of exploitation by developing a new law that 1) required the government to "nationalize" (repossess) all leased counties and send its own officials to administer them (this nationalization was called "shungdzin" [*gzhung 'dzin*] of "shungdzin phumpa silu" [*gzhung 'dzin bum pa sib blug*]; and 2) required county heads to pass on to the government in Lhasa everything they collected from the peasants. To compensate the county heads, the government now paid them better salaries and gave them adequate allowances for the servants who would accompany them.
>
> *ibid.*: 462

Shakabpa reproduces the entire detailed content of this 1954 *Five-Point Proclamation* (*don tshan lnga 'khod*), which shows that it was a general appeal to restore honesty and probity in the practices of tax collection, trade, and justice in the districts, with the obligation to present detailed and clear accounting of all income and expenditures to the government; to abandon former practices like "perpetrating fraudulent accounting", "misstating the quantities of taxes, goods and people", "deceptive commercial practices"; to conduct the headcount without those in charge taking anything for themselves (Shakabpa 2010: 964–70).[107] Such appeals had been made repeatedly in the past before the 1950s through decrees sent to all districts, which reiterates that the problem of corruption was neither a recent turn of events nor criticised for the first time by the Tibetan government.[108]

Trentsa Tamdrin Gyelpo concludes his account by referring to these reforms, that visibly also concerned the territories which were, by then, back under the Panchen Lama's direct authority. The author highlights first the fact that after 1951 only officials appointed by the government were allowed to work

107 See also the Tibetan version in Zhwa sgab pa 1976: 465–76.

108 To see but just one example of such decree that has been translated into English, see Chhodak 1978.

as District Commissioners, and privately appointed representatives would be unacceptable. Second, "except for the traditional various expenses like ritual allowances (*gtong sgo*), storage for the district (*bkar 'jug*), taxes in money and in kind (*sgrigs 'bul*), etc., accounts of all incomes had to be submitted to the *bla brang phyag mdzod* and to the *rtse phyag* by 'pouring the vase completely' (*bum pa sib blug kyis*)". Having himself taken part in this new process, he was awarded the bronze medal for having presented the second-best income.[109] It is not entirely clear here whether the author is referring to the two treasuries (*bla brang phyag mdzod* and *rtse phyag*) of the Ganden Phodrang administration or to the two eponymous treasuries in the administration of the Tashi Lhunpo *labrang*, these last two having been both created under the Fourth Panchen Lama (see Sle zur 'Jigs med dbang phyug and bDe zur Rin chen dbang 'dus 1991: 130 and 113 respectively). The latter is very likely, and would imply that this 1953 reform instituted by the Lhasa government and its "*gzhung 'dzin bum pa sib blug*" principle was implemented and adapted at the level of the semi-autonomous administration of the Tashi Lhunpo as well, as the "*bum pa sib blug*",[110] which by then had also taken over the direct administration of its districts and thus forced their incumbents to send over all their incomes.

5 Conclusion

This survey of the tax system in Ngamring district reflects several aspects of the Tibetan tax system in general. First, the district used a significant part of its income to sustain the monastic communities on its territories; second, it is apparent that new taxes and corvées were created at various historical points in time to meet the government's growing needs. In Ngamring, the military context for instance accounts for a number of the taxes mentioned. We have seen the specific taxes linked to the Gorkha wars in the 18th century, then to the Tibet-British wars, and also to the modernisation of the Tibetan army in the 20th century. These circumstances resulted in a complex layer of taxes that accumulated over time and that was constantly changing.

Trentsa Tamdrin Gyelpo's account exemplifies both the diversity of opportunities for enrichment that the tax collection process created—mainly through the over-collection of taxes and the subsequent diversion of part of

109 *gong lo nas rdzong gzhis tshang ma gzhung 'dzin gyis mi 'gro ngo las btang ste sngar lam gtong sgo khag dang / bkar 'jug /sgrigs 'bul sogs 'gro cha khag phud/ yong 'bab rnams bum pa sib blugs kyis bla brang phyag mdzod dang / rtse phyag tu rtsis zhu byed kyi yod de'i skabs nga rang yang las bya'i khongs mi yin pas yong 'bab zal thon ang gnyis pa byung gshis/ ang gnyis pa'i bya dga' yang thob byung /* (Phran rtsa rta mgrin rgyal po 1994: 78).

110 And thus, without the mention of the Tibetan Central Government (*gzhung*).

the collected taxes for private purposes, imposing fines and receiving gifts—and the authority over *mi ser* that agents of the tax collection process enjoyed. It is likely that the impermanence and the complexity of the tax system made it easier for the district administrators to profit from it, as the same agents who transmitted the information on the new taxes or on new decrees related to trade rules, for instance, were also the very individuals who levied these taxes for the Tibetan government.

Acknowledgments

I would like to thank Tashi Tsering Josayma (AMI) for his insightful comments on an earlier draft of this paper. I am also very grateful to Kalsang Norbu Gurung, Charles Ramble and Peter Schwieger for their valuable suggestions. All mistakes remain my own.

References

British Archives

Letter of the British trade agent, Gartok, dated 3rd/9th August 1931 (IOR/L/P&S/12/4163/P7900).

Who's Who 1937: Who's Who in Tibet, Corrected to the Autumn of 1937, with a few subsequent additions up to February 1938 (plus addenda), 1938, Calcutta, Government of India Press (IOR/L/P&S/12/4185 A).

Who's Who 1948: Who's Who in Tibet, Corrected with a few subsequent additions up to 30th September 1948, 1949, Calcutta, Printed by the Government of India Press (IOR/L/P&S/20D220/2 or V/27/270/26 with addenda until 1953).

Richardson, H.E. 1998 [1945]. *Tibetan precis*, Secret, For Official Use only, Printed by the Manager Government of India Press: Calcutta. *In* M. Aris (ed.) *High Peaks, Pure Earth: Collected Writings on Tibetan History and Culture*. London: Serindia Publications, 519–666.

Tibetan Archival Documents

Lcags lug zhib gzhung (document Hs.or.6898). *In* H. Schneider, 2012. *Tibetischsprachige Urkunden aus Südwesttibet (sPo-rong, Ding-ri und Shel-dkar)*, 2 vols, Stuttgart: Franz Steiner Verlag, 311–12.

DTAB: Digital Tibetan Archives Bonn: (https://dtab.crossasia.org). *Document DTAB ID 2677 (signatory in archives 0056_SBB6679)*.

Published Oral History

bDud 'dul chos dbyings. 1984. rDzong gi las drung nas dpal 'bar sa khul gyi zing slong dmag spyi'i bar [From being a *las drung* in a *rdzong* to a military representative in Pelbar]. *In Bod kyi rig gnas lo rgyus dpyad gzhi'i rgyu cha bdams bsgrigs* 3. Lhasa: Bod ljongs mi dmangs dpe skrun khang, 173–96.

bKa' rnying Blo bzang bde skyid. 2002. *bTsan 'og gi bod kyi bud med.* Dharamsala: Private publication [English abbreviated translation: Ka-Nying Phukhang Lobsang Dickye. 2002. *Tibetan Women under Oppression.* Dharamsala: Private publication].

bShad sgra dGa' ldan dpal 'byor, Chab tshom 'Chi med rgyal po, Sreg shing Blo bzang don grub. 1991. De snga'i bod sa gnas srid gzhung gi srid 'dzin sgrig gzhi [Organisation of the former local government of Tibet]. *In Bod kyi rig gnas lo rgyus dpyad gzhi'i rgyu cha bdams bsgrigs* 13. Lhasa: Bod ljongs mi dmangs dpe skrun khang.

Chos 'byor dar rgyas. 2005. Dwags po sku rnam rdzong gi sngar khral bsdu khrims gnon byed sgo'i skor [On the collection and tax and justice in Kunam Dzong]. *In Bod kyi rig gnas lo rgyus dpyad gzhi'i rgyu cha bdams bsgrigs* 25. Lhasa: Bod ljongs mi dmangs dpe skrun khang, 206–209.

lCam grwa nor bzang and Kun dga' chos bzang. 1991. De snga'i sa skya'i sgrig gzhi [The organisation of former Sakya]. *In Bod kyi rig gnas lo rgyus dpyad gzhi'i rgyu cha bdams bsgrigs* 13. Lhasa: Bod ljongs mi dmangs dpe skrun khang, 162–96.

gZhis rtse sa gnas srid gros lo rgyus rtsom 'bri tshogs chung nas. 2005. Ngam ring rdzong gi de snga'i lo rgyus rags tsam [Brief history of Ngamring district]. *In Bod kyi rig gnas lo rgyus dpyad gzhi'i rgyu cha bdams bsgrigs* 25. Lhasa: Bod ljongs mi dmangs dpe skrun khang, 32–65.

lHo kha sa gnas srid gros lo rgyus rgyu cha 'tshol bsdus tshogs chung. 1998. lHo brag lha khang rdzong gi khral bsdu khrims gnon byed phyogs dang 'brel yod 'khar chu dgon pa'i lo rgyus mdor bsdus [Condensed history of Karchu monastery and on the way Lhakhang rdzong in Lhobrag collected taxes and administred justice]. *In Bod kyi rig gnas lo rgyus dpyad gzhi'i rgyu cha bdams bsgrigs* 20. Lhasa: Bod ljongs mi dmangs dpe skrun khang, 154–76.

Phran rtsa rta mgrin rgyal po. 1985. sGer ru thog pa dang ngam ring mnga' 'du gnyis zlos gyar skor [On the conflict between the aristocrat Rutokpa and the people under Ngamring dzong]. *In Bod kyi rig gnas lo rgyus dpyad gzhi'i rgyu cha bdams bsgrigs* 5. Lhasa: Bod ljongs mi dmangs dpe skrun khang, 59–77.

Phran rtsa rta mgrin rgyal po. 1994. Ngam ring rdzong gi lo rgyus dang bar skabs rdzong sdod 'ga' zhig gi byed phyogs rang nyid las drung byed skabs bcas skor rags bsdus [A brief description of Ngamring district's history and of several District Commissioners' behaviour when I was myself a District Clerk there]. *In Bod kyi rig gnas lo rgyus dpyad gzhi'i rgyu cha bdams bsgrigs* 17. Lhasa: Bod ljongs mi dmangs dpe skrun khang, 67–78 (TBRC: W00KG01518).

Sle zur 'Jigs med dbang phyug and bDe zur Rin chen dbang 'dus. 1991. *De snga'i bla brang* rgyal mtshan mthon pa'i srid 'dzin sgrig gzhi'i spyi gnas tshul [General situation of the former organisation of the Tashi Lhunpo *labrang* administration]. *In Bod kyi rig gnas lo rgyus dpyad gzhi'i rgyu cha bdams bsgrigs* 13. Lhasa: Bod ljongs mi dmangs dpe skrun khang, 102–62.

Secondary Literature

Bell, C.A. [1928] 1992. *The People of Tibet*. Delhi: Motilal Banarsidass Publishers.

Bischoff, J. 2017. Completey, voluntarily and unalterably? Values and social regulation among Central Tibetan *mi ser* during the Ganden Phodrang period. *In* J. Bischoff and S. Mullard (eds) *Social Regulation: Case Studies from Tibetan History*. Leiden, Boston: Brill, 151–80.

Cassinelli, C.W. and R.B. Ekvall. 1969. *A Tibetan Principality: The Political System of Sa-sKya*. Ithaca, New York: Cornell University Press.

Chhodak, Tenzing. 1978. The 1901 proclamation of H.H. Dalai Lama XIII. *The Tibet Journal* 3(1), 30–38.

Colliard, J.-É. and C. Montalioux. 2007. Une brève histoire de l'impôt. *Regards croisés sur l'économie* 1, 56–65.

Cüppers, C. 2004. Ein Glossar zur Terminologie der tibetischen Urkundensprache. *Zentralasiatische Studien (ZAS)* 33, 25–98.

Goldstein, M.C. 1968. An Anthropological Study of the Tibetan Political System. Ph.D. thesis, University of Washington.

Goldstein, M.C. 1971a. Taxation and the structure of a Tibetan village. *Central Asiatic Journal* 15(1), 1–27.

Goldstein, M.C. 1971b. The balance between centralization and decentralization in the traditional Tibetan political system: an essay on the nature of Tibetan political macro-structure. *Central Asiatic Journal* 15(3), 170–82.

Goldstein, M.C. [1989] 1993. *A History of Modern Tibet, 1913–1951. The Demise of the Lamaist State*. New Delhi: Munshiram Manoharlal Publishers.

Goldstein, M.C. 2001. *The New Tibetan-English Dictionary of Modern Tibetan*. Berkeley: University of California Press.

Goldstein, M.C. 2009. *A History of Modern Tibet. Volume 2: The Calm before the Storm, 1951–1955*. Berkeley: University of California Press.

Gurung, Kalsang Norbu. 2016. Different copies of the *Iron-Tiger Land Settlement* and their historical value as taxation manuals. *In* J. Bischoff and S. Mullard (eds) *Social Regulation—Case Studies from Tibetan History*. Leiden: Brill, 209–30.

Gurung, Kalsang Norbu. 2018. The value of the Tibetan money: a study of the use of Srang in the late 19th century Tibet. *In* J. Bischoff and A. Travers (eds) *Commerce and Communities: Social and Political Status and the Exchange of Goods in Tibetan Societies*. Bonner Asienstudien Band 16. Berlin: EB-Verlag, 223–70.

Gurung, Kalsang Norbu. 2021. Measuring income inequality in Tibetan society: understanding the different amounts of offering and the status of Tibetan officials. *In* K.N. Gurung and L. Galli (eds) *Revue d'Etudes Tibétaines* 57 (Special issue: *The relationship between economic and social status in the Tibetan world until the mid-20th century*), 193–215.

Henrion-Dourcy, I. 2013. A look at the margins: autobiographical writing in Tibetan in the PRC. *In* S. Dauncey and M. Dryburgh (eds) *Writing lives in China*. London: Palgrave Macmillan, 206–35.

Jagou, F. [French version 2004] 2011. *The 9th Panchen Lama (1883–1937): A Life at the Crossroads of Sino-Tibetan Relations*. Bangkok: Silkworm.

Jamyang Norbu. 2008. Black annals: Goldstein and the negation of Tibetan history (Part II). Online article, consulted the 2 December 2013. URL: http://www.jamyangnorbu.com/blog/2008/07/27/black-annals-goldstein-the-negation-of-tibetan-history-part-ii/.

Karsten, J. 1979. Some notes on the house of lHa gya ri. *In* M. Aris and Aung San Suu Kyi (eds) *Tibetan Studies in Honour of Hugh Richardson. Proceedings of the International Seminar on Tibetan Studies, Oxford 1979*. Warminister: Aris & Phillips, 163–68.

Maitrot, J.-C. Impôt. Histoire de l'impôt. *Encyclopaedia Universalis*. Online article, consulted the 2 December 2013. URL: http://www.universalis.fr/encyclopedie/impot-histoire-de-l-impot/.

Okawa, K. 2016. A study on *nang zan*: on the reality of the "servant worker" in traditional Tibetan society. *Revue d'Etudes Tibétaines* 37, 278–92.

Petech, L. 1973. *Aristocracy and Government in Tibet 1728–1959*, Serie Orientale Roma XLV. Rome: Ismeo.

Ryavec, K.E. 2002. Land Use Change in Central Tibet, ca. 1830–2000. Ph.D. thesis, University of Minnesota.

Schwieger, P. 2018. Some remarks on the nature and terminology of gift exchange between Tibetan hierarchs and the Qing Emperor. *In* J. Bischoff and A. Travers (eds) *Commerce and Communities: Social and Political Status and the Exchange of Goods in Tibetan Societies*. Bonner Asienstudien Band 16. Berlin: EB-Verlag, 25–42.

Schwieger, P. 2021. Lenders and borrowers in Tibetan society. *In* Kalsang Norbu Gurung and L. Galli (eds) *Revue d'Etudes Tibétaines* 57 (Special issue: *The relationship between economic and social status in the Tibetan world until the mid-20th century*), 20–32.

Shakabpa, Tsepon Wangchuk Deden. 2010. *One Hundred Thousand Moons, An Advanced Political History of Tibet*, vol. 2, trans. Derek F. Maher. Leiden: Brill.

Surkhang, Wangchen Gelek. [1966] 1984. Tax measurement and *lag 'don* tax in Tibet. *The Tibet Journal* 9(1), 20–30.

Surkhang, Wangchen Gelek. 1986. Government, monastic and private taxation in Tibet. *The Tibet Journal* 11(1), 21–40.

Thupten Sangyay. 1986. Glossary of the "Government, monastic and private taxation in Tibet" (translated by Tsepag Rigzin). *The Tibet Journal* 11(1), 41–47.

Travers, A. 2009. La noblesse tibétaine du Ganden Phodrang (1895–1959): permanences et transitions. Ph.D. thesis, University Paris Ouest-Nanterre La Défense and INALCO.

Travers, A. 2012. Patrimonial aspects of public service: the careers of the Ganden Phodrang officials (1895–1959). *In* R. Vitali (ed.) *Studies on the History and Literature of Tibet and the Himalaya*. Kathmandu: Vajra Books, 157–81.

Travers, A. 2013. How should we define social status? The study of "intermediate groups" in Central Tibet (1895–1959). *In* C. Ramble, P. Schwieger and A. Travers (eds) *Tibetans who Escaped the Historian's Net. Studies in the Social History of Tibetan Societies*. Kathmandu: Vajra Books, 141–60.

Travers, A. 2020a. Renewing the United Front policy history through the writing of history: remarks on the production of collective memory in the *Materials for the Study of the History and Culture of Tibet* (1981–2014). *In* R. Barnett, F. Robin and B. Weiner (eds) *Conflicting Memories: Tibetan History under Mao Retold*. Leiden: Brill, 111–138.

Travers, A. 2020b. A compiled list of Tibetan districts (*rdzong*) and government estates of the Ganden Phodrang territory (1830–1959). *Revue d'Etudes Tibétaines* 56, October 2020, 5–47.

Tsarong, Paljor. 1998a. Economics of a Tibetan state treasury: the barley supply office. *The Tibet Journal* 23(2), 3–10.

Tsarong, Paljor. 1998b. Tseja: structure and economy of a Tibetan state treasury. *The Tibet Journal* 23(3), 23–33.

Zhwa sgab pa, dBang phyug bde ldan. 1976. *Bod kyi srid don rgyal rabs: An Advanced Political History of Tibet*, vol. 2. Kalimpong: T. Tsepal, Taikhang.

CHAPTER 4

Traditional Taxation Systems in Western Tibet: A Comparative Perspective

Nancy E. Levine

1 Introduction

This chapter focuses on traditional systems of taxation in Ngari (mNga' ris), or Western Tibet, and their integration with the system of land tenure and related features of social structure. These systems display tremendous regional diversity, due, no doubt, to particularities of history and idiosyncratic economic and geographical factors. Despite some noteworthy differences, they share fundamental commonalities with the taxation systems of Central Tibet: in the forms that taxation took and in its impact on social and economic life. As the conclusion to this paper argues, the taxation system must be understood in a broader economic context. If comparative perspectives shed any light on the matter, they suggest that this manner of taxation is the product of a particular kind of agrarian system, characterised by extensive agriculture, restrictions on land usage, low levels of production, limited monetisation, and restricted market systems. In traditional Tibet, taxation played a critical role in perpetuating this system and the social relations built up around it.

The data to be presented derive from a brief period of field research in summer 1990. They were collected in the course of interviews with ordinary men and women and local officials who also are members of Ruthog (Ru thog), Tholing (mTho lding) in Guge (Gu ge), Purang (sPu hreng), and Khochar (Kho char) villages. There are two caveats that must be offered in this regard. First, the data involve reconstructions of a system that had ended over thirty years ago, yet has remained a major issue in political consciousness.[1] It is difficult to assess the impact of such sensitivities on the recollections and interpretations of interviewees. Second, due to problems of recollection and restrictions

---

1 This reprinted article diverges from the original version, which was published in 1992 in a special issue of *China Tibetology*, in three regards. First, the spelling of Tibetan terms now uniformly follows the Wylie system of transliteration. Second, several terms now are used in translation. Third, an error concerning taxes owed to Darchen Labrang—kindly pointed out by Astrid Hovden—has been corrected.

 | DOI:10.1163/9789004529465_006

of research time, the accounts are not exhaustive. Thus the survey does not include comprehensive lists of all taxes of all tax statuses in the four villages, and there may be unrecognised lacunae in the summaries to follow.

Another set of issues concerns translation and the language of classification or terminology. Villagers in Ruthog, Guge, and the Purang valley refer today to their former socio-economic status by varying terms. They say that they were the *mi ser, khral pa,* and *g.yog* (using these terms in that order of frequency) of various landlords, whom they termed their *dpon po*. The meaning, and appropriate translation, of these and other terms associated with the traditional Tibetan land tenure system has occasioned a protracted debate in the European literature. In those arrangements some have seen parallels to past European feudal and serf systems, while others have stressed what they believe to be critical differences between the European systems and relations between Tibetan *dpon po* and *mi ser* or the latter's customary rights and obligations (see the summary in Goldstein 1986: 83–86).

To put this problem in perspective, it should be noted that similar debates have raged over the status of peasants and land tenure arrangements in South Asia and the Middle East in the past, with some scholars resting their analyses on models borrowed from European historical studies and others pointing to the idiosyncratic historical development of each society, thus reaffirming the value of particularistic analyses of each social system. None of these debates seems to have yielded permanent resolutions—although all may have prompted more focused, finer grained analyses of the relevant materials. Surely part of the problem lies in the constructs and models themselves. There is no single accepted definition of feudalism or serfdom even in the European historical literature. There different authors follow different paths in choosing among a constellation of features commonly found in pre-modern Europe. Thus each tends to cite a different set of facts as keys to understanding the relations between classes of society and their rights over land—whatever best fits the author's theoretical position or the time and place being described. Logically, such models must be even more greatly expanded and allow even greater slack to accommodate the vastly different experiences of Asian societies. For these and related reasons it seems advisable to slightly shift the orientation of discussions on Tibet. Instead of concerning ourselves with whether or not traditional Tibet was or was not a feudal society and whether or not the majority of its population was or was not in a relationship of serfdom to nobles, church, and state, we might begin to evaluate in exactly which ways Tibetan society was similar to pre-modern Europe, how it differed, and—most significantly—the reasons behind these variations. Because I hope to move toward the latter sorts of analyses, I deliberately have refrained from using terms that prejudge the issues and rely primarily on local terminology, which should be familiar to the reader.

2 Ruthog

I begin the discussion of taxation systems with Ruthog, because certain features of its taxation seem so distinctive, standing apart in several ways from the manner of assessments typically described in the literature on Tibet. Yet, at the same time, Ruthog taxation displays the same fundamental logic; it rests on similar relations of production and a similar organisation of distribution as taxation elsewhere in traditional Tibet—as well as bearing the same consequences.

2.1 *Control of the Land and Recipients of Taxation*

As one might find elsewhere in Tibet, offices of the central government and five monastic centres in the cluster of villages (*tsho*) known as Ruthog controlled land and held rights of taxation. This meant that taxes went to Lhasa, to the monasteries directly, and to the support of the Ruthog District Commissioner (*rdzong dpon*) and the government's representative in Gartok (*sgar dpon*). The vast majority of the population of the Ruthog valleys had some form of hereditary use-rights over sectors of land held from these institutions. Less usual, these people could loan out their land to anyone who would assume the tax obligations, they could mortgage it, and even sell the entire parcel, reportedly without seeking special permission from the taxing agency. The tax was automatically transferred.

The system, however, was less flexible in other ways. If someone, for any reason, failed to plant or harvest, the tax still was owed. If there was a natural disaster destroying the crops, the tax remained the same. There also was an inflexible adherence to the land records, which seem rarely to have been checked or revised. One seventy-one year old man said that he had never seen a revision of the records in his lifetime. Perhaps even more problematic, land reclamation was discouraged: there were fines imposed on people who cultivated or used any land which was not listed in the tax records. Elsewhere land reclamation occasionally was facilitated by temporary postponements or reductions in taxes (Goldstein 1971: 13). This, however, was not the case in Ruthog.

2.2 *Traditional Classes of Ruthog Social Structure*

In Ruthog, there was one person classed as a lord (*dpon*), who was descended from the ancient aristocracy. In recent centuries he acted as a hereditary tax collector and representative of the central government. He supervised a small group (*tsho*) of nomads and took a portion of the taxes he collected from them. Thus it seems that it would be inapt to speak of a true class of nobles, or *sger pa*, in Ruthog.

There were very few government officials, who were assigned to Ruthog by the central government and were only temporarily resident, typically for a term of three years. Among them were the lay and monastic officials in Gartok, which was relatively close to and thus able to exert considerable control in Ruthog. Ruthog also had its district officials, and in the fort complex also resided the head of all monastic estates in Ruthog (the *bla brang phyag mdzod*). He was sent from Sera monastery in Lhasa, collected the taxes due to these religious establishments, and served as their abbot, leading approximately 160 monks from the region, somewhat less than 5 per cent of the population.

In Ruthog there were three types of *mi ser*, or peasant subjects. Unlike Central Tibet and other areas of Ngari, the landholding subjects do not seem to have been internally differentiated as to the nature of their claims over land. More specifically, they were not subdivided into holders of hereditary *khral pa* allotments versus short-term or lifetime *dud chung*-type arrangements.[2] People simply farmed their parcels of land and paid taxes to the appropriate government and monastic agencies.

Among the peasant subjects was the class of *chos gzhis*, subjects of the five monasteries in the region, who held hereditary use-rights over arable or grazing lands and houses. Their primary tax obligations were to the monastic institution, but they also paid considerable tax to the government. While one person estimated them to constitute two ninths of the population, they were represented by one of five village leaders (*gtso ba*) in the region. Two thirds of these *mi ser* were government subjects, *gzhung rgyugs pa*, who had primary taxpaying obligations to the government, from whence they derived their hereditary rights to land. They constituted approximately two thirds of the population and were represented by four leaders in dealings with government officials.

Also counted among the subjects were *nang g.yog*, effectively servants, who worked within the various religious institutions. This was a smaller category of people, estimated to comprise about one ninth of the population. They were servants because they lacked rights to land on which to farm or graze animals. Thus they had to devote themselves fully to the labour of their monastic estate, cultivating its fields or raising its animals, and also providing various kinds of

2 As Goldstein (1971: 4) notes, an apt translation of the term *khral pa* is "taxpayer", while *dud chung* can be translated as "small household".

domestic services for the establishment. In payment they received only a small annual salary in food, tea, and so forth, but no pay for the specific tasks performed. Such a person might keep some goats and sheep of his own, but inasmuch as he had no rights to grazing, he had to pay grazing tax for land usage. A person became a *nang g.yog* only when he failed at farming or herding and became impoverished.

Also in Ruthog were a small number of artisans. There were *mgar ra*—ironworkers—who made tools. These people suffered special discrimination due to beliefs about their different origins, and they formed their own endogamous circle. Holding no land or productive property, they paid no tax, but were obliged to make or repair tools without pay when summoned by the district leaders. There were also traditional physicians, *em chi* or *sman pa*, who received pay for their services from patients. They too were obliged to go to the fort when called on and were not responsible for tax.

As always, there were a few beggars, *'bangs slong*. Needless to say, they paid no taxes, and tended to have no fixed residence either.

2.3 *The Logic and Varieties of Tax Payments*

Throughout Tibet, the basic unit of taxation was the household, not the individual or the married couple (Carrasco 1959: 212). Taxes ordinarily followed a fixed calculus of assessments, according to the extent of a household's rights over land—which, in most cases, were fixed over time. This was not the case in the border region of Ruthog. One of the distinctive features of taxation there was that the largest obligations involved what one might call income taxes, tithes, and head taxes, with relatively less tax accruing by virtue of hereditary rights to land.[3] The major categories of taxation incumbent on all Ruthog subjects included:

1. House tax (*them*). This was fixed in amount and was paid to the Ruthog *rdzong* administration annually.
2. Animal wealth tax (*sa phyug*), which was assessed and paid annually according to one's current animal holdings. The accounting would be made in mid-summer by a special official appointed for this purpose, together with the District Commissioner. The assessments were simple: 1 *srang* (a silver coin) for every ten goats, ten sheep, and two yaks owned. This too was paid to the administration.

---

3 This system appears to resemble conditions reported for Sikkim, where peasants were taxed on the basis of their general prosperity, rather than on the basis of the land they used and its productivity, as in Tibet. Note too that Bhutan in the past is reported as taxing peasants on the number of their family members (Carrasco 1959: 189, 204).

3. The major tax, combining features of an income and head tax, was known as *sleb*. This was annually assessed and paid to the government via its office in Gartok. The assessment involved a survey of subjects and their property: counting all the land a particular household farmed, whether hereditary, bought or borrowed, its animal holdings, and its human membership, then totalling these figures to arrive at the number of *sleb*. For taxation purposes, ten yak equalled 1 *sleb*, as did ten horses, some fifty goats or sheep, ten people, and the land on which 5 *khal* of barley can be sown.[4] Thus the assessment for a *mi ser* household with ten yaks, five horses, one hundred goats, five people, and 5 *khal* of land would be 5 *sleb*.

Each year, the government in Gartok would decide upon a target for taxation—for money, goods, and services needed that year—set partly in response to demands from the central government. The total tax burden would be assumed by Ruthog subjects according to the number of *sleb* each household held. These taxes had to be paid according to the targeted items: in cash, in kind, and in services, including shares in the annual corvée (*'u lag*) labour requirement for the region. People accordingly paid this tax in horses, yaks, sheep, salt, grain, wild potentilla tubers (*gro ma*), local whitewashes and dyes, home-produced soap, and so on. A commonly demanded item was wool, while also in demand were butter, dried cheese, and meat. People paid too in shares of the transport obligations, in days of labour on the construction and repair of buildings and the like, as they did in the obligation to buy goods sold under monopoly arrangements by the government and their contributions in support of the army (see below).

'U lag transport, specifically, had to be provided for local government officials and for anyone who turned up with a government pass. This meant assembling the requisite number of large pack animals (yaks and horses) (Goldstein 1971: 15–18). Due to the low density of population in the region, people were obliged to travel three stations (known here, as elsewhere in Tibet, as *rta zam* or *rta tshugs*). Thus transport in Ruthog was essentially long distance *rdzong skyel*, from administrative centre to centre. The extent of a family's obligations in this too depended on the number of their *sleb*.

4 A *khal* is equivalent to approximately 13 kilograms of barley, and a *khal* of land describes the amount of land requiring one *khal* of seed grain. Goldstein estimates that one *khal* of well-irrigated land, such as could be found in Ruthog, was equal to 0.22 acres (1971: 9). In upland agriculture in northwestern Nepal, one *khal* of barley seeds 0.30 acres of land, an amount it took one day to plough (Levine 1988a). A *khal* is further divided into 20 *bre*.

The *sleb* system thus appears to be different from modes of assessing taxes elsewhere in Tibet in two ways. First there are differences with regard to the basis on which it was assigned: it was a tax on current wealth, in land, animals, and people, rather than hereditary or tenancy rights in land. This system also subsumed within one category a whole host of taxation items often separately categorised, that is, taxes on grain and items of pastoral production, manufactured objects, cash, and labour.

4. Ruthog subjects also faced sporadic tithes (*bed*) imposed by the administration in Ruthog and Gartok, involving a percentage of their animals, but this tax was not consistently imposed, and the details now available, thirty years after the demise of the system, are very sketchy.
5. Gold tax. There was a so-called *gser dpon*, or Gold Officer, overseeing the several areas where gold was mined. These areas were inhospitable to agriculture and herding, and their inhabitants were very poor. Gold diggers had to pay a fee for their summer's work, upon which they would be relieved from certain corvée obligations.
6. Foreigners, that is, Indians, paid *tshong khral*, a trade tax, in the amount of 1/50 of any goods sold. Ruthog villagers had to pay 1 *srang* for every ten bags of salt (in recent years in Nepal, such bags have averaged 11 kilograms in weight) and 1 *srang* for the wool of every ten sheep they took abroad to sell.
7. Trade monopolies. Various government agencies imported tea, cloth, offering scarves, incense, paper, and the like to sell to people at high prices in cash. Agencies with trade monopolies included the central government, District Office, Gold Office, and monastic institutions. A household's obligation to buy correlated with the number of their *sleb*. This was known as *'bam tshong spos sgyur*.
8. Tax obligations in support of the army (*dmag khral*) also fell upon subjects in proportion to the number of their *sleb*. Households had a responsibility to provide soldiers and provide for their equipment and support. This was a national tax, conditional upon the existence of war, which had not occurred in recent memory.

In addition to these taxes, applied to all subjects, there were a variety of taxes paid to one's immediate lord, which differed by lord and village. In all cases—whether land rights extended from the government or monastic institutions—subjects had to work on estate fields (including some *rdzong* fields) or care for its animals (work described as *zhing las* and *'brog las*). These obligations superseded the demands of their own agricultural or pastoral work. In the case of monastic institutions, servants (*nang g.yog*) performed some of these duties. But government subjects were responsible for everything else. To give just a few examples, there were "exotic" taxes, like the so-called *na chung* or maiden tax, which required unmarried women to apply manure to the government's fields. There was the *gzhung lug rgyab mdun*, which required five government subjects to accompany some 500 government sheep to Kargil, Ladakh and exchange loads of salt for grain, flour, tea, and apricots to be delivered over to the Ruthog District Commissioner. The subjects had to consume their own food on the way.

For monastic subjects, there were various tithes, like the *gsum bcu khag gcig*, which required giving over one goat or sheep from one's herd for every thirty owned. There were also specially named tithes or payments of butter. Finally, there was work, on demand, in agriculture, construction of buildings, and animal care, for which no pay or food was provided. It is difficult to get a sense of what proportion of production went into taxes in former times; but Ruthog subjects may have been the poorest of all the populations I visited in Western Tibet. Older houses still standing were small and of poor condition, and both grazing and arable land are extremely limited.

3 Tholing

The second case concerns the small village of Tholing in the ancient kingdom of Guge, clustered around the famous Tholing monastery, one of the centres of Tibetan Buddhism in the "Second Diffusion". Seeing Guge now, it is difficult to imagine how a region so handicapped by its geographical isolation and poverty of natural resources once supported a major cultural efflorescence. Perhaps the later collapse of this area was aided by climatic changes or a drop in the level of the Sutlej River. But such conjectures are beyond the scope of this paper.

The questions of interest revolve around the possibilities for generalisation from the case of one small village and for constructing explanatory models of its circumstances. That is, how representative were the land and taxation circumstances of Tholing compared to Guge's fifty-five other small villages and what gave rise to them? Simple logic leads one to infer that differences must have existed in the content and direction of taxation obligations. Tholing villagers were responsible for the support of the major religious institution in the district, which retained a certain aura from its past glories and certainly was very expensive to maintain. Other villages had fewer responsibilities to the monastery, which probably were counterbalanced by greater obligations to government offices. More significant, Tholing's system of land rights seems atypical in the Tibetan context. To be specific, none of the villagers had any permanent or hereditary rights to land at all; all were tenants on monastery lands in an unstable status equivalent to Central Tibet's *dud chung rten med*. This leads to further questions. Was such tenancy widespread in Guge? Did its presence correlate with any particular fact of a village's history or any feature of its economic life, such as the nature of its tax obligations? And was the pattern equally widespread among nomads? While we know that Tholing monastery also rented grazing lands to nomads, those nomads also may have held more permanent titles to land from other sources.

3.1 *Control of the Land and Recipients of Taxation*

In Tholing, the monastery directly controlled all sources of productive property, including arable land. Technically, a certain portion of its lands were said to be designated as *khral zhing* and were said to constitute nine full taxpayer holdings. However, there were no *khral pa* taxpayers in the 20th century, and all this land was loaned out to people on so-called *'bogs ma* tenancy arrangements. The monastery held 500 *khal* of land, highlands and lowlands, in addition to large herds of sheep, milk cattle, plough animals, agricultural tools, and so on. Subjects of the monastery received land to cultivate according to the number of workers in their families. The allotment was somewhat less than 3 *khal* of land per adult worker aged fifteen to sixty, up to a maximum of 12 *khal*. Because of this system, a family would farm changing amounts and different parcels of land over its developmental history.

It is unclear how Tholing exercised control over its subjects. One elderly man recalled a situation which suggested that relations between lord and subject were quite tenuous in these border regions, far weaker than the circumstances reported for Central Tibet (Goldstein 1986: 85, 88). This man's father had lived in Diya, on the Indian border of Spiti, and was the *mi ser* of a Kagyupa religious institution. But he was overwhelmed by debts and unable to meet his tax obligations, so he abandoned that property. The father and three sons then moved to Tholing, where they took up a scant, one-quarter tenancy share of 3 *khal* of land. In this case the move severed the relationship: there were no ties maintained with or payments owed to their former lord.

As this man also recalled, such *'bogs ma* land was readily available in Tholing at that time. The 3 *khal* were, not surprisingly, wholly inadequate. They probably were equal to less than one acre of land and took less than two days to plough (see fn. 4 above). However, when the sons reached age fifteen, they received additional parcels.

3.2 *Traditional Classes of Tholing Social Structure*

Tholing village belonged to one of two Guge *rdzong*, which, in turn, stood under the jurisdiction of the *sgar dpon* in the provincial capital.[5] Gartok was not too distant but difficult to reach, being situated on the other side of remote country and a series of 5,000 metre passes. Both *rdzong* and provincial offices were led by temporary central government appointees far removed socially from their subjects. There were also three hereditary chiefs in nearby villages, two descended from the ancient rulers of Guge and one from a noble family that had emigrated from Central Tibet. The power of these chiefs was quite restricted. They were considered lords (*dpon po*), as they held relatively large (for the region), hereditary parcels of land, rights of corvée labour over villagers for the cultivation of those lands, and rights to punish recalcitrant workers. They also served as representatives of the central government—although over an area no larger than a cluster of villages, or *tsho*. At the same time, they themselves owed tax to the government and were, in a sense, no more than large-holder government taxpayers (*gzhung rgyugs pa khral pa*).

Tholing village was, as stated above, comprised only of tenant farmers, or *'bogs ma* holders, described as *chos gzhis rten med*. Families held no more than temporary rights to land, and only so long as their members aged fifteen to sixty could work and meet their share of corvée and tax obligations to the monastery. As soon as a man or woman turned age sixty, the monastery took one parcel away from the family. Ordinary families had no major agricultural tools or plough animals and would have to rent these from the monastery as well, with the payment made in animal feed. There seem to have been no permanently resident artisan families or other workers of any kind.

3.3 *The Logic and Varieties of Tax Payments*

The list of taxes was divided into "inner taxes" (*nang khral*) on the rented monastery fields and ten kinds of "outer taxes" (abbreviated as *phyi khral bcu*). Included within the inner taxes was rent on the land, in the amount of 1 *khal* of grain for every 3 *khal* planted. There also was work on estate lands controlled directly by the monastery. This involved work at planting, at harvest, in manuring, and in irrigating the fields. In addition, there was time spent taking the monastery animals out to and bringing them back from pasture areas. Several persons debated the amount of labour-time this occupied each year, with one person suggesting a full month, but the question seems irresolvable. The

5 In 1956, the two traditional *rdzong* of Tsaparang and Dawa were joined into the administrative office of Tsanda.

subjects would be supervised by a monastery steward (*gnyer pa*) who had the right to and would punish poor work.

Tholing subjects further were obliged to perform diverse domestic services for the monastery throughout the year: fetching water for the monks, tending cooking fires, and so on. Every day, the villagers had to send three among its number to perform these services. On major holidays, the demand for workers skyrocketed. Mönlam, for example, required twenty Tholing villagers for twenty days.[6] These services were a heavy burden, as might be indicated by the fact that Tholing was one of the largest monasteries in Ngari and was situated amidst villages which were small and impoverished. In the first half of the 20th century, there were between sixty and seventy monks in the monastery and seventy to eighty people in Tholing, the village which held the greatest service responsibilities.

On days that people devoted to monastery service they received some food (tea, soup, and one meal), and for a month's labour they received 15 *bre* measures of grain (equivalent to almost 10 kilograms). If they had to leave the village in the service of the monastery, they received half a *bre* of tsampa, plus some butter. There were no such arrangements for in-village labour on the monastery's fields, when people were expected to provide their own food.

The outer taxes were all-encompassing, involving various tithes, a bewildering variety of object taxes, a considerable amount of corvée services, and so on. Some of these taxes were allocated to a single village, falling upon village households according to the number of their workers granted a tenancy share, some were shared with a few other villages, and some were pooled among a number of village clusters. Some were assessed once annually; others recurred throughout the year. The taxes are so complicated that even with the aid of any still-extant tax documents, it would be difficult to assess the costs to a given Tholing household. I list them to add another example of the nature and scope of traditional tax obligations.

1. *tshwa shod*. A tax on the salt trade. One out of every ten measures of salt which were traded had to be paid to the government.
2. *gzhung tshong*. This was a corvée tax, which involved providing periodic transport to what now is the capital of Ngari province, Senge Khambab (Ch. Shiquanhe). Going there involved five days or five stations of travel, each station being a one-day round-trip yak journey. Those subjects who

6 Specifically, eight people to collect water, eight people to prepare tea, two people to help set up tables and bedding, one person to keep track of the time, and one person to guard over items which might be stolen—who was watched in turn by a monastery subject from another village.

lacked pack animals had to rent them from the monastery, for a payment in fodder (grass).

3. *sa skyod 'bum pa*. Each year villagers were obliged to contribute grain to a religious festival held concurrently in monasteries of the province. This festival was designed to ensure a good harvest, animal welfare, and good fortune for humans. Twelve pack animals would arrive in the administrative centre to collect the requisite grain and other tax items and then distribute them to the designated religious institutions.
4. *a drung khral*. This was a tax to support the services of the government messenger and mail carrier. Tholing villagers were periodically responsible for providing a horse for the mail carrier and all his food. When the need for payment of this tax arose, all *'bogs ma* holders would join together and contribute an amount according to the size of their shares.
5. *brgya phog pa*. This was a tax underwriting the salary of the District Commissioner. Taxpayers had to provide a host of goods necessary to his position, the pack animals to transport them to him, and food and lodging for the person accompanying the animals.
6. *mar 'bras*. This was one of two taxes which involved a division of labour between the two Guge districts. Dawa *rdzong* collected butter and grain from its subjects and transported these items to Tsaparang *rdzong* for the annual Mönlam festival. The monastery gave some payment for the grain and butter, but it is not recalled how much.
7. *shing dpon*. The subjects of Tsaparang *rdzong* collected wood and provided the animals and facilities to bring the wood to the local monasteries. Unlike the butter and grain described above, there was no payment made for this.
8. *sa mtshams skor khral*. This was a major corvée tax shared among four *tsho*, including six households in the *tsho* to which Tholing belonged. This tax accrued when the two District Commissioners and the government's representative in Gartok and their retinues had to patrol the border with India. The subjects of the designated *tsho* had to provide the requisite horses, pack animals, and their drivers.
9. *shing tog phar sgrub*. There was a favoured variety of apricots, known as Ngari Khambu, but grown in Ladakh. The central government used to transport them to Lhasa. Thus the subjects of this region annually were required to send a certain number of pack animals and drivers to bring the apricots, station by station, on the long route from Ladakh to Gyanima market, which is located outside of Guge, west of Mt Kailas.
10. *gar zhwa dpon po*. An official from Lahul, India would visit the major trade marts of Gartok, Gyanima and so on each autumn with a retinue of

twelve to fifteen men. Guge subjects were obliged to provide horses for the group once they crossed the Shipki pass into Tibet. Fifteen Tholing villagers took ten of their horses (or rented horses) on one station of this route—both on the way out to the trade marts and on the way back to India. Subjects were obliged to provide their own food, although they were also recompensed by one Indian rupee for each horse and a slightly smaller payment for each person attending the group.

As the list of taxes show, heavy corvée obligations were met in Tholing without the existence of a wealthy landholding and animal-owning peasant class. The animals used in transport could be—and, it seems, mostly were—rented from the monastery for simple payments involving animal feed. Those animals were raised as part of regular peasant duties on the estate. This appears to have been the case in Ruthog as well, where government taxpayers were obliged to lead *rdzong*-owned carrier sheep on long trading trips to Ladakh, with trading profits accruing to the *rdzong*. Goldstein has argued that the class of *khral pa* taxpayers served to fulfil heavy corvée carrying obligations: "They were given larger economic resources from which they were expected to generate the economic surplus necessary to maintain the animals and other expenses implicit in that tax" (1971: 27). Reliance on a class of corvée taxpayers who privately owned the transport animals may, in fact, have been the more effective system. This is because livestock owned by a lord or institution but reared by its subject labour force were more likely to receive poorer treatment and be in poorer condition (cf. Kula 1976: 48 on Poland).[7] Nonetheless transport could be and was accomplished without giving peasants control over large hereditary parcels of land and substantial economic resources.

This returns us to questions raised at the outset of the section. Why did Tholing rely exclusively on tenant farmers rather than the sort of hereditarily based taxpayers found not only in Central Tibet but also in the Purang valley? Perhaps it was because Tholing villagers were subjects of a monastery and had comparatively minor external corvée responsibilities, although this cannot be proven with the data at hand. Perhaps a contributing factor was the poverty of the region, which made it difficult to maintain both large landholding *khral pa* taxpayers and a large enough class of landless workers to meet the needs of the monks. Perhaps the conjuncture of land scarcity, a surfeit of potential workers,

7 In many cases this problem appears to have been anticipated and compensated for by contracting the animals out to individual peasant households on *skyed med shi med* arrangements. This meant that the family was able to keep any natural increase in the herd but had to make up any losses due to animal deaths. The Ruthog monasteries made such arrangements with their subjects, but, if the scarcity of family animal holdings is any indication, Tholing Gompa did not.

and political instability following the collapse of Guge made it easy to chip away at *khral pa* rights and reduce the peasants to a class of landless dependents. The way in which the land is classified suggests that a *khral pa* class may have existed in the past. But only further research, historical and comparative, can resolve these questions.

4 Purang Villages

Purang is the most productive agricultural region in Ngari, with perhaps twelve times the arable land as the districts of Ruthog and Guge. Unlike Ruthog and Guge, the land supported many purely farming villages, which were situated in an arid valley cut by the Karnali River and watered by streams from Memo Nani mountain. There were also pastoralists occupying highlands to the north of Memo Nani, but few *sa ma 'brog*, who require ready access to both pastoral and agricultural ecozones. The relatively greater wealth and greater density of population in the Purang valley surely are responsible for the more elaborate social stratification and for a taxation system more closely resembling those described for Central Tibet.

4.1 *Control of the Land and Recipients of Taxation*

There were several major landlords in the Purang valley. As elsewhere, the central government directly controlled a considerable share of the land. The other major landholders fell under the category of monastic-religious institutions, including the great Simbiling (Phyag pa gling) complex, located in an imposing site above the town of Purang. Smaller institutions, like Tashi Gang monastery, which was Sakya in sect, also held land in the region. Yet another major landlord was a branch of the Drukpa Kagyu sect, which maintained its summer headquarters in Darchen, fronting the pilgrimage trail around Mt Kailas. This estate was administered by clerics from Bhutan, and the way in which it gained control of land in far Western Tibet is discussed below.

Some of the villages belonged in their entirely to one of these landlords, but there were other villages whose memberships were divided among government and monastic estates. Also, the memberships of a few villages owed tax to several monastic institutions, although one of the monasteries clearly was dominant—in its control over local lands and its rights over local people—and readily identified as such. It is as if a large number of tax beneficiaries were vying for the support of a limited population in Purang.

4.2 *Traditional Classes of Purang Social Structure*

By the middle of the 20th century there remained just two large landed families in the Purang region. They are reported to have had their own subjects and to have served the government in an administrative role. Thus they supported themselves on a portion of the taxes they collected and on the labour of their subjects on their farms. As in Ruthog and Guge, however, they did not form a separate class of nobles and seem to have only limited wealth and influence in the region.

The vast majority of the agriculturalists in Purang were taxpayers, holding hereditary rights to fixed parcels of land and tax obligations concordant with their land holdings. They were subdivided into three categories. There were the government taxpayers (*gzhung rgyugs pa khral pa*), who had the greatest amounts of land and the heaviest taxation responsibilities. For them, a full tax holding (*khral pa gang po*) consisted of approximately 80 *khal* of land, although numerous taxpayers had just a half or a quarter of that amount—with correspondingly reduced tax obligations.[8]

A second type of government taxpayer was known as *rgyal ba*. This status was designed for the rapid staffing of an army in the event of war. Such people owed a special war tax (*dmag khral*), which obliged them to provide one soldier, either a son or a paid substitute, and all his equipment and expenses, when war broke out. Since there had been no military conscription in Purang in the 20th century there was no call for the tax, and people were obliged only to meet general obligations to the *rdzong*. And since their ordinary tax obligations were lighter than the other type of government taxpayer, the *rgyal ba* held less land: around 60 *khal* for a full tax holding. The third and largest set of taxpayers were subjects of the monasteries, for whom a full tax holding was also approximately 60 *khal*. As with the other taxpayer statuses, however, many households did not hold full tax shares, but part shares, such as 40 and even as few as 20 *khal*. There were also a small number of beggars and artisans, who paid virtually no tax or no tax whatsoever, and had little influence on the social life of the region.

Landlords in Purang seem to have exercised greater control over their taxpayers than was the case for the subjects of Ruthog and Guge. Here we find for the first time subjects having to ask permission to marry and complex negotiations having to be made if a woman of one lord was to marry and move

8 In the Purang valley, the calculus was in terms of *'bor*, which are a measurement equivalent to *khal*.

to the house of a man of another lord. This, however, was not a problem that arose often. Formal marriages with postmarital residential shifts seem mostly to have been the province of the wealthiest taxpayers on whom the lords depended the most.

4.3 *The Logic and Varieties of Tax Payments*

The subjects of the various monasteries and their organisational divisions were obliged to pay both inner and outer taxes. The inner taxes pertained to work for the monastery, mostly on the monastery lands. While approximately half the estate's land was in the hands of taxpayers, the other half was under the direct control of the monastery. Duties on the land were calculated and allocated according to the concept of the full taxpaying unit. The full unit for these taxpayers, as noted above, was 60 *khal* of land—well-irrigated, prime land in the Purang valley, equivalent to perhaps 14 acres. The holder of a full unit was obliged to send one man or woman to carry out agricultural work for the monastery for an entire year. If a household held only 40 *khal*, it would have to send one person for a portion of the year, and less time would be required of still-smaller holdings. At certain times the monastery would call upon three or four people for work, following upon which no one would have to go for the next three or four days. Another obligation was the collection of wood: each full taxpaying unit was obliged to collect wood for four days every year—but had to bring back an enormous quantity on each such day. If the wood did not suffice for the year, monastery subjects would be obliged to deliver more whenever needed. This could happen frequently in a monastery the size of Simbiling.

Monastery subjects participated in three difficult outer taxes, owed by all Purang taxpayer villagers. The difference was that they devoted fewer days and animals to these taxes than the government subjects, particularly the *gzhung rgyugs pa* category. These taxes primarily involved transporting the government's profits from trade in the region. Government subjects, furthermore, were continually on call for this sort of work, having to provide transport whenever someone arrived at the *rdzong* with a government pass.

The three taxes were organised around three occasions in which major numbers of transport animals were required. First was the annual visit of the government trade agent. When he came to the region, villager households had to provide grass for his horses and lodging and food for him and his party. They also had to provide pack animals to carry his loads to and from Barkha, below Mt Kailas and located close to many of the summer trade marts in the region. While Barkha was considered the next station for transport, or corvée, obligations, the round-trip took each man and his animals three days. The second transport tax was owed to the government's representative in Gartok. He came annually to Purang, whereupon village households were obliged to provide him a certain amount of food, as well as carrying his profits from regional trade all the way back to Gartok. The third and heaviest tax involved transporting all the summer's proceeds from government taxes on border trade. Village households had to carry the profits from five trade marts in the Mt Kailas and Lake Manasarowar area. These profits were partly, but not entirely cash, which is light in weight, but also Indian sugar, wooden bowls and the like. These taxes arose primarily in the busy summer months, demanding different numbers of pack animals and drivers from year to year. They were not terribly heavy for the monastic subjects; the average taxpayer household's share was perhaps eight transport trips per year. Government subjects assumed the major burden of these taxes, with a workload perhaps double that of their monastic counterparts.

There were also a few smaller taxes. Among them was the requirement to buy tea from the government monopoly. The price was said to be double what it would be on the local market, and households with a full taxpaying allotment were required to purchase about 3 kilograms of tea, although only once a year. These forced sales were especially problematic because people lacked cash; thus they had to sell some food or goods to get the necessary money.

5 Part IV: Khochar Village

5.1 *Control of the Land and Recipients of Taxation*

All but one Khochar village household belonged to the Drukpa Kagyu sect of Bhutan; they paid taxes to and were governed by hierarchs sent from Bhutan. Yet because this agency was present only in summer, they were under the direct jurisdiction of the Purang District Commissioner and the government's representative in Gartok for much of the year. Thus it was government officials who often played the major role and interceded, when necessary, in the affairs of the village. Concordantly, considerable taxes in food and corvée labour were paid to the government, in addition to the complex assessments of food, labour, and corvée transport owed to the Drukpa Labrang. At the same time, a certain amount of labour and food was provided to the famous Khochar monastery, located in the centre of the village, and a token amount of firewood had to be given over to Simbiling monastery. All this made for an elaborate, overlapping set of obligations to different agencies.

The Drukpa sect gained a place in this region during the early 17th century, at a time when Ngari was under the control of Ladakh. During this period, one devout Drukpa lama is said to have set up a small hermitage near Mt Kailas. The king of Ladakh granted him a number of villages, including Khochar, for his support. When Tibet wrested control over Ngari these rights were not abrogated. Under the patronage of the Fifth Dalai Lama, titles to land were granted in a number of villages along the major pilgrimage route. Over time, the establishment near Mt Kailas, known as Darchen, grew, as did the costs of maintaining it.

These arrangements continued unbroken until 1959. Beginning in 1952, villagers expressed resistance to paying taxes to the Drukpa establishment. Yet the latter was able to successfully exert its authority until the major land reforms and the elimination of all such taxation arrangements in Tibet.

5.2 *Traditional Classes of Khochar Social Structure*

The majority of Khochar villagers were classed as *khral pa* taxpayers: thirty-four households out of fifty-six, or 61 per cent, according to records compiled in 1959. All but one taxpayer household were the subjects of the Drukpa establishment in Darchen; that one was a government *rgyal ba* subject, the category which owed army tax in event of war, as was found elsewhere in Purang valley. Most of these households (twenty-one) held full tax allotments of approximately 60 *khal* of agricultural land (in one case a one-and-one-half share). Another two households held what were considered three-quarter allotments of land, ten households held one-half allotments, while one household had only a one-quarter allotment.

Another sixteen households, known as *grong chung*, or "small households", rented land and houses, mostly from *khral pa* taxpayers to whom they were related, and performed occasional labour for wages. They were described as the *mi khungs* of the higher status taxpayers, a term Goldstein has translated as being under the power of or belonging to another (1986: 86). Finally, there were a small number of people who held the status of "life servants" (*tshe g.yog*). There were four single individuals or couples in 1959, in the households of very wealthy taxpayers who were considered their employers (more precisely, *sbyin bdag*). Servants, male and female, helped out the taxpayer household in agriculture and in domestic service around the year. For this they were given a small room in the house, full meals on workdays, and some food the remainder of the year. Life servants formed a self-perpetuating, permanent class of society, in that their children were born as servants as well. This was congruent with the social discrimination against them: other people would neither marry nor share plates with them and considered them to be of inferior heredity. Their economic position was highly unstable, however, as they could be and were dismissed for presumed wrongdoing. They also could leave of their own accord, when they wished. Finally, there were two households of ironworkers (*mgar ba*), to whom even more deeply grounded norms of separation in marriage and commensality applied. This group faced predictably greater discrimination; they were said to be of mixed Indian and Tibetan descent and thought to be physically unclean.

5.3 *The Logic and Varieties of Tax Payments*

Khochar villagers cited a proverb that sums up how taxes were regarded. That is, however difficult, paying taxes gave people a standing in society and a house and fields to pass from father to son. Without tax fields, everything was lost—not least of which was social respect. Taxes in Khochar were not tremendously onerous, however. One local chronicle, which was compiled in 1959, estimates that a full taxpayer household paid the equivalent of 87 *khal* of grain for its total annual obligation (this figure incorporates grain, labour, object, and money taxes). Those 87 *khal* were equivalent to between 20 and 40 per cent of annual production and were considerably less than the taxes reportedly paid in Central Tibet. There taxation reportedly could reach two thirds and even up to three quarters of annual income (Survey 1984: 274–83).[9] It should be noted that total taxation demands were reported as roughly equivalent in the two small villages nearest Khochar: Sherwa, which included subjects of the Drukpa Labrang, and Gangtse, which included Simbiling subjects.

Khochar villagers made their major tax payments to the Drukpa Labrang in Darchen—all but the one *rgyal ba* household—and this was estimated to occupy 37 per cent of their total tax burden. Darchen required only token taxes in kind but considerable labour. Thus the closest equivalent to a land tax was annual payments in tsampa, for which the taxpayer would receive rights to a small quantity of wool in return. A full taxpaying household annually provided 4 *khal* of tsampa to Darchen Labrang and received the wool of four sheep—which they also were obliged to raise in the village.

The major inner taxes revolved around corvée transport obligations. The 1959 chronicle estimates that some twenty-five animal days were spent every year ferrying the Drukpa party and their goods from the Indian border up the Purang valley to Darchen and back again. Yet even these taxes were regarded as relatively light, so that the pack animals "could grow hair on their backs", as was said.[10] Although the number of trips made, their timing, and the number of animals required varied annually, one can reconstruct a hypothetical year's schedule:

---

9 This may be an exaggeration; it is high even by the standards of feudal Europe (Postan and Hatcher 1978: 32).

10 Although people also said that the obligation more than doubled since it was instituted, presumptively at some time during the 17th century.

> In springtime, Khochar taxpayers were obliged to assemble some ninety yak or yak crossbreeds—approximately three pack animals per household—plus a half-dozen riding horses to transport the Bhutanese representative, his retinue, and goods from Garbyang, India to Dowa village, further up the pilgrimage road toward Mt Kailas. In mid-summer another set of large pack animals—perhaps sixty yaks—would be required, together with a few horses, to carry additional items to the Labrang. And again in autumn, taxpayers would have to provide some fifty yaks, a half-dozen horses and seven human bearers to bring the Drukpa representative, his retinue, and goods from Dowa to the border again. If the steward, for example, left later in the year, it would be necessary to send another set of horses for his return journey. On these trips men were required to supervise the animals, to carry wood, and do the cooking. All food and cooking materials had to be taken on the road from the Khochar taxpaying households. And adding to the complications of the journey was the need to carry an amount of fodder for the pack animals, for the road passed through arid countryside.

As part of their taxes to the central Tibetan government, Khochar was required to provide corvée transport for the Purang District Commissioner and the government's representative in Gartok, which the chronicle of 1959 estimated cost every full taxpayer allotment eleven animal-days of work annually. Some of this transport appears to have involved sheep, which are less costly to maintain than the yak and horses used to ferry the Drukpa retinue toward Darchen and back again. These transport obligations took Khochar villagers several days away, to Barkha station.

These corvée obligations accrued to the village as a whole and were parcelled out among the various taxpayers according to their shares in land. Again, fodder was needed for the animals and food for the herdsmen. Each full taxpayer was therefore obliged to contribute a large amount of grain (8 to 12 *khal* each year) to a collective fund for food used on such journeys, and each time transport was required, two among the full taxpayer households were obliged to collect grass fodder for the animals. Finally, the officials from Barkha made an annual trip to Khochar, where they were stationed for a period each summer to collect taxes.[11] At that time, their accommodation, food, and fodder for their

11 It was not made clear what taxes these officials were collecting. Khochar, however, is the first major village beyond the Nepalese border, through which considerable amounts of Nepalese grain flowed. Possibly these officials were collecting taxes on trade.

animals had to be provided—obligations similarly pooled among the villagers. This cost approximately 8 to 10 *khal* of grain per full allotment taxpayer.

Finally, when the Purang district administration needed transport, Khochar village taxpayers could be called upon to provide animals. It might happen that the *rdzong* sent its own animals, in which case they would have to provide grass. Even though they were not subjects of Purang and paid no direct tax to them, they were also obliged to provide food and lodging when the District Commissioner visited in the village. It was estimated that this would happen five times a year, with the associated obligations rotating among village households.

Another part of their inner taxes was the labour which Khochar taxpayers were obliged to provide on estate lands held by Darchen Labrang and situated within the village. While this amounted to only 60 *khal* of land, villagers still were responsible for every aspect of their cultivation. Thus they were expected to prepare and apply fertiliser to the fields. At planting time, every full taxpayer had to contribute one plough animal and four workers, so that all the fields could be planted in a day. At harvest time, one worker per household would be expected to labour from three to five days, and one yak or yak crossbreed would be pressed into service for three days to thresh the grain. The responsibilities of partial taxpayers were proportionately reduced, so, for example, one person from a half-allotment household would join in the harvesting for two days, and the quarter-allotment taxpayer would work in alternate years. The combination of agricultural labour and the work expended on corvée trips for Darchen Labrang was estimated as costing each full taxpayer forty-five person-work days per year.

Finally, there were some 55 *khal* of Khochar monastery land in the village. This was planted and harvested by villagers, who received food from the monastery on the day they worked. The chores were rotated, following general taxpayer status in the village (a full share of work from a full allotment, a half share of work from a half allotment, and so forth), although this seems not to have formed a part of the official Khochar tax responsibilities. That is, work for Khochar monastery was described as "voluntary" and as not supported by external coercion. The primary organisational responsibilities lay with the family members of the two monks currently serving as monastery stewards (*gnyer pa*, which involved a two-year term).[12] Village households were also responsible for making tea for the monastery six times a year. This required

12 The Khochar monastery, of the Sakya sect, recruited its monks from the village. Each village household with at least two sons was required to deliver one over to be a monk in the monastery.

contributions of firewood, tea, and work time. It also seems that butter was given to the monastery. A document listing "Income and Expenditures in 1958" reports receipt of a large amount (seemingly 80 kilograms) from villagers in 1958, but it is not clear how this was assessed.

The small households were obliged to help the taxpayers in agriculture, mostly during the period of heaviest demand at harvest time, and in other chores of property maintenance. Thus they threshed grain, fertilised fields, whitewashed houses, and so forth, along with taxpayer families. During their work days—the number of which is unclear—they would be given food and would sleep in the taxpayer's house. Some of the more generous taxpayers are said to have fed their dependents during those days as well. Each worker also would be given a payment of 3 *khal* of grain after the harvest (*ston gla khal gsum*). Finally, a number of the wealthiest taxpayers had servants, who carried out occasional field and domestic labour for them.

5.4 *Insufficiencies of Production in Khochar*

Although tax obligations in Khochar were not exceedingly heavy compared to other villages in Tibet, and although full taxpayers held what seems to be a respectable amount of land, most of the villagers could be considered poor. Certainly none could be considered rich. This is why even the wealthiest taxpayers with servants were classed no higher than the middle (*'bring ba*) serf class at the onset of land reforms in 1959. In that year too, thirty-two households were recorded as having taken out grain loans. The Khochar monastery seems to have been the main lender; for 1958, it was able to collect 481 *khal* of grain from its loans, including the return of principal and interest payments. In addition it acquired 80 *khal* of grain from rented land and 120 *khal* of grain profits from its own cultivated fields.

Food did not last the year-round for these villagers, and food shortages led many people to go south in the winter. The members of small households suffered particularly from lack of food, and many lacked adequate clothing for harsh weather. Because they relied on meals from taxpayers during workdays, the lack of work during the winter slack season could mean serious hardship for them. Thus they were most likely to pack up after the autumn harvest was over. They would seek odd jobs in villages to the south, where they might card wool, tan skins, or apply manure to the fields of lower-lying hill villages with longer growing seasons. If possible, they would trek on to pilgrimage sites. Some among the taxpayers with partial allotments—quarter and even half shares—had trouble meeting their tax obligations. They too would pack up in winter, to look for work, sometimes trying to conceal this by saying they were going on pilgrimage. Some would never return, leaving their land to be redistributed in the village. Even some middle-level taxpayers would leave in the winter, due to the absence of adequate food and harsh weather. The wealthier a family was, the likelier it would be to spend the winter seeing the holy sites in Nepal and India.

That grain would be insufficient is obvious when one considers the demographics of the village. In 1959, there were approximately 500 people in Khochar and the two small villages near it, but only 2,124 *khal* under cultivation. This averages out to 4.24 *khal* per person. So few *khal* of land could not possibly produce enough food in a bad agricultural year, when it is estimated that production was only four times the grain sown. Thus most taxpayers and even more the small households and servants were balanced on the economic margins, alternating between conditions of bare sufficiency of production and periodic insufficiencies.

The fact is that this sort of situation commonly has confronted traditional peasants in past and present. For one pertinent example, villagers settled just a few hours' walk across the border in northwest Nepal continue to live under similar conditions. Some villages are more favoured than others and have relatively greater economic security, but the inhabitants of most live in circumstances of chronic food shortages and face extraordinary burdens of agricultural debt. The situation in modern Nepal is the product of different economic and social conditions and a different history from Tibet, which I lack the space to discuss here. What I would like to devote consideration to is why the socio-economic dynamic of small peasant villages in Western Tibet took the shape that it did, the ways in which it was similar to that of other pre-modern agrarian societies, particularly in well-studied Europe, and what factors perpetuated the low level of productivity and impediments to positive change.

6 Discussion and Conclusions

Western Tibet in the first part of the 20th century offers an example of a traditional agrarian society which bears many resemblances to the feudal systems of pre-modern Europe. There also are many differences between Tibet as it was under the Dalai Lamas and feudalism as classically depicted—which we know to follow a model abstracted from the European experience. Among commonly cited features of European feudalism which do not apply to Tibet are parcellised sovereignty or feudal decentralisation and the associated fragmentation of authority, which culminated in limited state intervention in economic life (cf. Goldstein 1986: 82). Nor do we find in Tibet strong military, private armies, and land granted specifically for military service. Moreover, the personal element in ties of dependence between lord and subject seem much attenuated in Tibet, in comparison to descriptions of Europe. Thus traditional Tibet seems to differ in fundamental ways—not only cultural but also structural—from the European feudal society which Marc Bloch described as a "hierarchically-organized system of peasant subjection and military vassalage" (1961: 247).

Recently it has been argued that these classic, political-legal definitional criteria are derivative from what may be more central features of the feudal dynamic (cf. Wickham 1985: 169). When we examine the comparative literature we find that societies which historians analyse in terms of a feudal model share other, possibly more fundamental, political and economic attributes. Invariably such societies are agrarian in nature, they also are "traditional" or "pre-modern" in their economies. They manifest what might be termed a "natural economy", characterised by low levels of productivity and capable of little more than basic reproduction (Kula 1976: 9, 17). As Carrasco finds for Tibet, such societies are "only to a limited extent a money economy. Most exchanges take place in the form of direct exchanges of services, of goods [...] the exchanges follow the patterns determined by the existing social structure rather than by the demands of a market" (1959: 84). For this and other reasons, peasants in such societies are obliged to pay much of their taxes and rent in-kind and in the form of labour service. The scarcity of money, together with limited access to markets, thus becomes associated with an often byzantine hodgepodge of taxes in services and kind, as was illustrated in this paper and has marked the literature on Tibet.[13] It is for similar reasons that the name for equally multifarious taxes in France, *banalités*, has come to refer to triviality in French and in its English derivative (Bloch 1961: 251). Taxation of this kind has further consequences, which will be discussed below.

Perhaps the most important parallel between the socio-economic system of early 20th century Tibet and feudal Europe is how each created conditions which inhibited the further development of factors of production (Bray 1986: 176). Such systems have their own intrinsic logic and momentum which rationalise what to an outsider may seem to be limitations and contradictions. Thus, given the level of socio-economic development, there seemed to be great logic

13 Carrasco describes this as "a multiplicity of taxes, a specific tax or labor service being required for practically every need of the state, and a direct relation between the source of revenue and the end to which it applied, particular items of revenue being used to meet particular expenses" (1959: 85).

in relying on simple peasants and their labour services to run a government. As Goldstein notes:

> The *miser* system prevalent in Tibet, consequently, was intrinsically linked with economic production and labor. It was an efficient system of economic exploitation that guaranteed the country's religious and secular elites both land resources and a permanent and secure labor force to cultivate that land without burdening them with any day-to-day direct responsibility for the *miser's* subsistence.
>
> GOLDSTEIN 1986: 90

Yet this system could be considered problematic in that it precluded actions on the part of the peasants which would contribute to agricultural intensification and raise levels of production. For that matter, such systems characteristically fail to encourage investments of this kind on the part of land-owning bodies. I can offer some examples of concrete consequences from the commentaries provided to me by Western Tibetan villagers.

First, land reclamation and thus expansion of agriculture seem to have been negatively sanctioned in every area I surveyed. There was a positive restriction on using land which was not enumerated in the rarely revised tax documents. Accordingly, one can only assume that land use was frozen at some time in the past, impeding efforts at supplementing production to insure against shortfalls in lean years—let alone to place a regular grain surplus in the hands of the peasants. In Central Tibet, there were instances of government sponsorship of reclamation of fallow land, seemingly at the advice of the Amban in Lhasa (Goldstein 1971: 13). Carrasco also mentions provisions for the allotment of land to new settlers in certain areas (1959: 20) But the otherwise pervasive restrictions on land reclamation, even if justified by efforts to retain the land under official control, were particularly insidious, as they eliminated the simplest avenue to increased production.

Second, major obstacles seem to have been built up against small-scale trade. Trade, it should be noted, was the one factor which has saved land-short Tibetan speakers on the Nepalese side of the border. The ethnic Tibetans of northwest Nepal, for example, earned annual profits of twelve times their initial investment during the first half of this century (Levine 1988a: 225) By contrast, all but the wealthiest households in Ruthog, Guge, Purang, and Khochar villages did not engage in trade. Men would travel to trade marts in the course of corvée labour for their landlord, yet fail to trade themselves. Men without such corvée obligations would rarely cross the Indian or Nepalese border for trade. As in feudal Europe, people would sell just enough produce or handicrafts to meet their tax obligations.

Kula has argued that feudalism in Poland led inexorably either to the diminution of peasant plots or amplification of tax obligations until the ratio of persons to land reached a sub-optimal level, that is, land barely enough to feed a family in good agricultural years (1976: 66). Others suggest that these sorts of processes are not so much the outcome of class relations as of demographic factors (Postan and Hatcher 1978). Without adequate historical data one cannot determine whether such processes occurred in Tibet and, if they did, what the underlying causes might be. There is no doubt, however, of a similar outcome in Western Tibet: inadequate land for all but a small portion of the peasant population, leading to chronic indebtedness.

It is accurate to speak of a heavy load of debt shared among most peasant subjects.[14] In grain-short years, people would have to borrow, to feed their families or meet tax obligations. Such was the recollection of a number of people to whom I spoke. Interest rates were not tremendously usurious, at twenty to twenty-five per cent per annum. Yet the same factors that produced grain shortages in one year were likely to produce grain shortages the next, so that most Western Tibetans with smaller allotments became caught in a spiral of debt they could not repay. Thus in Khochar we find that 57 per cent of households had taken out some sort of loan in 1958; an uncertain number of households repaid these loans promptly in 1959. A man from the area of Purang closest to the Indian border estimated a far higher rate of indebtedness there, possibly because the level of taxation was higher.

The result of these combined constraints was the perpetuation of a class of peasants producing only for subsistence, who invested only enough labour to meet immediate needs.[15] Labour tax obligations may have further complicated these efforts. In Western Tibet, the time of peak demand for labour service, corvée transport, and the like was summer. Competing work obligations surely undermined attempts to gain the fullest yield from the household's own plots of land and often placed heavy demands on transport animals, leaving them in poor condition.

---

14 The major beneficiaries of peasant debt were the landlords who loaned grain, as noted above. By contrast, in Nepal, debt divided the peasantry. There were a few households who won extraordinary profits from their lending activities and hoarded grain and a great majority who slowly fell deeper and deeper into debt and lacked adequate food for their families (Levine 1988b).

15 Seemingly the same approach to domestic economy that Chayanov described for the Russian peasantry (1966).

All of these factors militated against improvements in agriculture, the production of a surplus, and the creation of other income to supplement an agricultural regime subject to natural constraints of altitude, a correspondingly limited growing season, and aridity. In this way, through a kind of positive feedback, these factors supported the persistence of a subsistence, pre-modern agrarian regime well into the 20th century. Expansion of agriculture or improved agricultural techniques could have contributed to a very different outcome. In addition to intrinsically desirable improvements in the standard of living, increased production might have led in Tibet, as it has elsewhere, to the demise of what have been described as feudal relations. In Japan, for example, agricultural improvements and resulting higher yields in rice production led to changes in relations of production. As Francesca Bray describes these consequences and the broad social changes they produced:

> The social and legal status of the dependent rural classes improved rapidly. The servant classes decreased in number while the lower echelons of the landholding class grew, and tenants who had previously been obliged to provide their landlords with various free labour-services acquired a far greater measure of economic independence. With the expansion of agricultural production and the growth of non-agricultural sources of income, labour became a marketable commodity [...] Technical improvements [...] tended to increase the tenants' degree of independence from the landlord.
>
> BRAY 1986: 212–13

Thus the taxation system described in this paper was central to the system of land tenure and the socio-economic dynamic of traditional Tibet. Whether light or heavy in relative terms, many tax obligations duplicated efforts and dispersed investments of time between individual agricultural and pastoral production and the similar enterprises of landlord and government. It is not unlikely that taxpayers were reluctant to earn too much from farming or herding, lest that inspire landlords to increase their tax base. In Western Tibet too, difficulties in agriculture coupled with the weight of taxation left many villagers without adequate food for their support. The result was widespread debt, which further undermined the possibility of building up the necessary resource base for investments in diversified production strategies such as trade. Debt also led an unknown number of villagers to abandon their home and kin and take their chances elsewhere in Tibet, Nepal, or India. And the most direct way of improving the situation—expansion of the land under agriculture—was blocked. Thus it seems that economic stagnation was a characteristic of traditional Tibet, and a characteristic shared with many other pre-modern, predominantly agrarian or rural societies. This consequence, I have argued, was supported by and in turn perpetuated a particular kind of land tenure system, particular forms of taxation, and a special kind of economy.

References

Bloch, M. 1961. *Feudal Society*. Chicago: University of Chicago Press.

Bray, F. 1986. *The Rice Economies*. Oxford: Basil Blackwell.

Carrasco, P. 1959. *Land and Polity in Tibet*. Seattle: University of Washington Press.

Chayanov, A.V. 1966. *The Theory of Peasant Economy*, ed. by D. Thorner, B. Kerblay and R. Smith. Homewood, Illinois: Irwin Press (1st Russian edn. 1925).

Goldstein, M.C. 1971. Taxation and the structure of a Tibetan village. *Central Asiatic Journal* 15, 1–27.

Goldstein, M.C. 1986. Reexamining choice, dependency and command in the Tibetan social system: "tax appendages" and other landless serfs. *The Tibet Journal* 11, 79–112.

Kula, W. 1976. *An Economic Theory of the Feudal System: Towards a Model of the Polish Economy 1500–1800*. Translated by Lawrence Garner. London: Verso. First published as *Teoria Ekonomiczna Ustroju Feudalnego*. (Warsaw: Państwowe Wydawnictwo Naukowe, 1962).

Levine, N.E. 1988a. *The Dynamics of Polyandry*. Chicago: University of Chicago Press.

Levine, N.E. 1988b. Webs of dependence in rural Nepal: debt, poverty and depopulation in the far northwest. *Contributions to Nepalese Studies* 15, 213–45.

Postan, M.M. and J. Hatcher. 1978. Agrarian class structure and economic development in pre-industrial Europe. *Past and Present* 78: 24–37.

Survey of the Tibetan Autonomous Region. 1984. Lhasa: Tibet People's Publishing House.

Wickham, C. 1985. The uniqueness of the East. *Journal of Peasant Studies* 12, 166–96.

CHAPTER 5

Lam yig—An Official Document Granting Travel Privileges in Tibet

Saadet Arslan

1 Introduction

The subject of the present chapter[1] is a type of document called *lam yig*, a specific legal document in the collection of historical documents in the database Digital Archives Material Bonn.[2] *Lam yig* literally means "route letter": issued by the Ganden Phodrang (dGa' ldan pho brang) administration (1642–1959) and its subordinate departments, it is an official paper granting travel privileges to designated people. As Wylie already mentioned in 1969, a *lam yig* document had three functions: first, it gives permission to travel (*'gro chog pa'i lam yig*); second, it serves as an entry visa to Tibet (for foreigners); and finally, it authorises the requisition of supplies and transport services (*rta khal khral 'ul skul 'ded chog pa'i lam yig*). The latter function of this document type renders it central to the understanding of corvée labour in Tibet. The holder of such a *lam yig* was entitled to benefit from services that others had to provide as a form of tax obligation. These other persons were both the farmers themselves who had to perform the corvée labour, and also their landlords, who regarded such obligations as a burden.

1 This article is a short summary of my Magister Artium thesis, "Tibetisches Reisebegleitschreiben (*lam yig*)—Einordnung und Klassifikation" (2005). The thesis, supervised by Professors Peter Schwieger and Dieter Schuh, is a critical analysis of *lam yig* documents, and is still unpublished. All the information contained in the present paper, as well as the conclusions, are presented in detail in the thesis. The theoretical background of the thesis—socio-economic structures such as taxation and the governmental transport and postal system—was based mainly on works by Goldstein (1971a, 1971b) and Carrasco 1972; the methodology employed for the analysis of the actual documents is based on Western diplomatics, which proved to be applicable to Tibetan documents. This approach was initiated by Dieter Schuh in Tibetology in the 1970s. Important insights were provided by informants, former officials of the Tibetan Central Government, who were interviewed in 2004 in Dharamsala, namely Zhebo Lozang Dargyas and Ngawang Thondup Narkyid; Arslan 2005: 100 ff.

2 https://dtab.crossasia.org.

 | DOI:10.1163/9789004529465_007

The characteristics of Tibetan documents reveal a general accordance with the formal apparatus of Western medieval documents.[3] Therefore the methodology of Western diplomatics (the study of legal documents) can be applied to characterise Tibetan legal documents. A document may be defined as the record of a legal act which observes certain formalities and must be validated by a sign. Documents are usually classified under two groups: official documents, which are those of emperors, kings and rulers in general, and private documents, which comprise all others.

Official or state documents in Tibet were called *bka' shog*, *bka' gtan* or *gtan tshig*. The Ganden Phodrang administration had two chanceries, the Council of Ministers (*spyi khyab bka' shag las khungs* or *bka' shag* and the Office for Ecclesiastic Affairs (*rtse yig tshang las khungs* or *yig tshang*), which were involved in the proceedings of legal enactment, and all petitions (*snyan zhu*) to the government had to be submitted there: broadly speaking it can be said that the *yig tshang* was the highest clerical office issuing documents from the Dalai Lama or the Regent (with special scribes called *e pa*), while the *bka' shag* was responsible for all other points of law. The *lam yig* document belongs to this group of official or governmental documents (*bka' shog*) issued by the Ganden Phodrang administration, mainly the *bka' shag* chancery or by subordinate departments such as the Trade Agency of Gyantse (*tshong spyi lhan khang*).

The *lam yig* document is very much reduced to its external and internal features, since the travelling privileges granted do not concern rights in perpetuity: externally it is plain and short, written in the cursive *'khyug yig* handwritten script, without ornamental embellishments. Furthermore, the context is reduced to the most indispensable features: it begins immediately with the main text, the *publicatio* (addressing the people in charge), followed by the *dispositio* (declaring the purpose) and concludes with the date and the sign of execution, the seal.

1.1 *Authorities Granting Travelling Privileges*

Which authorities were legitimised to issue *lam yig* travel documents during the Ganden Phodrang administration? According to informants in Dharamsala, former officials of Tibet, as well as Sino-Tibetan edicts from the 18th century, the following authorities had the legal capacity to grant travelling privileges: 1. "Rulers" (Dalai Lama, Regent or "King", i.e. the Qoshot Khan), 2. Council of Ministers (*bka' shag*) and 3. Subordinate Departments such as:

3 The external features of a document are taken from the physical appearance (style of writing, written material, medium for writing, seals, etc.). The internal features emerge from the text itself (structure, fixed formulae, terminology, etc.).

the general governor of a province (*spyi khyab*) and the governmental trade agency (*tshong spyi lhan khang*), and 4. Ambans (*bod bzhugs am ban*; these *lam yig* documents are bilingual).

The *lam yig* granted by the Dalai Lama and issued in the *yig tshang* office were called *sbug dam lam yig*;[4] when the *lam yig* was issued by the *bka' shag*, it was known as *bka' dam lam yig*, in which *bka' dam* is an abbreviation of *bka' shag dam phrug bde skyid ma* or *bka' dam bde skyid ma*, "seal of the Council of Ministers with the inscription *bde skyid* (i.e. happiness and well-being)".

There were two kinds of *lam yig* documents, either permanent/annual or temporary ones. Beneficiaries of permanent *lam yig* documents were: the postman (*sbrag pa*); the governmental carrier (*a drung*); and trade agencies (*tshong spyi lhan khang*) delivering goods for the government. Beneficiaries of temporary or one-time *lam yig* documents were mainly governmental officials like tax collectors, district officials etc., and foreigners. This will be discussed in more detail below.

1.2 *Disambiguation: Travel Accompanying Letters and Documents*

The secondary literature contains an assortment of travel accompanying letters, but some are (legal) travel documents and many are not. It is noteworthy that the terminus *lam yig* is used in an undifferentiated way because not all travel accompanying letters are the type of *lam yig* with its legal character as issued by official rulers discussed in this paper. It is important to disambiguate the diverse travel letters such as *lam yig, lag 'khyer, mda' yig, ngos sbyor, lam son* and *ngos lam*. The differentiation of these travel letters is in brief as follows:

- *lag 'khyer*: a letter of introduction or of official credentials plus a certification of the identity, (most closely equating the term "passport", later authorising travel to foreign countries as well);[5]
- *mda' yig*: an official "express-letter";[6]
- *ngos sbyor*: a letter of introduction or recommendation (*ngos sprod kyi yi ge*); issued at a local level, for example by members of estate-holding nobility;
- *lam son*: a letter of authorisation in order to ask for transport services but at a local level, not issued by the *bka' shag*, for example;
- *ngos lam*: an abbreviation of *ngos sbyor* and *lam son*.

4 Note that *sbug dam* is a term generally designating seals of the Dalai Lama.

5 Cf. the passport of Finance Minister Shakabpa issued 1947 by the Tibetan Government for the Tibetan Trade Delegation that travelled around the world.

6 *mda' yig*: the "arrow letter" was an "express letter", which preceded the traveller by one or more days and announced the arrival of the official guests. Thus, unnecessary waiting times at the stations for travellers could be avoided and the service staff had enough time to prepare the supplies; cf. Arslan forthcoming Dec. 2022.

These last three documents have legal components but just on a local level: they were never issued by the Central Government or the Ambans obliging local people legally to provide services of public or state interest as the *lam yig* documents did. It should be noted that the term *lam yig* may also be used as a synonym for *gnas yig*, pilgrims' guidebook.

The most precise definition of a *lam yig* would thus be as follows: a legal travel paper belonging to the category of governmental documents (*bka' shog*) which grants privileges to officials or state guests. It was issued by the Ganden Phodrang administration with its two chanceries (*bka' shag* and *yig tshang*). It had three functions: 1) permission to travel, 2) entry visa to Tibet or transit visa and 3) authorisation for requisition of supplies including means of transport, accommodation and food. It was allotted just for public purposes or the public weal (*gzhung don rigs*), not for private use (*rang don du*).

In this paper, after setting the socio-cultural background of *lam yig* documents, I will examine, using the methodology of Western diplomatics, their general characteristics and prevailing formulae, before presenting a transcription, translation and detailed analysis of two particular examples of *lam yig* archive documents issued by the Cabinet of Ministers (*bka' dam lam yig*) in 1937 and 1954. A final glossary completes this study.

2 The Socio-Cultural Background of Tibet under the Administration of the Ganden Phodrang Government

In order to classify the *lam yig* document as a primary source for the study of the Tibetan (social) history, one has to look at the socio-cultural background of Tibet under the administration of the Ganden Phodrang Government between 1642 and 1959, in particular at a) territory and land property, b) social order, c) taxation and d) the transport and communication network: postal stations and the *'u lag*-system introduced to Tibet during the Yuan period (1247–1386) under Mongol rule.

2.1 *Territory, Land Property*

The territory of the Tibetan Central Government, Ganden Phodrang, under the rule of the Dalai Lama, stretched over the two central provinces of Ü (dBus), with its capital Lhasa, and Tsang (gTsang), with its two major cities Shigatse (gZhis ka rtse) and Gyantse (rGyal rtse), Ngari (mNga' ris), parts of Eastern Tibet, Kham, and the northern plateau, the Changthang (Byang thang). The resident population of this area, estimated at 470,000 km^2, amounted to 3.9 million people spread across 130,000 villages and (a few) cities. This information is based on results of Carrasco who uses data from the British Trade Representative David Macdonald, who in turn takes his data from a poll tax that the Lhasa government calculated in 1915.[7]

The religious and secular powers of Tibet, predominant up to the time of the establishment of the Central Government, remained, but stood in a (quasi-feudal) relation of rights and duties to the Dalai Lama as the supreme ruler of the country: the demanded duty was the strict loyalty to the supreme ruler and the obligation to provide taxes and services (especially *'u lag*), and the granted rights included the possession or usufruct of the allotted tenure (manorial landlordship) and were recorded in documents called *gtan tshig*.

Tibet knew three kinds of landlords: the Central Government itself, the nobility and the clergy (*gzhung sger chos gsum*). In Central Tibet—in contrast to the north, west and east of the country, where the nomadic economy dominated—agriculture played an overriding role. The typical arrangement was the estate (*gzhis ka*) and the peasant farm on it: this was the economic management unit for tax revenues. In percentage terms, the manorial system was divided as follows:

1) 37 per cent belonged to the governmental estates (*gzhung gzhis*)
2) 21 per cent to noble estates (*sger gzhis*)
3) 42 per cent to monastic estates (*chos gzhis*).[8]

Thus, noble families and monasteries were landowners of 63 per cent of the cultivated land in Central Tibet. Their lands were not geographically connected complexes, but consisted of different, distant and independent *gzhis ka*. Several *gzhis ka* together formed a district (*rdzong*) with a District Capital. Depending on the size and significance of a district, one or two District Commissioners (*rdzong dpon*) of the Central Government had their headquarters there, and were mainly responsible for the collection of taxes for the government. Taken together, districts in turn formed a province that was administered by a provincial governor (*spyi khyab*).

The area over which the bureaucratic reach of the Central Government extended can be illustrated by a diagram of the geographer Karl Ryavec (2001):[9] based on a document dating back from 1830, entitled *lCags stag zhib gzhung*,

7 Carrasco 1972: 78.

8 Carrasco 1978: 86.

9 Ryavec's work is based on a source which includes only fifty-nine out of the traditional 200 or so districts and government estates that the Ganden Phodrang territory comprised, as Travers (2020) points out. She compares the districts mentioned in the 1830 *Iron-Tiger Land Settlement* and those included in later Tibetan sources, and presents a compiled list of 166 districts and government estates of the Ganden Phodrang.

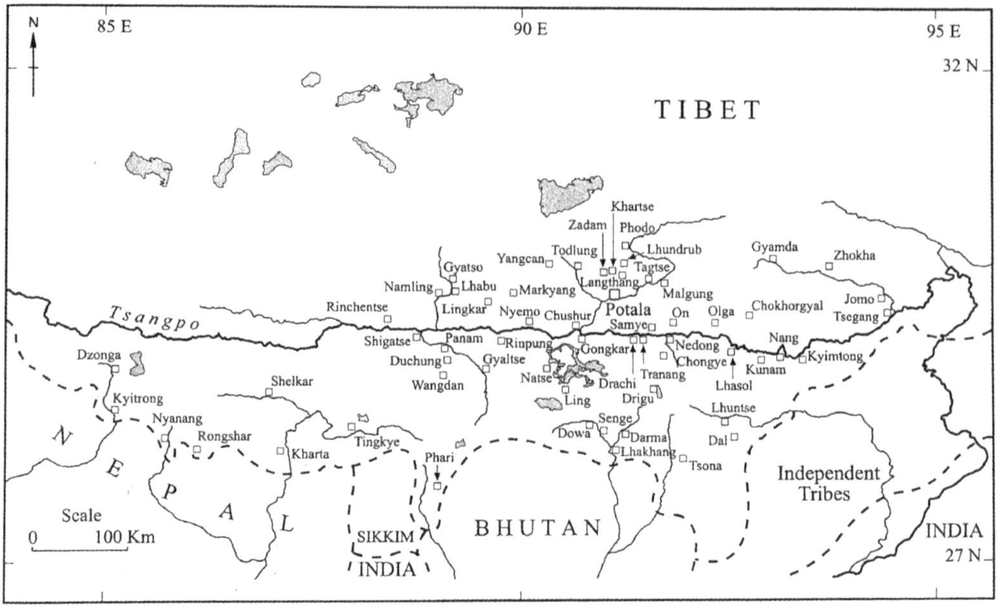

MAP 5.1 Area of arable land in Central Tibet
RYAVEC 2001: 343

i.e. an (official) "land register" of the Iron-Tiger Year,[10] he tries to reconstruct and map the area of the arable soil of Central Tibet (see Map 5.1).

In this land register all estates, which are spread over fifty-nine districts,[11] are listed by name according to the land value tax (*rkang*)[12] to be paid.

The size of the estates (*gzhis ka*) was not uniform; estates consisted of one or several villages. They were divided into personal property (*phyag 'debs*) or leased property (*khral rten*): the lease was left to peasants (*mi ser*) for cultivation; for that they were obliged to pay taxes and to carry out corvée labour for the landlords (*mi bdag*: government, nobility and monastery). These obligations were ensured by either the monastic and aristocratic landlords

10 See Gurung 2016 for different copies of the *Iron-Tiger Land Settlement* and their historical value as taxation manuals.

11 See footnote 9.

12 "The method of land taxation in Tibet was different from methods employed by state bureaucracies in traditional Chinese and Indian peasant-based civilisations. The *kang* [sic!], a basic unit of measurement of land for taxation purposes, was calculated by the amount of barley seed normally sown in a given area, though the actual land size was related to other variables such as soil fertility and local climatic conditions (Gelek [*sic*! Surkhang] 1986)", Ryavec 2001: 354–55.

or their representative or manager, or, in the case of government estates, by government-appointed stewards (*gzhis sdod*) who were under the control of the District Commissioner. Governmental estate administrators are summarised under the term *rdzong gzhis*, an abbreviation of the composita *rdzong sdod dang gzhis sdod*.

The term of office of the District Commissioner was generally three years but extensions were also possible. As permanent representatives of the Central Government their responsibilities were mainly: to collect the taxes for the government (the sum was dependent on the output of the soil and the harvest within the district); to mediate in conflicts of interest; to organise government transport.

In addition to the *rdzong dpon*, other important position in the local administration was that of the village elders (*rgan po*).

2.2 *Social Order: Landlords* (mi bdag) *and Peasants* (mi ser)

As stated above, Tibet had three kinds of landlords (*gzhung sger chos gsum*):

1) The Central Government as landlord: the property of the Central Government (*gzhung gzhis*) was divided into plots and transferred to peasants for use. Documents called *lag 'dzin* acknowledged this lease. For this "right" the peasants were obliged to pay taxes to the government in kind and corvée labour;
2) Monasteries as landlords: the monasteries or the *bla brang* (i.e. the household of reincarnate lamas) as landowners[13] were often exempted from the tax levy obligation (*chag yangs*) but the tax exemption did not include exemption from transport service obligation (*'u lag*), which involved the supply and transportation of government officials, messengers and guests while traveling.
3) Nobility as landlord: the nobility as landowners were committed to the "state"; depending on the size of a *gzhis ka* they were obliged to provide soldiers, to dress and cater for them; to pay taxes regardless of the size of a *gzhis ka*; to give one son to be trained for government service; to organise transport services for governmental transport (whether these were goods or people: organised by the stewards, the villages had to provide animals and accompanying people in order to carry out the transport).

The peasants (*mi ser*)[14] served the three landlords (nobility, clergy and central government) and were obliged to provide taxes and corvée labour. A *mi ser* "belonged" either to a noble family, the clergy or the central government, in

---

13 On reincarnates' land property, cf. Schwieger 2015.

14 Cf. Bischoff 2017.

which case they were called *gzhung rgyugs*. Landlords and subjects were based on a mutual relationship of power and welfare on the one hand, and devotion and service obligations on the other. The classification *mi ser* can further be differentiated into *khral pa, dud chung* and *tshong pa*, among other categories.[15]

The non-noble population which cultivated the "leased" land on the property of the clergy, the nobility and the central government was *the* tax delivery force in the country. The peasants in the monasteries and nobility estates were doubly affected by their tax liability, as they were obliged to two institutions: on the one hand to the central government, represented by the district officers, and secondly to their "direct" landlords, the nobility or a monastery, represented by the estate manager or steward. Since the *chos gzhis* were often exempted from taxes to the government, except for the transport service obligations (*'u lag*), the monastery benefited from the total tax incomes of the peasants living on their estates.

2.3 *Taxation and Service Obligations*

As stated above, the tax burden was imposed on the entire population (except the clergy), from which the Central Government drew its resources. This tax burden was shouldered both by the peasants, who had to deliver a fixed proportion of their profits in kind (and also in cash after 1850)[16] and to perform obligatory labour, and also by noble families, who also had to pay taxes in cash or kind to the government, depending on the size of their estates.

Every *mi ser*, male or female, between thirteen and sixty years of age, had two types of obligations: tax payments and obligatory labour. These obligations were also classified as taxes because they served public needs (administration, organisation of religious celebrations and festivals, etc.). Corvée labour was allocated only to areas where agriculture formed the basis of the economy. Nomads were therefore exempt from compulsory labour, but did have to pay taxes.

The *mi ser*, the peasants of the government, the nobility and the monasteries, had to pay taxes as obligatory corvée labour (*rkang 'gro*) and taxes in kind (*lag 'don*), both obligations together being subsumed by the term *rkang 'gro lag 'don*. The most important corvée labour was called *'u lag* and included only obligatory services to the Central Government, including military and civil construction works.

The heaviest *'u lag* service was the duty of transport: transportation as well as the provision of board and lodging for individual officials, and perhaps also

15 Travers 2013.
16 Rauber-Schweizer 1976: 52.

their families, as well as groups of people (like soldiers), and the transportation of state-sanctioned goods.

The totality of the taxes to the Central Government were designated by the term *phyi khral*, while levies to the "direct" landlords (nobility and clergy) came under the rubric of *nang khral*. These obligations were recorded in documents: the Central Government held a register book on land ownership (*zhib gzhung*), which formed the basis for taxation and listed the taxes to be paid. In addition to a copy in Lhasa, another register was kept by the village administration. Based on these documents, the annual tax was collected by the government officials.

The taxes and services to which the peasants were obliged—limited to relevant points in the *lam yig* study—are summarised in the following sketch (see Figure 5.1).

2.4 *The Transport and Communication Network:*[17] *Postal Stations and the* 'u lag *System Introduced to Tibet during the Yuan Period (1247–1386) under Mongol Rule*

The second aspect of the socio-cultural background concerns the transport and communication network, in particular the introduction of a postal service to Tibet. Census, tax collection, armed forces and postal services constituted the four pillars of Mongol rule in all territories of their empire, and this principle was also applied in Tibet. A census (*rtsa ba'i dud chen rtsis pa*) was carried out (1267) and the routes for the location of postal stations (Mong. *ǰam*, Tib. *'jam lam*) were established.[18]

Based on the census, the tax burden was calculated. This was divided into three obligations (*dmag khral las gsum*): 1. military service, 2. tributes, which is tax in kind, and 3. labour service which included the postal service (*'jam*) that served as an important institution for the administration of the country. With the census, the taxable families were registered. According to the population register and tax lists, the management of the regional postal network was imposed on families. For this service they were exempted from other taxes and compulsory labour. Representatives and leaders of the families concerned, the "elders", supervised the service, while other "staff" such as stable boys, cooks, kitchen helpers, wardens and so on were bound to its upkeep. The stations had lodges, stables, storage facilities, fields and pastures. Water-routes were

17 The paper on which this article is based was presented at the conference "History and Organisation of Labour in Tibetan Societies (mid-17th to mid-20th centuries)", Bonn, 9–11 December 2015. It was available to P. Maurer, who in 2020 published an article entitled "The Tibetan governmental transport and postal system: horse services and other taxes from the 13th to the 20th centuries" (*Buddhism, Law and Society* 5, 1–58).

18 Petech 1979: 233–34; Olbricht 1954: 36 ff.

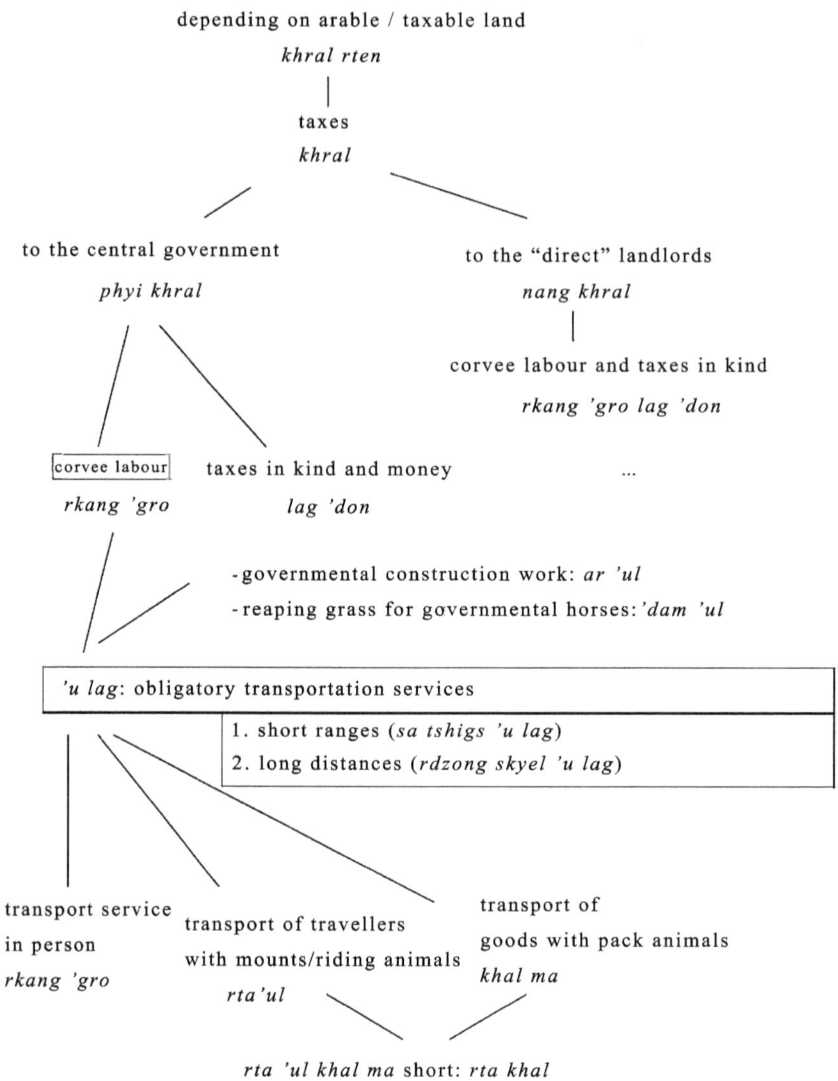

FIGURE 5.1 Taxation (with regard to *lam yig* obligations): corvée labour—*'u lag*

also used. Riding horses, pack animals, porters, boats and other facilities were ready for people and goods.

Even though the postal stations were called *'jam lam* (*'jam chen* or *'jam chung* according to size) after the Mongolian loan-word *'jam*, in the documents considered here the term *rta zam* is more common[19] for designating the governmental postal stations or a halting spot to exchange postal horses, and the

19 E.g. Document 012 2-1/#/19/1/4 (https://dtab.crossasia.org): *lha sa nas bkra shis lhun po phyin gyi rta zam so … so nges dgos.*

FIGURE 5.2 Courier station for the postal service along the Gyantse-Lhasa route
BELL 1992: 177

responsible people were called *rta zam pa*. The term *sa tshigs* is used synonymously for postal station.[20] Since the postal stations and the *sa tshigs* service stations[21] (e.g. for the exchange of animals, supply of food etc.) coincided, it is not surprising that these two terms are often used interchangeably.

The mandatory service obligation—the maintenance of postal stations—was called *'u lag*, again borrowed from the Mongolian loan-word *ulaγa*.[22] The postal route, with stations at regular intervals, was a supporting organ for the main functions of the state: the administration of the country, the management of the state budget and the defence of the borders.

This postal system, which was introduced in the Yuan period, with the characteristic feature of imposing the *'u lag* obligations upon the peasants, existed in Tibet until 1959. The Ganden Phodrang administration issued legal documents called *lam yig* in its two chanceries (mainly the Cabinet of Ministers or *bka' shag*) which legitimated its beneficiary to claim the granted travel privileges at those postal routes or halting stations (see Figures 5.2 to 5.4).

---

20 Cf. Petech who defines *sa tshigs* as "stazioni postali"; Petech 1953: 199.

21 See the next paragraph: "Transportation Network Detail: *sa tshigs* and *rdzong skyel* (relays)".

22 For the Turkish/Mongolian origin of the term *'u lag*, see Arslan 2005: 25 fn. 92.

FIGURE 5.3 "Food given to Bell in Gyantse by Tibetan government"
THE TIBET ALBUM 05 DEC. 2006. THE PITT RIVERS MUSEUM: <http://tibet.prm.ox.ac.uk/photo_1998.285.498.html>

FIGURE 5.4 A service area in East Tibet
TEICHMANN 1922, PLATE VII

2.5 *Details of the Transportation Network:* sa tshigs *and* rdzong skyel (*Relays*)

A distinction was made between two types of transportation corvée, i.e. *sa tshigs 'u lag* and *rdzong skyel 'u lag*. *Sa tshigs* are stops or stations on a route, often corresponding to the postal stations called *'jam lam* during the Mongol period or later *zam* or *rta zam* (governmental post station); the distance between two *sa tshigs* was varying, the shortest was approximately 13 km, and the longest distance between them could be about 37 km.[23] This network of stations served not only for the postal traffic and official courier service but also for carriage of state approved goods, as well as for business trips of officials (see Figure 5.6).

The task of the villagers who lived around a *sa tshigs* stop was to provide helpers and transport animals and to ensure the transport of passengers and goods to the next station, where people from the neighbouring villages would take over the onward transport. To take advantage of this service, the traveller had to carry a *lam yig*, in which the granted privileges were fixed firmly: depending on the specifications in the *lam yig* the villagers had to provide animals, firewood, lodging and persons to load, unload, and accompany the goods to the next *sa tshigs*.

This *sa tshigs* duty was limited to a maximum of ten horses and fifteen mules.[24] The change of the animals was managed at short intervals within a district, unlike the *rdzong skyel* tax obligation. If the number of animals required exceeded the limit of ten mounts and fifteen mules, the transport tax was called *rdzong skyel*. It concerned primarily the transport of goods, but also the supply of government troops travelling across two to more districts (see Figure 5.5).

The *mi ser* of an entire district were needed for this obligation: the pack animals of an entire district had to be taken to the district capital in order to ensure the transfer to the next district capital.

This transport relay from one district capital to another is called *rdzong skyel*. This service was ordered by the District Commissioner and organised by the *tsho dpon*, head of the county or *brgya tsho* (or by the village head or *rgan po* as mentioned in the documents).

When government troops travelled from one place to another, their provisions of grain needed to be transported without any damage and loss. At each *rdzong* the sacks containing the grain needed to be changed. If there was some loss from the original amount the *mi ser* were liable for the lost grain; besides horses and mules, they had also to provide accommodation with furnishings to any person carrying a government *lam yig*, whether it concerned the *sa tshigs* or *rdzong skyel* category.

23 Goldstein 1968: 73ff. For details concerning the Tibetan postal network, see Arslan 2022.

24 *Ibid.*

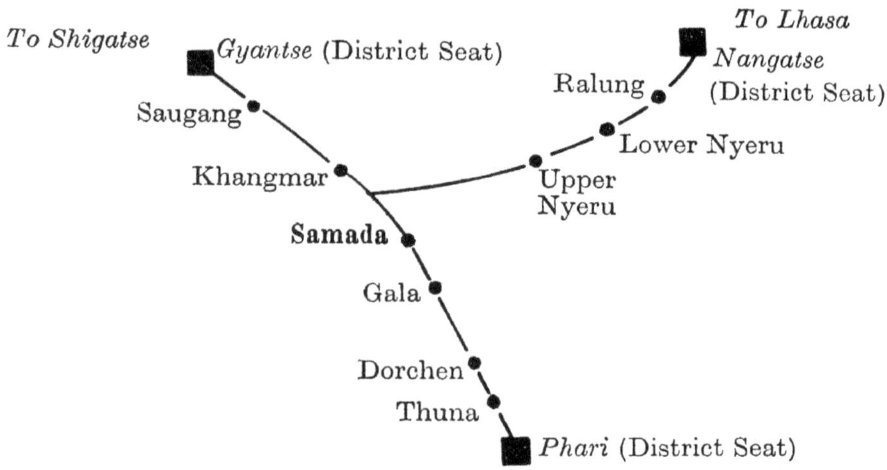

FIGURE 5.5 Relay stations for transport services (*sa tshigs* and *rdzong skyel*, short: *sa rdzong*) in the vicinity of Samada
GOLDSTEIN 1971: 15

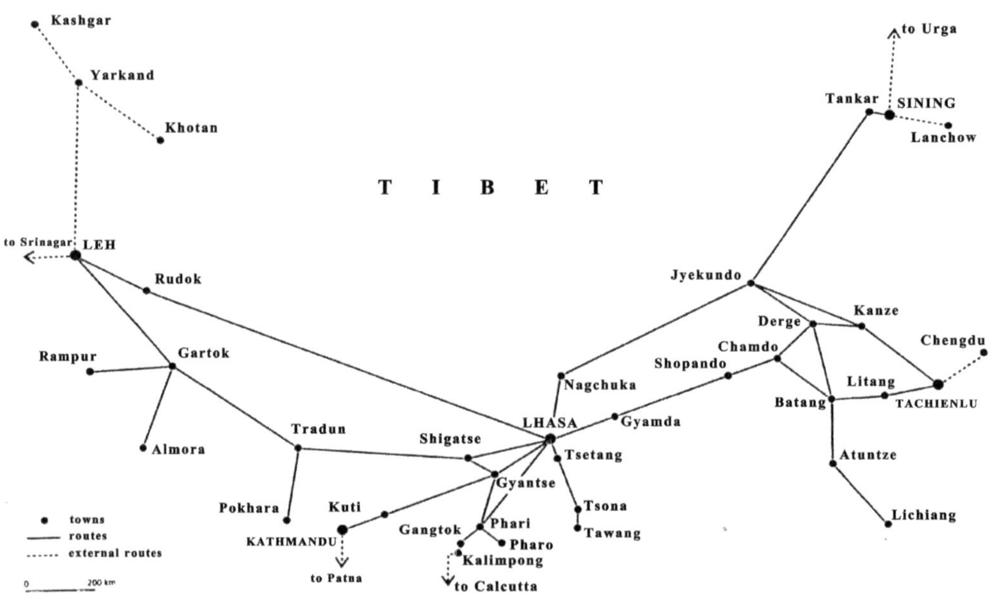

FIGURE 5.6 The trade and transport network before 1959
VAN SPENGEN 2000: 83

3 *Lam yig* Characteristics and Document Formula[25]

When studying a *lam yig* document several questions need to be raised. The first question is who was authorised to issue a *lam yig* (*originator* or *issuer*)? Official documents from rulers usually contain an *intitulatio*, a formula that gives the name and title of the sender; this element is missing in the *lam yig* document, and the method of validating the document consists instead in appending a seal to it. The issuing authority of *lam yig* was primarily the Dalai Lama or the *bka' shag*, but there were other bodies besides:

a. Dalai Lama: travel privileges granted directly by the Dalai Lama, the highest ruler, were issued in the *yig tshang* chancery and were called *sbug dam lam yig*; *sbug dam* indicates the Dalai Lama's office seal;
b. *bKa' shag*: if the Cabinet of Ministers granted the travel privileges, the document was called *bka' dam lam yig*; *bka' dam* indicates the use of the official seal of the Council of Ministers with the seal inscription *bde skyid*, an abbreviation for *bka' shag dam phrug bde skyid ma* and its shorter form, *bka' dam bde skyid ma*;
c. Subordinate departments like provincial governors (*spyi khyab pa*), whose authority was limited to the area under their jurisdiction, and governmental trade agents (*tshong spyi*), for trade transactions of the government;
d. Ambans (*bod bzhugs am ban*, who had this authority after the decree of 1793).

In order to stop misuse, several decrees such as the Thirteen-Point Decree of 1751[26] and the Twenty-Nine Point Decree of 1793,[27] with threats of punishment, were issued. The transport services and so forth were intended for official purposes (*gzhung don rigs*) only, and not for personal use (*rang don du*). After the reforms of the Thirteenth Dalai Lama, only the *sbug dam lam yig* and the *bka' dam lam yig* were approved as official travel documents for using transport services. Besides, he ordered the stop of compulsory corvée practice. Those

25 In general, chanceries kept copies of outgoing documents in registers. They usually did not compose each new text afresh but rather made copies from books in which such text formulae had been collected. Tibet had no such tradition of keeping books of templates (cf. fn. 54). Instead, copies and drafts were used as models: legally relevant passages are repetitively used formulae, while the individually applicable parts, such as names, figures, and dates which varied were filled.

26 *Bod kyi lo rgyus yig tshags dang gzhung yig phyogs bsdus dwangs shel me long* 1989: 97–112 and Dung dkar blo bzang 'phrin las 1991: 111. See also Arslan 2005: 39–40.

27 *Gong ma'i bka' 'brel lugs srol gsar 'dzugs kyi don tshan nyer dgu. A Collection of Historical Archives of Tibet* 1994: Abb. 50f. Compare also with Arslan 2005: 40–41.

travelling on official business had to pay the symbolic governmental rate (*gzhung srol*) and other travellers like foreigners the local rate (*yul srol*).[28]

The second question to be raised is what types of travellers (*beneficiaries* or *usufructuaries*) were entitled to receive a *lam yig*? Those to whom travel privileges were granted were called *beneficiaries* ("recipient" is a misleading term, since the recipients of the travel document were the subjects who had to execute the orders, the officials who had to guard the services and the peasants who had to provide the services specified).

There were two kind of *lam yig* as mentioned before: permanent or annual *lam yig*, called *gtan 'jags lam yig*, and temporary *lam yig* for single use, in which the travel route was set in advance and the letter had to be returned after the journey.

Permanent/annual *lam yig* holders were:

a. postmen (*sbrag pa*, see Figure 5.7)
b. officials in charge of post stations (*rta zam pa*)
c. governmental messengers or couriers (*a drung*)
d. representatives of warehouses and trade agents for the transport of goods[29] to Lhasa.[30]

Temporary *lam yig* for single use were issued mainly for:

a. governmental/administrative officials, for collecting taxes, carrying out inspections, or travelling to their new headquarters and take up their posts in the province or in the district (see *lam yig* n°2, presented in the final part of this paper, for a representative of the Trapshi Regiment); and for

28 Cf. interview Zhebo Lozang Dargyas and Ngawang Thondup Narkyid; Arslan 2005: 100 ff; Wylie 1969: 150.

29 The transportation of goods for the Central Government (meat, rice, butter, tea, salt, paper, dried fruits, wool, grain, etc., see Figure 5.8) was carried out at regular intervals, in addition to unscheduled transports. This obligation was feared most, since the villagers had to spare a lot of animals and people for it. If any loss or damage occurred—a constant danger with bad roads and steep slopes in Tibet—they were obliged to pay for it. If they were unable to assemble enough animals, they would have to borrow as many as were needed, and/or had to bribe the agents of the transport to carry out the transports in several trips.

30 Such as the Phag ri 'bras khang and the Dong ri 'bras khang: Phag ri 'bras khang came twice a year and required 200–300 pack animals; *shog grub*: paper transport from Phakri (Phag ri) to Lhasa and Gyantse, roughly 200 pack animals needed; from Phakri and Dromo (Gro mo): New Year transport of dried fruits to Lhasa. The Dong ri 'bras khang supplied Lhasa with rice twice a year, and for this they needed 150–160 pack animals for each tour. Cf. Goldstein 1968: 76–78 and Arslan 2005: 51ff.

FIGURE 5.7 Postman in Phari Dzong, Tibet 1938/1939
"Phari Dzong, tibetischer Postläufer mit Kurzspeer, an dem Glocken befestigt sind."
BUNDESARCHIV, IMAGE 135-BB-064-0

b. foreigners, such as ambassadors and other state guests (see *lam yig* n°1, presented in the final part of this paper, for the Cutting couple).

At the end of the Nepal-Tibet Gorkha War (1788-1792), the contact of Tibetans with foreign countries was strictly regimented. The Twenty-Nine Point Decree (1793) lists the following points:

– Registration (*deb sbyor*) and inspection (*zhib 'jug*) of all foreigners entering the country

FIGURE 5.8 Peasants carrying supplies (tea) to the Potala
JIN HUI AND NAIHUI 1995: 57

- Permit requirement for Tibetans travelling abroad
- Penalties for unauthorised trespassing the borders without travel permit ("Anyone caught crossing the border without a passport shall be punished" (Article 22); and "Lamas on pilgrimage outside Tibet must also have passports [*lam yig*] issued by the Resident Ministers [Ambans] in Tibet" (Article 23);[31]
- Supervision of all correspondence with foreign countries;
- Inspection of the boundary markers.

31 Cf. *A Collection of Historical Archives of Tibet*, 1994: Abb. 50ff.

Finally, in 1942 the "Bureau of Foreign Affairs" (*phyi rgyal las khungs*) was set up by the Central Government. It was an administrative department of ministers. All incoming foreigners first had to make an application, a kind of "visa requirement", to enter the country. The entry permit was called *lam yig*.[32]

The third significant question to be asked is which categories of people were obliged to perform services such as corvée labour (the *addressees*): documents usually contain an address (*inscriptio*) that identifies those to whom it is directed. However, *lam yig* documents begin immediately with the main text, the *publicatio*, by addressing the people in charge, and this is followed by the *dispositio* (declaration of the purpose).

Often the formula used for the addressees is: *rdzong gzhis, rgan, dmangs*, followed by the expression *nas nges dgos*, "[these] should take notice":

a. *rdzong gzhis* is short for *rdzong sdod dang gzhis sdod*, i.e. the *rdzong dpon* and the government estate steward; the *rdzong dpon*'s duty was to validate the travel document, a procedure called (*m*)*thong 'dzin*, which consisted of making handwritten notes below the seal mark on the *lam yig*. Without this validation note, the villagers would not have to perform the services. The (*m*)*thong 'dzin* was also a certification about the tax obligation provided, comparable to a receipt (as the documents show). This office rule was laid down by the *bka' shag* in order to keep records about expenses and to check the proper course of events. The *lam yig* thefore generally contains the formula: [...] *lam yig 'di yang phyir 'bul yong ba gyis*, "[...]this travel document also must be returned."

In addition, the District Commissioner was obliged to deliver an annual written report on the services provided within six months.

b. *rgan*: *rgan po*, the headman of a village (see Figure 5.9). The village elder or headman was the first contact point for travellers. He was the district officer's representative. The travellers had to wait at the relay station (*sa tshigs*) until he had checked their papers with the district officer and the papers had been confirmed. Without valid travel papers, which had to be issued by the Central Government and certified by the district officials, the services would not be performed.

c. *dmangs* (also *dmangs thun mongs*), the common people, mostly peasants (*mi ser*). Sometimes there is a more precise identification of of the addressee: *rdzong gzhis dang* ***sa tshigs kyi*** *rgan dmangs rnams*—common or local people and the headman of the relay stations. However, a mandatory differentiation is always the formula: ... *nas* ... *phyin gyi lam 'khel* (or

32 For further explanations and sources, cf. Arslan 2005: 52 ff. and Goldstein 1989: 381 ff.

FIGURE 5.9 Reception of officials by the village elder or headman
O'CONNOR 1937: 96

lam 'khod), "along the route from ... to ...", a formula which clearly defines the area within which the *lam yig* is valid.

The *publicatio* ends with an order using the wording (... *nas*) *nges dgos*, "to be taken note of (by ...)".

Last, what kind of corvée labour had to be provided for travellers holding a *lam yig*? The *dispositio* (declaration of purpose) contains the actual ordinance. The name of the person who is provided with a *lam yig*, as well as his or her position (*gro spyi rim bzhi, dmag sgar gyi ngo tshab, rdzong sdod*) or nationality (*a mi ri ka'i sa heb, i ta li pa'i mi rigs*) are given. Also, the purpose of the trip (*phyir log la, gsar pa rtsis len du..., lha bskyod la dmigs gsal*) and any companions (*g.yog bcas*) are specified.

After this follows the actual directive, with the granted travel privileges being strictly defined—what, how, how much and so forth—and are marked with the following *dispositive* verb: ... *gtong ngos*, "... are to be provided" or ... *'phral gtong ngos*, "... are immediately to be provided", or ... *bkag med 'phral gtong ngos* ".... shall be provided immediately without hindrance". The various arrangements for transport and logistics (see Figures 5.10–5.12) specified within a *lam yig* are, for example:

a. defined area of applicability, the route (*lam 'khel*) with place names;
b. fixed number of riding and pack animals (*rta 'ul khal ma*) to be provided;
c. supply of hay (*gzan*) for animals;

d. firewood for cooking (*me kha'i thab shing*);
e. ferry transport across rivers (*ko gru'i sgrol*);
f. ferry costs, food sales and rental fees (*gla*) at fixed prices (*rgyas dpyad gtan 'bebs*);
g. provision of stable boys and kitchen helpers (*rta thab g.yog*) at resting places and lodges (*tsha zhag*) and other accompanying persons (*mi hreng*);
h. possibly also catering and accommodation (*mtshams la za nyal chas*).

The *dispositio* normally ends with the formula: ... *lam yig 'di yang phyir 'bul yong ba gyis*, "... this travel document must also be returned".

The *final protocol* is extremely concise: it contains the time of the law enforcement (*datum*) and the *subscriptiones* (validation of the act by the seal of the issuer). The *lam yig* documents that are used and returned include later additions below the seal and aligned with its left side, one below the other: handwritten notes of District Commissioners about the inspection and utilisation of the *lam yig* in their area of jurisdiction: ... (*m*)*thong 'dzin song* "checked, confirmed".

FIGURE 5.10 Transport staff of a trade caravan at rest
TUCCI 1956: 34

FIGURE 5.11 Ferrymen at the Tsangpo River
TUCCI 1956: 34

FIGURE 5.12 Mrs Shelton and daughters in a yak-leather boat
REYNOLDS 1998: 23

To sum up, the Central Tibetan Government issued *lam yig* to ensure facilities for their government employees on business trips, as well as to transport goods into the capital. *Lam yig* not only provided travel amenities for foreigners, but also possessed other legal components. A *lam yig* was like a visa, that is, a document granting approval to cross the border and take up temporary residence. For traders, this was a kind of license to carry on their profession.

The *lam yig* document is linked to the obligatory transportation service along the road linking the postal stations. Through this network and manpower the state administered the country, managed its budget and defended its borders.

4 Examples of *lam yig* as Primary Sources[33]

4.1 Lam yig *n°1*

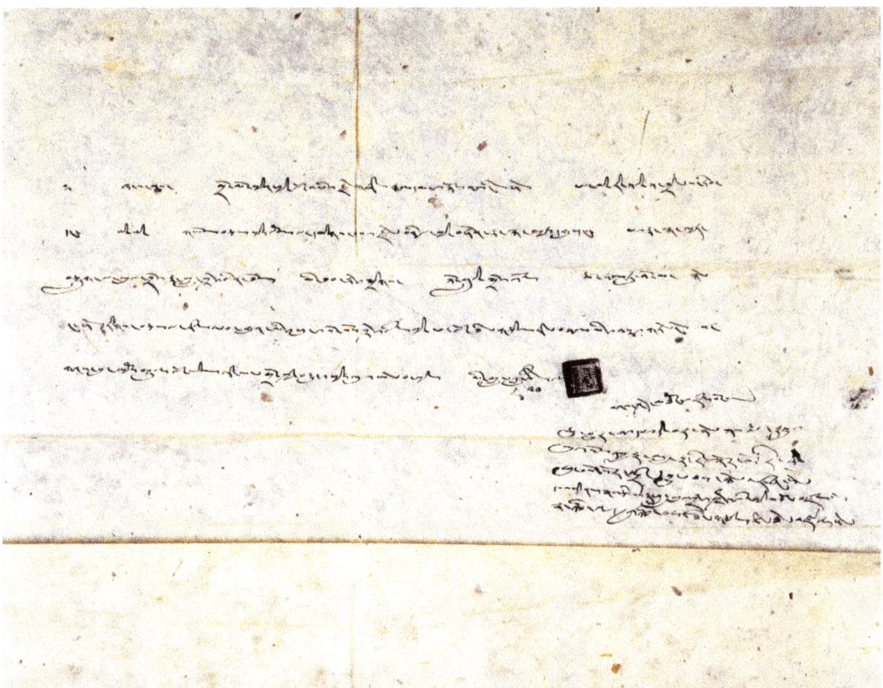

FIGURE 5.13A *Lam yig* issued by the *bka' shag* to the Cutting couple in 1937
THE NEWARK MUSEUM: ARCHIV-NR. 73.38 // A black and white photocopy is available in DigiBonn: 1105_LTWA_316

33 For a compilation of several *lam yig* documents as well as other travel documents, issued for example by *mi dbang* Pho lha nas and *sde srid* bSod nams chos 'phel (1651, 1657), see Arslan 2005: 72 ff.

External Description:[34]
Handmade, rough paper. 53.1 × 79.4 cm. 16 times folded. *'Khyug yig* handwriting.

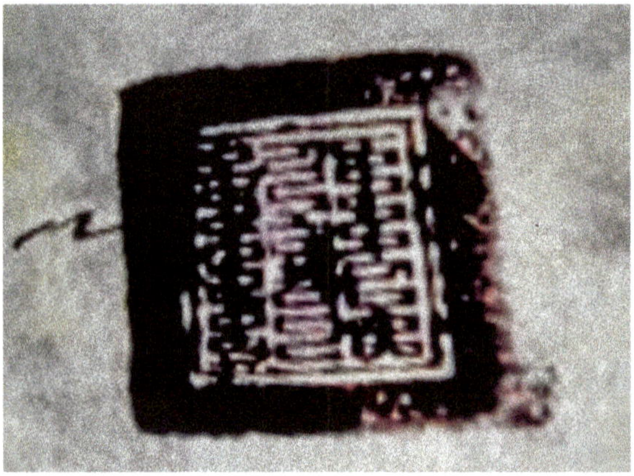

FIGURE 5.13B
Seal: *bka' dam bde skyid ma.*
Edge length
Approx. 2 × 2 cm.
Three-column inscription.
Central column:
bde skyid

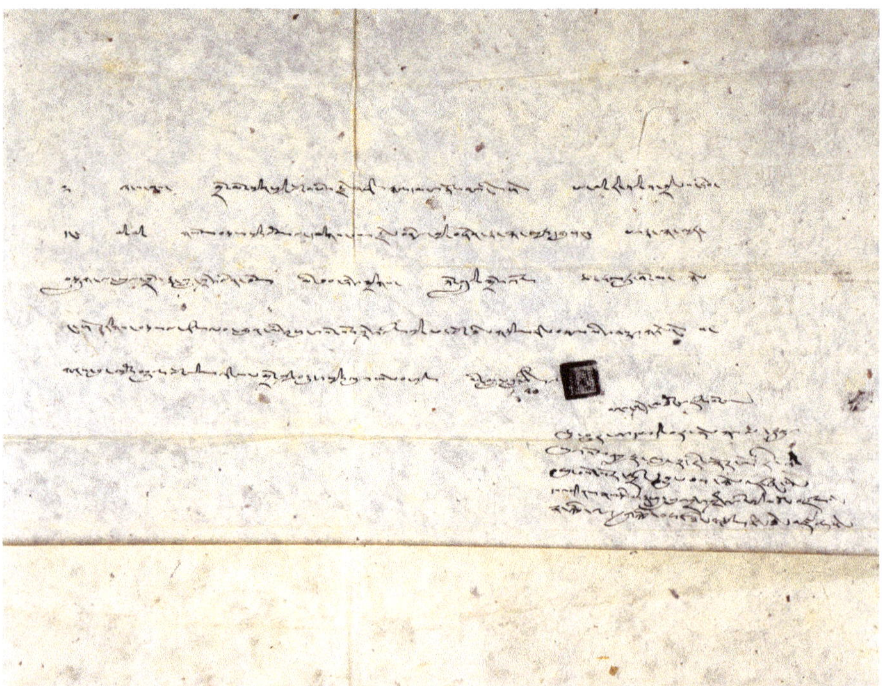

FIGURE 5.13C *Lam yig* issued by the *bka' shag* to the Cutting couple in 1937 (detail)

34 From the catalogue of the Newark Museum: Nr. 73.38.

Transcription of the document:

1. lha sa nas gro mo phyin gyi lam 'khel rdzong gzhis rgan dmangs rnams nas nges dgos a mi ri ka'i ka kring sa heb
2. dang mi mi g.yog bcas phyir log la dmigs bsal rdzong bskyel gyi bzhon rta sga 'byar dgu dang khal rta sga 'byar
3. bcu drug la yul srol rta gla sprod len thog me thab sdod sgrigs ko gru'i sgrol 'don tsha zhag tu 'o ma sgong
4. nga dgos rigs bcas la rin 'bab gun med khungs so sor sprod len gyi {gyis} phar lam then {thengs} gcig ring bkag med 'phral gtong ngos sa
5. gnas su 'byor bstun lam yig 'di yang gro spyi brgyud phyir 'bul yong ba gyis me glang zla ba tshes la

8 10 [Seal]

– bka' shod mthong 'dzin song

– chu shur nas dpal di bar gong gsal rta 'ul
yul sol {srol} rta gla rta re sgor mo re khri {'khri}
khungs so sor sprod [?len] byung bas thong 'dzin song
– dpal di nas sna rtse bar rta gla yul srol sprod len gyi mthong 'dzin
– sna rtse nas rgyal rtse bar theng {thengs}gcig ring thong 'dzin

Translation:

[*Publicatio, line 1*] To be noted by all the district officers and estate stewards, the village elders and local people along the route from Lhasa to Gro mo:[35]

[*Dispositio, lines 1–5*] The American Sahib Cutting,[36] his lady[37] and their servants are on the way back with a special permission.[38]

[They must be provided with] nine saddled riding horses from the district exchange station[39] and 16 saddled pack horses to local lending fees.

In addition, stove and accommodation are to be arranged, ferry services to be provided,

35 Corresponds to Yadong, i.e. the border area to India between Phari and Sikkim.

36 Suydam Cutting travelled to Tibet several times; in 1937 he was accompanied by his wife, Helen McMahon Cutting. His travel experiences are recorded in Cutting 1947.

37 *mi mi*: probably representing the Hindi and Nepali *mim* or *mem*, "A European lady" (Turner 1937).

38 *dmigs bsal*: special; *dmigs bsal byed*: to give preferential treatment.

39 *rdzong bskyel gyi*.

and if required (?)[40] at overnight rest stations[41] milk and eggs [to be provided]

The costs are to be handed over without loss[42] to the respective office.

[The services] must be carried out once during the return journey without reservations!

Upon their arrival, also the return of this travel document must be carried out by the provincial goveneur of Gro mo.

[*Final protocol, line 5, datum*:] On the 10th day of the 8th month of the Fire-Ox [Year].

Seal: *bka 'dam bde skyid ma*

[*Validation/Certification Remarks*:]

- Certified by the *bka' shag* secretary!
- From Chu shur up to dPal di: Confirmation that—as stated above—per horse
  the horse rental fee [was levied] at local prices for transport riding animals [and that] the money[43] has been handed over to the respective office!
- From dPal di up to sNa [dkar] rtse: Certificate of the delivery of horses at local prices.
- From sNa [dkar] rtse up to rGyal rtse: Certificate [for] once during [the return journey].

4.2 Lam yig *n*°2

External description:
The document, written on paper, is 48 cm wide and 64 cm long. Centred text block: approx. 12 × 15 cm. Right edge: approx. 9.5 cm. Top margin: 20 cm. Left border: 10 cm. Lower edge: 30 cm. Folded 14 times. *'Khyug yig* handwriting.

Transcription of the document:

1. lha sa **nas** rong brgyud mkhar rta **phyin gyi lam 'khel rdzong gzhis rgan dmangs rnams nas nges dgos mkhar rta gzhis sdod**
2. gsar pa rtsis len du thon **mi gra {grwa} bzhi dmag sgar gyi ngo tshab** 'di par **sa tshig gi rta'ul gcig dos khal ma gcig rta thab**

40 *dgos rigs la*: *dgos mtshams la*?

41 *tsha zhag*: abbr. of *tsha 'bog* und *zhag sdod*.

42 *rin 'bab gun med*.

43 *sgor mo*.

3. **g.yog me kha'i thab shing ko gru'i sgrol 'don** bcas dgos pa dpyad don nyin tshugs rer rta gla dngul zho bzhi re dang khal ma rer
4. dngul zho do re rtsis sa gnas 'khri khungs so sor 'tshims {'tshems} med sprod len thog yar lam theng {thengs} gcig ring **'phral gtong ngos** sa gnas su 'byor
5. bstun **lam yig 'di yang phyir 'bul yong ba gyis** shing rta zla ba tshes la
 6 27

– bka' shod thong 'dzin[44] song

?[45]

- gdong dkar nas thong 'dzin song
- mnyes thang nas gnam bar thong 'dzin song
- gnam nas ljang bar thon 'dzin song
- chu shur nas dpal thog thong 'dzin song
- dpal di nas yar gzigs bar thong 'dzin song
- rin spungs nas gzhis rtse bar thong 'dzin song
- gzhis rtse nas thong 'dzin song

Translation:

[*Publicatio, line 1*] Along the route from Lhasa via the steep valleys [between Nepal and Tibet][46] to mKhar rta, the (following) is to be noted by all the district officers and estate stewards,[47] village elders and local people:

[*Dispositio, lines 1–5*] (Supply) this representative of the Trapshi Regiment, who has set off to take up his new [position as] estate manager of mKhar rta, with the [following] requirements needed [on his way]:

- 1 riding animal out of the *sa tshigs* exchange station[48]
- 1 pack animal,
- a stable boy and a cooking aid,[49]
- firewood for his stove,
- ferry crossing.

44 (*m*)*thong 'dzin*: validation, certification.
45 The vertical line is unclear.
46 *rong brgyud*.
47 *rdzong gzhis*.
48 Along the *sa tshigs* relay stations.
49 *rta thab g.yog*.

In accordance with the fixed [amount] the horse lending fee for a day's journey shall be set at 4 silver *zho* and per load animal at 2 silver *zho*; it shall be handed over without deduction to the respective responsible office of the region. Concerning the above [mentioned services], they are to be provided immediately [only] once during the outward journey [to mKhar rta]!

Upon arrival [of the official], also this travel document must be given back!

[*Final protocol, line 5, datum*:] On the 27th day of the 6th month of the Wood-Horse [Year].

Seal: *bka 'dam bde skyid ma*
[*Validation/Certification Remarks*:[50]]

- Certified by the *bka' shag* secretary![51]
- Attested within gDong dkar!
- Attested from mNyes thang up to gNam!
- Attested from gNam up to lJang!
- Attested from Chu shur [up to] dPal [?thog]!
- Attested from dPal di up to Yar gzigs!
- Attested from Rin spungs up to gZhis [ka] rtse!
- Attested within gZhis [ka] rtse!

50 (*m*)*thong 'dzin*: certificate of authorisation.
51 *bka' shod*: abbr. for *bka' shag shod pa*.

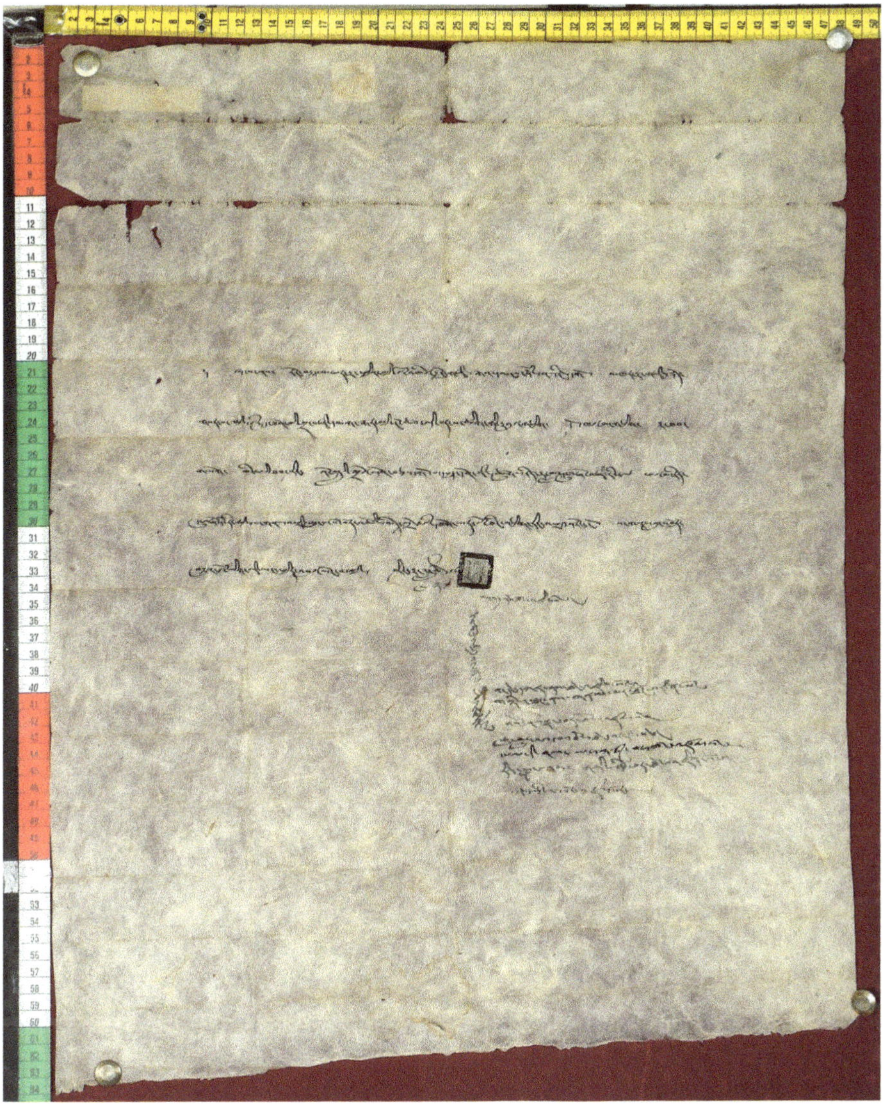

FIGURE 5.14A *Lam yig* issued by the *bka' shag* (*bka' dam lam yig*) to a representative of the Trapshi regiment in 1954
DIGIBONN: 0902_LTWA_77

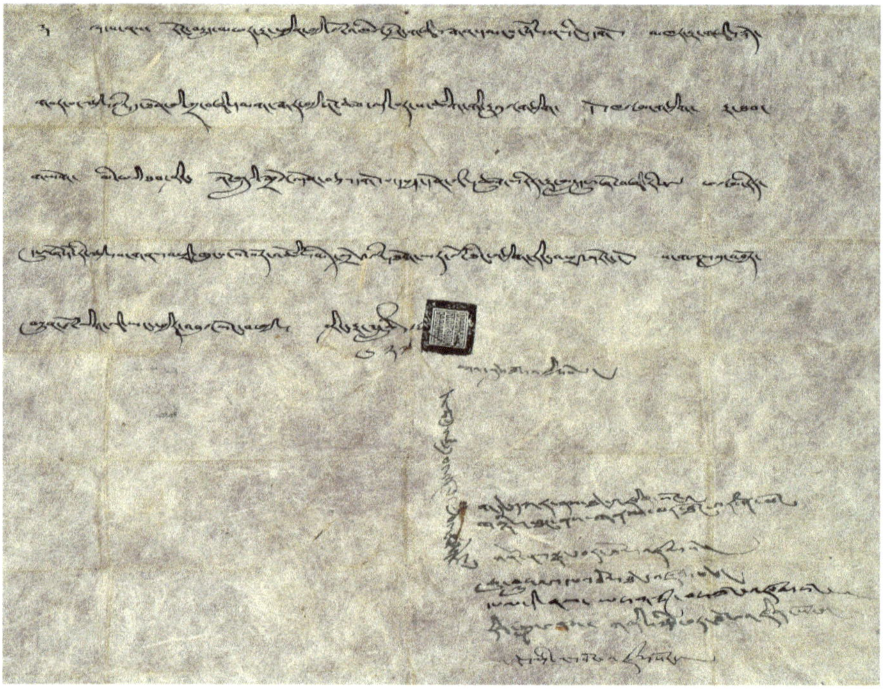

FIGURE 5.14B *Lam yig* issued by the *bka' shag* (*bka' dam lam yig*) to a representative of the Trapshi regiment in 1954 (detail)

FIGURE 5.14C Seal: *bka 'dam bde skyid ma*. Edge length approx. 2 × 2 cm. Three-column inscription. Central column reads *bde skyid*

5 Formal Aspects[52] of the *bka' dam lam yig* Document

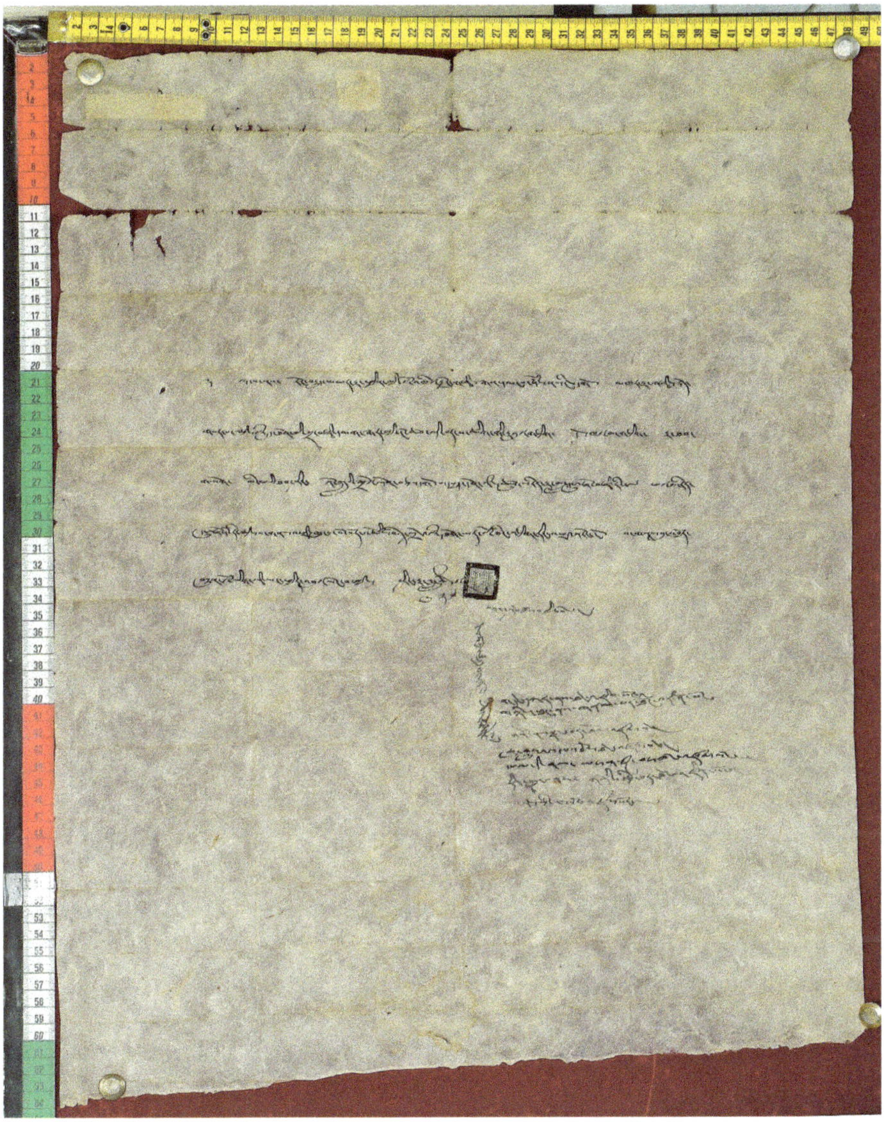

FIGURE 5.15A Digibonn: 0902_LTWA_77

52 Documents are bound to fixed forms. Therefore, the structure of the document follows a particular form insofar as certain formulae are necessary to produce the legal force of the document and to secure its credibility.

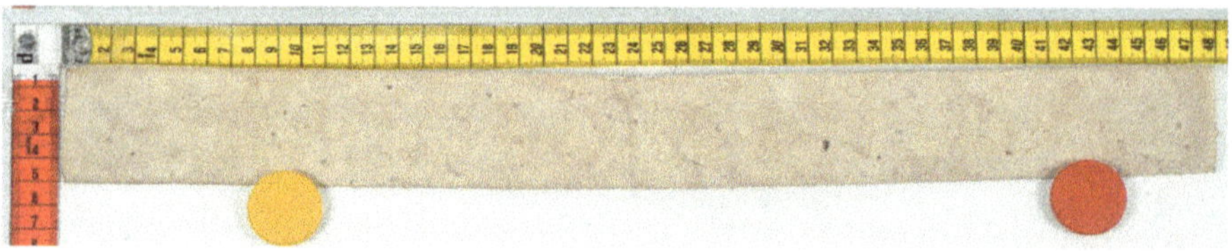

FIGURES 5.15B, 5.15C Two folded *lam yig*

5.1 *External Characteristics of the* bka' dam lam yig

In general the external form in the composition of a document is determined by the type of document and the position of the issuer and the beneficiary.

The *bka 'dam lam yig* is an administrative functional document for practical use and with an average significance, for which paper was the most common material used in Tibet.

There is nothing general to say about the paper size of the high-format documents; the two examples of *bka 'dam lam yig* presented here are 48 × 64 cm and 53.1 × 79.4 cm. The marginal strips left and right are identical whereas the distance from the last line of the main text to the lower edge is always longer than the distance from the first line to the upper edge, since there needs to be space for the notes (*mthong 'dzin*) of the District Commissioner.

The entire text of the document is written with black ink in the *'khyug yig* handwriting, which can be classified as simple letters without any particular ornamental style. It was primarily used for administrative instructions as well as for internal use in offices, chanceries and so forth.

The documents consist of a centrally positioned part (standard measure approx. 12 × 15 cm), comprising four to five lines. This block includes the context of the document and the dating. However, these two structural elements are not visibly offset from each other. The first line always begins with the *publicatio* addressing the addressee, and the last line ends with the *datum*.

A black imprint of a square seal (*tham ga*)[53] measuring roughly 2 × 2 cm (*tham 'byar ma*) is placed at the end of the last line (*tham 'byar ma*). As a concrete act of documentary execution or means of authentication it testifies the issuer of the document (*bka 'dam*, seal of the Council of Ministers). A three-column inscription can be seen as seal image (*zhal ris*): the first and third columns are pseudographs, but the middle line contains the following inscription in the vertical *'phags pa*-script (*hor yig gsar pa*): *bde skyid*, "happiness and well-being!"

The document is folded from bottom to top. The cross folds have a width of approx. 4 to 5 cm. The "rolled up" document is also folded in the middle.

5.2 *Formulary and Phraseology of the* bka' dam lam yig

In the making up of a *lam yig* document there are two structural elements, which are not formally separated: *context* and final *protocol*.

a) The context of the *bka' dam lam yig* document contains following *formula*:[54]

Publicatio: Beginning with the first line, it mentions the persons to whom the travelling document is addressed. The addressees from whom the beneficiary or usufructuary (i.e. the owner of the *lam yig*) can claim the granted privileges are specified as: *rdzong gzhis*, *rgan*, *dmangs*; that is the district officer and estate steward,[55] the village headman and the local people. Sometimes these people are further specified by the prefix *sa tshigs*, i.e. the enumerated persons along the *sa tshigs* relay stations. An obligatory differentiation, however, is always the formula: ... *nas* ... *phyin gyi lam 'khel* (or *lam'khod*), "along the route from ... up to ...". This formula also clearly defines the area of application of the *lam yig*. The *publicatio* ends with the command [... *nas*] *nges dgos*, "[these] must note that". Right after the *publicatio* follows the concrete decree (*dispositio*).

Dispositio: The declaration of purpose contains the actual legal order. The person who is the usufructuary of the travel document is named together with his position (e.g. *gro spyi rim bzhi, dmag sgar gyi ngo tshab, rdzong sdod*) or

---

53 The spelling of the term is variable: *tham ga*, *tham kha* or *dam ga*.

54 In the early Middle Ages, European chanceries had sample books with collections of stock phrases (formulae) and used them as models for drawing up new documents. According to Dieter Schuh there were no formula books in Tibet, but the drawing up of a new document was based on formulae of earlier documents and on experience and knowledge acquired during the course of many years of administrative practice. Cf. Schuh 1983: 326. See also footnote 25.

55 *rdzong gzhis*: short for *rdzong sdod dang gzhis sdod*, i.e. the *rdzong dpon* and the estate steward.

nationality (e.g. *a mi ri ka'i sa heb, i ta li pa'i mi rigs*). The purpose of the trip (*phyir log la, gsar pa rtsis len du…, lha bskyod la dmigs gsal*) and any accompanying persons (*g.yog bcas*) are also mentioned. This is followed by the actual instructions: issued travel privileges are precisely defined (what, how, how much etc.) and are marked with the following dispositive verb: … *gtong ngos*, "… must be provided" or … *'phral gtong ngos* or … *bkag med 'phral gtong ngos*, "… must be provided immediately" or ".… must be provided immediately without hindrance". The *dispositio* normally ends with the formula: … *lam yig 'di yang phyir 'bul yong ba gyis*, "… this travel document must be returned as well".

Final protocol: The final protocol of the *lam yig* document is extremely concise: it contains the time of the law enforcement (*datum*) and the *subscriptiones* (legalisation of the act by the seal of the issuer). The documents which had to be returned after their use contain, under the seal, handwritten notes of District Commissioners about inspection and utilisation of the *lam yig* in their office area: … (*m*)*thong 'dzin song*, "Checked! Confirmed!"

6 Glossary

A *lam yig* document is a representative source exemplifying the official language of the traditional Tibetan Government (*gzhung skad*), which is characterised by the usage of administrative *termini technici*. In the *New Tibetan Dictionary of Modern Tibetan* (2001)[56] Goldstein marks these entries with the signum "shung" for "the genre of government Tibetan" and "tt." for "traditional Tibetan society". These entries are used verbatim below. Additions taken from my previous work (2006) are marked with "SAA".[57]

The glossary below lists relevant terms that have been useful for the analysis of *lam yig* documents.

KA

ko gru – coracle, boat

ko gru'i sgrol 'don – *ko sgrol* – SAA: crossing a river by coracle

bka' dam – the seal of the *bka' shag*; SAA: legal letter, seal

bka' drung – secretary to the *bka' shag*

56 See bibliography.

57 Another helpful reference is a compilation in German by Christoph Cüppers entitled "Glossar zur Terminologie der tibetischen Urkundensprache" (Cüppers 2004).

bka' rtsa – abb. *bka' rgya dang rtsa tshig* – an ordinance, rule, edict;
bka' shod – abbr. *bka' shag shod pa*: the secretaries of the seventh rank who are under the *bka' shag*'s *bka' drung*
bka' shog – an official order, edict, document;
rkang 'gro – taking/delivering things on foot (e.g., a porter, messenger)
rkang 'gro lag 'don – two types of taxes: those taxes that involve sending corvée people and animals to work and those that involve sending goods in kind or money
rkang – a land unit in tt. for which one full tax unit had to be paid

KHA

khal rta – a pack horse
khal pa – people who go with transport animals, e.g., muleteers
khal phyugs – carrying animals, transport animals
khal 'phyags – form of taxation wherein the government uses private animals as a special tax for transportation
khal ma – an animal used for carrying or transport, a pack animal
khra bzung dam bsgrag(s) – being selective and demanding
khral – tax, custom's duty
khral rten – the land basis for paying a tax
khral pa – taxpayer serf/subject, name of a category of serf who held taxable land
khral dpon – officals in charge of tax collection

GA

gro chas – sm. *gro kha*: food provisions carried for a journey or when herding
'gro chas – provisions/money for travelling or for a journey
gla rin – wage and cost or price (of materials)
'gel khal – transport animals
rgan po – SAA: elder, headman of a village
sger rta – SAA: horse for use of private party
sger gzhis – aristocratic estate
sgrol 'don – to cross a river/stream

NGA

ngos lam – SAA: abbr. *ngos sbyor* and *lam son* (*lam son*: a letter of authorisation in order to ask for transport services but at a local level, not issued by the *bka' shag*, for example)
ngos sbyor – SAA: a letter of introduction or recommendation (*ngos sprod kyi yi ge*); issued at a local level, for example by members of estate-holding nobility
ngo tshab – agent, representative
dngos po – materials, things, objects, goods

CH

chos gzhis – estate of a monastery

NYA

gnyis gun med – incurring no loss for both sides
gnyer 'dzin – *gnyer pa*: steward, manager
gnyer las 'dzin – SAA: administrative officials
mnyan pa – SAA: ferrymen

TA

gtan tshig – land tenure document
rta khal – riding horses and transport/carrying animals; SAA: abb. *rta'ul khal ma*
rta gla – price to rent a horse
rta sga 'byar – SAA: saddled horse
rta thab – abbr. *rta thab g.yog* – peasants who as a corvée tax have to care for individuals traveling with a government travel permit when they stay overnight (this involves looking after the traveller's animals, cooking, etc.); SAA: provision of grooms and kitchen help for travellers
rta drel – transport animals
rta 'ul – horse corvée tax (*-gtong/-rgyugs*: to pay/perfom the horse corvée tax), SAA: transport horses (tax obligation)
rta g.yog – SAA: provision of grooms (tax obligation)

THA

thab shing – firewood (for cooking)
thong 'dzin – a certificate of authorisation for levying a corvée tax on animals
mthong 'dzin – SAA: handwritten certification notes below the seal mark on the *lam yig*, approval by officials; also certification about the tax obligation provided, comparable to a receipt

DA

dud chung – a type of lower status peasant (or peasant household) in tt. who belonged to a lord but normally had no land as a tax base so did not have to perform extensive corvée labour
dos khal – loading a pack animal
dos 'go – SAA: transport load
dos rgyab pa – muleteer, people who accompany transport animals; SAA: transport attendants
drung 'khor – lay official in the tt. government

drung yig chen mo – same as *drung yig che mo* the four monk officials who headed the tt. government's *yig tshang*
gdan sa gsum – the three great monastic seats of the dGe lugs pa: Se ra, 'Bras spungs and dGa' ldan
sdod sgrigs – making accommodation for travellers; SAA: providing accommodation
mda' yig – SAA: official express letter
(*b*)*rdal gla* – transportation fee (for truck, yak, etc.)

NA

nang khral – inner tax (tax paid to one's lord); SAA: levies to the "direct" landlords (nobility and clergy), opposite to *phyi khral*
gnas yig – a traditional guidebook to a pilgrimage site or sites; SAA: pilgrim's guide

PA

dpyad mtshams – SAA: agreements, regulations
spyi khyab – governor-general, overall head of an area; SAA: provincial governor
sprad mchan – the notations a person makes when keeping a record of expenses,

PHA

phyag 'debs – to found (monasteries, institutions, etc.)
phyi khral – tax paid to the government (rather then one's lord); SAA: totality of the taxes/levies to the central government
'phral gtong – sending at once/urgently; SAA: provide without delay, immediately

BA

bla brang – residence/ household cooperation of a *bla ma*
sbug dam – the personal seal of the Dalai Lama
sbrag pa – postman, postrunner, mailman

MA

mi bdag – lord, serf owner; SAA: landlord
mi ser – SAA: peasants
mi hreng- sm. *mi hrang hrang*: a single individual (with no family), an individual who is alone
me kha gso – to light a fire
me thab – stove (? SAA: abbr. *me kha'i thab shing* – firewood for cooking)

TSA

rtsa tshig – a public notice, proclamation, ordinance

rtse drung – monk official
rtswa chag – SAA: hay and cattle fodder

TSHA

tsha 'bog – a stop for a meal/tea on a journey
tsha zhag – abbr. *tsha 'bog* and *zhag sdod*; SAA: rest and hostel
tsha zhag gar babs su – SAA: wherever you stop to rest and spend overnight
tshong pa – trader, merchant
tshong spyi – trade agent (of tt. government)

DZA

rdzong skyel – tax requiring corvée labour to transport goods from one district to another
rdzong skyel rta 'ul – tax requiring corvée people and animals to transport goods from one district to another
rdzong skyel 'u lag – SAA: tax-imposed transport service obligation for longer distances, i.e. from district to district (cf. *sa tshigs 'u lag*)
rdzong sdod – synonym for *rdzong dpon*
rdzong dpon – District Commissioner
rdzong gzhis – 1. districts and estates 2. estates held by a district, SAA: *rdzong sdod dang gzhis sdod*

ZHA

zhag sa – halting place/station for travellers, a place to stop overnight on a trip; SAA: hostel
zhag sdod – staying overnight on a trip
zhib(s) gzhung – SAA: register book on land ownership, land registry
zho – traditional Tibetan monetary unit (10 *skar* = 1 *zho*; 10 *zho* = 1 *srang*)
gzhis ka – estate (agricultural)
gzhis sdod – s. *gzhis gnyer*: manager/foreman/steward of an estate (who generally lives on the estate)
gzhung srol – governmental rules and regulations; SAA: "governmental customs" = governmental rate
gzhung zhabs – government official
gzhung gzhis – government estate
(b)zhon rta – SAA: riding horse

ZA

za nyal chas – SAA: "things to eat and sleep": food and sleeping blankets
gzan shing – SAA: hay and firewood

'A

'u(l) lag – corvée labour; SAA: transport service, transport service obligation of the population to the central government for the transport of loads and persons

YA

yig tshang – highest monk official office in tt.; SAA: abbr. *rtse yig tshang las khungs*: one of the two chanceries, the office for ecclesiastic affairs
yul thang – local price
yul srol – local customs; SAA: local rate
yul srol brdal 'bab – SAA: charge at local rates

LA

lag 'khyer – 1. pass, permit, certificate, diploma 2. passport, SAA: letter of introduction or of official credentials plus a certification of the identity
lag 'don – a type of traditional tax payment in kind/cash (in contrast to work
lag 'dzin – document authorizing something; SAA: acknowledgment of lease
lam 'khel – place on a road/trail where one's journey will pass, a place one will encounter along on a journey; SAA: (travel) route
lam son – 1. travel documents permitting the requisition of corvée labour and transport animals, 2. passport; SAA: legal letter, letter of authorisation in order to ask for transport services but at a local level

SHA

sho – a tax, customs duty
sho 'bab – SAA: tax levies, customs revenue

SA

sa rdzong – 1. abbr. of *sa tshigs* and *rdzong skyel*, SAA: relay stations for transport services
sa tshigs – a station/stage in the corvée transportation system in tt.; SAA: station, rest stop, also exchange stop, service and postal station, relay station
sa tshigs kyi khral – corvée tax requiring taxpayer peasants to provide animals to transport goods from one stage on a transport network to the next
sa tshigs kyi mi hreng – a corvée person accompanying corvée transport animals from one stage to the next; SAA: porter, carrier
sa tshigs sgrub rten – land basis for having to perform the corvée transportation tax
sa tshigs rta khal mi gsum – corvée transport tax consisting of horses, carrying animals and people
sa tshigs dod – money paid as a substitute for performing the corvée transportation tax

sa tshigs 'u lag – SAA: tax-imposed transport service obligation for shorter distances, i.e. within a district (cf. *rdzong skyel 'u lag*)
sa rim – the stages/posts/stations of the corvée transportation system
sa rim skyel – to transport loads from one corvée station to another
srang – a Tibetan currency unit equal to 10 *zho*

A
a drung – a governmental messenger (on horseback)
e drung – clerk in the *e khang* (an office in the tt. where letters and documents were copied)
e pa – a person trained for copying government documents who works in the *e khang*

References

A Collection of Historical Archives of Tibet. 1994. Compiled by the Archives of the Tibet Autonomous Region. Lhasa: Cultural Relics Publishing House.

Arslan, S. Forthcoming Dec. 2022. Official travel documents in Tibet—Quick mail using the example of an express letter (*mda' yig*). *In* C. Cüppers and K.H. Everding (eds) *A Life for Tibetan Studies*. Lumbini International Research Institute, Nepal, 2022.

Arslan, S. 2005. Tibetisches Reisebegleitschreiben (*lam yig*)—Einordnung und Klassifikation. Magisterarbeit Universität Bonn.

Bell, C.A. 1992. *Tibet. Past and Present*. New Delhi, Madras: Asian Educational Services.

Bischoff, J. 2017. Completely, voluntarily and unalterably? Values and social regulation among Central Tibetan *mi ser* during the Ganden Phodrang period. *In* J. Bischoff and S. Mullard (eds) *Social Regulation: Case Studies from Tibetan History*. Leiden, Boston: Brill, 151–80.

Bod kyi lo rgyus yig tshags dang gzhung yig phyogs bsdus dvangs shel me long. 1989. Lhasa: Bod ljongs mi dmangs dpe skrun khang.

Carrasco, P. 1972. *Land and Polity in Tibet*. Seattle: University of Washington Press. 2nd print.

Cutting, S. 1936. In Lhasa-The Forbidden. *Natural History* 37, 102–126.

Cutting, S. 1947. *The Fire Ox and Other Years*. London: Collins.

Cüppers, C. 2004. Ein Glossar zur Terminologie der tibetischen Urkundensprache. *Zentralasiatische Studien* (*ZAS*) 33, 25–98.

Dung dkar Blo bzang 'phrin las. 1991. *The Merging of Religious and Secular Rule in Tibet*. Beijing: Foreign Languages Press.

Goldstein, M.C. 1968. An Anthropological Study of the Tibetan Political System. Ph.D. thesis, University of Washington.

Goldstein, M.C. 1971a. Serfdom and mobility: an examination of the institution of "human lease" in traditional Tibetan society. *Journal of Asian Studies* 30(2), 521–34.

Goldstein, M.C. 1971b. Taxation and the structure of a Tibetan village. *Central Asiatic Journal* 15(1), 1–27.

Goldstein, M.C. 1989. *A History of Modern Tibet, Volume 1: The Demise of the Lamaist State (1913–1951)*. Berkeley: University of California Press.

Goldstein, M.C. 2001. *The New Tibetan-English Dictionary of Modern Tibetan*. Edited with T.N. Shelling and J.T. Surkhang. California: University of California Press.

Gurung, Kalsang Norbu. 2016. Different copies of the *Iron-Tiger Land Settlement* and their historical value as taxation manuals. *In* J. Bischoff and S. Mullard (eds) *Social Regulation—Case Studies from Tibetan History*. Leiden: Brill, 209–230.

Hofmann, R.A. 2002. Zur Tibetpolitik der Qing-Regierung am Ende des 18. Jahrhunderts. Das „29-Punkte-Dekret zur Reorganisation in Tibet“ (1793). Magisterarbeit Universität Leipzig.

Jin Hui, R.Y. and M. Naihui (eds). 1995. *Dokumente und Illustrationen zur Sozialgeschichte Tibets, China*. Beijing: China Intercontinental Press.

Körös, A.C. 1833. Translation of a Tibetan passport, dated A.D. 1688. *Journal of the Asiatic Society of Bengal* 2, 201–202.

O'Connor, S.F. 1937. Tibet in the modern world. *The Geographical Magazine* 6. London.

Olbricht, P. 1954. *Das Postwesen in China unter der Mongolenherrschaft im 13. und 14. Jahrhundert*. Wiesbaden: Otto Harrassowitz.

Petech, L. 1953. *I Missionari italiani nel Tibet e nel Nepal. I Cappuccini marchigiani. Parte IV*. Rome: La Libreria Dello Stato.

Petech, L. 1979. The Mongol census in Tibet. *In* M. Aris and Aung San Suu Kyi (eds) *Tibetan Studies in Honour of Hugh Richardson. PIATS Oxford 1979*, 233–38.

Rauber-Schweizer, H. 1976. Der Schmied und sein Handwerk im traditionellen Tibet. Ph.D. thesis. Zürich: Robert Hofmann Druck.

Reynolds, V. 1998. The journey to Tibet of Dr. Albert L. Shelton 1904–1922. *Lungta 11. Christian Missionaries and Tibet*. Dharamsala: Amnye Machen Institute.

Richardson, H.E. 1998. Reflection on a Tibetan passport. *In* M. Aris *High Peaks, Pure Earth. Collected Writings on Tibetan History and Culture*. London: Serindia Publications, 483–85.

Ryavec, K.E. 2001. Land use/cover change in Central Tibet, c. 1830–1990: Devising a GIS methodology to study a historical Tibetan land decree. *The Geographical Journal* 167(4), 342–57.

Schuh, D. 1978. Ergebnisse und Aspekte tibetischer Urkundenforschung. *In* L. Ligeti (ed.) *Proceedings of the Csoma de Körös Memorial Symposium*. Budapest: Akademiai Kiado, 411–25.

Schuh, D. 1981. *Grundlagen tibetischer Siegelkunde. Eine Untersuchung über tibetische Siegelaufschriften*. Monumenta Tibetica Historica. Abteilung III. Band 5. Sankt Augustin: VGH Wissenschaftsverlag.

Schuh, D. 1983. Zum Entstehungsprozess von Urkunden in den tibetischen Herrscherkanzleien. *In* E. Steinkellner and H. Tauscher (eds) *Contributions on Tibetan*

Language, History and Culture. Proceedings of the Csoma de Körös, vol.1. Universität Wien: Arbeitskreis für Tibetische und Buddhistische Studien, 303–328.

Schuh, D. 1984. Recht und Gesetz in Tibet. *In* L. Ligeti (ed.) *Tibetan and Buddhist Studies. Commemorating the 200th Anniversary of the Birth of Alexander Csoma de Körös*. Budapest: Akademiai Kiado, 291–311.

Schwieger, P. 2015. *The Dalai Lama and the Emperor of China: A Political History of the Tibetan Institution of Reincarnation*. New York: Columbia University Press.

Shakabpa, Tsepon Wangchuk Deden. 1967. *Tibet. A Political History*. New Haven: Yale University Press.

Surkhang, Wangchen Gelek. 1986. Government, monastic and private taxation in Tibet. *The Tibet Journal* 11(1), 21–40.

Teichmann, E. 1922. *Travels in Eastern Tibet*. Cambridge: University Press.

Thupten Sangyay. 1986. Glossary of the "Government, Monastic and Private Taxation in Tibet". *The Tibet Journal* 11(1), 41–47.

Travers, A. 2013. How should we define social status? The study of "intermediate groups" in Central Tibet (1895–1959). *In* C. Ramble, P. Schwieger and A. Travers (eds) *Tibetans who Escaped the Historian's Net. Studies in the Social History of Tibetan Societies*. Kathmandu: Vajra Books, 141–160.

Travers, A. 2020. A compiled list of Tibetan districts (*rdzong*) and government estates of the Ganden Phodrang territory (1830–1959). *Revue d'Études Tibétaines* 56, 5–47.

Tucci, G. 1956. *To Lhasa and Beyond. Diary of the Expedition to Tibet in the Year MCMXLVIII*. Rome: La Libreria Dello Stato.

Turner, R.L. 1931. *A Comparative and Etymological Dictionary of the Nepali Language*. London: Routledge and Kegan Paul.

van Spengen, W. 2000. *Tibetan Border Worlds. A Geohistorical Analysis of Trade and Traders*. London: Kegan Paul International.

Wylie, T.V. 1965. The Tibetan tradition of geography. *Bulletin of Tibetology* 2(1), 17–25.

Wylie, T.V. 1969. Tibetan passports. Their function and significance. CAJ 68, 149–152.

Wylie, T.V. 1987. Notes on Csoma de Körös's Translation of a Tibetan Passport. *In* C.I. Beckwith (ed.) *Silver on Lapis. Tibetan Literary Culture and History*. Bloomington: The Tibet Society, 111–22.

CHAPTER 6

"My Karma Selected Me to Become a Ferryman": The Role of Waterways and Watercraft in the Corvée Tax System in Pre-1959 Tibet

Diana Lange

1 Introduction

This chapter addresses one aspect of my research on the significance of waterways for infrastructure, economy and socio-cultural life in pre-1959 Tibet. In an earlier article, "'The government forced us to send the boat in the middle of the night:' water transport in pre-1959 Tibet", I gave a general overview on the use of waterways in Tibet to demonstrate the role that water transport played in pre-1959 Tibet (Lange 2014). In this essay I will focus on ferry and transport services in the Tibetan corvée tax system. In this context I will concentrate on the nature of taxation on a specific Tibetan village—the fishing village of Jun ('Jun) in Chushur (Chu shur) county in Central Tibet (see Figures 6.1 to 6.4).

I conducted fieldwork in this fishing village on several occasions between 2003 and 2012. For my Ph.D. project I documented and analysed the economic, technical and socio-cultural aspects of Tibetan fishing communities in Southern and Central Tibet. I investigated how fishermen adapted to the geographical, ecological and cultural conditions of their environment and how they utilised the potential of their environment for their own economies. My two main research questions were: (1) how have the fishermen adapted to the changes of the last decades in relation to new infrastructure, ecology, new technologies, politics and society, and (2) in what way can material culture be used as an indicator for these transformations in the socio-cultural and economic fields. Jun—the last remaining fishing village in Central Tibet[1]—provided the opportunity for a detailed case study, and the yak hide boat was exemplary for my analysis of the fishermen's material culture. Since many fishermen of

1 Fishery never played an important role in the Tibetan economic system and a fishing culture only developed in places in Central and Southern Tibet where the local residents depended on that source of income or food due to geographical circumstances, such as the lack of fertile land. Next to Jun there existed only a few places that had depended upon fishing for their livelihoods for a long time: Lungpa (close to Jun) and a few communities at the western shore of the Yamdrok Lake in Southern Tibet; see Altner [Lange] 2009a and 2009b.

 | DOI:10.1163/9789004529465_008

the older generation had also worked as ferrymen in the past, I came in contact with the subject of waterways and water transport on many occasions and from different perspectives. These impressions inspired me to pursue research on the traditional water transport system in pre-1959 Tibet (see Figures 6.5 to 6.7).

The study of water transport as part of the transport system of pre-1959 Tibet has generally been neglected, and so too has the role of ferry and transport services in the tax system. Neither in Tibetan nor in Western sources could I find any information about the integration of water transport in the Tibetan corvée tax system. Most of the information on this taxation I collected during my fieldwork. Nevertheless, I have so far only scratched the surface of this topic, and further research certainly needs to be conducted. In this paper, I want to demonstrate how taxation in the fishing village of Jun was integrated into the local and regional tax system and how ferry and transport services relating to water transport worked in practice. These insights will give us a chance to answer the questions of how the tax system in pre-1959 Tibet was adapted to the environmental and economic conditions of the particular taxpayers.

2 The Fishing Village of Jun

The village of Jun is situated around sixty kilometres to the south of Lhasa, on the east bank of the southern part of the Kyichu (sKyid chu), close to Kyitsang Drilsa (sKyid gtsang 'gril sa)[2]—the place where the Kyichu flows into the Yarlung Tsangpo (Yar klungs gTsang po). The earliest written Tibetan source I have been able to find that refers to the place dates from the 17th century and mentions "Jun at the lower Kyichu" (*skyid smad Jun*) (Ngawang Lobsang Gyatso 1678, Vol. 17: 239). Compared to the pre-1959 era, when around 150 people lived in Jun, in 2004 the village had around 400 inhabitants (eighty households). With the rising population, the built area also increased, but is still less than 1 km^2. Until 2004, the location of Jun was comparable to an island. It was only possible to reach the place by boat. There was no bridge or road at all. The village's proximity to the river was one reason for the development of a fishing tradition there; the shortage of arable land was another.[3] Apart from the fact that there was a lack of arable land, a large part of the available land was damaged regularly by flooding of the Kyichu. Before 1959, all inhabitants of

2 sKyid gtsang 'gril sa: "place where Kyichu and Tsangpo merge".

3 In 1946, the villagers asked the central government for the last time for additional land, but without success.

Jun engaged in fishery and all were considered as "low-caste".[4] Next to fishing they lived largely by providing ferry transport services on both the Kyichu and Yarlung Tsangpo rivers. They also paid a part of their taxes in the form of these services.

3 The System of Taxes in Jun

There were different kinds of taxes in pre-1959 Tibet. The taxpayers were taxable to their landlords and to the central Tibetan government in Lhasa. In those days, the village of Jun was subordinated to Drepung ('Bras spungs) monastery. Every villager between the ages of eighteen and sixty was subject to taxation by Drepung and by the central government in Lhasa. The tax load was the same for everybody regardless of age. There were two segments of tax: those based on land holdings and those not so based. The former were subdivided into *rkang 'gro*, which designated corvée tax,[5] and *lag 'don*,[6] paid in kind or money (see Surkhang 1966: 23). The depön (*sde dpon*), who was responsible for tax collection, was appointed by the local government and lived in the village.[7] Furthermore, there were five more leaders living in Lhasa who were responsible for all decisions concerning the village.[8]

As *rkang 'gro*, the inhabitants of Jun were committed to providing ferry and transport services in this system, mainly in the area between Lhasa and Tsetang. For instance, the Chaksam ferry station—the gate to Lhasa—was served by villagers from Jun during the whole year. These services were imposed by the central government and by Drepung monastery. They had to be conducted irregularly and the villagers took it in turns[9] to provide them. Actually, these

4 The status of the villagers has not really changed until today; they are still regarded as "dirty fishermen" by most of the neighbouring (non-fishing) villagers although some have given up fishing due to alternative sources of income.

5 See Goldstein 2001: 37; *rkang 'gro*: a corvée tax involving the sending of people for work.

6 See also *ibid.*: 1060; *lag 'don*: a type of traditional tax payment in kind/cash (in contrast to work).

7 According to elderly villagers the name of the last depön who led the village until 1959 was Sonam Tobgyal. In 1983 he moved to Lhasa, where he lived until his death. He had been a shoemaker before his appointment as depön. In contrast to many villagers he was able to read and write.

8 The old people in the village remember that these leaders treated them "like animals".

9 I cannot say for sure how the ferry and transport services were divided between the village's households. Today, the inhabitants of Jun still practise a system of dividing the herding of their animals (cattle and sheep).

services were exclusively provided by men; women were excluded from fishing and also from boat building.

The villagers of Jun were responsible not only for the ferry services on the Kyichu and Yarlung Tsangpo Rivers before 1959. During the Saga Dawa festival they were also responsible for the ferry service on the Lukhang lake to the north of the Potala. Visitors usually wanted to visit the Lukhang temple or to search for the *lu* (*klu*)—a kind of spirit being that is believed to live in water, among other environments—that they believed to be in the lake. After visiting several other temples the Tibetan ministers and government officials toured the Lukhang lake in the company of musicians who sang and played in honour of the *lu*. The residents of Lhasa customarily watched this boating trip and camped at Lubuk for a picnic (Tsepak Rigzin 1993: 35f). After the end of their ferry service the boatmen carried the boats on their backs and made a circumambulation around the Tsuglakhang temple on Lhasa's Barkhor before they went back home (see also Altner 2010: 5).

In addition to this and as *lag 'don*, the villagers of Jun had to pay a fixed tax rate from the yields of their land, in terms of barley and fish. Fish is generally considered a "dirty food" by most Tibetans and the attitude towards fish as food had a hindering effect on the development of a fishery tradition. Nevertheless, dried fish played an important role as an item of trade,[10] and spring fish was very popular. Tibetans have the popular belief that spring fish is very healthy, and the fact that it is sought after is often emphasised by the following proverb: *dpyid nya rgyal por ma rag, ston ka khyi yis za* ("The spring fish is hard to get even for the king, the autumn fish is eaten by dogs").[11] According to local informants in Jun and at the Yamdrok Lake, the Tibetans believe that all fish in the lakes and rivers are females and married to the snow frog (*gangs sbal*) living up in the snow mountains. In spring, this frog sends his semen with the melting water into the lakes and rivers where the (female) fish are already waiting for it. It is said that the fish are excepionally tender at that time.

Generally, fish is also regarded as a very good medicine for several diseases. Dried fish is said to be an excellent treatment for pregnant women—not only during their pregnancy but also while they give birth (see also Altner 2009a: 47).

Heinrich Harrer visited Jun in 1950 and he described the fishing activities as well as the tax payment as follows:

10 There used to be an extensive trade in dried fish at the Yamdrok Lake, with mainly Bhutanese coming to buy the fish.

11 Actually, most fish are available and caught in autum; in spring only a few fish are available.

> [...] in the morning we arrived in Djum. This is a little village that does not have a single field. The people here are the only ones in Tibet that are allowed to fish and to do business with fish. As tax they have to hand over fish to the government.
>
> From an unpublished diary, 1 October 1950[12]

The popularity of spring fish allowed the fishermen of Jun to trade the spring fish against barley at a ratio of 1:3 in the surrounding villages. The grain they acquired in this way was also used for their tax payment in case their fields did not yield enough barley, which was very often the case. Nowadays the village has around 600 *mu*[13] of land. Around 300 *mu* of the land are not usable because of the regular flooding. 300 of the 400 inhabitants of Jun are authorised to have allotted land—that means around 1 *mu* of land for each person. In contrast, the neighbouring villages on the other side of the Kyichu have around 3 *mu* per person on average. According to my local informants the quantity of available land was the same before 1959. In any case the land often did not yield enough to subsist on.

4 Water Transport Services in General as Taxes and as a Private Enterprise in Tibet

In general, transport services were carried out mainly along the most important water transportation route between Lhasa and Tsetang, via the Chaksam ferry station and Samye (bSam yas) monastery. There were three ports or ferry stations at the Kyichu in Lhasa: the Ramagang (Ra ma sgang) ferry, the Tsecholing (Tshe mchog gling) ferry and the Lhatong (lHa gtong) ferry. The Tsecholing ferry was only used for river crossing. The ferry service was provided as a corvée tax by three families[14] who lived in the Tsecholing village closed to the ferry station.[15] The other two stations were used for river crossing as well as for long distance water transport. The boats started in Lhasa and travelled downstream for around 60 km. In Chushur the boats that were continuing to the east down the Yarlung Tsangpo were usually bound together with ropes by means of

12 My translation. The diaries are kept in the Völkerkundemuseum Zürich.

13 1 *mu* correspondends roughly to 1/15 hectare (1 ha = 10,000m^2).

14 These families were only responsible for the ferry service, and had no fishermen among them.

15 This information I received from monks of the Tsecholing monastery during a field trip in 2012.

two special wooden sections fixed to the side of the boats.[16] Such connected boats were called 'kodrel' (*ko sbrel*). All kinds of commodities were transported along this route including wool, grain and firewood (see also Lange 2014: 81). While some of these goods were intended for consumption at places such as monasteries along the way, others were part of long-distance trade networks. Depending on the season, the terrain, the distance, the goods to be transported and the water level, Tibetans used either hide boats or wooden ferries to cross and travel along waterways. The wooden ferries were only used for river crossing at fixed ferry stations like Chaksam. While they were only usable at low water levels, hide boats were not dependent on the water level and could be used throughout the year (*ibid.*: 83). Sarat Chandra Das described his own experience with this ferry station in his travel account:

> Two miles beyond this point we came to the famous Palchen chuvori monastery and the chain bridge (*chag-zam*) over the Tsang-po. This bridge, built, tradition says, by Tang-tong gyal-po in the fifteenth century, consists of two heavy cables attached at each end to huge logs, around which have been built large *chorten*. The bed of the river here is about 400 feet broad, but at this season of the year it spreads out several hundred feet beyond the extremities of the bridge, and travellers are taken across in boats. [...] The Palchen chuvori monastery, where there are upwards of one hundred monks, is supported by the toll collected at the ferry. We and our ponies crossed the river in a roughly made boat about 20 feet long, but a number of skin coracles were also carrying travellers and freight from one side to the other.
>
> DAS 1902: 143

Apart from the descriptions by the pundits there are plenty of accounts of the ferry service at the Chaksam ferry station by Western travellers, since nearly all those who came from the south had to use this ferry on their way to Lhasa. But they and their goods were not transported as part of the corvée service; they had to pay for their transport. There are different descriptions of the payment of the boatmen. Ippolito Desideri, for example, states that: "One has to pay something to the boatmen, [but] the King's, Lamá's and Governor's messengers pay no fee" (de Filippi 1932: 127). According to the statements of older Tibetans I interviewed during my fieldwork who still remember travelling by boat before 1959, the passengers paid their fares not only in cash but also in kind—butter,

16 This practice was also described by the Tibetans I interviewed and by Western travellers; see Thomas 1952: 123 and Tucci 1956: 16.

tsampa, tea and so forth. The men remembered it as a relatively cheap service for passengers. The boatmen and owners of the boats made much more profit by transporting goods such as wool on behalf of businessmen and traders. The way in which boats were named gives us information about the economic scope of their users. The so-called "government boat" *shungdru* (*gzhung gru*) was used for tax payments—as a ferry service or for carrying goods. Next to the "government boats" the Tibetans used the term "profit boat" *beko* (*bed ko*) for the boats from which—depending on the distance and the quantity of goods and people they had to transport—they frequently made good money (see also Lange 2014: 80). Some of the people in Jun lived all the year round by providing transport services to businessmen.

Not only was transport on the water integrated into the tax system as corvée service, but so too was the transport of the boats back to their starting points on land. Due to the rapid currents of most Tibetan rivers, it was not possible to navigate non-motorised boats upstream after ferrying goods and people downstream. The hide boats had to be carried upstream. According to legend, after having a fight with a boatman over the ferry price, the Tibetan saint Rechungpa (Ras chung rdo rje grags pa; 1084–1161) condemned the boatmen with the words: "May your boat be swept away downstream! May it have to be carried on your backs upstream!"[17] In fact, after being in the water the hide boats were quite heavy (even a dry boat weighed around 60 kg) and needed to be dried out before being carried upstream. There were two methods by which this return journey was made. In the case of boats used for government services, these were carried by local villagers and passed along from village to village along the river—as a form of corvée tax payment by the particular villagers. When the boats were used for private transport, they were carried on the backs of the boatmen. When the terrain permitted, the boats could be carried across shortcuts over the mountains. That procedure was described by Western travellers such as Lowell Thomas, who visited the country in 1949 and noted that:

> The Tibetan boatmen cannot row their coracles upstream against the roaring current. When we reached Chushul, our *kobos* had to carry their skin boats back home along the river bank. Every boatman takes a pet sheep on the journey downstream. On the homeward trek the sheep carried the boatman's personal effects.
>
> THOMAS 1952: 124–25

---

17 Tibetan: *mar zhor chu mo'i gzhung la 'khyer ba shog/ yar zhor sgal par'kyer rgyu yong ba shog* (Grothmann 2011: 68).

To motivate the sheep to follow their masters, they were fed with tsampa, the Tibetan staple made from roasted barley flour. For carrying the boats the Tibetans developed a special technique. With the help of a carrying strap and the two oars the boat is balanced on the back (see also Lange 2014: 82).

The title of this paper, "My karma selected me to become a ferryman",[18] represents an extract from one of the songs that were sung to entertain the boat passengers by the boatmen in the past. The text refers to the social status and the reputation of ferrymen in pre-1959 Tibetan society that in general was not a good one. As occupational groups who benefited directly from the deaths of living beings, the ferrymen belonged to the lowest level in this society—next to butchers, fishermen, *ragyepa* (*rags rgyab pa*),[19] and beggars (Lange 1976: 111 and Ronge 1978: 31). They mostly lived in poverty and economic uncertainty, were sometimes forced to beg, and were regarded as "impure". According to Veronika Ronge, in the eyes of the Tibetans the ferrymen offended against every proper sense of cleanness since they accepted food and drinks from strangers. Also they loaded the dirt left by passengers and animals onto their heads when carrying the boats on their backs. An unflattering Tibetan proverb says about the boatmen: *gru pa'i kha las lha ris pa'i rkub gtsang*—"The backside of a painter is cleaner than the mouth of a boatman" (*ibid.*: 31f).

5 Conclusion

Waterways not only had an important function in the local and long-distance transport system in pre-1959 Tibet, but the ferry and transport services were essential for Tibet's trade and economy. The transportation system in pre-1959 Tibet was primarily adapted to the natural conditions of the landscape and its fauna. So was the tax system. The transport services were integrated into the local and regional tax system as corvée tax. In particular, communities that did not have enough fertile land due to geographical circumstances had to pay their tax dues in terms of corvée service. The case of the fishing village of Jun demonstrates how the tax payment was adapted to a community's economic and environmental conditions: though the *lag 'don* was traditionally paid in barley in Tibet, the village's fishing tradition allowed it to pay a part of this tax in fish. Its geographical location at the junction of the Yarlung Tsangpo and the

18 Tibetan: *las la mnyan dpon bskos song*. During my research I collected a large number of such songs that I publish in the paper "'The boatman is more beautiful than a god': poetizing and singing on the rivers in Central and Southern Tibet" (Lange 2016).

19 The *ragyepa* were responsible for carrying corpses out of the town in traditional Tibet.

Kyichu, and its relative proximity to the Chaksam ferry, to Lhasa and Tsetang led to an inclusion of the villagers in the ferry and transport service—as corvée tax. The village's boat-building and fishing tradition provided the essential equipment in terms of boats as well as technical skills and knowledge in terms of river navigation. Although the ferrymen belonged to the lowest level of the society and were regarded as "dirty", Tibetan society essentially depended on their ferry and transport services.

The ferry and transport services were abolished by the new government after 1959. In addition, over the last decades, through the modernisation of infrastructure, the old water craft—the hide boats and horse-head wooden ferries—have been replaced with bridges in many places. Apart from a few exceptions, such as the ferry services over the Yarlung Tsangpo to the monasteries of Samye and Dorje Drak (rDo rje brag), water transport has almost completely lost the significance it had previously held due to extensive road construction.[20]

Traces of the old transport and ferry system can still be found in present-day Tibet. The local colloquial Tibetan name of the longest bridge to the southeast of Lhasa is one example. The so-called Kuru bridge (Ku ru zam pa) is built where the former Lhatong ferry station used to stand. The term *kuru* is used in Tibet for the wooden X-shaped cross placed over the mouth of a calf to stop it from suckling. In recollection of the former ferrymen who lost their source of income (their "milk") due to the construction of the bridge, the Tibetans named it after the *kuru* (Lange 2014: 85f.)

Within the context of the construction of the new shortcut road between Lhasa and Gongkar (Gong dkar) airport—with two new bridges crossing the Kyichu and the Yarlung Tsangpo and one tunnel in between—Jun was connected to the local road network. Among the many consequences of that road, the villagers now no longer depend on boats as a means of transport.[21]

References

Altner [Lange], D. 2009a. Fishery in Southern and Central Tibet: an economic niche is going to disappear. *In* B. Dotson, K.N. Gurung, G. Halkias and T. Myatt (eds)

20 For further information on the surviving ferry stations in Southern and Central Tibet, see Lange 2014.

21 For a detailed study on the recent changes in Jun see my publications: Altner 2009a, 2009b and 2010.

Contemporary Visions in Tibetan Studies. Proceedings of the International Seminar of Young Tibetologists, SOAS 2007. Chicago: Serindia, 45–67.

Altner [Lange], D. 2009b. *Die Verkleinerung der Yakhautboote. Fischerkulturen in Zentral- und Südtibet im sozioökonomischen Wandel des modernen China*. Wiesbaden: Harrassowitz.

Altner [Lange], D. 2010. From water radish to fish restaurant: recent development of fisheries in Central Tibet. *AAS Working Papers in Social Anthropology* 18, 1–13.

Das, S.C. 1902. *Journey to Lhasa and Central Tibet*. London: John Murray.

Filippi de, F. (ed.) 1932. *An Account of Tibet. The Travels of Ippolito Desideri of Pistoia, S.J., 1712–1727*. London: Routledge.

Goldstein, M.C. 2001. *The New Tibetan-English Dictionary of Modern Tibetan*. Berkeley, Los Angeles, London: University of California Press.

Grothmann, K. 2011. *Die Arshe. Arbeitslieder aus dem traditionellen tibetischen Handwerk*. Wiesbaden: Harrassowitz.

Harrer, H. 1950. Unpublished Diary.

Lange, D. 2014. "The government forced us to send the boat in the middle of the night": water transport in pre-1959 Tibet. *In* J. Bray, A. McKay and E. Sulek (eds) *Wim van Spengen Commemoration Volume, The Tibet Journal* special volume 39(1), 73–91.

Lange, D. 2016. "The boatman is more beautiful than a god": poetizing and singing on the rivers in Central and Southern Tibet. *In* O. Czaja and G. Hazod (eds) *The Illuminating Mirror: Tibetan Studies in Honour of Per K. Sørensen on the Occasion of his 65th Birthday*. Wiesbaden: Dr. Ludwig Reichert Verlag, 269–82.

Lange, K. 1976. *Die Werke des Regenten Sans Rgyas Rgya mc'o (1653–1705)*: eine philologisch-historische Studie zum tibetischsprachigen Schrifttum. Veröffentlichungen des Museums für Völkerkunde zu Leipzig, 27. Berlin: Akademie Verlag.

Ngawang Lobsang Gyatso. 1991 (1678). Ngag dbang blo bzang rgya mtsho'i rnam thar (Collected Works of the Fifth Dalai Lama). Vol. 17. Lhasa.

Ronge, V. 1978. *Das tibetische Handwerkertum vor 1959*. Beiträge zur Südasienforschung Vol. 43. Wiesbaden: F. Steiner.

Surkhang, Wangchen Gelek. 1966. Tax measurement and *lag 'don* tax. *Bulletin of Tibetology* 3(1), 15–28.

Thomas, L. 1952. *Out of this World. Across the Himalayas to Tibet*. London: Macdonald.

Tsepak Rigzin. 1993. *Festivals of Tibet*. Dharamsala: Library of Tibetan Works and Archives.

Tucci, G. 1956. *To Lhasa and Beyond. Diary of the Expedition to Tibet in the Year MCMXLVIII*. Rome: Istituto Poligrafico Dello Stato.

FIGURE 6.1 Overview of the village Jun in 2004; the Kyichu can be seen on the left side, photo by Diana Lange

FIGURE 6.2
A yak-hide boat set up to dry in Jun in 2012, photo by Diana Lange

FIGURE 6.3 A yak-hide boat being carried to the Kyichu River in Jun in 2012, photo by Diana Lange

FIGURE 6.4 A yak-hide boat being placed into water near Jun in 2012, photo by Diana Lange

FIGURE 6.5 Yak-hide boats are being carried by ferrymen at the Chakzam ferry station in 1938/1939; the sheep carry their luggage, photo by Ernst Schäfer
BUNDESARCHIV, IMAGE 135-BB-082-10-1

FIGURE 6.6 Yak-hide boats being loaded with wool at one of the ports in Lhasa in 1938/1939, photo by Ernst Schäfer
BUNDESARCHIV, IMAGE 135-S-12-43-07

FIGURE 6.7 River crossing at the Chakzam ferry station with a horse head wooden ferry in 1938/1939, photo by Ernst Schäfer
BUNDESARCHIV, IMAGE 135-S-15-07-20

CHAPTER 7

Performing Tibetan Opera As *khral* in the First Half of the 20th Century: In Principle a "Tax", in Experience a Pervasive Obligation

Isabelle Henrion-Dourcy

1 Introduction

Until the takeover of Tibet by the People's Republic of China (PRC), the Curd Festival (*zho ston*) was one of the most important festivals of the Lhasa year, certainly the most significant and attended one in the summer.[1] It was initiated by the Fifth Dalai Lama at his palace, the Ganden Phodrang (dGa' ldan pho brang), in Drepung ('Bras spungs) monastery in the middle of the monastic summer retreat.[2] The name of the festival is said to have come from the large amount of curd (*zho*) that was served to monks at the time.[3] Over time, it featured, among other events, the investiture of the two discipline masters of 'Bras spungs (*tshogs chen zhal ngo*) for the coming year and the display of a giant appliqué thangka (*gos sku*). It was enhanced with a multitude of songs, dances and recitations executed by lay performers from various places in Central Tibet. In 1848, at the time of the Eleventh Dalai Lama, the festival was extended for a few days into the 7th month, with additional shows in the gardens of the Dalai Lama's summer palace, the Norbu Lingkha (Nor bu gling kha; Zhol khang bSod nams dar rgyas 1993: 18). This is how the *zho ston* was mostly known in late premodern Tibet: as lavish performances of opera (*a lce lha mo*, often simply called *lha mo*) that would draw all and sundry to Norbu Lingkha. Opera troupes were summoned to Lhasa by the Tibetan government. These performances were considered a "tax" (*khral*), and were therefore overseen

1 See Richardson (1993: 97–107) for fine photographs of the *zho ston* in the 1930s and 1940s.

2 The summer retreat extends from the 15th day of the 6th month to the last day of the 7th month. The *zho ston* was held in Drepung ('Bras spungs) on the last two days of the 6th month (see Figure 7.1). It is said that popular rejoicing during that ascetic period was a ruse to prevent a demon living in the rocky mountain behind the monastery from harming the studious monks, as he would be satisfied to see that the monks were distracted enough.

3 Blo bzang rdo rje (1988). Alternative etymologies include *zhog ston*, "festival held in the morning" (Rak ra Rin po che 1996: 11).

DOI:10.1163/9789004529465_009

by officials in charge of the fiscal matters of the state, more exactly by one of the three state treasuries, the Dalai Lama's private treasury at the Potala (*rtse phyag las khungs*).

lHa mo was a popular entertainment, especially in Tsang (gTsang), and was of course not solely performed as a tax at the *zho ston*. The Curd Festival was an exceptional occasion for opera shows, its splendour and repute having shaped much of the popularity of this tradition among Central Tibetans. As we will see, *lha mo* was also performed as "tax" on other occasions, for private landowners, yet most of the time, it was simply performed as a remunerated activity. In this paper, I shall focus the discussion on opera as *khral*, but I will also briefly evoke the other non-*khral* occasions, to show how the integration of the ritual and economic dimensions of opera, an activity related to Buddhist notions of merit, sheds light on the understanding of *khral* by the actors.

It is well known that the Tibetan government (Ganden Phodrang) levied tax (*khral*) in kind and corvée labour, and that taxes included services—such as religious rituals, acrobatic exploits and secular performances, that could be temporary or lifelong duties. *lHa mo* was such a service, but how was the system of performance-as-tax conceptualised and practically organised in this case? What was the relationship between the government and the actors, and was this relationship different whether it was a performance-tax for the Tibetan state (*phyi khral*, as in the case of *zho ston*), or for the actors' landowners (*nang khral*)? As I will give voice to some of these actors themselves, as they remembered in their old age the practicalities of acquitting a "tax" for their landlords, it will become clear that the tax principle was conveniently loose for the beneficiaries of the tax. More often than not, it was experienced as a pervasive obligation by the performers. In this paper, I aim to show that *lha mo* performed as a *khral* is an example of a general characteristic of the Tibetan tax system: the structural domination between landlords (be they government, monastic or aristocratic) and taxpayers resulted in the taxpayers being generally, and somewhat indiscriminately, obliged towards their landlords. Their services were not always precisely quantified or limited.[4]

This paper is thus a foray into the sociology of traditional Tibetan opera. This aspect has been largely overlooked, previous publications having concentrated on the repertoire (with translations of the plays) and the general features of a *lha mo* performance. Very few studies have tried to document how drama was

4 I wish to thank Alice Travers for her thorough revision of this paper, which has greatly enriched my understanding of the taxation system in Central Tibet. Any misconstruction is of course entirely my own.

FIGURE 7.1 Actors performing as *khral* at the *zho ston* in Drepung monastery, date and photographer unknown
© LTWA PHOTOGRAPHIC ARCHIVE

embedded into the Tibetan social fabric.[5] There is a dearth of information on the social status of actors, their livelihoods, the economic and social relationship they had with patrons, gender issues, or the maintenance of discipline and order within the troupes. This chapter falls short of addressing all these points but will look more specifically at the social relations surrounding *lha*

5 Snyder (1979: 29–35) for an overview of the *zho ston*; Schuh 1976 (translated into English: 2001) and Norbu Tsering 1999 for the Kyormolungpa (sKyor mo lung pa) troupe; Dikey Drokar 2008 for the Gyelkhar, Tshome and Nyangdren (rGyal mkhar, mTsho smad, Nyang bran) troupes. See Henrion-Dourcy (2017: 287–384) for an overall discussion of the social fabric of *a lce lha mo*. Publications in either Tibetan or Chinese are very scant and short: bDe skyid sgrol dkar 2001 for the Gyelkhar troupe; Jiala 2012 and Sangjidongzhi 2015b for the Kyormolung troupe; and Sangjidongzhi 2015a for a sociology of peasant actors.

mo performance as an economic activity that was integrated into the taxation system of premodern Tibet.

The research presented here relies on oral history data[6] gathered during three years of doctoral fieldwork carried out at the end of the 1990s. As the practice of *lha mo* was shifting in the last three decades of the Ganden Phodrang rule, it is important to stress here that the following descriptions are limited to the first half of 20th century, which represents the span of the informants' living memory. I have collected testimonies from over seventy *lha mo* actors in Central Tibet (mostly in Lhasa, but also among the most famous troupes of Tsang), and exile in Nepal (mostly Kathmandu), India (Dharamsala) and the West (the United States, Switzerland, France, Canada, Belgium and Holland). Most of them have now passed away. I crossed their accounts with the reflections of about fifteen Tibetan historians, scholars and folklorists in either Lhasa or Dharamsala.[7] I have updated the materials with two field trips in the 2000s and publications, in Tibetan and Chinese, by young scholars working in the Tibet Autonomous Region (bDe skyid sgrol dkar 2001, Jiala 2012, Sangjidongzhi 2015 a).

2 A Typology of *lha mo* Troupes up to the 1950s

As a first step into the sociology of *lha mo*, let us delineate the various types of troupes extant until the end of the 1950s. *lHa mo* was first and foremost a peasant (*zhing pa*) culture. It expressed the preoccupations of farmers and the key occasions for opera performances were inscribed in the agricultural cycle: the *'ong skor* festival, at the beginning of autumn, with the ritual circumambulation of the fields; and the New Year. Pastoralists (*'brog pa*) did not usually have a taste for this dramatic style or his stories, to which they preferred the more martial Ge sar epic.

lHa mo is also predominantly a Central Tibetan cultural practice. Some troupes, performing an archaic-looking form of opera, are found in the fringes of the Tibetan plateau: among Sherpas of Southern Tibet (Sangjidongzhi 2015 c), further west in Humla and in Spiti (sPi ti), as well as, to the east, in

6 I still sorely miss access to archival documents. It would have shed a much clearer light on the matter of this chapter, especially terminology, than the sole memory of my informants, who were young and inexperienced actors at the time. This is one of the many methodological difficulties of working on an orally transmitted tradition inserted in a very textual cultural environment. My attempts to peruse the archives of the *rtse phyag las khungs* related to *zho ston*, if still extant, have not been fruitful so far.

7 For a complete list of the informants and scholars and their background, see Henrion-Dourcy (2017: 753–62).

several places of Mon and among the Sherdukpen (Sher stug spen). *lHa mo* also spread from Lhasa eastwards, first to some monasteries in Kham in the second half of the 19th and at the beginning of the 20th centuries; then, from 1946 onwards, a new style emerged in Amdo, named *rnam thar*, partially inspired by *a lce lha mo*.[8] But the heartland of *lha mo* remained in Ütsang (dBus gTsang), though it was not evenly popular everywhere. It was widespread all over Tsang, where the style originated. It was also popular in Lhokha (lHo kha), mostly around Tsethang, Chonggye and Kunga.[9] As for Ü (dBus), it was concentrated in the Tölung (sTod lung) valley and of course Lhasa.

Moreover, opera was predominantly performed by laypeople.[10] Early accounts (Bacot 1914, 1921; Duncan 1955, 1967), perpetuated by later commentators, gave the impression that *lha mo* was performed by monks, reading aloud a hand-held libretto. Actually, these first observations were done in Kham, where a late and idiosyncratic form of *lha mo* had developed, unrepresentative of the overall style in Tibet. *lHa mo* was indeed performed by monks in Kham—as was the case in Amdo—emulating back home what the monks had seen, as students in Lhasa, during the *zho ston*.

Troupes were nearly always named after the village or region of the actors, adding a nominaliser -pa or -ba, as in Kyormolungpa (sKyor mo lung **pa**), Gyelkhar**wa** (rGyal mkhar **ba**), and so forth, underlying the importance of territorial anchoring. Three main terms are used nowadays to signify "troupe", but it is unclear whether they were common before 1959. *lHa mo* is probably an old designation; it is a noun that first meant "troupe", before it was used to refer to the dramatic style. The term *skyid sdug*, or the composed *lha mo'i skyid sdug*, is best translated as "company" rather than "guild", since it does not entail for *lha mo* the usual bonds of mutual assistance found in other professional or regional *skyid sdug* (Miller 1956). Finally, *tshogs pa*, "association", is probably a term that has emerged after the Chinese take-over (a possible translation of 团 *tuan*) and has now become the most widely used denomination. Except for the 'Phyongs rgyas spun bdun, troupes did not generally keep records of their history, not even those summoned to the *zho ston*. The number of actors within troupes appears to have increased over time to reach, in the first half of

8 On the historical diffusion of *lha mo* outside of Central Tibet, see Henrion-Dourcy (2017: 135–56).

9 rTsed thang, 'Phyong rgyas, Kun dga'.

10 Sometimes by women (see below), and also, in the 1940s, by monks in Lhasa (Henrion-Dourcy 2017: 385–409), and even by the nuns of Michungri (Mi chung ri) and Gadong (dGa' gdong) nunneries (Takla 2005: 207). It is important to emphasise that two of the *zho ston* troupes, the Gyelkharwa and the Chungpa were *ser khyim pa* (married religious practitioners), the latter having been defrocked at the time of the Dzungar invasions in the 18th century.

the 20th century, about twenty performers for the full-fledged *lha mo* performances, and seven to ten actors for the *bkra shis zhol pa* style of performances that will be detailed below. Both types of troupes were enlisted at the *zho ston*.

There was no such thing as a uniform "social status of opera performers", as *lha mo ba* did not hail from a single, homogeneous social category, and because their social status did not actually derive from their practice of *lha mo*. One often reads in vulgarisations about Tibetan opera or in Chinese propaganda that the actors hailed from the lower social ranks and were despised. This form of marginality did indeed exist, and applied to most performers of the famed Lhasa-based Kyormolung troupe, for example (see Figure 7.6). But it was in no way coextensive with the whole *lha mo* practice. Tibetans have not produced a traditional classification of the various opera troupes, but in my interviews, it was clear that they compared troupes in terms of, on one hand, prestige (higher or lower) and, on the other hand, socioeconomic status (higher or lower). If we combine these to criteria, we can delineate four types of troupes in premodern Tibet (see Table 7.1).

As for socioeconomic status, the first criterion, actors were peasants before being performers. *lHa mo* was a folk genre performed as a side-activity by *khral pa*, farmers attached to a piece of land (*sa zhing*) and to a landowner (*mnga' bdag*). Their social status was thus derived from their position in the wider socio-economic estate system. Performing *lha mo* was an activity of commoners (*mi ser*). Aristocrats were on the whole fond of *lha mo* and several of them learned the songs (*rnam thar*) and a few moves. Some even did put up shows at one of the summer picnics in Lhasa, but this was dilettante entertainment, not real performances for everyone to watch. Among the commoners (*mi ser*), those who did not have a land to cultivate could not eke out a living, and therefore had to roam the land as beggars (*sprang po*) or specialised professionals (activities far less honourable than agriculture). They were considered poorly and encountered contempt. Among these social dropouts were several troupes of vagrant *lha mo* actors, who could go as far as Darjeeling or Kalimpong in the winter (see Figure 7.2). Most of them hailed from Tsang, which is famous for, and very prolific in, songs, dances and ritual exploits. A famous adage evoked the vagrancy of the Kyormolung actors, who were based in the Lhasa region: "Instead of holding an estate in Kyormolung, take an old drum and roam the land!"[11]

11 *sKyor mo lung gi pha gzhis zin pa las / rnga gog 'khyer nas rgyal khams skor nas 'gro.* This adage knows a few variants. One of them, for the second half, is: "Take Dangzang and go on a pilgrimage!" (*Dwangs bzang 'khrid nas gnas bzang mjal na dga'*). Dangzang was the lady who is said to have founded the Kyormolung troupe at the turn of the 20th century.

TABLE 7.1 Typology of premodern *lha mo* troupes in Central Tibet

Socioeconomic status / **Prestige**	HIGHER **Attached to a land (amateur troupes)**	LOWER **Not attached to a land (professional troupes)**
HIGHER Troupes summoned to the *zho ston* as a tax obligation (*khral*)	9 troupes: 3 full-fledged *lha mo* troupes: 1. rGyal mkhar ba 2. gCung pa 3. Shangs pa and 6 *bkra shis zhol pa* troupes: 4. 'Phyongs rgyas bkra shis spun bdun 5. Yar lung bkra shis zhol pa 6. Dar grong sNye mo ba 7. Thon pa Snye mo ba 8. mTsho smad ba 9. sNang rtse ba	1 full-fledged *lha mo* troupe: sKyor mo lung pa
LOWER Troupes **not** participating at the *zho ston*	about a hundred *lha mo* troupes?[a] (most of them in gTsang and lHo kha, but also in dBus)	a dozen *lha mo* troupes?[b] (mainly in gTsang)

a A common estimate by actors I met across and out of Tibet. Liu Zhiqun believes there were "between 300 and 400 such troupes" (interview, Lhasa, 2005). As a point of comparison, since *lha mo* has been recognised as an Intangible Cultural Heritage, first of the PRC (2006) then of humanity (2009, under the auspices of UNESCO), 117 troupes have been officially inscribed on that list in the Tibet Autonomous Region.

b Estimation by Norbu Tshering, interview, 2001. One well-known such troupe was the Yamdrok Chökhortsewa (Yar 'brog chos 'khor rtse ba; Sangs rgyas don grub [cf. Sangjidongzhi 2015 a], interview, 2017). *lHa mo* was performed in Chökhortse (Chos 'khor rtse) for a long time, as we find a mention of this troupe's name in sDe srid Sangs rgyas rgya mtsho's *Rab gsal gser gyi snye ma*, on the occasion of the enthronement of the Sixth Dalai Lama in 1697 (passage translated in Henrion-Dourcy 2017: 122). The Indian pundit S.C. Das (1988 [1902]: 217) also mentions having seem a *lha mo* performance from a troupe from Chökhortse in 1881–1882.

In Table 7.1, I have named the lower socioeconomic status troupes "professional", but this does not correspond to a Tibetan labelling. Professional (*ched las*) and amateur (*las zhor*) are modern categories that were not in use then, at least not in that sense and for *lha mo* actors. My designation as "professionals" is sociological (performing was their only income) rather than aesthetical (actors devoted to an art that they sought to perfect, for example). They were fugitives fleeing oppressive conditions on their estate, orphans, or of mixed Chinese and Tibetan parentage (a few in the Kyormolungpa troupe, such as Lenden Pao and his family).

The social status of the performers attached to a land was higher. They were commoners (*mi ser*), internally differentiated between the "tax payers" (*khral pa*) and, somewhat lower, the "small hearths" (*dud chung*), who had no hereditary rights to a land and had to sell their work force. In principle, all the troupes selected to perform at the *zho ston* had to come from the *khral pa* class. But they were not requested to be from affluent *khral pa* families, as was the case for the *gar phrug pa*,[12] the dance troupe of the Dalai Lama, composed of young boys uprooted from their families and sent to be trained in Lhasa as a "tax" (*khral*). In practice, some troupes did send *dud chung* actors to the *zho ston*, or at least so did the Gyelkharwa troupe (see Figure 7.4) on a few occasions.[13] Actually, the status of the Gyelkharwa troupe was higher than that of the other troupes—for those who were *khral pa*, of course—because they were also married religious practitioners (*ser khyim pa*).[14] They were literate and engaged in religious rituals on top of their domestic activities. This troupe's style was highly regarded, considered the most classical, pure and sedate, yet I wonder if this aura of respectability was not owed to their higher social status, rather than the actual artistic quality of their production on the stage.

Furthermore, status was unrelated to both popularity and wealth. In the last two decades before the PRC annexation, the Kyormolungpa troupe was the most popular troupe at the *zho ston*, but it was also the one with the lowest social status. Aristocrats sought and fought to invite them to perform at their mansion after the *zho ston*, but as these "beggars" were thought to be bringing bad luck, the nobles also tried to invite the famed Yarlung Trashi Zhölpa (Yar lung bkra shis zhol pa) troupe, to perform just a few dances of good luck (*bkra shis*) after the show, to get rid of infortune. If they were unavailable, the Kyormolungpa would perform the auspicious songs and dances of the *bkra*

12 Tashi Tsering, Goldstein and Siebenschuh (1997: 11).

13 More exactly, it was not a first choice or a deliberate deception on the part of the troupe. It was a make-do solution in case a regular actor of the troupe had died or was not able to go to the *zho ston*. This was made easier among the Gyelkharwa by the fact that there were two performing traditions in their village: the *khral pa* performed *a lce lha mo* (and went to the *zho ston*), and the *dud chung* performed the same librettos, but in *bla ma ma ṇi* (recitation only) style (and were not allowed at the *zho ston*). Since the *dud chung* already knew the librettos well, replacements were easy to do.

14 Kapstein (2006: 186) mentions how *ser khyim pa* enjoyed a social status higher than other commoners.

shis zhol pa themselves, without costumes. Wealth was also variable, not only between troupes, but also within them. Some Kyormolung actors were quite prosperous in the 1950s, more so than *khral pa* actors, while others barely made ends meet. In *khral pa* troupes like the Thonpa Nyemowa (Thon pa sNye mo ba), there were also considerable differences of wealth within the troupe.

On the whole, socioeconomic status played into the life of actors in two main ways. First, it implied different motivations for playing *lha mo*: it was a part-time activity for the actors attached to a land; but a full-time necessity for those with no roots in a piece of land. In actuality, as we will see below, some amateur *zho ston* troupes did perform for money as well—their *lha mo* practice was not limited to paying a tax in Lhasa. Likewise, the Kyormolung troupe performed both as a tax at the *zho ston* and as a necessity, to eke out a living, elsewhere.[15] Besides, for amateur troupes not participating at the Curd Festival, it was neither a duty nor a necessity, but rather a choice, or an inclination, to play opera at one's village festivals and in the vicinity.

Second, the internal organisation of the troupes was different, following their status. Amateur troupes were composed of villagers, gathered on a somewhat egalitarian basis, the director of the troupe (*dge rgan*, "teacher") claiming a larger share of the earnings.[16] Professional troupes were mostly family-based (usually one, sometimes two families), and relations were subject to intra-family dynamics. They usually shared income equally, and children, elders, women, etc., all did their chores, on and off the stage. They were thus the only troupes that featured female performers. Some *lha mo* actresses from the Kyormolung troupe, such as Ama Lhakpa (A ma lHag pa),[17] did even achieve a high level of popularity, but they were not allowed to perform at the *zho ston*, or even in the performances right after the *zho ston* in Lhasa. Expressive female movements were considered bad luck and also unsuitable in the presence of monks—even more so in front of the Dalai Lama.

Let us now turn to the second criterion: prestige (my term), depending on whether or not the troupe was enlisted in the Curd Festival. The *zho ston* was a tax (*khral*) for all the troupes involved. They did consider this *khral* a burden, since the 6th and 7th months were the busiest time of year to attend the

15 In many regards, such as social status and acting style, the Kyormolungpa troupe stood out as totally exceptional. What opera has now become, both in Tibet and in exile, is the product of a long process of standardisation building on the Kyormolungpa tradition. See Henrion-Dourcy (2017: 348–72) for a detailed description of this troupe and the various lifestyles of its actors at the end of the Ganden Phodrang rule.

16 This could also be the case for the vice-director (*dge rgan gzhon pa*) and the keeper of the troupe's belongings (*gnyer pa*, or *bdag gnyer*).

17 See Henrion-Dourcy (2005: 209–17) for her life story and achievements.

fields. This was not a good time to leave home. Actors used to say that "a *lha mo ba*'s life is short" (*lha mo ba tshe thung thung red*), alluding to this arduous obligation. Yet, at the same time, this duty filled them with pride and they were highly regarded (*mthong chen*) by other commoners. They were entrusted to perform for the highest tier of Tibetan society, and their performance was considered, by others as well by themselves, an "offering" (*mchod pa*) to the Dalai Lama. The fact that one could even make such an offering was considered a privilege, bestowing upon the actors a special blessing in return. It is thus an interesting reversal, where an obligation (tax) doubles up as a voluntary gift (devotional offering). The old actors I met, who had been at the *zho ston* in the 1950s, did not voice any criticism, nor the slightest ironic comment, on what could be considered a hypocritical rhetorical device to make coercive taxes more acceptable to commoners by appealing to the Dalai Lama's paramount charisma. They unanimously shared a sense of pride in the exclusiveness of their proximity to the Dalai Lama through this offering, which brought them merit as well as blessings. Actors were, for example, given protective cords (*srung mdud*) blessed by the Dalai Lama to wear around their necks, and that they carried back home.

Troupes summoned to *zho ston*, which comprised ten *lha mo* troupes and two troupes performing other acts, were ranked in two categories (see Table 7.2). Out of the ten *lha mo* troupes, the four troupes performing full-fledged *lha mo* performances, what PRC folklorists now call "blue mask *lha mo*" (*'bag sngon po'i lha mo*, translating the Chinese 蓝面剧 *lanmianju*) were considered more prestigious than the six troupes that were performing the drum dances and good wishes of the *bkra shis zhol pa* style, what PRC folklorists have termed "white mask *lha mo*" (*'bag dkar po'i lha mo*, translating the Chinese 白面剧 *baimianju*). This distinction is based on the colour of the mask of the main characters that first take the stage.[18] Actually, the traditional categorisation used by Tibetans opposed "the four great troupes" (*lha mo che khag bzhi*) and the "six lesser troupes" (*lha mo chung ba drug*). The four great ones played opera as we usually understand it. The other troupes were primarily dancers and reciters of good wishes, brought to attract good luck onto official ceremonies, but they could also perform a shorter and more archaic-looking[19] style of

18 The hunter, *rngon pa*, in the first case has a blue mask; and wishers of good fortune, *bkra shis zhol pa*, in the second case mostly have a white mask—but this mask could be yellow in some troupes!

19 A thorough research is needed to confirm the claim of PRC folklorists that the *bkra shis zhol pa* troupes had kept the primitive form of *lha mo* that developed elsewhere into *a lce lha mo* as we know it today. There definitely are some ancient and rough looking elements in their performances, but it is not sufficient to say that one is the origin of the

lha mo, from the standard repertoire of plays, but with less vocal and gestural complexity than the full-fledged *lha mo* troupes.

Moreover, some troupes were singled out as being a hierarch's "favourite" troupe (*spyan bsal lha mo*).[20] It is said that the 'Phyongs rgyas spun bdun were the *spyan bsal* troupe of the Fifth Dalai Lama (they were in fact from his native village), whereas the Chungpa (gCung pa) were the *spyan bsal* troupe of the Thirteenth Dalai Lama.[21] The Kyormolungpa were the favourite troupe of the Fourteenth Dalai Lama, but it is unclear if they were publicly recognised with the status of *spyan bsal lha mo*. The Shangpa (Shangs pa) were the Seventh Panchen Lama's *spyan bsal lha mo*, even his own private troupe. The Darong Nyemowa (Dar grong sNye mo ba), for their part, were the favourites of the Karmapa in Tshurpu (mTshur phu), who enjoyed *lha mo* and had organised a summer festival (mTshur phu'i dbyar 'cham). Likewise, the village troupe of Drigung ('Bri gung) was the Reting (Rwa sgreng) regent's private troupe when he was in power (1934–1941), although it was not enrolled in the *zho ston*.[22]

Differentiating troupes according to prestige had three main implications. First, as attendance was mandatory, the *zho ston* troupes were more permanent than the others. Second, the quality of the performance was better. These troupes had probably been chosen for symbolic reasons (see next section, below), and not because they were the best performers. But they did become the best exactly because they were selected for the *zho ston*: their yearly performances were monitored by officials of the *rtse phyag*, and they were fined if they made mistakes. Finally, the prestigious troupes could capitalise, so to

other (Zhol khang 2003). An examination of *lha mo* played in the fringes of the Tibetan plateau, in Mon, Spiti (sPi ti), or among the Sherpas, would be a useful departure point for comparison.

20 *sPyan bsal*: "in old times, someone who had attracted in a specific manner (*dmigs **bsal***) the gaze (***spyan***) of the king, and then received a charge in government" (*Bod rgya tshig mdzod chen mo*: 1675).

21 Ex-Kyormolungpa Norbu Tshering (Nor bu tshe ring; interview, 2001), is of the opinion that the Thirteenth Dalai Lama supported this troupe not really because he thought they were the best (it may have actually been the opposite), but to deflect the craze that the Kyormolungpa troupe was gradually gaining in the 1920s and 1930s, under the tenure of its charismatic director Migmar Gyaltsen (Mig dmar rgyal mtshan). The Dalai Lama publicly criticised this actor, not because he genuinely thought he was not talented, but to prevent him from getting sick from all the talk that was generated by his fame. Furthermore, the Chungpa (gCung pa) were a relatively new (1918) re-addition to the *zho ston*, after several decades of absence, and their first performances may not have met the standards expected by the *lHa sa ba*. Their journey to Lhasa was also the longest among the *zho ston* participants, so this *spyan bsal* status may have actually been a form of encouragement.

22 See Henrion-Dourcy (2017: 320–21) for the gifts and prerogatives associated, for *lha mo* actors, with the *spyan bsal* status, especially for the Chungpa troupe.

FIGURE 7.2 Two *lha mo* actors, probably from a roaming troupe. Das studio, Darjeeling, 1930s
PRIVATE COLLECTION OF TASHI TSERING (AMNYE MACHEN INSTITUTE)

speak, on their repute and sell their performing skills, including their performance libretto (*'khrab gzhung*) to "branch" troupes, along the familiar terminology of "mother troupe" and "son troupes" (*ma/bu*). I interviewed an actor from a Gyelkhar "son troupe" in Lhasa in 1997, who stated that his itinerant troupe had learnt the skills from the original Gyelkhar troupe before the 1950s and advertised it as a Gyelkhar style of performances. Once "mother" troupes finished teaching *lha mo* to other troupes, they did not keep relations with them.

3 Overview of the Ten Troupes Performing at the *zho ston* as a Tax

A detailed description of each troupe performing at the *zho ston* would be too lengthy here.[23] I will centre the discussion of the socio-economic relations mobilised by the performance-as-*khral* during the Curd Festival. Table 7.2 summarises the most important data related to each troupe, including their name, location, landowner, time of foundation (when kept in oral tradition), specialised repertoire, and finally, family or institution responsible for their upkeep when they were staying in Lhasa for the *zho ston*—surprisingly, their landowners did not all care for their maintenance.

The logic for drafting troupes at the *zho ston* was to fulfil a *khral* for the government. Three troupes depended on a monastic estate; three troupes lived on an aristocratic estate; and three troupes had a combination of two landlords (either monastic and government; or monastic and aristocratic).[24] The latter situation concerned troupes comprising members from a same area, but attached to pieces of land belonging to different landlords because of the patchy land distribution in premodern Tibet, as a result of centuries of land donations, confiscations or redistributions, following landlords' promotions, appreciations or destitutions. For the troupes hailing from an aristocratic estate, i.e. the two Nyemo troupes and the Chonggye Pündün ('Phyongs rgyas spun bdun), the *zho ston* was not a *khral* on the actors, but explicitly targeted the landowners (respectively Shedra, Thönpa and Phalha),[25] who counted among the most powerful noble families of Tibet.

None of the troupes I have interviewed has kept in oral history the reason or time of its conscription at the Curd Festival. If the archives of the *rtse phyag* (supervising the *zho ston*) are still extant, they may give some clues to future researchers. Most of the troupes enlisted in the 20th century had unquestionably been part of the *zho ston* for a very long time. In Ngor dpal ldan chos skyong's autobiography (1702–1759), Tashi Tsering[26] has found a lengthy passage where the Sakyapa hierarch relates his donations to actors during the 1755

23 See their full description in Henrion-Dourcy (2017: 326–72).

24 The three types of estates until the 1950s were held by either a monastery, an aristocratic family or the government (*chos sger srid gsum*).

25 bShad gra, Thon pa, Pha lha.

26 Tashi Tsering (2001: 58) for a translation in English. See Henrion-Dourcy (2017: 127) for a translation in French of a more extensive passage of the Tibetan original.

FIGURE 7.3 Performers of the Karma Shar *'cham* dance at the Norbu Lingkha, receiving *kha btags* after their duty at the *zho ston*. Rhenock Tse Ten Tashi, Lhasa, *c.*1950

zho ston. He lists a number of troupes among which we find the familiar names (see Table 7.2) of performers from Nangtse (sNang rtse; three troupes), Yarlung (three troupes), Chonggye (two troupes), Tshome (mTsho smad), as well as "eighteen dancers of the *Bya khri spyan gcig* entourage", that is, the *'cham* dance (performed at the *zho ston* until 1959) of Lhasa city's protective deity, by the Karma Shar oracle and his retinue of constables (*skor 'chag pa*), petty criminals, and *rags rgyab pa*[27] serving in the lesser roles (see Figure 7.3).[28] Of special interest in this passage is the fact that Ngor dpal ldan chos skyong gives a much longer list of actors than the twelve troupes registered in the 20th century. Moreover, in addition to *lha mo* performers, he mentions several *bro pa* (dancers) and *glu pa* (singers) that have disappeared in the 20th-century *zho ston*. It is thus clear that the troupes and genres of performance enlisted to fulfil a *khral* at the *zho ston* have varied over time, and that the standard

27 Outcastes in Lhasa who performed various polluting chores, including transporting the corpses of indigent people to sky burial sites. They also supervised the beggars of Lhasa and the criminals who were released from jail and had nowhere to go (Jamyang Norbu 2015: 241–42). See the photograph in Richardson (1993: 102).

28 Nebesky-Wojkowitz (1993 [1956]: 122, 425), Tsepak Rigzin (1993: 50–51), Jamyang Norbu (2015: 237).

TABLE 7.2 The twelve troupes performing at the *zho ston* as tax in Lhasa in the first half of the 20th century

Name of the troupe First are the "four great troupes" (*lha mo che khag bzhi*), then the "six lesser troupes" (*lha mo chung ba drug*). The last two did not perform *lha mo*	**From: village (district, *rdzong*) [region]**	**Type of estate (landowner)**	**Foundation at the time of …**	**Specialised repertoire: in decreasing order of excellence**	**Upkeep of the actors while in Lhasa for the *zho ston***
rGyal mkhar **ba**	rGyal mkhar chos rdzong (Rin spungs) [gTsang]	Monastic (bSam sding) and government (district of Rin spungs)	Seventh (Fifth?) Dalai Lama?[a] (mid-18th century)	Specialised: CN, Rech[b] Other: No, GZBZ, DK	[Yab gzhis] Phun khang (aristocratic) family
gCung pa	[gCung] Ri bo che (Ngam ring) [gTsang/ sTod]	Monastic bKra shis lhun po)	Thang stong rgyal po? (15th century)	Specialised: CDD Other: No, CN, DK	gNas chung monastery
Shangs pa	Gram bKra shis rtse (rNam gling) [gTsang]	Monastic (bKra shis lhun po) and partially government (district of rNam gling)	Third Panchen Lama (mid-18th century)	Specialised: DK, GZBZ Other: No, DZ	Bla brang of Zhi bde monastery (Rva sgreng Rin po che)
sKyor mo lung **pa**	Actors not attached to an estate, coming from all over Tibet (mostly Lhasa, gTsang, Kong po)	/	Thirteenth Dalai Lama (*c.*1913)	Specialised: Po, ZN, DZ Other: No, CN, GZBZ, DK	Bla brang of Kun bde gling (rTa tshags Rin po che)

a The Gyelkhar actors told me the Seventh Dalai Lama. Le'u kre chun (1980: 256) mentions the Eighth Dalai Lama. bDe skyid sgrol dkar (2001: 79, see also Dekyi Drokar 2008: 215) cites the Fifth Dalai Lama.

b For the correspondence of the abbreviations, see below.

TABLE 7.2 The twelve troupes performing at the *zho ston* as tax in Lhasa (*cont.*)

Name of the troupe First are the "four great troupes" (*lha mo che khag bzhi*), then the "six lesser troupes" (*lha mo chung ba drug*). The last two did not perform *lha mo*	**From: village (district, *rdzong*) [region]**	**Type of estate (landowner)**	**Foundation at the time of …**	**Specialised repertoire: in decreasing order of excellence**	**Upkeep of the actors while in Lhasa for the *zho ston***
'Phyongs rgyas bkra shis spun bdun	sPun bdun ('Phyongs rgyas) [lHo kha]	Aristocratic (Pha lha family)	Fifth Dalai Lama (mid-17th century)	CN, DZ [excerpts only, did not play full-fledged *lha mo*]	Pha lha (aristocratic) family
Yar lung bkra shis zhol pa	bSam grub bde chen (sNe'u gdong, near Yum bu bla sgang) [lHo kha]	Monastic (bKra shis chos sde) and aristocratic (Khe smad family)	Fifth Dalai Lama (mid-17th century) Or end of 18th century?	*lJon pa'i yul gyi rnam thar* (local variant of CN)	Khe smad / Kun bzang rtse (aristo-cratic) family
Dar grong [or bShad sgra] sNye mo ba	Dar grong (sNye mo) [gTsang][c]	Aristocratic (bShad sgra family)	Seventh Dalai Lama (mid-18th century)	Main: CN, DZ Other: No, DK, GZBZ (as full-fledged *lha mo*)	bShad sgra (aristocratic) family
Thon pa Snye mo ba	lHun [grub] sgang (sNye mo) [gTsang]	Aristocratic (Thon pa family)	?	Main: CN Other: DZ, No, Po (as full-fledged *lha mo*)	Thon pa (aristocratic) family
mTsho smad ba	mTsho smad (sTod lung) [dBus]	Monastic ('Bras spungs spyi so)[d]	Fifth Dalai Lama (mid-17th century)	CN, DK, DZ, No	'Bras spungs spyi so
sNang rtse ba	sNang rtse (sTod lung) [dBus]	Monastic (sDe drug bla brang, in rMe ru grva tshang)	?	?	rMe ru grwa tshang

c Nyemo was considered as being part of Tsang before 1959 but is nowadays considered as part of Ü.
d Snyder (1979: 32) noted that they hailed from a government estate (located in the district or *rdzong* of Tshede), but this is not what the actors from Tshome told me in the 1990s.

TABLE 7.2 The twelve troupes performing at the *zho ston* as tax in Lhasa (*cont.*)

Name of the troupe First are the "four great troupes" (*lha mo che khag bzhi*), then the "six lesser troupes" (*lha mo chung ba drug*). The last two did not perform *lha mo*	**From: village (district, *rdzong*) [region]**	**Type of estate (landowner)**	**Foundation at the time of ...**	**Specialised repertoire: in decreasing order of excellence**	**Upkeep of the actors while in Lhasa for the *zho ston***
Shel grong 'brong rtsed (the play of the wild yaks of Shel grong)[e]	Shel grong (Chu shur) [dBus]	?	Fifth Dalai Lama (mid-17th century)? Seventh Dalai Lama (mid-18th century)?	(did not perform *lha mo*)	?
Kong po'i bro pa[f]	rGya mda' [Kong po]	?	Khri srong lde'u btsan (8th century)?	(did not perform *lha mo*)	?

e Richardson (1993: 106) shows a picture of this troupe, which is not performing *lha mo* but a related genre. It features performers playing two wild yaks, a reciter wearing a white goat skin mask reciting good wishes (close to the recitations of the *bkra shis zhol pa*) and singing in a vocal style reminiscent of Tibetan opera, and two percussionists (the rhythms are very close to *lha mo*). These are still performed nowadays, though in a very modernised fashion.

f Also named *Kong po'i rkyang 'khrab* ("the solo performer from Kongpo"). I have not been able to find much information about this performer. He was not from Kongpo during the last years of the Ganden Phodrang rule. He was a descendant of the first *bro pa* dancers brought from Kongpo at the court of the Fifth Dalai Lama, as a reminiscence of the shows of songs and dances of the royal period. *Bro* dancers, with big drums attached to their waists, featured prominently at the inauguration of Samye in 779, for example (Interview with Zhölkhang Sonam Dargye [Zhol khang bSod nams dar rgyas], 1996).

Abbreviations for the titles of the plays:

CDD	*Chung po Don yod dang Don grub*
CN	*Chos rgyal Nor bzang*
DK	*Dri med Kun ldan*
DZ	*'Gro ba bzang mo*
GZBZ	*rGya bza' Bal bza'*
No	*sNang sa 'od 'bum*
Po	*Padma 'od 'bar*
Rech	*Ras chung pa (or Ras chung dBus la phebs)*
ZN	*gZugs kyi nyi ma*

twelve-troupe list of the 20th century is the product of a reorganisation, about which we unfortunately do not have any details.

Why did the *khral* of the Curd Festival fall onto these specific troupes? At this point, we can only produce conjectures. Is it because the quality of their erstwhile performances that some troupes were summoned to the *zho ston*? Or because an aristocratic official was promoted and considered it an honour to bring performers from his estate to perform in Lhasa? Or was it a punishment? From the scant available oral data, with no access to potential written archives, I shall, for four of these troupes, tentatively propose an interpretation resting more on political symbolism than artistic excellence. The Chonggye Pündün, for example, were from the native village of the Fifth Dalai Lama, who not only initiated the *zho ston*, but also represents, in Tibetan history, the recovered splendour of a unified Tibet. He rekindled much of the political symbolism of the royal period. The Yarlung Trashi Zhölpa were from Yarlung, near Yumbu Lagang (Yum bu bla sgang), the origin of the Tibetan royalty. These were the two most important *bkra shis zhol pa* troupes in the whole of Tibet. The Chungpa came from Riwoche (Ri bo che), more precisely from the monastic seat of Thangtong Gyelpo (Thang stong rgyal po), the purported founder of *a lce lha mo* in oral lore. They were married religious practitioners of the Nyingma school until the Dzungar invasion at the beginning of the 18th century forced them to defrock. They were held to be direct heirs to Thangtong Gyelpo's tradition, so their participation at the *zho ston* may have been a late[29] symbolic caution to the *zho ston*, bringing "authentic" *lha mo* and the aura of Thangtong Gyelpo onto the Norbu Lingkha stage.

Finally, the Gyelkhar troupe in Tsang was composed of *ser khyim pa* of the Kagyü school. They were often requested to perform the libretto *Ras chung dBus la phebs* (Rechung [Milarepa's disciple] goes to Ü), deriding some aspects of the Kagyü masters' lives. Had they been conscripted to perform in Lhasa as a humiliating commemoration of the 1642 victory of the Dalai Lama and the Gelukpa over the princes of Tsang and the Kagyüpa? This was already the case for another well-known performance-as-*khral* during the New Year celebrations, the *byang khar* [*mkhan*?] *thag shur*. It was carried out by peasants from Tsang, who had to "fly down a rope" tied between the Potala and a stele in the courtyard below, head first, to retell year after year of the demise of the Tsangpa.[30] The Thirteenth Dalai Lama abolished these risky acrobatics after a fatal accident, and replaced them with the *gnam bro thag rtsed* (dance in the

29 They were enrolled in the *zho ston* again in 1918.

30 Chapman (1940: 313), Stein (1987: 147, 149), Richardson (1993: 18–20), Snellgrove (1957: 133–34).

sky, play on the rope).[31] Shortly after, in the 1940s, the libretto *Ras chung dBus la phebs* fell out of fashion at the *zho ston*. The Gyelkharwa actors I interviewed in the 1990s could only sing a few songs (*rnam thar*) and had forgotten, or never known, the libretto—which I could photocopy at the Tibet Opera Troupe (*Bod ljongs lha mo tshogs pa*) in the 1990s.

4 Performance-as-*khral* in the Taxation System

How were the *lha mo* performances of the *zho ston* integrated into the taxation system of the Ganden Phodrang? I shall review in this section the principles of the system and, in the following section, the complications of its practical implementation.

The literature on taxation in Central Tibet[32] has documented how taxes (*khral*) were divided into two main categories. The first one included two types of taxes: tax in kind (*lag 'don*), on the products of agriculture and husbandry,[33] and corvée (*rkang 'gro*). The latter category comprised various types of mandatory labour (*'u lag*), such as building a house or temple, drying up swamps, fetching water, weaving textiles, repairing bridges and roads, as well as the most dreaded and burdensome obligation, the "corvée about the way" (*lam thog*), for which the *mi ser* had to provide free transportation animals for officials, their family and their belongings, as well as holders of a special permit from the government.[34] The taxation practices of estates under the Ganden Phodrang jurisdiction were not uniform, and the burden of the levy, or the social pressure from the landowners in general, knew considerable variation across Central Tibet. There were also different types of taxes: on the village, on the household (Aziz 1978: 111), and, especially on the monastic estates, on individuals (Dargyay 1982: 22–26).

As for the taxes collected by the government, they were calculated by the Ministry of Finance (*rtsis khang*) in Lhasa, and divided between the three government Treasuries.[35] The private Treasury of the Dalai Lama (*bla brang phyag mdzod*, or *bla phyag*), at the Jo khang, received the money, meat, and butter; the Potala Reserve Treasury (*rnam sras gan mdzod*) collected the precious

31 See the photograph in Richardson (1993: 19).

32 See Carrasco (1972 [1959]), Goldstein (1968, 1971), Surkhang (1984, 1986), Thupten Sangyay (1986), Schwieger (in this volume) for the most important contributions.

33 The *lag 'don* had gradually and partially been converted in money from the second half from the 19th century for easier conveyance to Lhasa.

34 Surkhang (1986: 24–25). This corvée did not apply to monastic estates.

35 Petech (1973: 11), Thupten Sangyay (1986: 44–46).

materials; and the Dalai Lama's private Treasury at the Potala (*'phral sde phyag mdzod*, or *rtse phyag*) managed the cereals, felt, tea and minerals. The income generated was mostly spent on religious purposes, especially at *dge lugs pa* monastic institutions. It is the office of the Dalai Lama's private Treasury at the Potala (*rtse phyag las khungs*) that supervised the ceremonial expenditures of the State (Tsarong 1998: 24), which included religious rituals for the prosperity of the Dalai Lama and the Ganden Phodrang regime, as well as for the collective well-being of all Tibetans. The Lhasa year was punctuated, month after month, by such recurring rituals.[36]

Tax in kind could be adapted in the case of particular environmental conditions, or specialised local productions. Those local specialties were then levied in total or partial replacement of the usual agricultural and pastoral goods. In this category were found natural products (oil, medicines, furs, salt, rare or specific kinds of fruit, wood, or minerals), manufactured goods (textiles, incense, metalwork, paper, felt, arrows, dyes, molasses, etc.), and specialised skills (carpentry, masonry, painting, music, or other forms of entertainment). We can now understand how cultural productions such as *lha mo* performances have become subsumed into the Tibetan State taxation system. They were a local production, a part of which was handed over to the central power. Conceptually, although they were intangible, they were understood to be a type of tax in kind (*lag 'don*), and not a corvée (*rkang 'gro*)—an association a Western sensibility would be inclined to make intuitively, since performances imply labour or service. But in the Tibetan case, these performances were thought to be characteristic local productions (alongside incense or medicines in specific regions) that would benefit the welfare of the State. There was no specific terminology in Tibetan for these types of performance-taxes, which could also include religious rituals performed by monks. They were simply called *khral*,[37] and, in principle, they meant a partial or total exemption from other taxes (Stein 1987: 80): the *mi ser* met all or part of their tax obligations by means of that performance, thereby alleviating their burden of other taxes, for instance payments of grain or butter.

Actually, despite the sparse population and the simplicity of both life conditions and the administrative structure in Central Tibet, the State ceremonies were extremely sophisticated and profusely ornamented. This is where most of the spending of the dGa' ldan pho brang was directed. In a way, rather

36 See the powerfully evocative photographs of those yearly rituals in Richardson (1993).

37 In the Chonggye Pündün troupe, the tax was called *khral dgu bsdus* ("tax on the nine [actors] together"), since they were seven dancers/reciters, plus the troupe director and a percussionist.

than the official denomination "combination of religion and political power" (*chos srid zung 'brel*), the core ideology prevalent in premodern Tibet may have simply been: ritualism. Rituals were omnipresent in social and religious life, as they were in the exercise of power. What the State needed for its survival was indeed landed revenue—but the administration was limited to about 500 officials overseeing the whole range of public affairs (Goldstein 1993 [1989]: 6). But it also relied on rituals for immaterial sustenance, not only Buddhist liturgies and actions devoted to the upkeep of monasteries,[38] but also opulent spectacles enhancing the prestige and legitimacy of rulers. To be efficient, these performances had to be rooted in the Tibetan imaginary: not only salvific Buddhist rituals, but also, as during the New Year celebrations,[39] sports competitions exalting strength, courage and speed—auspicious signs of vitality—acrobatic skills, apotropaic rituals ridding the community of evil,[40] as well as, closer to our topic, songs, dances and displays of popular merriment under the ruler's political order. Moreover, the show was also partly in the audience: for major ceremonies, all the religious dignitaries, government members and officials, and foreign representatives were seated according to an elaborate protocol of decreasing importance—a showcase for the political winds in the capital. In other words, power was as much a matter of performance as it was about administration.

In the realm of the secular songs, dances and spectacles demanded as *khral* by the government, *lha mo* actors were thus far from exceptions. The two key festivities that drafted the most significant number of performers to Lhasa were the New Year in winter, and, on a smaller scale, the *zho ston* in summer. Nearly all the thousands of participants of the lengthy New Year celebrations had to perform their part as a *khral*. Song and dance performers were a mere fraction of them. Alongside the various sorts of reciters of praises, wishes of luck and prayers for happiness, including the well-known *'bras dkar* ("white result", sometimes *'dre dkar*, "white demons"), we can cite the *bro pa gzhas*

38 Carrasco (1972 [1959]: 123), Goldstein (1993 [1989]: 2).

39 Bell (1992 [1928]: 272–84), Richardson (1993: 11–59). All the participants at the various New Year festivities were fulfilling a *khral*, from the commoners engaging in the sports competitions to the sumptuously dressed ministers, high-ranking nobles and religious officials, or aristocratic waitresses who had to play their part in the pageant (and pay for the expenses themselves).

40 Such as the two scapegoat-like "ransoms" (*glud gong rgyal po*) who were also enlisted as acquitting a *khral*, at the end of the 2nd month (Richardson 1993: 61–71, with a photograph on p. 65).

ma,[41] the *'bras bu gling pa*,[42] the *gzim chung ba*[43] and of course the renowned *gar* [*phrug*] *pa*.[44] In the summer, during the *zho ston*, alongside *lha mo ba* were also called a variety of performers that changed over time, but that included, in the first half of the 20th century, the *shel grong 'brong rtsed* (the play of the wild yaks of Shelgrong [Shel gong], near Chushur [Chu shur]) and the *kong po'i bro pa* (see Table 7.2). More surprisingly, the monks of Meru Sarba (rMe ru gsar ba) in Lhasa were also subjected to a performance-as-*khral*: the government required them to perform on the Norbu Lingkha stage, officially every twelve years (actually only occasionally), a two- or three-day grandiose drama-like spectacle, quite innovative and different from *a lce lha mo*, in front of the Dalai Lama and a packed crowd.[45]

41 The *bro pa gzhas ma* were originally from Lhokha, and featured male dancers with a drum, female singers, and a male character wearing a white goatskin mask reciting wishes of happiness and prosperity.

42 The *'bras bu gling pa*, or *'bras gling mchod sprin gar pa* ("dancers [who present] clouds of offerings, from Dre[bu] Ling"), were peasants from Kumbum Thang (sKu 'bum thang), east of Lhasa (Zhol khang bSod nams dar rgyas, 1993: 1), or from a village named Drebu Ling ('Bras bu gling) near Tsethang (rTsed thang) in Lhokha (Richardson, 1993: 18). Their performance was very different from the other genres, deemed very elegant, and featured poetic songs, and dances of celestial beings on flute music. The style had been founded during the Rinpung (Rin spungs) dynasty (1481–1565) and integrated as a mandatory *khral* performance at the court of the Princes of Tsang (1565–1642). The Ganden Phodrang took them over from the previous rulers, as it did with the *gar* style.

43 The *gzim chung ba* ("those from the small residence [of the Dalai Lama]") or *gzim spyong ba* ("the soldiers of the residence [of the Dalai Lama]") were mostly part of the personal guard of the Dalai Lama, but also comprised peasants who had been conscribed through the military taxation system (*dmag khral*) from monastic estates in Ü, Kongpo and Dakpo (Dwags po) belonging to Drepung monastery or the Namgyal college (rNam rgyal grwa tshang) at the Potala. About fifty men were selected for this ritual one-month-service every year. They had to wear what was considered to be the military uniform of the royal period and execute archaic-looking performances such as *rbad* or *ljags rkyang*. During the two official *gtor rgyag* on the 29th day of the 12th month and on the 24th day of the 1st month, they had to do a *kha 'tshad* (?), shooting their firearms in all directions (Surkhang 1986: 31; Richardson, 1993: 40–41, 116, and interview with Norbu Tshering).

44 This troupe was different in that it was permanent and composed of highly trained young boys who took years to master their skills and remained in Lhasa. On the *khral* affecting the *gar phrug pa*, see Tethong (1979), Jamyang Norbu and Tashi Dondhup (1986: 139) and Tashi Tsering, Melvyn Goldstein & William Siebenschuh (1997: 11, 44). The drafting of a boy to Lhasa was a *khral* only on his household, not on the whole village, as was the case for several other performance-as-*khral* genres. This created resentment in the village, as his family, who was usually wealthy, was totally exempted of taxes, but the loss of income by the government had to be compensated for by the other households.

45 See Henrion-Dourcy (2017: 402–408) on the performances of the monks of Meru, that span from 1909 to 1940.

In addition to their yearly obligation, the performers could be called to Lhasa at other times to partake at exceptional celebrations associated with specific events in the life of the Dalai Lama. These events were named "good news and raise the flag" (*gtam snyan dar 'phyar*) and included his enthronement, ordination, final *dge bshes* examination, investiture as a ruler, or laying down the relics of the former Dalai Lama in the Potala. Again, these were major State ceremonies that needed a display of popular rejoicing to consolidate political legitimacy. A good example in historical documents is the thorough account, by the regent Sanggye Gyatso (Sangs rgyas rgya mtsho; 1653–1703), of the performances held for the inauguration of the Fifth Dalai Lama's Cenotaph and extension of the Potala Palace in 1690–1694. He lists hundreds of performers, their place of origin, their style of performance and the total amount of donations that were made to them.[46]

Furthermore, on top of their duties for the government, *lha mo* actors also had to perform as *khral*, on certain occasions, for their respective landlords. The Dardrong Nyemowa, for example, were sent by their landowner (the Shedra [bShad sgra] family) to Chede Zhöl (lCe bde zhol) monastery in Lhokha, to perform for three days, starting on the 3rd day of the 1st month. The obligation to the monastery was actually that of the aristocratic family, but the aristocrats sent in performers from their estates to acquit this *khral* in their stead. The Nyemowa found this *khral* burdensome, as they needed to walk for a week to Lhokha, and could therefore not spend New Year at home. *Khral* therefore also appears as a system of piled-up obligations, rather than an exclusive relation between the government and the subjects.

Other examples of peasants called to perform songs and dances as a *khral* to their landowners include the peasants on the land of the Sakya hierarch (Sa skya khri 'dzin), who had to offer a performance of *gzhas chen* every year.[47] Other *mi ser*, on the land of the Panchen Lama, yearly owed him not only *gzhas chen*, but also *bro*, other folk dances, and *gar*, just as for the Dalai Lama.[48]

46 A famous mural in the Potala palace depicts these elaborate celebrations (see a photograph in Lhading Jampa Kesang, 2000: 120). The regent's account is included in his *Catalogue of the Tomb* ([sDe srid] Sangs rgyas rgya mtsho 1990 [1696]: 736–37). For a translation and discussion of this passage, see Henrion-Dourcy (2017: 117–21). See also Schwieger 2021.

47 According to oral tradition, *gzhas chen* ("great songs") are held to have been composed at the time of Songtsen Gampo (7th century). To a contemporary ear, they do carry a flair of antiquity, although their precise genealogy is difficult to establish. They contain many historical references. They are performed in several places of Central Tibet, but are especially famous in Tsang.

48 Interview with Trashi Dondrub (bKra shis don grub), director of the Shangpa troupe, Namling (rNam gling), August 1997.

Peasants under the joint landownership of Sera monastery and the Tibetan government in Ruthog had to perform a "song tax" (*gzhas khral*) of *gshon* (a song-and dance genre specific to that region, with historical allusions) every three years, when the District Commissioner (*rdzong dpon*) and the Sera abbot visited Ruthog.[49] Closer to Lhasa, in Taktse (sTag rtse), more precisely in the villages of Dromthö ('Brom thod) and Dechen (bDe chen), villagers had to offer a *khral* of *bro* (dance) during the butter lamp festival of the monastery (*bde chen gsang sngags mkhar*)[50] in the 6th month. The creation of the *bro* dance is credited to the legendary trickster Akhu Tönpa in a well-known oral story: he had borrowed wheat grains (*gro*) from that monastery and was trying to find ways to avoid paying his debt back. On the due date, he went to the monastery and performed a dance (*bro*, perfectly homonymous with *gro*). When the monks asked him "Where is your *gro*?", he replied "I have just performed it for you". Contrary to all the shows mentioned until now, no spectator was allowed to watch this particular *bro*; it was called the "sealed *bro*" (*bro bka' rgya ma*).[51]

Most of these performances-as-*khral* were obligations inherited over many generations, typically with no oral record of their historical origins. How come that some commoners were enlisted to perform-as-*khral*, and why did the obligation befall onto them rather than commoners from other villages, for example? Reasons probably vary locally, but an ironic adage gives a first hint: "The tea and beer that we offer [to celebrate] propitious times, become a lasting tax in bad times (*skal pa bzang po'i ja chang / Dus tshod ngan pa'i khral 'jags*).[52] In other words, what was once a good-hearted offering, because it was appreciated, becomes a recurrent obligation. This may have been the case for some of those *khral*, but as Carrasco reminds, "the Tibetan economic system is such that special services can be considered either to be paid for by grants of tax-free land or to be the special due rendered by the holders of that land" (Carrasco [1972] 1959: 91). That means that some singers and dancers may have been the descendants of vagrant performers that a landowner had chosen to attach to his estate by giving them a plot of land and requesting an occasional performance in return. This was frequently the case for other wandering professionals, whose skills were sought after, such as sorcerers, artisans, doctors and blacksmiths (Stein 1987: 80). Conversely, in other cases, as one actor from Nyemo remembered,[53] the *khral* applied to itinerant performers who had been freed from the attachment to their land. He evoked singers who roamed the

49 Ngag dbang gsung rab (1997: 50), Karma mkhas grub (1998: 15).

50 This particular monastery is said to have kept "relics" of Akhu Tönpa (A khu ston pa).

51 Grong khyer lha sa chab gros rig gnas lo rgyus rtsom 'bri u yon lhan khang (1989–4: 148).

52 Information from Tashi Tsering (Amnye Machen Institute).

53 Interview with Tashi, Nyemo Dardrong, 1997.

FIGURE 7.4 Gyelkharwa actors performing *lha mo*, two actors performing *bkra shis zhol pa*, and other actors seemingly performing *bro* (on the left side) at Tshe smon gling monastery during the 7th month. Note: Thanks to Diana Lange for informing me about this source, and contextual details. Wise-Drew roll, c.1854

land with their *sgra snyan* (lute) and lived in tents, but who still owed once a year an "ear tax" (*am khral*), in the form of a few songs, to the landlord of their original estate.

5 On the Loose Interpretation of *khral*: a Tax Perceived as a Pervasive Obligation

How was the performance-as-*khral* concretely experienced from the actors' side? What were the other taxes that they were exempted from? Were their performances a substitute for the tax in kind (*lag 'don*) or the corvée service (*rkang 'gro*)? Or were their obligations thought to belong to a third category of tax? One thing is sure in my informants' minds: these "taxes" did not substitute for the particular corvée service of transportation (*'u lag*), considered an altogether different category of tax. As Carrasco already noted, the conceptual differences between taxes in kind and taxes in services (or labour) were not always clear for the Tibetans themselves (Carrasco 1972 [1959]: 90). In the specific case of the *zho ston*, it seems that only one troupe, the Chungpa, benefitted from a total tax exemption in return for servicing the Curd Festival. It may have been because they came from the furthest away from Lhasa (Riwoche [Ri bo che]), or because they were the last troupe to have been (re-)enrolled in the *zho ston* (1918). In their case, performing in Lhasa was considered a collective obligation for the whole village, which was not very difficult to fulfil given the fact that Riwoche was very large. Out of the sixty families, twelve had to produce the twenty actors of the troupe going to Lhasa. They were *mi ser* of the Tashi Lhunpo monastery, and they were relieved from tax in kind and corvée for the government. However, they were still subjected to the military conscription (*dmag khral*) and the monk-tax (*grva khral*).[54]

For all the other troupes that I interviewed, participation at the *zho ston* did not convert into any form of exemption whatsoever, be it exemption from grain tax or corvée labour.[55] So *khral*, in this case, was just unpaid labour. *Zho*

---

54 Interview with Pang Dorje (Pang rDo rje), Chung Riwoche, 1997.

55 If one day we have access to the archives of the Tibet Autonomous Region, we should look for possible official documents (*bka' shog*), letters of exemption that would tell us about the exact agreement between the State and the troupes: what was the counterpart of a performance at the *zho ston*? Which tax exactly, or series of taxes, and in which amount, was exempted in exchange for a performance in Lhasa? What is remarkable is that, in the memory of *all* my informants (but they were young actors and not the directors of the troupes in the 1950s) except the Chungpa, performing at the *zho ston* did not translate into *any* exemption. It is conceivable I have either misunderstood my informants, or

ston performances were indeed qualified as *khral*, but were not recognised as a clear and quantified item in the fiscal system, and were not identified as the precise counterpart of a specific right to a piece of land, for example. *Khral* translates here as a pervasive obligation: it was a type of binding relation between two unequal parties, where one had to produce an activity for free and the other one had to receive it formally. As the director of the Chonggye Pündün explained tongue-in-cheek, "Well, the idea of *khral*, that's very simple: you just do a mandatory work for a leader, and you don't get any food or salary".[56] Bell (1992 [1928]: 278) had also provided an ironic definition of *khral*: "[...] a tax or forced service: there is no profit, but only loss [...]". In some (maybe rare?) cases, performing *lha mo* was even a "surtax" (Snyder 1979: 23), that is, the actors had to deliver (perform) the same duty twice or more. Snyder does not give an example, but the case of the Dardrong Nyemowa, cited above, is instructive: the troupe was sent by its landowner (Shedra), on his behalf, to *zho ston* in the summer, then to Chede Zhöl monastery in the winter. There had also been a few other compulsory performances. Here again, the actors did not recall any concrete tax exemption for these performances, either in their taxes due to the State (*phyi khral*) or those owed to their landowners (*nang khral*). It was just understood that this troupe was on call to perform for free whenever the landowner needed it.

Proverbs and sayings abound in popular culture to complain about the burden of *khral*. In Lhamo Pemba's collection of proverbs, for example, we can read "*Ko la sprod rgyu dang rgyab chu brgal rgyu*", translated in the following manner by the editor: "Double taxation: To pay for the skin-boat and yet have to wade through the narrow stream" (Lhamo Pemba 1996: 2). Or, further down, "*mgo spu med la ral pa'i khral / rkang lham med la zhabs bro'i khral*", translated as: "No hair on my head, but taxed for a wig. No shoes on my feet, but forced to dance (To be called to perform beyond one's ability)" (Lhamo Pemba 1996: 43). *Khral* appears as a form of outright extortion in these formulations. The *bkra shis zhol pa*, on their part, found a comical, yet somewhat coarse, way to express their grudges. Drum rhythms are quite difficult to teach to young recruits, so they devised a "drum mnemonic" (*rnga tshig*) that was voiced aloud as they were learning the beats:[57]

that they themselves do not have a clear memory of the prevailing situation in the 1940s and 1950s.

56 Interview with Phüntsok Gyelpo (Phun tshogs rgyal po), Chonggye Pündün, 1997.

57 Underlined syllables indicate the strong beats.

> ***Khral** red **khral** red / **rkub** btsum **rkub** btsum* (3 times)
> *gZims chung **steng** / gzims chung **shod*** (3 times)
> ***sTeng shod min** pa **nyang mas rgyang***
>
> (It's a *khral*, it's a *khral*, shut your arse up, shut your arse up! [i.e. there is nothing you can do about it]
> Small residence [of a master] above, Small residence below!
> Whether it is above or below, fill it up with diarrhoea!)[58]

Despite the resentment generated by the unrewarded obligations of *khral*, every old actor I met still remembers fondly the *zho ston*. First, performing in front of the Dalai Lama was thought to be an offering with a sense of moral and spiritual fulfilment. As many actors said, "the heart was happy", and this intangible gratification should also be taken into consideration when understanding the nature of *khral* in an official/religious context. Second, their accomplishments in Lhasa definitely granted them pride and an enhanced status in the eyes of other commoners, in addition to the many interesting anecdotes they were bound to tell after their experiences. Finally, if indeed they could not receive any payment for their performances, they ended the *zho ston* season with considerable gains—some of the troupes did, however, drink all of these earnings away on the way back home. The *khral* of the *zho ston* did in fact only apply to the first two days of performance, at the Potala and in 'Bras spungs, at the very end of the 6th month. For the following performances in the Norbu Lingkha at the beginning of the 7th month, they received many gifts from the government, such as *rtsam pa*, butter, tea, meat and scarves—in later days, these were partially replaced with cash, more convenient to carry around. According to old informants, the situation of the *zho ston* was actually shifting during the first half of the 20th century, to the extent that, on the eve of the PRC annexation, this tax (*khral*) was slowly evolving into a remunerated service: the efforts of unpaid labour during the 6th month were balanced with the substantial presents of the 7th month.

Moreover, the earnings of the actors did not stop at the official *zho ston*. The journey to Lhasa and back was, for most of the troupes, a slow voyage interspersed with performances given for occasional patrons. They of course

58 Interview with Jamyang Tobgyel ('Jam dbyangs stobs rgyal), Tshome (*bkra shis zhol pa* troupe), 1997. This drum-mnemonic is actually well-known among the Kyormolungpa as well, as I could see from the students of Norbu Tshering (1927–2013), the main *lha mo* master at the Tibetan Institute of Performing Arts of Dharamsala, and a Kyormolungpa himself.

FIGURE 7.5 Lhamo performers in Western Tibet. Place and date unknown, beginning of 20th c.
FILIPPI 1924: 188, COURTESY ZANICHELLI

cashed in on their reputation as *zho ston* troupes, and this enhanced the prestige (*dbu 'phang*) of local patrons as well, who were aristocrats or monastic leaders. The Chungpa troupe, however, did not engage so much in performances along the way. This could be due to the distance—it took three weeks on foot from Riwoche to Lhasa—but it was probably owed to the contractual nature of their *khral*. They were the only troupe that was exempted from other taxes in exchange for service at the *zho ston*, so they probably adhered to the official regulation preventing them from playing for other sponsors against payment. Most of the troupes had actually established a yearly calendar of recurring patrons, right before or right after the *zho ston*. The Gyelkharwa seem to have had eight such appointments a year in the 1950s.[59] The Dar grong sNye mo ba had over fifteen engagements, including the *mTshur phu'i dbyar 'cham* for their privileged patron the Karmapa, right before the *zho ston*. After the Norbu Lingkha performances, the *lha mo* season extended over into the city of Lhasa: until the 15th day of the 7th month. Private patrons, be they aristocratic

59 Dikey Drokar (2008: 222), who gives a complete table of their performances, with the names of the patrons, the dates and the gifts usually received.

or monastic, vied for securing a performance by one of the *zho ston* troupes in the courtyard of their Lhasa mansion, and they ostentatiously displayed their wealth, not only when paying the actors at the end of the show, but also by making for them enhanced masks and costumes, with precious materials. All in all, attending the *zho ston* as a *khral* did not seem to entail the "losses" evoked by Bacot. Because the *lha mo* actors could successfully make the period surrounding the *khral* profitable, they enjoyed a fairly positive balance at the end.

6 On the Supervision of the Actors during the *zho ston*

What were the relations between the actors and those to whom they owed performances as tax? Snyder has outlined the main elements of the organisation of the *zho ston* and its chronological unfolding (Snyder 1979: 33–35), so I will concentrate here on the role of the Treasury office (*rtse phyag las khungs*), in charge of the supervision of the performances, and on that of the actors' landlords.

The *khral* of the *zho ston* was considered by Tibetan actors as both an obligation to the Tibetan government and an offering to the Dalai Lama. The Dalai Lamas did not interfere much with the *lha mo ba*. They had closer ties with their *spyan bsal* troupe, but that often simply meant dispensing fine presents to the actors.[60] Besides, the Fourteenth Dalai Lama once remarked, as the Kyormolungpa were taking the stage in Norbu Lingkha, that the young actor Norbu Tshering, famous for his impersonation of female roles, had changed characters that day and was about to play a male role. This was interpreted as a criticism and the actor was immediately rushed backstage where he changed to his familiar female role. The actual interference with the content and quality of the show on stage was done by four officials of the *rtse phyag las khungs*, including the director of this office. Actors came to Lhasa a few days before the start of the *zho ston* and rehearsed under the *rtse phyag*'s supervision in the 'Phral sde gling kha, attracting many onlookers. At that moment, a play was chosen for each troupe for their performance at the Norbu Lingkha, and

60 The gifts of the Thirteenth Dalai Lama to the Chungpa troupe were highly symbolic. He gave a golden ring and a golden *sog byil* earring (worn by middle range officials on the left ear) to the teacher of the troupe, Chungpa Tshewang (gCung pa Tshe dbang), as well as an ornate mask and costume. To the characters playing the princes (*rgya lu*) in the prologue, he offered small white hats (*ar kon*) similar to those worn by the aristocratic officials (*drung 'khor*) wearing the *rgya lu'i chas* during the New Year celebrations. The Chungpa troupe still wears today these exclusive insignias conferred by the Thirteenth Dalai Lama.

the officials verified that the actors could do a faultless recitation of their text. Perfection was important in the Tibetan Buddhist cultural context: the librettos, modelled on *jātaka*s and (typically) featuring previous lives of the Buddha (or Padmasambhava or Avalokiteśvara, among others) were considered equal to words of the Buddha. Their flawless recitation produced ritual efficacy, a blessing falling down onto the audience as general prosperity. During the Norbu Lingkha shows, the *rtse phyag* officials sat at the side of the stage and checked correct utterance. It was most stressful on the director of the troupe, as he had to recite most of the text by heart. The troupe directors were also habitually appointed by the Treasury Office.

The second task of the *rtse phyag* officials was to verify attendance. All names were registered in what the actors called the "mother book" (*ma deb*). Presence was duly taken: no actor could evade his duty, and absences, deaths, or substitutions had to be justified. Fines were imposed if actors arrived late in Lhasa, or did not show up. At the end of the *zho ston* season (that is, after the last performances in the private mansions of Lhasa on the 15th day of the 7th month), all the actors had to take an oath to come back the next year.

The main preoccupation of the *rtse phyag* was to ensure that the *khral* would to be fulfilled as planned. The treasury officials had to attend a vast range of other taxes throughout the year, so their personal interest in the *zho ston* or in *lha mo* was probably varying. But, within this rather formal fiscal system, one individual in particular came to play a major transformative role in late premodern Tibet: Mindrukbuk (or Möndrubuk) Thubten Gyelpo (1902–1973).[61] He was a monk official (*rtse 'khor*), from a *shag tshang* family, who was heading the *rtse phyag las khungs* (dates unknown, maybe from the late 1930s throughout the 1940s or even 1950s?). He was deeply interested in *lha mo*, had learnt it himself with the best Kyormolungpa actors, presumably from the great actor Migmar Gyaltsen. During the summer picnics of the aristocrats, he even performed himself with a few colleagues. He was said to sing some of the best *rnam thar* in Tibet, especially for the songs of the mother of Norzang (Nor bzang) in the *Chos rgyal nor bzang* libretto. His voice is actually recorded in the HMV Dum-dum recordings made by Basil Gould in Lhasa in the 1940s.[62] At a time when snippets of modernity were influencing Tibet,

61 sMin 'brug/sMon grub sbug Thub bstan rgyal po; see Blo bzang chos bdag (1990: 58) and the *Dung dkar tshig mzod chen mo* (2002: 1645) for entries on this monk official. His role in the *zho ston* and his passion for *lha mo* are mentioned.

62 For example, the Musée Guimet holds excerpts of the librettos *gZugs kyi nyi ma* [HMV N 16623, side A; HMV P.8863, side A], *Chos rgyal nor bzang* [HMV P. 8860, side A; HMV P.8863, side B], *sNang sa 'od 'bum* [HMV P. 8861, side A], *'Gro ba bzang mo* [HMV P.8862, side A], *Dri med kun ldan* [HMV P.8862, side B], *rGya bza' bal bza'* [HMV P. 8864, side A] and *Padma*

especially through the British Raj, during the troubled first half of the 20th century, he sought to straighten out the *lha mo* tradition. As he was literate, he clarified some passages sung by the actors that were perceived as incoherent after several generations of oral transmission. He also put order in the performance style, in the costumes, the melodies and in the refinement of some dance movements. He further requested that the teachers of a few troupes, at least those of the Kyormolungpa and the Chungpa, stay over in Lhasa for a whole year—some say it was two years—to train with him and in the end produce a better-quality show on the Norbu Lingkha stage. He shortened the *Chos ryal nor bzang* play of the Gyelkharwa from the original three days to a single day.[63] According to one informant, "the Kyormolungpa troupe was his 'vocal laboratory' par excellence".[64] He undoubtedly had a strong impact on what was until then a locally diverse folk tradition. He initiated what can be retrospectively described as a standardisation process. Many aspects of the *lha mo* that we know today, which mostly represents the Kyormolung tradition, are owed to his reforms.

Surely, Mindrubuk did not singlehandedly change a whole tradition. He came at a time when *lha mo* was already undergoing important changes, contrary to its image as timeless static tradition nowadays. This drama style had been slowly shifting with the emergence of a new, professional, type of troupe (the Kyormolungpa) at the turn of the 20th century. Is it because of that troupe, or for other reasons, that *lha mo* was going through a process of amplification since the early 20th century? Under the Thirteenth Dalai Lama's tenure, the *zho ston* in Norbu Lingkha became a big show. The number of actors on stage expanded,[65] the costumes became richer, the masks were enlarged—especially the mask of the hunter (*rngon pa*), doubled or tripled in size to accommodate the jewels and ornaments designed by the patrons of the performance, hindering the actors' performance.[66] The economic dynamics around *lha mo* were also changing, with patrons investing larger sums of money to display their wealth as they invited *lha mo* troupes.

'od 'bar [HMV P. 8864, side B]. The All-India Radio in Delhi and Tashi Tsering (Amnye Machen) also have a few of these 78 rpm records.

63 Interview with Rakra Trethong (Rak ra bkras mthong), 2001.

64 Interview with Norbu Tshering, 2001.

65 In the absence of witnesses still alive, we are left to wonder if the occasional and impressive performances of the Meru monks in Norbu Lingkha, featuring up to 200 actors at once on the stage, have not left a mark on subsequent *lha mo* performances.

66 It is striking to notice how, in early 20th century photographs (see Figure 7.5), the hunter's mask was quite small (about the size of the face) in comparison with its proportions in the 1950s. See Henrion-Dourcy (2017: 790–94) for a list of photographs of *a lce lha mo* ranging from the 1880s to the 1950s, by about forty different photographers.

FIGURE 7.6
Ama Tshering (A ma Tshe ring), who was to become the last teacher of the Kyormolungpa troupe, *c.*1950
PHOTOGRAPH BY CHEN ZONGLIE (陈宗烈) http://www.tibetinfor.com/tibetzt/zangxi/10/xiandai/003.htm (last accessed 13 April 2009)

Let us now briefly turn to the role of the landlords of the actors in the *khral* dynamics of *zho ston*.[67] As for the taxes in general, their attitude was often limited to "a passive role" (Goldstein 1971: 180). As long as the taxes were given over to the State, the landlords interfered minimally with the life of the actors and the content of the shows. They never attended rehearsals. In some troupes, they were consulted to appoint a new director. Drama was not an important preoccupation for them. What mattered was to stay out of trouble with the government, because they had to pay a fine if the actors failed to show up for the *khral*. They usually did not comment on the performances of the actors, but congratulated them if they had recited their text correctly, since this was their major task. If a performance was popular and got the whole Lhasa crowd talking about the troupe, it would make them have a "big name" (*ming chen po*) and could derive some pride from it.

67 The Kyormolungpa were landless actors, so this section does not apply to them. In the 1940s and 1950s, however, the *bla brang* of Kundeling, more precisely the Twelfth Tsatsak Rinpoche (rTsa tshags rin po che; 1924–1957), who was personally fond of *lha mo* and secular performances in general, shouldered a type of tutelage of the troupe, mostly as it related to the upkeep (*'tsho 'dzin*) of the actors (Henrion-Dourcy, 2017: 357–51).

In principle, the landowners' counterpart was to provide for the costs generated by the performance of the *khral* by the actors. This included the basic supplies enabling them to perform at the *zho ston*, such as the costumes of the prologue and the percussion instruments. The situation for the two Nyemo troupes were different: Thönpa paid for the instruments and a few masks, but never for costumes. Shedra refused to give anything to the Dardrongwa and asked them to go and perform for money in the countryside, so that they could pay for their props and costumes. The landlords were also supposed to provide for the upkeep (*'tsho 'dzin*) of the actors during the *zho ston* by accommodating them in the courtyard of their mansion or monastery in Lhasa, and giving them food. But some landlords did not want to get involved (as for the Gyelkharwa and the Shangpa), so other figures of authority stepped in in their stead (respectively: the Phünkhang [Phun khang] family and the *bla brang* of Zhide monastery). After the Norbu Lingkha performances, the actors played for a whole day in the courtyard of their landowner (or host). Some landlords gave them payment, and some did not (such as the Phala family, for the Chonggye Pündün).

7 The Economy of *lha mo*: a Merit-making Activity Situated between Religion and Entertainment

This article has focused on performance-as-*khral*, when opera was performed as an unpaid obligation. However, to avoid a distorted view of the social fabric of *a lce lha mo* before the 1950s, it is important to keep in mind that it was far from the only social configuration of performance—it was closer to the exception than the rule, as mentioned in the introduction. It was the most remarkable instance because of the splendour of the *zho ston* and its eminent attendance. It was less spectacular when it was owed to local landlords as a tax—and more begrudged because it did not yield the same spiritual and material perks. But, in the greater picture, *lha mo* was fundamentally a folk genre performed in villages, and a cultural activity of a specific kind, ambiguously situated between religion and entertainment. The nature of this performance style impacted its economic features. The religious constituent of *lha mo* culturally precluded it from being a commodity for trade, contrary to traditional Chinese opera, for example, where self-managed troupes could function as businesses selling tickets. Tibetan actors did not sell their show to individual onlookers, and they were not supposed to make any profit (*khe bzang*) from their activity. They were invited by a patron (*sbyin bdag*), who sponsored the show for the whole community—who thus attended for free. The actors did receive a compensation for their performance, but it was not considered a payment or salary (*phogs*), as for other types of labour. It was considered a donation (*gnang sbyin*), a terminology reminiscent of both religious service, and of the alms given to the poor and the beggars (*sbyin pa*). These gifts were in principle solely aimed at the troupe's basic maintenance (as for beggars), or in exchange for exemplary activities benefitting all beings (as for monks). They were not meant to facilitate the actors' accumulation of income. This conceptualisation of the social and economic dimension of *a lce lha mo* is already expressed in its very legend of origin. Oral tradition credits Thang stong rgyal po for creating opera as a fund-raising activity, but not for self-profit, for the construction of bridges for the benefit of all (facilitating pilgrimage to holy places, allowing humans and animals to cross rivers safely, etc.). Patronage is at the core of *lha mo*, but only inasmuch it assists virtuous and altruistic deeds.

The main occasions for a patron to host a *lha mo* performance were during community festivals associated with the agricultural cycle, such as the field circumambulation (*'ong skor*) preceding the harvest, and New Year announcing the spring renewal. It was also performed for monastic patrons at other important community festivals, such as the local monastery's annual feast—often a commemoration of the founding of the monastery, or a festival set on a propitious day of the Buddhist calendar—extended for a few days with secular performances. Moreover, aristocratic or well-to-do people could call a *lha mo* troupe to enhance an important family celebration, such as a wedding (see Figure 7.7) or an administrative promotion. Performances could also be hosted by officials, such newly appointed District Commissioners (*rdzong dpon*), making themselves known to their new constituents by offering them a show. All these occasions were meant to highlight merriment, luck and happiness for the community.

The donations (*gnang byin*) were agreed upon before the performance, and made in kind (*skya skya*) after the show. They included barley, *rtsam pa*, butter, salt, tea and sheep carcasses, as well as ceremonial scarves (*kha btags*). Later, in the 19th–20th centuries, they included cash (*dmar skya*). Patrons additionally had to provide for the actors' needs during the whole performance, with food and drinks—the consumption of large quantities of beer making the end of the shows rather euphoric. When actors were touring Tibet, especially for the landless roaming troupes, they converted their donations into money to ease their journey. Sometimes, they could also receive letters of credit: when the Gyelkharwa performed in the courtyard of the Lhalu (lHa klu) family on the 25th day of the 6th month (in Lhasa, right before the *zho ston*), they gave a

FIGURE 7.7 The Gyelkharwa troupe performing at a marriage. Performers and donations are represented. Wise-Drew Roll, *c.*1854

letter to the director of the troupe, who could receive the credit from the Lhalu estate that was conveniently close to their home.[68]

A lce lha mo performances served a double ritual purpose. As recitations of valued Buddhist librettos, they brought blessings (*byin rlabs*) of Buddhist deities, translating as peace and general wellness for the community and beyond. As offerings of entertainment to the local worldly gods (*gzhi bdag*) responsible for life sustenance, the performances brought fertility and prosperity to the village and its environment. This duality is again expressed in the very legend of origin of *lha mo*: some versions emphasise that Thang stong rgyal po performed stories to turn the common people's minds to the Dharma; other versions stress that he created a show to distract a rock demon that was undoing at night all the work on the bridge carried out during the day. *lHa mo* therefore catered not only for the two polarities of performance according to Schechner (1988: 122)'s model (efficacy and entertainment), it also addressed to the two main sets of pursuits of religious life in Tibet: the other-worldly (*'jig rten las 'das pa*) concerns of salvation found in Buddhism; and the worldly (*'jig rten pa*)

68 Interview with Tshering, director of the Gyelkharwa troupe, 1997.

concerns of good fortune, protection from the local gods, and leading a happy, prosperous and joyful life.

As they were sponsoring what could be framed as a Buddhist activity, the patrons (*sbyin bdag*) of *lha mo* performances were, like patrons of Buddhist art or religious rituals in general, involved in a specific type of exchange that brought positive results onto themselves: they paid for a virtuous specialised service and in return personally accumulated merit (*bsod nams*)—a type of intangible "storable wealth" that was (and still is) much sought after. The religious nature of Tibetan opera thus makes it stand out from other forms of secular songs and dances that do not attract merit-making donations. The term *sbyin bdag* is a widely used and polysemic one in Tibet (Dikey Drokar 2008: 2017), with religious and secular overtones linking it to religious offerings, positions of authority and various forms of tribute. In the present discussion, suffice is to say that the *sbyin bdag* enjoyed prestige (*dbu 'phang*), and that his enhanced status and offerings were conspicuous. He sat at a place of choice in the audience, and his donations were ostentatious, presented to the performers in what looked like a "ceremony" in its own right, with a public proclamation of what was being given out. Actors also sang praises and good wishes for him at the end of the show. Besides, the other spectators could also offer personal contributions named *gsol ras*: a few coins wrapped in a *kha btags* and thrown onto the stage at emotional moments of the play or at the end of the show. These were considered more tips than donations, although they were also said to allow for the accumulation of merit. Lastly, some popular *lha mo* actors could receive individual gratifications from their (male and female) admirers (a piece of jewellery, clothing or material). This was done in private, outside performances, and was thus never declared aloud publicly. In this case, the gift was not about accumulating merit, but about creating a privileged relationship with one performer.[69]

Finally, at the other end of the exchange, the actors received the donations. A well-known saying used in the dice game (*sho bshad*) relates that "the *mahāsiddha* Thang stong rgyal po himself had something of a beggar."[70] The *lha mo ba* thus also had "something" of mendicants, but among the three types of beggars outlined by Jamyang Norbu (2015: 241–42), it is clear that *lha mo ba* were not "outright beggars" (with a lowly social status). They were both

69 Especially for the Kyormolungpa, this comprised, but was not limited to, homosexual relations with monks and religious officials (*rtse drung*). See Tashi Tsering (1997: 28) for similar experiences among the *gar phrug pa*.

70 *Grub thob Thang stong rgyal po la sprang po'i g.ya' gcig 'dug*. Cited in Tashi Tsering (2001: 56–57).

"spiritual beggars" (such as the *bla ma ma ni*, or the *phyag 'tshal bla ma*) and "mendicant-entertainers" (as the singers in beer taverns). The term for the donations to the *lha mo ba* (*gnang sbyin*; appears to be an honorific of *sbyin pa*) is clearly differentiated from alms to beggars (*sbyin pa*). The verb is also different: giving alms to beggars is *sbyin pa* ***gtong ba*** (or *gnang sbyin* ***gnang ba*** in the honorific form), whereas giving donations to actors is *gnang sbyin* ***stsal ba*** or ***sprod pa***, verbs that do not imply the same movement of going "down". As we can see from this survey of the economic dimension of opera acting, *lha mo* was in a conceptual *entre-deux* between mendicancy and ritual, economy (earning) and religion (devotion), as well as Buddhism and local pagan cults, making it a rich and significant cultural institution of premodern Tibet.

8 Conclusion

I hope that this long account of the social, political and economic fabric of Tibetan opera performance has managed to convey not only a lively picture of the world of *lha mo ba*, but also an insight into the complexity and inconsistency of the category of *khral* for performances at the beginning of the 20th century. There were discrepancies between the general principles of the taxation system and their practical implementation. According to the old actors and former aristocrats whom I interviewed, a performance-as-*khral* was understood to pertain to tax in kind (*lag 'don*), despite it being intangible, and not to corvée (*rkang 'gro*). In theory, a performance would be a quantified equivalent to all or part of the taxes-in-kind owed by the actors, to the State or to their landowners. These taxes were thus expected to be balanced by some level of exemption, since a part had already been acquitted in drama form. This was the case for at least one troupe (Chungpa), that was exempted from all taxes, even the transportation corvée, in exchange for coming to the *zho ston*. In actuality, for all the other troupes of the *zho ston*, it never entailed any form of exemption—at least in the few last decades of the Ganden Phodrang rule.[71] In the actors' memory, the tax was felt as a pervasive obligation. But *lha mo* was also undergoing changes during that period, not only on the stage, but also in its social setting, as the *zho ston* "tax" was gradually evolving towards a remunerated service. The wider social context of *lha mo* was a complex and

71 I have not been able to survey a large number of performances done as tax for landowners (as part of *nang khral*) and therefore I cannot say whether it was the same mistreatment as was encountered with the State was or not generalised.

FIGURE 7.8
"Tibetan masked dancers" (original caption); a *lha mo* troupe from West Tibet
SHERRING 1906: 77

unequal economic exchange based on merit-making, between patrons, who accumulated merits and prestige, and actors who received ambiguous donations situated between alms to beggars and offerings for religious service.

Lastly, I hope that the main contribution of this paper is to have shown that there was contingency and opportunity within the overall structure of the taxation system in Tibet. Confronting theory and practice, bringing together social history's taste for patterns, and anthropology's propensity to value agency, I have shown that the *zho ston* was undergoing important changes under the Thirteenth and Fourteenth Dalai Lamas, not only because of the general shifting economic and political conditions of the early 20th century, but also because of the vision and passion of a particular individual, Mindrubuk. In today's Tibet, *lha mo* has become a commodity, and *lha mo ba* are mostly mendicants of a new type, hankering for government subsidies and variable money from the tourism industry. The next chapter to be written on performance-as-obligation concerns now the mandatory shows of opera and other genres demanded by the PRC State in the wide, though repetitive, range of its local, regional and national ceremonies.

References

Sources in Tibetan

[sDe srid] Sangs rgyas rgya mtsho. 1990 [1696]. [*rTse pho brang gser gyi*] *mChod sdong 'dzam gling rgyan gcig gi dkar chag thar gling rgya mtshor bgrod pa'i gru gzings*. Lhasa: Bod ljongs mi dmangs dpe skrun khang.

bDe skyid sgrol dkar. 2001. rGyal mkhar lha mo tshogs par brtags dpyad byas pa'i snyan zhu. *Bod ljongs zhib 'jug* 3, 78–93.

Blo bzang rdo rje. 1988. Bod ljongs kyi rig rtsal dus chen zho ston gyi 'phel rim skor gleng ba. *Bod ljongs sgyu rtsel zhib 'jug* 2, 9–19.

Grong khyer lHa sa chab gros rig gnas lo rgyus rtsom 'bri u yon lhan khang. 1989. sTag rtse rdzong gi lo rgyus. *Bod ljongs zhib 'jug* 2, 118–31; 3, 131–39; 4, 135–53.

Karma mKhas grub (ed.). 1998. *mNga' ris rong chung khul gyi thun mong ma yin pa'i gna' srol glu gar phyogs bsgrigs.* Dharamsala: Karma Khedup, Indraprastha Press.

Le'u kre chun [= Liu Zhiqun 刘志群]. 1980. Bod kyi lha mo'i lugs khag ngo sprod byed pa. *In* Bod rang skyong ljongs mang tshogs sgyu rtsal khang (ed.) *Bod ljongs dmangs khrod kyi rig rtsal dpyad gzhi'i yig rigs phyogs bsgrigs (vol.1) / Bod rang skyong ljongs skabs dang po'i las zhor lha mo'i lhan tshogs 'khrab ston gyi rtsom yig ched sgrig.* Lhasa: Bod rang skyong ljongs mang tshogs sgyu rtsal khang, 249–65.

Ngag dbang gsung rab. 1997. Bod kyi mNga' ris sa khul du dar ba'i dmangs khrod zhabs bro gar shon gyi sgyu rtsal skor la rags tsam dpyad pa. *Bod ljongs zhib 'jug* 1997-1, 48–55.

Rak ra Rin po che. 1996. Zho ston. *Bod kyi zho ston dus chen* 96. Dharamsala: TIPA, 11–12.

Zhol khang bSod nams dar rgyas. 1992. *Glu gar tshangs pa'i chab rgyun.* Lhasa: Bod ljongs mi dmangs dpe skrun khang.

Zhol khang bSod nams dar rgyas. 2003. Bod ljongs kyi rgyun srol a lce lha mo khag gi khyad par dang 'Phyongs rgyas kha bro sPun bdun bKra shis zholpa lha mo'i 'byung khungs skor bshad pa, *Bod ljongs sgyu rtsal zhib 'jug* 2, 9–29.

Sources in Chinese

Jiala 加拉 [rGyal lags]. 2012. Zao qi jue mu long zang xi tuan ji qi zhu ming xi shi li shi hui gu 早期觉木隆藏戏团及其著名戏师历史回顾 (A Historical Overview of the Early skyor mo lung and its Leading Artists). *Xizang daxue xuebao* 西藏大学学报 (*Journal of Tibet University*) 2, 141–44.

Sangjidongzhi 桑吉东智 [Tib. Sangs rgyas don grub]. 2015a. *Xiangmin yu xiju: Xizang de ajilamu jiqi yiren yanjiu* 乡民与戏剧：西藏的阿吉拉姆及其艺人研究 (*Villagers and drama: Research on ache lhamo in Central Tibet and on its actors*). Beijing: Ethnic Peoples' Press (Minzu chubanshe 民族出版社).

Sangjidongzhi 桑吉东智 [Sangs rgyas don grub]. 2015b. Jiemulongba de qianshi jinsheng 觉木隆巴的前世 今生 (The past generations and present lives of the Kyomolunga actors). Zhongguo zangxue 中国藏学 (*China Tibetology*) 3, 184–90.

Sangjidongzhi 桑吉东智 [Sangs rgyas don grub]. 2015c. Xiju biaoyan yu cunluo zhixu: Chentang xia'erba ren de "mani" biaoyan jiqi yiyi 戏剧表演与村落秩序：陈塘夏尔巴人的 "嘛呢" 表演及其意义 (Drama performance and village order: the performance of "Mani" by the Sherpas of 'Dren thang and its meaning). *Nei mengu daxue yishu xueyuan xuebao* 内蒙古大学艺术学院学报 (Journal of the Arts Department of Inner Mongolia) 3, 28–32.

Sources in Western languages

Aziz, B.N. 1978. *Tibetan Frontier families. Reflections of Three generations from D'ing-ri.* New Delhi: Vikas Publishing House.

Bacot, J. 1914, Drimedkundan. Une version tibétaine dialoguée du Vessantara Jâtaka. *Journal Asiatique* 9, 221–305.

Bacot, J. 1921. *Trois mystères tibétains: Tchrimekundan, Djroazanmo, Nangsal.* Paris: Bossard.

Bell, C.A. 1992 [1928]. *The People of Tibet.* Delhi: Motilal Barnasidass.

Carrasco, P. 1972 [1959]. *Land and Polity in Tibet.* Seattle: University of Washington Press.

Chapman, S.F. 1940. *Lhasa the Holy City.* London: Chatto and Windus.

Dargyay, E. 1982. *Tibetan Village Communities: Structure and Change.* New Delhi: Vikas Publishing House.

Das, S.C. 1988 [1902]. *Journey to Lhasa and Central Tibet.* Delhi: Mehra Offset.

Dikey D. 2008. The relationship between *A-lce lha-mo* troupes and their sponsors. *Inner Asia* 10, 211–40.

Duncan, M.H. 1955. *Harvest Festival Dramas of Tibet.* Hong Kong: Orient Publishing Co.

Duncan, M.H. 1967. *More Harvest Festival Dramas of Tibet.* London: The Mitre Press.

Goldstein, M.C. 1968. An Anthropological Analysis of the Tibetan Political System. Ph.D. thesis, University of Washington.

Goldstein, M.C. 1971. Taxation and the structure of a Tibetan village. *Central Asiatic Journal* 15(1), 1–27.

Goldstein, M.C. 1993 [1989]. *A History of Modern Tibet, 1913–1951. The Demise of the Lamaist State.* New Delhi: Munshiram Manoharlal Publishers.

Henrion-Dourcy, I. 2005. Women in Tibetan performing arts: portraits of six contemporary singers. *In* J. Gyatso and H. Havnevik (eds) *Women in Tibet.* London/New York: Hurst & Co./Columbia University Press, 195–258.

Henrion-Dourcy, I. 2017. *Le Théâtre ache lhamo : Jeux et enjeux d'une tradition tibétaine.* Mélanges chinois et bouddhiques (Vol. 33). Bruxelles-Leuven: Peeters.

Jamyang Norbu and Tashi Dondhup. 1986. A preliminary study of *gar*, the court dance and music of Tibet. *In* Jamyang Norbu (ed.) *Zlos-Gar. Performing Traditions of Tibet: Commemorative Issue on the Occasion of the 25th Anniversary of the Founding of Tibetan Institute of Performing Arts (1959–84).* Dharamsala: Library of Tibetan Works and Archives, 132–42.

Jamyang Norbu. 2015. The Lhasa Ripper: a preliminary investigation into the "dark underbelly" of social life in the Holy City. *In* R. Vitali (ed.) *Trails of The Tibetan Tradition: Papers for Elliot Sperling. Revue d'Études Tibétaines* 31, 233–50.

Kapstein, M.T. 2006. *The Tibetans.* London: Wiley-Blackwell.

Lhading Jampa Kesang (ed.). 2000. *Pho brang Po ta la'i ldebs bris ri mo'i 'byung khungs lo rgyus gsal ba'i me long / Budalagong bihua yuanliu / A mirror of the Murals in the Potala* [trilingual book]. Jiuzhou: Jiuzhou tushu chubanshe.

Lhamo Pemba. 1996. *Tibetan Proverbs*. Dharamsala: Library of Tibetan Works and Archives.

Miller, B.D. 1956. Ganye and kidu: two formalized systems of mutual aid among the Tibetans. *Southwestern Journal of Anthropology* 12, 157–70.

Nebesky-Wojkowitz, René de. 1993 [1956]. *Oracles and demons of Tibet. The Cult and Iconography of the Tibetan Protective Deities*. Kathmandu: Tiwari Pilgrims Book House.

Norbu Tsering. 1999. *Ache Lhamo is my Life*. Torino: Legenda.

Petech, L. 1973. *Aristocracy and Government in Tibet: 1728–1959*. Rome: ISMEO.

Richardson, H.E. 1993. *Ceremonies of the Lhasa Year*. London: Serindia.

Schechner, R. 1988. *Performance Theory*. London: Routledge.

Sherring, C.A. 1906. *Western Tibet and the British Borderland: The Sacred Country of Hindus and Buddhists, with an Account of the Government, Religion, and Customs of its Peoples*. London: Edward Arnold.

Schuh, D. 1976. Der Schauspieler des tibetischen Lha-mo Theaters. *Zentralasiatische Studien* 10. Kommissionsverlag Otto Harrassowitz, 1976: 339–384. (Translated into English by Monika Lange: The actor in the Tibetan *lha mo* theatre. *Lungta, Journal of Tibetan History and Culture* (Special issue, *The Singing Mask, Echoes from Tibetan Opera*) 15, 97–118.

Schwieger, P. 2021. Rule and labour in Tibet: constructing the Red Palace of the Potala. *In* L. Galli and K.N. Gurung (eds) *Revue d'Études Tibétaines* 57 (Special issue, *The Power of Wealth—Economy and Social Status in Pre-modern Tibetan Communities*), 216–40.

Snellgrove, D.L. 1957. *Buddhist Himâlaya: Travels and Studies in Quest of the Origins and Nature of Tibetan Religion*. Oxford: Bruno Cassirer.

Snyder, J. 1979. Preliminary study of the Lha-mo. *Asian Music* 10(2), 23–62.

Stein, R.A. 1987 [1962]. *La Civilisation tibétaine*. Paris: L'Asiathèque.

Surkhang, Wangchen Gelek. 1984. Tax measurement and *lag-don* tax in Tibet. *The Tibet Journal* 9(1), 20–30.

Surkhang, Wangchen Gelek. 1986. Government monastic and private taxation in Tibet. *The Tibet Journal* 11(1), 21–40.

Takla, Namgyal Lhamo. 2005. *Women of Tibet*. Dehradun: Songtsen Library.

Tashi Tsering, M.C. Goldstein and W. Siebenschuh. 1997. *The Struggle for Modern Tibet. The Autobiography of Tashi Tsering*. Armonk: M.E. Sharpe.

Tashi Tsering. 2001. Reflections on Thang stong rgyal po as the founder of the A lce lha mo tradition of Tibetan performing arts. *Lungta, Journal of Tibetan History and Culture* (Amnye Machen Institute, Tibetan Centre for Advanced Studies) 15, Winter 2001 (*The Singing Mask: Echoes from Tibetan Opera*), 36–60.

Tethong, Rakra. 1979. Conversations on Tibetan musical traditions. *Asian Music* 10(2), 5–22.

Thupten Sangyay. 1986. Glossary of the "Government, monastic and private taxation in Tibet". *The Tibet Journal* 11(1), 41–47.

Tsarong, Paljor. 1998. Tseja: structure and economy of a Tibetan state treasury. *The Tibet Journal* 23(3), 23–33.

Tsepak Rigzin. 1993. *Festivals of Tibet*. Dharamsala: Library of Tibetan Works and Archives.

CHAPTER 8

A Preliminary Investigation Into Monk-Tax: The Concept of *grwa khral/btsun khral/ban khral* and Its Meanings

Berthe Jansen

1 Introduction[1]

At first glance, the phenomenon of monk-tax (*grwa khral/btsun khral/ban khral*) appears to be well understood among scholars of Tibet. Mainly thanks to Goldstein we understand it to mean the tax levied on families with three or more sons. These families were required to send their second-oldest boy to the monastery (*bu gsum bar ma'i/ba'i grwa khral*). This tax is occasionally cited as a prime example of the far-reaching influence institutionalised monasticism has had on ordinary families, or even as an illustration of the supposed despotic power exercised by "the old theocratic regime" in Tibet (e.g. Parenti 2003). While the fact that this phenomenon existed cannot be disputed, neither the prevalence of this tax in time and space nor the underlying reasons for imposing this policy have been appropriately researched. The extent of the current limited understanding of this phenomenon is highlighted by its appearance in a textbook on Tibetan Buddhism:

> [...] within the Tibetan political system, it was *common* for villages in *centralized areas* to have a tax-obligation of providing a certain number of young men to serve as monks in a nearby monastery. Thus *quite a few monks* were, effectively, conscripts not volunteers. This had a political and strategic element, since many *large monasteries* were situated in strategically important locations that governed major trade routes.
>
> SAMUEL 2012: 132, italics added

1 The research for and writing of this article has been made possible by the VICI grant "Buddhism and Social Justice" at Leiden, the visiting research fellowship at the Cluster of Excellence "Asia and Europe" at Universität Heidelberg, and my VENI grant on the interchange between Buddhism and law at Leiden.

 | DOI:10.1163/9789004529465_010

Unfortunately, this description is far from accurate. This tax-obligation was not common. It did not just occur in centralised areas. "Conscripts" never formed any significant portion of the total Tibetan Buddhist monk population. Monk-tax was highly unusual (and unnecessary) in large (successful) monasteries. It should be clear that this often misunderstood issue needs to be considered more carefully. In this article, I discuss the concept, the history, and the occurrences of monk-tax in Tibetan Buddhist regions before the 1950s. In addition to putting forward the hypothesis that the documented presence of this tax at a given monastery can be seen as an indicator of the unstable socio-economic circumstances of that particular institution and its networks at a certain point in time, the occurrence of two other meanings of the word *grwa khral* (alternatively *btsun khral*)—the glosses of which are (so far) not attested in any dictionary—are also discussed.

1.1 Grwa khral *and* btsun khral*: Monk-Tax or Monk-Levy*

Monk-tax or monk-levy is generally understood to be a tax that ordinary Tibetans "paid" to the monastery.[2] It usually meant sending a son to the monastery where he would be made a monk. This particular understanding adds fuel to the fire of certain authors reporting on the forceful nature of the Tibetan theocracy: "[…] it would appear that compulsion is also exercised by the despotic priestly government in the shape of a recognised tax of children to be made Lāmas, named bTsun gral [*sic*]" (Waddell 1895: 170). A more recent commentator posits that once these Tibetan children were taken from their families to take up robes "they became bonded for life" (Parenti 2003: 581). The mountaineer Spencer Chapman also observes this obligatory recruitment: "Many of the smaller monasteries and nunneries are founded and supported by wealthy families, and the monks and nuns therein recruited from their tenantry" (Spencer Chapman 1984 [1938]: 179).

It is tempting to associate this conscription of people into the monastery with certain governmental (i.e. Ganden Phodrang; dGa' ldan pho brang) policies

2 Here the main terms that I deal with are *grwa khral* and *btsun khral*. Caumanns has brought another possible relevant term to my attention, namely *'thus/thus btsun* (literally "gathered monks"). This word occurs in Shākya mchog ldan's (1428–1507) biography, written by Kun dga' grol mchog (1507–1565), in the context of Shākya mchog ldan's discussion regarding the continuation of the Teachings at Chökhortse (Chos 'khor rtse) in Central Tibet. rJe mkhan po Shākya rin chen (1709/10–1759), in a parallel passage, refers to the same event, but uses the term *grwa phral* [*sic*: *khral*] (Caumanns 2015: 192, see further 219 and 263). The term *thus btsun* is also used in the legend regarding Drukpa Kunlek's ('Brug pa Kun legs) building of the first Drukpa ('Brug pa) temple in Bhutan, Sip *lhakhang* (Sribs lha khang), for which thirty Bhutanese (*mon pa'i thus btsun*) were conscripted (Si tu paṇ chen chos kyi byung gnas and 'Be lo Tshe dbang kun khyab's *Chu shel gyi phreng ba* vol. 2, 1775: 214a; Ardussi 1977: 129).

largely directed at Central Tibetan monasteries and the tendency toward mass monasticism mainly ascribed to the Geluk (dGe lugs) school. Khenrap, in his account of life in Ruthog (Ru thog) before the Chinese occupation, remarks that most monks "entered Ru thog monastery in compliance with the government's requirement that every middle son of each family must be sent to the relevant local monastery" (Khenrap 2000: 41). However, I argue here that closer investigation reveals that this was not necessarily a "tax" levied by the state, and furthermore that policies of regulated, or forced, monastic recruitment predated the establishment of the Ganden Phodrang government—they were in place hundreds of years before the 17th century, and they last well into the 21st century. Moreover, the occurrence of monk-tax in Tibetan Buddhist monasteries *and* nunneries is not limited to Central Tibet, but is geographically very widespread: from Nepal to Mongolia and from Ladakh to Amdo.

A relatively early mention of this type of conscription is found in Tāranātha's (1575–1634) autobiography. He mentions that he stayed in Drangphu ('Brang phu), in Tölung (sTod lung) for half a month. While he was there, he cut the tufts of hair of the new monks, who were conscripted under the monk-tax (*ban khral*) from the monastic estates (*mchod gzhis*) of Lhagyal Ling (lHa rgyal gling) and Dethung ('De thung).[3] The casual mention of this practice indicates that this was seen as a normal state of affairs and the *Jo nang* master appears to have had no objections to being a part of their ordination.[4] In contrast, in 2014 during a public teaching session in Ladakh, the Dalai Lama condemned the old system of monk-tax—every family "donating" one child to the monastery—saying that true Sangha-members should be volunteers.[5] That said, there appears to be an Indian precedent for a monk-tax of sorts. In the *Vinayavibhaṅgha*, for example, we find the narrative in which Buddha Śākyamuni returns to his ancestral home. His father Śuddhodana, the ruler of the Śākyas, is so impressed by his son's achievements that he decides to

3 Tāranātha's *bDag nyid kyi rnam thar* vol.1: 357: *lha rgyal gling dang 'de thung la sogs pa'i mchod gzhis la/ ban khral lam pa zhig byas pa'i grwa gsar rnams kyi skra phud re yang blang/ 'di res zla phyed tsam bsdad/.*

4 Similar casual references are found in the autobiography of 'Be lo Tshe dbang kun khyab (18th c.). In this work he speaks of his travels in Eastern Tibet (Barkham, Gyalrong ['Bar khams, rGyal rong]) and mentions the number of monks levied at two different Karma Kagyü (Karma bka' rgyud) monasteries. Sixty monks at T'rochu Shuba monastery (Khro chu shu b+ha dgon) and a hundred at the newly founded Namgyel Teng monastery (rNam rgyal steng dgon), the latter of whom he himself ordained, were instated as part of the monk-tax ('Be lo rnam thar; page numbers not provided). I am grateful to Jann Ronis for providing me with this reference.

5 http://buddhism-controversy-blog.com/2014/07/14/dalai-lama-good-and-bad-buddhist-monks-in-tibetan-buddhism/.

become ordained and to let his younger brother take over his rule. Still, he decrees that one young man from every Śākya household should be made to become ordained. This resulted in 500 Śākya boys joining the entourage of the Buddha.[6] While this passage can certainly be interpreted and indeed used as a "Buddhist" justification for the existence of monk-tax, it appears that Tibetan authors have never done so—the works I have examined so far never once mention this "precedent".

Leaving aside the ethical qualms that the conscription of monks may evoke for the moment, for many monasteries this forceful way of recruiting monks among Tibetan communities was simply a way to increase or maintain the monastic population in accord with the original *numerus fixus*. Tucci presents this as an obligation: "If for some reason the monasteries had places to spare, it was the duty of all families to supply novices. This duty was called *tr'a-thrê*, 'monk-tax'" (Tucci 1967: 97; for references in other secondary sources see Caple 2019: 23; Dagyab 2009: 22; Goldstein 2009: 7; Whitecross 2008: 49; Mills 2003: 40; Samuel 1993: 514; Michael 1982: 144).

As appears to be the case with many discussions on regulations of any kind we find the lines between legal duties, moral obligations, and (religious) customs in Tibetan and Himalayan areas to be blurred if not occasionally non-existent, and the issue of monk-tax can perhaps be seen as a prime example of the complexity involved in these matters. The practice of sending a son to the monastery in the case of there being two boys or more in the family is well known and still in place among Tibetan Buddhist communities.[7] This, at least in the past, may have had more to do with issues of inheritance than with any locally or nationally imposed tax regulations. Doubtlessly, however, monasteries or those in charge of managing monasteries that were in need of new

---

6 This potential link between this narrative and monk-tax was made by Robert Mayer (personal communication, August 2020), who pointed to the passage being cited by Lamotte (1944: 177 n. 2), who in turn quotes Feer (1883: 62–63), whose translations tend to be far from accurate. I have traced this translated passage to the *Vinayavibhaṅgha* (D3): 79a–80a: *rgyal pos smras pa/ khyim re re nas re re rab tu phyung shig /lhas bka'* (80a) *stsal pa bzhin 'tshal lo /rgyal po zas gtsang gis shAkya gzhon nu rnams kyis khyim re re nas re re rab tu dbyung bar bya'o zhes dril bsgrags pa byas so/ /gang gi tshe rgyal po zas gtsang gis dril bsgrags pa de'i tshe na bzang ldan dang ma 'gags pa dang / nam gru la sogs pa shAkya'i gzhon nu lnga brgya rab tu byung ngo /*. According to Lamotte, another version of this narrative can be found in Aśvaghoṣa's Sūtrālaṃkāra, which was translated from the Chinese by Huber (1908: 222). This "mandate" by the king of Śākyas and its potential ramifications for later Buddhist rulers in South Asia and beyond would benefit from further research.

7 This was for example in place in some areas in Kham, where households were "obliged to furnish one monk to the local monastery, Galen Gon, if it had at least two sons" (Thargyal 2007: 159).

recruits capitalised on an already well-established practice that later became a cultural norm among some Tibetan Buddhist groups.

In only a few cases was this rather flexible "rule" and occasionally strategic socio-economic practice of sending a son to the monastery presented as an iron law. According to a decree concerning the restoration of Phakpa Lhacupa ('Phags pa lha bcu pa) monastery from 1919 (*sa lug*) issued by the administration of the Geluk "mother" monastery (*ma dgon*) Chamdo Jampa Ling (Chab mdo byams pa gling), families belonging to the eight lay communities that were allied to the monastery that had two sons or more were ordered to send one boy to the monastery. While the document does not mention the word "monk-tax", a more recent work on the history of the Chamdo area refers to this text and calls this practice monk-tax (*grwa khral*) (*Bod kyi rig gnas* 9(18): 233). The decree itself, however, is in a way more revealing regarding the position taken on recruitment practices:

> One has to act, without postponement, according to what has been settled upon in the register regarding the allotments and decisions of the dependencies. This is to say that families that have two sons will make one son 'enter the gate of Dharma', which is in accordance with the previously established chief practices in the mother monastery. Therefore, when people—on account of certain misconceptions—try to find fault with or slander this command, be they incarnated lamas, monasteries, monastery officials or lay dependents (*mi ser*), due to which disputes regarding the monk-entrance and turmoil may arise, they will certainly be legally prosecuted.
>
> *'Phags pa lha bcu pa'i dgon pa nyams gso'i rtsa tshigs*: 416–17[8]

The decree goes on to state that other parties, including monks, complicit in helping people shirk their responsibilities in sending a son to the monastery are equally liable for prosecution. While we cannot know whether the above threats were actually followed up on, the authors clearly show that here sending the second son to become a monk was not conceived of as a simple "moral obligation". Furthermore, it is also worth noting that the monastery in question actually purported to have legal powers according to which they could in fact prosecute and punish families for their non-compliance. It is clear, however,

8 *ma dgon gtso bor 'don pa'i sngar lam bzhin bu gnyis yod dud re'i bu re chos sgor 'jug pa'i thob khongs gtan 'bebs cha bgos deb 'khod ring min bya rgyu yin pas go ba log sgrub kyis bla sprul/ dgon khag dbon khag mi ser sogs che khra sus kyang bka' sher snyad pas mtshon ban rgyun la rtsod 'then ka kor byung tshe khrims kyis bda' 'ded bya nges dang/.*

that the decree in question has as its main aim to restore and rejuvenate an ailing monastery, which might explain the level of force it employs.

Goldstein lists *grwa khral* (or *btsun khral*) as a tax that was occasionally levied: only when a monastery's monk-population could not be maintained through voluntary entrance. He also remarks that—like many other types of tax—this obligation could be relatively easily evaded (Goldstein 1971: 20). Sometimes monks were recruited by levying a monk-tax when a monastery was newly founded so as to ensure its success. The Fifth Dalai Lama proclaims in an edict dated to 1680 and directed to the Mon pa community that there had been a collection of monk-tax (*ban khral*) in order to found a number of religious institutions in all regions of Mon, which here refers to current-day Arunachal Pradesh.[9] Another example of this type of recruitment is found in *The Ladakh Chronicles* (*La dwags rgyal rabs*), the composition of which probably started in the 17th century and continued on until the early 20th century. This text states that in the late 16th century the king of Ladakh Trashi Namgyal (bKra shis rnam rgyal), together with Chöje Denma Künga Drakpa (Chos rje lDan ma kun dga' grags pa),[10] founded Gangngön Trashi Chödzong (sGang sngon bkra shis chos rdzong), nowadays more commonly known as Phiyang (Phyi dbang), a monastery not far from the capital Leh. The work informs us that "from the area he levied monk-tax and thus instated the Teachings of the practice lineage" (Francke 1926: 37, 38, 103).[11] This information is corroborated by Tshe dbang nor bu's (1698–1755) account of this king's activities, written in the 17th century.[12] *Antiquities of Indian Tibet vol. 2*, the work that presents *The Ladakh Chronicles* both in Tibetan and in an English translation, provides additional notes on this phenomenon, penned by a certain Karl Marx.[13] He writes:

> Regarding btsun-gral [*sic*][14] 'tax order of children to be made lamas'. Under the old regime every family of more than one of two male children

9 This edict is transliterated and translated by Aris 1979: 13, 15: *mon shar nub stod smad rnams su chos sde 'ga' zhig rgyab pa'i ban khral bsdus/.*

10 This is a Drigung ('Bri gung) lama from Denma, who was active in South Tibet in the 16th century. His dates are unknown.

11 *yul nas btsun khral btab nas/ bsgrub rgyud kyi bstan pa btsugs/.* I asked a number of elderly monks at this monastery in 2012 about this monk-tax. Among them there is no living memory of this particular obligation. Rather, it was denied that such a practice had ever existed.

12 See *Tshe dbang nor bu gsung 'bum* vol. 3: 128. The word for monk-tax used here is *btsun khral*.

13 This Karl Marx (1857–1891) was a Moravian missionary and ophthalmologist who lived and died in Ladakh.

14 On page 280 the correct spelling of *khral* reappears.

> had to give up one—not the eldest, however—to be made lamas. At present, of course, this tax is no longer compulsory, and hence the great falling off in the number of lamas.
>
> *ibid.*: 104

Writing toward the end of the 19th century, Marx observes that monk-tax had become obsolete in Ladakh.[15] He further reasons that the fact that monk-tax was no longer compulsory caused the monk-population to dwindle. In this regard, a more recent work by the Tibetan author Dung dkar rin po che claims the exact opposite regarding Geluk monasteries in Central Tibet. It is argued that *because* monk-numbers declined a monk-tax *had* to be levied:

> During the period starting with the time of the Fifth Dalai Lama's death (1682) up until 1959 only the few powerful monasteries that received a high income (*phogs mthon po*) could increase their monk-numbers yearly. Except for those, the number of monks of most monasteries decreased many-fold (*ldab kha shas bar chag yod pa dang*) and many monasteries disintegrated and reverted to lay-residencies (*grong khyim*). Because of that, in order for the monasteries not to disintegrate, a *numerus fixus* of monks (*grwa grangs gtan 'bebs*) and a fixed monk-tax consisting of the middle son (*bu gsum bar pa'i grwa khral*) had to be put in place. However, the number of monks only decreased, and did not reach the required amount.
>
> *Dung dkar tshig mdzod*: 78

Dung dkar here suggests that despite the fact that monk-tax was in place at a number of monasteries the policy failed to accomplish its objective.

The autobiography of Ngor Khenchen Penden Chökyong (Ngor mkhan chen dpal ldan chos skyong; 1701–1760) acknowledges that the mere (re-)instatement of monk-tax at the temple and monastic institutions in Washül T'rom (Wa shul khrom), in Kham (Khams), was not enough to ensure their revival. In addition, there needed to be a sponsorship for the tea, the shrines had to be restored, and the discipline of the monks needed to be tightened. This is because, according to the text, the monastic population had previously been slightly too lax, which is given as the main reason why the monk-numbers had

15 Similarly, Dargyay's informants from Western Tibet remembered there being a monk-tax in place but they noted that it had become an "obsolete rule" (Dargyay 1982: 76). Furthermore, Dreyfus mentions that, generally speaking, "monk-tax was rare" (Dreyfus 2003: 345, n. 26).

dwindled in the first place. As in other texts, this manner of planning to preserve or revive religious institutions was in order to help the precious Teachings flourish (e.g. *bstan pa rin po che gong 'phel gyi zhabs tog*) (*Ngor mkhan chen dpal ldan chos skyong zhabs kyi rnam thar*: 12a, b).[16]

In the main Sakya (Sa skya) monasteries during the first half of the 20th century monk-tax appeared to have been levied on a large scale. It is suggested that two thirds of the monks in Sakya were "levy monks", as they are called by Cassinelli and Ekvall. Not all households were liable to pay this tax: traders, artisans, Nepalese, subjects of the palace, and the nobility were exempted from having to send a son to the monastery (Cassinelli and Ekvall 1969: 294–95). This suggests that most of these monks had an agricultural background, which strengthens the hypothesis that this policy was in line with inheritance strategies already practised by land-holding farmers. According to Cassinelli and Ekvall:

> Levy monks had certain advantages over volunteer monks, especially the opportunity for attaining personal wealth. This opportunity—and the general advantages of monkhood, such as education, high prestige, material comfort, proximity to the sources of power and authority, and the chance to become a *sKu drag* official—apparently made the levy of monks a quite bearable institution. Moreover, the family that produced a boy upon call had its revenue lowered in compensation. It must also be remembered that the average Tibetan family felt a kind of duty of providing at least one son to the monkhood.
>
> *ibid.*: 296

Similarly, Miller—researching monasteries in the Himalayas in the 1950s—notes the existence of "lama tax" but comments that it was not widespread. In addition, she reasons that as this policy, for example in Sakyong (Sa skyong) monastery in Northern Sikkim, was geared toward keeping up the numbers, it thus did not amount to "not adhering to a real tax as such" (Miller 1958: 193).

The provisional nature of monk-tax is also witnessed in the Fifth Dalai Lama's autobiography. He mentions Chökhor Ling, a college of Drepung ('Bras spungs) that had been temporarily dissolved. To rebuild it a monk-tax (*btsun khral*) was put in place by the head-disciplinarian (*zhal ngo*), consisting of around thirty men (*Ngag dbang blo bzang rgya mtsho gsung 'bum* vol. 5: 45).[17] In a later

16 I am grateful to Jann Ronis for bringing this passage to my attention.

17 *gra tshang chos 'khor gling pa bar skabs su 'thor ba zhal ngos btsun khral sum cu tsam dang bcas btsugs* [...]/.

volume of his autobiography, he writes that the managing lamas of that same college had put a stop to registering "wanderers from outside" and that, from that time onward, volunteer monks (*dad btsun*, literally "faith monks") were not allowed admission. Instead, he writes, a monk-tax of about three hundred was instated. According to the Great Fifth, in previous years, the monks at this college had been living together with the monks of Drepung Losel Ling ('Bras spungs blo gsal gling), but the two parties had become hostile toward each other. It was announced that the mingling of the two monastic sections was no longer necessary as Chökhor Ling was given its own monk-quarters as well as its own monks (*ibid.* vol. 6: 94).[18]

In the above instance of monk-tax, it is not stated where the monks were drafted from, although it is likely that the levy of three hundred monks was a one-off measure and did not end up becoming a periodic tax. In other texts, however, it is clearly stated that boys were collected as monk-tax from among the subjects (*mnga' zhabs* or *mnga' 'bangs*). In the context of Chökhor Ling, however, it is more likely that the monks in both cases were levied from the other colleges at Drepung, especially because it is mentioned that the practice of taking in outside wanderers had been discontinued and that instead monks were brought in from elsewhere in the monastic community. The Fifth Dalai Lama's uncritical stance regarding the non-admittance of volunteer monks is striking here, in particular when seen in the light of the current policy advocated by the Fourteenth Dalai Lama. However, when seen in a historical context—Drepung during that time was seeing a sizeable influx of monks with questionable motives and equally dubious reputation—the Fifth Dalai Lama's position is strategically sound (see Jansen 2013a).

Much like other types of taxes levied in Central Tibet, such as the military tax, neither the individual nor the households were taxed separately. Rather, whole communities—usually villages—were to pay the monk-tax together (Aziz 1978: 111).[19] Aziz notes for example that in the Dingri (lDing ri) region Yöldong (Yol dong) village was to send five men to Phelgye Ling ('Phel rgyas gling) monastery to become monks (*ibid.*: 239). Presumably, however, the families that had to send one of their sons away were elected on a local level by village headmen, who would take into account the amount of sons each family had and possibly also the boys' suitability for life in the monastery.

---

18 *bla ma sne mo ba sogs yong mi rnams la phyi 'khyar mi yong ba'i rtsi kha bkag gra tshang la dad btsun de nas bzung ma bcug pa'i btsun khral gsar pa sum brgya tsam brgyab chos 'khor gling rang du gra shag dang bcas gra tshang gnyis dang 'dres 'dres mi dgos pa byed par dril bsgrags/.*

19 Other mentioned taxes that are fulfilled by the village as a whole are transport tax and other service tax (ibid.: 198).

Contrary to what one might expect, the males who were levied as part of a monk-tax did not necessarily go to a monastery. Cakpori (lCags po ri), the medical college founded in 1696 by Desi Sangye Gyatso (sDe srid Sangs rgyas rgya mtsho), recruited thirty people from the Büri (sBus ri) region in Central Tibet as "monk-tax" (*dGa' ldan chos 'byung*: 464; Meyer 2003: 111).[20] Another perhaps surprising feature of this manner of recruitment is that it did not just affect the male population: in a number of cases females were to join the nunnery to fulfil part of their community's tax-obligation. The nun-tax for communities in the Sakya area is described by Cassinelli and Ekvall:

> There was also a levy of nuns to staff the two nunneries near the capital, Sa bzang and Rin chen sgang, with a total of about 110 nuns, of whom not more than 10 percent were volunteers. The nun levy was also based on the schedule of revenue in kind, and a family that gave up a little girl also had its revenue lowered. The levy of nuns, like the levy of monks, no doubt helped tie the policy together, but in a much less significant way. [...] The life of a nun had few attractions.
>
> CASSINELLI AND EKVALL 1969: 297

While becoming a monk could provide social mobility (see for example Jansen 2013b), ordination as a nun did not offer this opportunity—nuns were often illiterate and had a relatively low standing in society. Nonetheless, just as with monasteries, once a nunnery was built, the number of inhabitants had to remain constant. Therefore "[t]he levy of nuns was probably the only way to keep enough nuns in the capital nunneries in order to maintain the religious prestige of the sect" (Cassinelli and Ekvall 1969: 297). Cassinelli and Ekvall's information is based on interviews they conducted with high-placed people from Sakya. A similar "nun-tax" is also reported in an interview with an ex-nun from Sera Lung (Se ra lung) in South-west Tibet who recounted that she was made a nun at eight years old, probably during the 1940s, at the request of the authorities and that she went to live at the small nunnery in her birthplace when she was thirteen.[21] Until now, however, the few times that this nun-tax is mentioned in Western language works the sources have been oral.[22]

---

20 *sbus ri rgyud nas grwa khral sum cu skor bsdus/ rten brten par zhig gso dang gsar bzhengs sogs byas pa'i lcags ri baidū rya 'gro phan lta na ngo mtshar rig byed gling btsugs/.*

21 http://www.tibetoralhistory.org/Interviews/05_Chonzom.pdf. Unfortunately, this interview only contains the English translation and not the original Tibetan.

22 Nicolas Sihlé informed me that Cooke has reported the occurrence of nun-tax in Nyishang (Cooke 1985). Unfortunately, I was unable to consult this work.

In my endeavour to understand the phenomenon of monk- and nun-tax, I came across a document that is contained in the database Digital Tibetan Archives Bonn (DTAB, 0967_LTWA_179), which mentions *btsun ma'i khral*: nun-tax. This heavily damaged manuscript contains an agreement between the Dedruk Teu Rapa (sDe drug Te'u ra pa)—a community from an area in South-west Tibet (Nyel; gNyal), where six Geluk monasteries can be found, with which the Dedruk incarnation lineage is associated[23]—and the Sertengpa (gSer steng pa), referring to inhabitants of Nyel Serteng (gNyal gSer steng). It is dated to the Water-Bird Year, which could be 1814, 1874, or 1934. As it has large holes in the middle, portions of the document are missing, making it difficult to understand. It is clear, however, that the manuscript deals with the issue of monk-tax (*btsun khral*).

The document speaks of an old monastery where a community of monks was established with Chöje Künzang (Chos rje Kung bzang) as the monastery's head (*dgon bdag*). The authors of the text then note that there existed a written agreement (*gan rgya*) that attested that this person "had created a trust fund so that rNam rgyal and Kun rigs [*sic*: *rig*][24] rituals would be performed for us."[25] It appears that things did not work out and a request was made to the Fifth Dalai Lama, after which a nunnery (*mo dgon*) was established. The document states that the Great Fifth gave instructions—it is damaged at the place where one would expect some sort of specification—and it furthermore remarks that it was made clear that it was allowed, for the accumulation of merit of the living and the dead, to levy a monk-tax, consisting of the second boy, in the case of there being three sons and a nun-tax, which meant that when there were at least two girls the youngest would be made a nun.[26] The document further suggests that previously there had been a problem in actively collecting this tax and its authors seek the communities' full support in heeding their obligations.

It appears that defaulting on this type of tax-obligation was not unique: Bischoff mentions a document dated to 1761 in which it is stated that this tax regulation had to be re-enforced as previously people had not complied out of

23 For a short description of Te'u ra (or rTe'u ra) monastery, see *dGa' ldan chos 'byung*: 209–10. According to *Dung dkar tshig mdzod* (936.6), the six monasteries are 1. gNyal gra skor; 2. Zangs chen; 3. Ri steng; 4. Ngang skyal; 5. gSer phye kha; 6. rTe'u ra.

24 These are rituals propitiating protectors and rituals to bring about long life, respectively.

25 *DTAB*, 0967_LTWA_179: r. 8: *dgon bdag chos rje kun bzang zer bas phran tshor rnaM rgyal kun rigs sogs kyi cho ga gtong theb du sbyor 'jags byas* (r. 9) *pa gan rgya zur gsal ltar lags par/.*

26 *Ibid.* r. 9: *^gong sa mchog la stan* (r. 10) *zhus phul ba'i thog nas mo dgon gsar 'dzugs la ^gong sa lnga pa chen po'i bka' xxxxxxxxx gshig son la skor pa dge khongs gang yin la bu gsum byung la bar par btsun khral dang bumo gnyis pa de rjes gzhon par btsun ma'i khral rgyab chog pa gsal ba bzhin/.*

disregard or stubbornness (Bischoff 2013: 17; the document itself is published in Schuh 1981: 113). In another Central Tibetan official document it is suggested that families could also buy off this duty of sending a son to the monastery (Schneider 2012: 83). Similarly, an agreement dating to 1916 regarding the obligation of the community of Te in Mustang demonstrates that the obligation of sending one out of three daughters born to each family to become a nun with the (Nyingma) Lama of Tshognam (Tshogs rnams) could be lifted by paying the sum of 500 rupees to the representative of the government and 100 rupees to the head of the community (*HMA/UTshognam/Tib/36*, Ramble 2016: 258–60).[27]

These occurrences are certainly in line with statements made by elderly monks, now living in exile, whom I interviewed in 2012. They noted that sons of the wealthier families usually did not end up becoming monks as they were able to compensate their tax-obligations in other ways, although, as I demonstrate below, notable exceptions occurred. Based on oral histories, Bingaman's research on a Naxi community who were subjects of the Muli kingdom, the monk-tax was both levied and frequently evaded. Muli (Mu li/ sMi li) monastery aggressively levied this tax among families with three or more sons until it was abandoned in 1956. One way this community, which had a more than ambiguous stance toward Tibetan Buddhism, evaded this tax was by having one of the sons adopted by another family. The son would return to his natal family once he reached adulthood. The data collected by Bingaman show that this evasion occurred on a large scale (Bingaman 2020: 268–97; 2021: 56–59).

In more recent Tibetan local histories, occasional references to monk-tax can sometimes be found. As these works unfortunately tend not to refer to original historical sources, they are somewhat problematic. However, they appear to be more often than not based on oral history or personal experience, and thus they occasionally prove to be valuable sources indeed. One such work, *Sa skyong 'bur ba'i gdung rabs*, published in 2009 in Dharamsala, relates the history of the Porong (sPo rong) area in South-west Tibet.[28] In the chapter that narrates the history of the *Bo dong* monastic institution of Pemo Chöding (dPal mo chos sdings),[29] founded by Chokle Namgyel (Phyogs las rnam rgyal,

27 I am grateful to Charles Ramble for bringing this to my attention. This agreement is part of a larger and more complex saga of the collapse of a nunnery, a quarrel and a relocation of nuns, which the documents collected by Ramble attest to. It would lead too far to detail these issues here.

28 Doubtlessly, this work is based on a much older history of the Porong area, which was completed in 1820. For more on this text see Ramble 2002.

29 This monastery is alternatively known as Padma chos sdings.

1375–1451), the way in which the eight monastic communities in the area maintained their population numbers is described in the following way:

> With regard to maintaining and keeping up the monk- and nun-populations in the eight Bodong (Bo dong) religious communities, the way in which the monk-tax and nun-tax worked was as follows: for Pemo Chöding there is a monk-tax of the middle son in the case of there being three boys [levied] from Yala (g.Ya' la).[30] In the monastic institution of Shekar (Shel dkar) there was a monk-tax of twenty-five [males] and they were taken from the higher-class agriculturalists (*grong pa*)[31] in the Zurtsho (Zur mtsho) area. The monk-tax for Ngönga (mNgon dga') monastery was taken from the five regions in Tibet and from north and south Pel (dPal), thus among the six sectors (*tsho*) it was the middle son of three. Regarding the origin of the nun [-tax], for Porong nunnery and Gamchok (sGam mchog) nunnery it concerns the middle of three daughters [levied] from Yala, and even the middle daughter of the hereditary ruler (*rje dbon*) of Porong had to go to Gamchok. The nun-tax for the other nunneries came from other regions in Tibet.[32]
>
> *Sa skyong 'bur ba'i gdung rabs*: 99–100

Interestingly, while in most other instances, *btsun khral* and *grwa khral* are treated more or less synonymously, in this work *grwa khral* is used for monk-tax and *btsun khral* for nun-tax. We see here that the monk- and nun-tax appear to be levied on the communities that had previously established tax-obligations, either with the religious institution itself or with the secular ruler in that area. While this is in itself unsurprising, the fact that the higher echelons of society—and even the hereditary ruler himself—are here pointed out as being liable to "pay" this tax is worth noting. This is likely to have served as an example for the rest of the lay population.

---

30 Yala is a mountain pass near the monastery, so presumably it concerns the inhabitants of that area. I am grateful to Charles Ramble for pointing this out.

31 In South-west Tibet the *grong pa*, lacking real "aristocrats", form a kind of elite group (Aziz 1978: 70).

32 *bo dong chos brgyud pa'i grwa rgyun dang btsun rgyun 'dzin skyong ched grwa khral dang btsun khral gyi 'gro lugs 'di ltar te/ dpal mo chos sdings dgon pa'i ched/ g.ya' la yas nas bu gsum bar pa'i grwa khral yod/ shel dkar chos sder grwa khral 25 yod pas yong khungs zur mtsho yul gyi grong pa drag gras yin/ mngon dga' chos sde'i grwa khral yong khungs ni bod gzhis khag lnga dang dpal lho byang gnyis 'then pas tsho drug gi bu gsum bar pa yin/ btsun ma yong khungs ni spo rong btsun dgon dang sgam mchog btsun dgon gnyis la g.ya' la yas nas bu mo gsum gyi bar ma dang sgam mchog tu spo rong rje dbon gyi sras mo bar ma phebs dgos kyi yod/ de min btsun dgon gzhan gyi btsun khral bod gzhis khag nas yong/.*

The above shows the variegated nature of this clerical tax, which has affected both males and females at certain times and place. It also serves to demonstrate that this policy—although widespread—was by no means in place everywhere and at all times. In fact, some monasteries, such as Tashi Lhunpo (bKra shis lhun po) in the 19th century, imposed an upper limit to the number of people entering there as monks (Jansen 2013b). The author of the monastic guidelines for this monastery, the Eighth Panchen Lama, even speaks of the drawbacks of having too many monks in the monastery (*bKra shis lhun po bca' yig*: 67). While the levying of monk-tax might be given in support of the existence of the "ideology of mass monasticism" (Goldstein 1998: 15), there are many indications that this mass monasticism was never part of any sort of self-conscious monastic or state policy (also see Jansen 2013a: 121), despite the simple fact that there were indeed masses of monks in Tibet. It is clear that the concern with having the right number of monks at the monastery had to do with monk-population control and, perhaps more importantly, with the type of agreement in place among the institution's donors.[33] Depending on the context, the levying of monk-tax can be interpreted as a sign of a monastic institution being in decline and trying to keep up its numbers or alternatively as an indication of a monastery with a strong hold on the lay population. All things being equal however, it is evident that this tax has never been imposed across the board and that it has not been part of state policy over any sustained period of time.

Among both most historians and Tibetan Buddhist monks alike we find the notion that monk-tax, in whatever form, has now been relegated to the past. One monk from Ladakh, belonging to the Drigung Kagyü school, whom I interviewed, was able to tell me that somewhere in Nepal there existed a monastery of the same school where this custom (*lugs srol*) is currently in place. Indeed, this monastery in Limi (Humla district) currently imposes monastic recruitment at three village communities, where a written agreement (*gan rgya*) from 1890 concerning monastic recruitment is still being followed (Hovden 2013: 218–20). Be this as it may, the fact that this monk-tax is upheld in Limi appears to be viewed by other monks in the Tibetan Buddhist tradition—even by those belonging to the same school—as idiosyncratic, if not more than slightly

33 This is to say, it would not be seen as correct if a group of donors committed themselves to paying for the monastic tea-round for eighty monks and there were only forty monks actually there to perform rituals and recite prayers. Remedying this was thus seen to be in the interest of both the monastery and the donors.

problematic, and, as indicated above, not entirely in line with the current Dalai Lama's views regarding monk-tax.[34]

1.2 Grwa khral: *Chores*

Understanding the concept of *grwa khral* (and *btsun khral*) is further complicated by the fact that, while it has been so far mostly translated as "monk-tax", it does not unequivocally mean a tax levied by the monastery on families that were required to provide a son. There are at least two other uses of the word. A contemporary work on the history of Tshurpu (Tshur phu) monastery refers to the term *grwa khral* with quite a divergent meaning attached to it. Here, the compound is not taken to mean a tax consisting of monks, but refers to duties to be fulfilled by monks,[35] such as serving tea and sweeping. The word is elaborated further as "monk duties attached to the lower garment" (*so so'i gsham thab* [*sic*: *thabs*] *la 'khri ba'i grwa khral*) (*mTshur phu dgon gyi dkar chag*: 259). This concept occurs elsewhere as "youth tax" (*gzhon khral*). In Tashi Lhunpo monastery in the 19th century this "tax" was called "chore tax" (*las khral*). The text in which this is mentioned states that studying monks were to be given as few chores as possible (*bKra shis lhun po bca' yig*: 73). This particular duty could—in almost all cases—be bought off. In Tshurpu,

> Some relatives of a newly enrolled monk, in order to prevent him from having to perform youth tax (*gzhon khral*) for the studying monks, held something called 'the burning light of the message: a confession to the rows [of monks]' (*gral bshags*), during the assembly of the Sangha. This involved giving an enrolment tea (*sgrig ja*) and along with that there was the custom of giving each member of the Sangha (*dge 'dun*) an offering of money. Previously, this was half a silver *zho* each, but later on this became, in Tibetan currency, five *zho* for each member as an offering of money. Then one did not have to perform 'youth tax'.
>
> *mTshur phu dgon gyi dkar chag*: 258[36]

---

34 Similarly Gyatso remarks that the Fourteenth Dalai Lama regularly suggests that "the emphasis should be upon monastic quality rather than quantity" (Gyatso 2003: 239).

35 For example: *'dul ba'i spyi sgrigs/ tshogs bsags kyi ched du dmigs te grwa khral rgyugs mi dgos pa dang* [...]/ (*mTshur phu dgon gyi dkar chag*: 259).

36 *yang sgrig zhugs grwa pa rnams kyi khyim bdag 'ga' zhig gis gsar zhugs nas gsham thab* [*sic*: *thabs*] *bslab gral gyi gzhon khral rgyugs mi dgos pa'i phyir du dge 'dun 'dus tshogs rnams la bshags 'bul snyan sgron gyi mtsho byed* (*gral bshags*) *zhes pa sgrig ja dang mnyam du dge 'dun rer sngar lam phyag 'gyed dngul kyang zho med skar rnga* [*sic*: *lnga*] *re 'bul srol 'dug kyang phyis bod dngul srang med zho lnga re phyag 'gyed du phul phyin gzhon khral rgyugs mi dgos/*.

This process of buying off duties by means of sponsoring a ceremony also took place in the process of becoming a "monk-sponsor" (*chos mdzad*) (see Jansen 2018: 61–64; Dreyfus 2003: 51; Cabezón 1997: 348). This essentially meant that such a monk would gain certain privileges, which included securing a place in the front of the monastic rows during assembly. This particular concept has only been briefly referred to by Goldstein, who notes that certain monks "had some intermittent monastic work obligations in their early years (as a kind of 'new monk tax'), but otherwise were free to do what they liked within the overall framework of monastic (vinaya) rules" (Goldstein 2009: 10).

In brief then, we see that in some instances, *las khral*, *gzhon khral* and *grwa khral* all carry the same meaning: the chores that a junior monk is expected to perform at the monastery. However, to my knowledge, none of the dictionaries currently attests to this particular gloss of the word *grwa khral*.

1.3 Grwa khral: *Sustenance Payments Made to Monks*

The elderly monk Sherab Gyatso (Shes rab rgya mtsho) who lived in Sakya monastery in the 1940s and 50s indicated that there is another meaning to the word *grwa khral*. When I asked him what it meant to him, he said:

> In the past, the general population (*mi dmangs*) of the surrounding villages had to come together and give roasted barley flour (*rtsam pa*) to feed the monks from their community, this is what was understood to be *grwa khral*—it was not considered to be a heavy tax. The other understanding of *grwa khral* was not practised in Sakya: there was no need for families to give a son to the monastery. The habit of giving one son to the monastery when you have three boys is a "*khams pa*" habit. It is not good to force (*'tshe dbang btang na*) a family to make their son a monk, it should be the child's own wish.[37]

This statement appears to contradict the findings of Cassinelli and Ekvall regarding the prevalence of monastic recruitment in Sakya. It is possible that their oral sources were better informed on the monastic policies than this monk of humble origins, who was in his late teens or early twenties when he was living in Sakya. This apparent contradiction will be further discussed below. Regardless of who was right, Sherab Gyatso's opinion very much reflects current ideas among Tibetans in exile with regard to monastic recruitment. Interestingly, the type of "tax" he refers to—that of certain communities

37 This monk, who was in his late seventies, was interviewed in August, 2012 in Sakya monastery in Rajpur.

coming together to give financial aid to a select group of monks—occurred, and still occurs, in many Tibetan Buddhist communities. Davidson, writing about a much earlier time, also remarks upon this type of fundraising. The "tax" or "contributions" collected in order to support a temple or a group of monks was—as early as the 13th and 14th centuries—called *khral* or, alternatively, *sham thabs khral* (lower robe tax), which Davidson translates with "monk-tax" and explains it as what certain "funding groups" would contribute to support monasteries and temples during this early era in the history of Tibetan monasticism. He notes that "the term might better be understood in the period as something like obligatory professional dues" because "whatever weak governmental structures may have existed, there is no sense that they had anything to do with the collection and distribution of such funds" (Davidson 2008 [2005]: 103).

The concept of *sham thabs khral* as something intended to support (a certain group of) monks continued to be used centuries later, for example by the Fifth Dalai Lama. In his monastic guidelines for Drepung monastery, he notes that monks originally from faraway monasteries studying at Drepung should not be allowed to go on certain centrally organised outings, during which rituals were performed and donations were collected. This is because:

> The monks who were sent by their native monasteries (*gzhis dgon*) as students are sent shares (*skal*). Therefore they will need to bring about their own *sham thabs khral* by means of doing rituals and the like.
>
> *'Bras spungs bca' yig*: 304[38]

The author appears to suggest that monks from areas outside Central Tibet were thought to be self-sufficient and thus were not to be given any extra help by letting them participate in certain monastic events.

Turek also notes the occurrence of the concept of *sham thabs kha khral* in monasteries in Nangchen (Nang chen) in Kham (see Turek in this volume). Here it is explained as the contribution the monks at the monastery were expected to make toward paying for the rituals, which confirms Goldstein's gloss of the *sham thabs khral* as "tax collected from monks" (Goldstein 2001: 1093). In line with this particular understanding of "monk contribution", Nornang suggests yet another meaning of *grwa khral*, namely as an alternative to *grwa chags*: a tax that monks themselves were obliged to pay—presumably to the Central

38 *gzhis dgon pa'i rigs nas grwa pa tshor bslab gnyer lta bur song ba la skal ba gtong ba ni tshul sgrub mchod kyis mtshon so so'i sham thabs khral sgrub dgos pa'i rgyu mtshan yin 'dug/.* For more on the monastic guidelines for this monastery see Jansen 2013a.

authorities. He acknowledges, however, that this tax was never levied in the 20th century (Nornang 1990: 266).[39] So far, there is no textual evidence that can confirm this gloss.

2 Concluding Remarks

The above discussion demonstrates that when we come across the word *grwa khral* or even *btsun khral*, we should not immediately assume that it refers to the levying of monks; the two other meanings should also be taken into account. This being said, the remaining remarks I make here pertain exclusively to the first meaning of the word: that of monk-tax or monk-levy. At first glance, the source materials for the study of this phenomenon appear scarce: there is a small number of official documents that detail the levying of monks in certain communities, and additionally the concept is often employed—albeit only in passing—in a number of hagiographies and biographies. It is noteworthy that when monk-tax is mentioned, as in the case of Tāranātha's autobiography, the notion is used merely to highlight the grand acts of certain masters in certain localities and *never* to criticise the practice. Furthermore, particularly in earlier (pre-Ganden Phodrang) works, monk-levy appears to be part of an agreement between a religious figure and the ruler or leaders of a community. The underlying notion may be that it was thought to be beneficial for a Buddhist community to have a religious institution in the neighbourhood: it meant that the necessary rituals could be performed regularly. It was then the community's responsibility to make sure that that nunnery or monastery would be sufficiently populated. In some Tibetan and Himalayan areas the way to fulfil this duty was to introduce a monk-tax. As is usual in the history of Tibetan communities, the "state" was conspicuous by its absence and was not an effective agent in imposing this tax, regardless of the geographical location of that state.[40] The phenomenon of monk-tax was geographically widespread: it occurred not just in Central Tibet, but also in Ladakh, Amdo, Nepal, Arunachal Pradesh and Kham. It was not simply a Geluk affair, but all Tibetan

39 The general contention is that monastic estates were exempted from taxation (i.e. Carrasco 1959). However, there are Tibetan documents that demonstrate that monasteries (even the Geluk ones) were made to pay tax and contribute to the work-force (see Schwieger in this volume).

40 Perhaps an exception to this is the King of Derge's instatement of a monk-tax of five hundred in order to populate the newly founded monastery Pelpung in 1729 (Ronis 2010). There are no indications that this monk-tax remained in place for a sustained period of time. I am grateful to Maria Turek for pointing me to Ronis' article.

Buddhist schools appear to be represented among the monasteries (and nunneries) where monk-tax existed at certain points in time.

From the small sample of occurrences of monk-tax in the sense of the obligatory recruitment of monks given here, it appears that the smaller "branch" monasteries were more likely to have a monk-tax. The larger "mother" monasteries often did not need to draw in monks, because they received a steady flow of monks joining to study or to climb the socio-economic ladder. This may in fact explain the contradictory findings regarding Sakya monastery: Cassinelli and Ekvall treated the main monastery of Sakya and its branch monasteries as one "polity" and could thus make the claim that two thirds of the monastic population were levy-monks, while the former resident of Sakya, Sherab Gyatso, resolutely stated that there was no monk-tax at Sakya: both may have been right if the monk-tax was actually only in place for the branch monasteries and not the main monastery.

As the title of this article suggests, the treatment of the phenomenon of *grwa khral/btsun khral* in this article is nothing more than preliminary: as the digitisation of Tibetan texts continues, many more references to this concept will become more easily available, and some of these yet-to-be searchable works may well contradict—but hopefully further clarify and elaborate on—the findings presented here. The fluidity and diversity of the concept and implementation of this monk-tax cannot be stressed enough. It is clear that the tax could be negotiated and circumvented (by the wealthier families) and communities could also outright refuse to heed the call to send out sons to the monastery. Decrees that call upon the people of certain areas to comply with previously made agreements point exactly to the occasional non-compliance of local communities and the relatively weak position of the monastery in question among the lay population.

Viewing monk-tax more broadly, when in place in whatever form, it appears to be an indicator not of "masses of monks", but rather of a chronic *shortage* of monks. Even though the major monasteries may have been full to the brim at certain times, it seems that many less prominent monasteries regularly failed, as indicated by various Tibetan sources—be they modern or historical—that comment on the Ganden Phodrang period's state of the monastic institutions. Without exception, the works cited in this article convey a perception of enduring low levels of monastic population, which was seen to endanger the continuity of mostly local monasteries. This appears to have been one of the main justifications for instating a monk-tax, particularly as these local monasteries served the communities in the neighbourhood with vital religious services, which were mostly of a ritual nature. Elsewhere, I have called into question the supposed ideology of mass monasticism. I see two main reasons why this notion is highly problematic: first of all, because large numbers of monks were seen by important "policy-makers" such as the Fifth Dalai Lama and the Eighth Panchen Lama as a security threat and a nuisance, and thus they sought to curtail the influx of monks (Jansen 2013a), and secondly because the monkhood was not always open to all: certain groups were systematically excluded from entering (Jansen 2013b). Even though there does not appear to have been any ideology of mass monasticism among Tibetan Buddhists there were of course massive numbers of monks. What the issue of monk-tax highlights most of all is that the monk population was very unevenly spread throughout the Tibetan and Himalayan areas. Various methods of regulating this appear to have been in place at certain points in time, of which monk-tax was but one. Monk-tax was, however, never and has nowhere been applied universally and it was something that could be circumvented in a number of ways. At the same time—at least in one pocket of the Tibetan Buddhist world—this tax has managed to survive the changed sensibilities of the majority of the 21st-century monastic population.

References

Tibetan Language Sources

'Be lo rnam thar

'Be lo Tshe dbang kun khyab (b. 18th century). 2013 edition. *Ma hA paN+Di ta tshe dbang kun khyab kyi rnam thar rtogs brjod rin chen nor bu'i phreng ba*. In *'Be lo tshe dbang kun khyab kyi gsung thor bu'i skor*. Byang chub ljon bzang, vol. 7. Lhasa: Bod ljongs bod yig dpe rnying dpe skrun khang.

bKra shis lhun po bca' yig

bsTan pa'i dbang phyug. 1876. 1989 edition. bKra shis lhun po dpal gyi bde chen phyogs thams cad las rnam par rgyal ba'i gling gi dge 'dun dbu dmangs dang/ bla brang nang ma sogs lto zan khongs gtogs dang bcas pa spyi khyab tu nges dgos pa'i yi ge khrims gnyis srog gi chad mthud rab brjid gser gyi rdo rje'i gnya' shing dge. *In* mGon po dar rgyas (ed.) *Gangs can rig brgya'i sgo 'byed lde mig ces bya ba bzhugs so: bca' yig phyogs sgrig*. Beijing: Mi rigs dpe skrun khang, 35–158.

Bod kyi rig gnas 9(18)

Collective (Bod rang skyong ljongs srid gros lo rgyus rig gnas dpyad gzhi'i rgyu cha u yon lhan khang). 1995. *Bod kyi rig gnas lo rgyus dpyad gzhi'i rgyu cha bdams bsgrigs* 9(18). Beijing: Mi rigs dpe skrun khang.

'Bras spungs bca' yig

Ngag dbang blo bzang rgya mtsho (the Fifth Dalai Lama). 1682. 1989 edition. *Chos sde chen po dpal ldan 'bras dkar spungs pa'i dgon gyi bca' yig tshul 'chal sa srung 'dul ba'i lcags kyo kun gsal me long. In Bod kyi snga rabs khrims srol yig cha bdams bsgrigs.* Tshe ring dpal 'byor *et al.* (ed.). Lhasa: Bod yig dpe rnying dpe skrun khang, 275–323.

Chu shel gyi phreng ba vol 2

Si tu paṇ chen chos kyi byung gnas and 'Be lo Tshe dbang kun khyab. 1775. 2013 edition. *sGrub brgyud karma kaM tshang gi brgyud pa rin po che'i rnam par thar pa rab 'byams nor bu zla ba chu shel gyi phreng ba* vol. 2.

dGa' ldan chos 'byung

sDe srid Sangs rgyas rgya mtsho (1653–1705). 1991 [1938] edition. *dGa' ldan chos 'byung baiDUrya ser po*. Xining: Krung go'i bod kyi shes rig dpe skrun khang.

Digital Tibetan Archives Bonn (DTAB)

Document number 0967_LTWA_179. Anonymous. Digital (https://crossasia.org/en/service/crossasia-lab/dtab/).

Dung dkar gsung rtsom

Dung dkar blo bzang phrin las. 1997. *Dung dkar blo bzang phrin las kyi gsung rtsom phyogs bsgrigs*. Beijing: Krung go'i bod kyi shes rig dpe skrun khang.

Dung dkar tshig mdzod

Dung dkar blo bzang 'phrin las. 2002. *Bod rig pa'i tshig mdzod chen mo shes bya rab gsal.* Beijing: Krung go'i bod rig pa dpe skrun khang.

mTshur phu dgon gyi dkar chag

Rin chen dpal bzang. 1995. *Mtshur phu dgon gyi dkar chag kun gsal me long*. Beijing: Mi rigs dpe skrun khang.

Ngag dbang blo bzang rgya mtsho gsung 'bum

Ngag dbang blo bzang rgya mtsho (1617–1682) 1991–1995 edition. *Za hor gyi ban de ngag dbang blo bzang rgya mtsho'i 'di snang 'khrul ba'i rol rtsed rtogs brjod kyi tshul du bkod pa du ku la'i gos bzang. In gSung 'bum* vols 5 and 6. Gangtok: Sikkim research institute of Tibetology.

Ngor mkhan chen dpal ldan chos skyong zhabs kyi rnam thar

Ngor mkhan chen dpal ldan chos skyong (1702–1760) and Zhu chen Tshul khrims rin chen (1697–1774). 1974 edition. *Ngor mkhan chen dpal ldan chos skyong zhabs kyi rnam thar, vol. 3*. Palampur: Sungrab nyamso gyunpel parkhang, Tashijong (sde dge par ma bskyar par).

'Phags pa lha bcu pa'i dgon pa nyams gso'i rtsa tshigs

'Phags pa lha bcu pa'i dgon pa nyams gso'i rtsa tshigs. 1919. 2007 edition. *In* Blo bzang shes rab, *Chab mdo'i yig tshang rin chen spungs pa* vol. 2. Delhi?: N.P.

Sa skyong 'bur ba'i gdung rabs

Zla ba dar rgyas. 2009. *Sa skyong 'bur ba'i gdung rabs las 'phros pa'i 'brog sde chen po spo rong gi byung ba brjod pa dwangs gsal me long*. Dharamsala: A myes rma chen bod kyi rig gzhung zhib 'jug khang.

Tāranātha bDag nyid kyi rnam thar

Tāranātha kun dga' snying po (1575–1634). 1982–1987 edition. rGyal khams pa tā ra nā thas bdag nyid kyi rnam thar nges par brjod pa'i deb gter shin tu zhib mo ma bcos lhug pa'i rtogs brjod. *In* gSung 'bum vol. 1. Leh: C. Namgyal and Tsewang Taru.

Tshe dbang nor bu gsung 'bum

Rig 'dzin tshe dbang nor bu (1698–1755). *gSung 'bum vol. 3*. Dalhousie (1976–1977): N.P.

Western Language Sources

Ardussi, J. 1977. Bhutan before the British: A Historical Study. Ph.D. thesis, Australian National University.

Aris, M. 1979. *Bhutan*. Warminster: Aris and Phillips Ltd.

Aziz, B.A. 1978. *Tibetan Frontier Families: Reflections of Three Generations from D'ing-ri*. Durham: Carolina Academic Press.

Bingaman, M.E. 2020. The Art of Being Governed under the Muli Tibetan Regime: A Case Study of Naxi House Kinship. Ph.D. thesis, National Tsing-Hua University.

Bingaman, M.E. 2021. Monk levies and kinship in the Sino-Tibetan borderland. *Inner Asia* 23(1), 51–78.

Bischoff, J. 2013. Right there but still unnoticed: information on dGa' ldan pho brang *mi ser*. *In* C. Ramble, P. Schwieger and A. Travers (eds) *Tibetans who Escaped the Historian's Net: Studies in the Social History of Tibetan Societies*. Kathmandu: Vajra Books, 9–26.

Cabezón, J.I. 1997. The regulations of a monastery. *In* D.S. Lopez (ed.) *Religions of Tibet in Practice*. Princeton: Princeton University Press, 335–51.

Caple, J. 2019. *Morality and Monastic Revival in Post-Mao Tibet*. Honolulu: University of Hawai'i Press.

Cassinelli, C.W. and R.B. Ekvall. 1969. *A Tibetan Principality: The Political System of Sakya*. Ithaca: Cornell University Press.

Caumanns, V. 2015. *Shākya-mchog-ldan, Mahāpaṇḍita des Klosters gSer-mdog-can: Leben und Werk nach den tibetischen Quellen*. Wiesbaden: Dr. Ludwig Reichert Verlag.

Cooke, M.T. 1985. The People of Nyishang: Identity, Tradition and Change in the Nepal-Tibet Borderland. Ph.D. thesis, University of California.

Dagyab, N. 2009. Vergleich von Verwaltungsstrukturen und wirtschaftlichen Entscheidungsprozessen tibetisch-buddhistischer Klöster in der Autonomen Region Tibet, China und Indien. Ph.D. thesis, Rheinischen Friedrich-Wilhelms-Universität.

Dargyay, E.K. 1982. *Tibetan Village Communities: Structure and Change*. Warminster: Aris and Philips Ltd.

Davidson, R.M. 2008 [2005]. *Tibetan Renaissance: Tantric Buddhism in the Rebirth of Tibetan Culture*. New York: Columbia University Press.

Dreyfus, G. 2003. *The Sound of Two Hands Clapping: The Education of a Tibetan Buddhist Monk*. Berkeley: California University Press.

Feer, L. 1883. *Fragments extraits du Kandjour*. Paris: E. Leroux.

Francke, A.H. 1926. *Antiquities of Indian Tibet, Part II: The Chronicles of Ladakh and Minor Chronicles*. Calcutta: Superintendent Government Printing.

Goldstein, M.C. 1971. Serfdom and mobility: an examination of the institution of human lease in traditional Tibetan society. *The Journal of Asian Studies* 30(3), 521–34.

Goldstein, M.C. 1998. The revival of monastic life in Drepung monastery. *In* M. Goldstein (ed.) *Buddhism in Contemporary Tibet: Religious Revival and Cultural Identity*. Berkeley: University of California Press, 15–52.

Goldstein, M.C. (ed.). 2001. *The New Tibetan-English Dictionary of Modern Tibetan*. Berkeley: University of California Press.

Goldstein, M.C. 2009. Tibetan Buddhism and mass monasticism. *In* A. Herrou and G. Krauskopff (eds) *Moines et moniales de par le monde : la vie monastique au miroir de la parenté*. Paris: L'Harmattan. English version at: www.case.edu/affil/.../Tibetan_Buddhism_and_Mass_Monasticism.doc.

Gyatso, S. 2003. Of monks and monasteries. *In* D. Bernstorff and H. von Welck (eds) *Exile as Challenge: the Tibetan Diaspora*. Hyderabad: Orient Longman: 213–43.

Huber, E. (trans.) 1908. Aśvaghoṣa's Sūtrālaṃkāra: traduit en Français de la version Chinoise de Kumārajīva. Paris: E. Leroux.

Hovden, A. 2013. Who were the sponsors? Reflections on recruitment and ritual economy in three Himalayan village monasteries. *In* C. Ramble, P. Schwieger and A. Travers (eds) *Tibetans who Escaped the Historian's Net: Studies in the Social History of Tibetan Societies*. Kathmandu: Vajra Books, 209–30.

Jansen, B. 2013a. How to tame a wild monastic elephant: Drepung monastery according to the Great Fifth. *In* C. Ramble, P. Schwieger and A. Travers (eds) *Tibetans who Escaped the Historian's Net. Studies in the Social History of Tibetan Societies*. Kathmandu: Vajra Books, 111–39.

Jansen, B. 2013b. Selection at the gate: access to the monkhood and social mobility in traditional Tibet. *In* T. Takeuchi, K. Iwao, A. Nishida, S. Kumagai and M. Yamamoto (eds) *Current Issues and Progress in Tibetan Studies: Proceedings of the Third International Seminar of Young Tibetologists, Kobe 2012* (*Journal of Research Institute, vol. 51*). Kobe: Kobe City University of Foreign Studies, 137–64.

Jansen, B. 2018. *The Monastery Rules: Buddhist Monastic Organization in Pre-modern Tibet*. Oakland: University of California Press.

Khenrap, K.L. 2000. Ru thog district before the Chinese occupation (1900–1958): a preliminary study of its cultural history. *The Tibet Journal* 25(4), 33–78.

Lamotte, E. 1944. *Le traité de la grande vertu de sagesse de Nāgārjuna* (*Mahāprajñāpāramitāśāstra*) vol. 1. Louvain: Bureaux du Muséon.

Meyer, F. 2003. The golden century of Tibetan medicine. *In* F. Pommaret (ed.) *Lhasa in the Seventeenth Century: the Capital of the Dalai Lamas*. Leiden: Brill, 99–117.

Michael, F.H. 1982. *Rule by Incarnation: Tibetan Buddhism and its Role in Society and State*. Boulder: Westview Press.

Miller, B.D. 1958. Lamas and Laymen: a Historico-functional Study of the Secular Integration of Monastery and Community. Ph.D. thesis, University of Washington.

Mills, M.A. 2003. *Identity, Ritual and State in Tibetan Buddhism: the Foundations of Authority in Gelukpa Monasticism*. London: Routledge Curzon.

Nornang, N.L. 1990. Monastic organization and economy at Dwags-po bShad-grub-gling. *In* L. Epstein and R.F. Sherburne (eds) *Reflections on Tibetan Culture: Essays in Memory of Turrell V. Wylie*. Lewiston: The Edward Mellen Press, 249–68.

Parenti, M. 2003. Friendly feudalism: the Tibet myth. *New Political Science* 25(4), 579–90.

Ramble, C. 2002. The victory song of Porong. *In* K. Buffetrille and H. Diemberger (eds) *Territory and Identity in Tibet and the Himalayas*. Leiden: Brill, 59–84.

Ramble, C., with N. Drandul. 2016. *Tibetan Sources for a Social History of Mustang, Nepal, Vol. 2: The Archives of the Tantric Lamas of Tshognam*. Andiast: International Institute for Tibetan and Buddhist Studies.

Samuel, G. 1993. *Civilized Shamans: Buddhism in Tibetan Societies*. Washington DC: Smithsonian Institution Press.

Samuel, G. 2012. *Introducing Tibetan Buddhism*. New York: Routledge.

Schuh, D. 1981. *Grundlagen tibetischer Siegelkunde: eine Untersuchung über tibetische Siegelaufschriften in 'Phags-pa-Schrift*. Sankt Augustin: VGH Wissenschaftsverlag.

Schneider, H. 2012. *Tibetischsprachige Urkunden aus Südwesttibet (sPo-rong, Ding-ri und Shel-dkar): Band 2: Verpflichtungserklärungen, Vergleichsurkunden, Schlichtungs- und Teilungsurkunden*. Verzeichnis der Orientalischen Handschriften in Deutschland, Band XI, 17. Stuttgart: Steiner.

Spencer Chapman, F. 1984 [1938]. *Memoirs of a Mountaineer: Lhasa the Holy City*. Gloucester: Alan Sutton.

Thargyal, R. 2007. *Nomads of Eastern Tibet: Social Organization and Economy of a Pastoral Estate in the Kingdom of Dege*. Leiden: Brill.

Tucci, G. 1967. *Tibet, Land of Snows*. New York: Stein and Day.

Waddell, L.A. 1895. *The Buddhism of Tibet: or Lamaism, with its Mystic Cults, Symbolism and Mythology, and in its Relation to Indian Buddhism*. London: W.H. Allen and Co.

Whitecross, R.W. 2008. Transgressing the law: karma, theft and its punishment. *Revue d'Études Tibétaines* 13, 45–74.

Oral Sources

Interview with Shes rab rgya mtsho, August 2012, Sa skya chos 'khor gling, Rajpur, India.

http://www.tibetoralhistory.org/Interviews/05_Chonzom.pdf/ consulted 19-04 2017.

Internet Resources

http://buddhism-controversy-blog.com/2014/07/14/dalai-lama-good-and-bad-buddhist-monks-in-tibetan-buddhism/ consulted 19-04 2017.

Ronis, J. 2010. Pelpung Monastery. http://places.thlib.org/features/17172/descriptions/1207/ consulted 19-04 2017.

CHAPTER 9

Monastic Obligations, Hat Change and Lhasa Encroachment: Taxation Rights Among Politico-Religious Shifts in the Kingdom of Nangchen

M. Maria Turek

The tent pole over here is gold
The tent pole over there is silver
Between the two tent poles
Dwells the Victorious Protector (=Dalai Lama).
A song from Nangchen[1]

1 Introduction

The kingdom of Nangchen (Nang chen rgyal khab) (1300–1951) counts among those historical Tibetan polities which have so far received only minimal scholarly attention. This is partially due to its ambiguous status: culturally speaking, Nangchen belongs to Kham (Khams), but since its former territories became incorporated into the southern part of present-day Qinghai province already in the 18th century, it is also often mistakenly counted as part of Amdo.

Moreover, most sources discussing Nangchen and known to Western scholarship often amount to reiterating colonial narratives, where the position of the realm is "peripherised" and reduced to an outpost of the different powers dominating or neighbouring the realm: the Kokonor Qoshots, the Central Tibetan Ganden Phodrang (dGa' ldan Pho brang) government, the Qing empire or the territories of the Muslim warlord Ma Bufang.[2]

1 Causemann 1989: 79; translation mine.

2 The inaugural publication on Nangchen, Elliot Sperling's introduction to one of the chronicles (Sperling 2003: 7–37) quoted in this contribution, has so far been the most extensive treatment of the polity. However, Sperling's analysis deals with Chinese registers of officials excerpted from elsewhere and not with the actual local publication, the subject of the

 | DOI:10.1163/9789004529465_011

Available sources speak of Nangchen from the perspective of an external centre and until now, local literature has remained virtually unknown. Consequently, Nangchen, much like Kham itself, to borrow a phrase coined by Geoffrey Samuel, has become "artificially peripheral" (Samuel 2005: 296). On the ground however, Nangchen was a self-referential sphere with a long legacy of religious and political power and autonomy. What is more, it was known far beyond its boundaries to be one of the most important cultural centres in Eastern Tibet: in terms of the religious vitality of the *sgrub brgyud* schools, the kingdom was perhaps only matched by the neighbouring Derge (sDe dge), with which Nangchen maintained close relations of competition or mutual support.

During the 17th to 20th centuries, Nangchen was the scene of a series of shifts in political and religious authority, involving the Lhasa-centred dGe lugs school, the Qoshot princes, the Qing authorities and, later, the Muslim warlord Ma Bufeng, among other protagonists. If changes in political control brought clear benefits in terms of taxation for any new ruler, this was no less the case where transfers of religious control were concerned: the Ganden Phodrang had much to gain by its displacement of the earlier bKa' brgyud pa presence in the region. On the basis of contemporary accounts and also more recent Tibetan publications, this contribution will examine features of the fiscal regimes that prevailed in Nangchen at different points over the course of these three centuries.

1.1 *Locating Nangchen*

Locating Nangchen will pose the kind of difficulties that arise when describing all decentralised polities, additionally positioned at the crossroads of larger powers. Thus, depending on a source, we will find a slightly different delineation of the kingdom, whose territory has shifted many times over the course of history. It must also be said that the loyalty of chiefs of the principalities (*dpon khag*) inhabiting areas further away from the power centre in Nangchen sGar (for instance the twenty-five principalities of Yus hru'u) and their de facto submission to the Nangchen kings is unclear. Regardless of the definition of the border as a newer concept embedded in the political-martial drama of modern nation-states, in which as we shall see, Nangchen has also played its part, the boundaries of the kingdom enveloped a network of economic, religious and political relationships, and as such were fixed for each community—this fact is also expressed in local narratives. The heart of this network roughly

introduction. A brief overview of Nangchen's history based on local sources is found in my dissertation (Turek 2013: 115–21).

corresponds to that of today's Nangchen county (Nangqen Xian) in Yushu Tibetan Autonomous Prefecture (TAP), Qinghai. However, the entire territory of the historical kingdom was much larger and extended far beyond the modern county on the vast plains and mountainous areas centring on the Dzachu (rDza chu) basin, but also stretching beyond the 'Bri chu, and is approximately comparable with Yushu TAP in shape and size. From the south, 20th-century Nangchen bordered on the Central Tibetan dominion, notably on its Chamdo (Chab mdo) and Riwoche (Ri bo che) principalities; from the east, on other Khampa kingdoms of Derge and Lhathok (lHa thog), and from the northeast, on Golok (mGo log). The northern and northwestern borders were less apparent due to the fact that the adjacent wastelands of Changthang (Byang thang) and Yarmo Thang (dByar mo thang) were practically depopulated (Gruschke 2004: 33, 103).

1.2 *Sources and Methods*

To the best of my current knowledge, no Tibetan-language archives containing material on Nangchen are accessible today. In the absence of historical records or original documents, a plethora of new accounts of the local religious tradition has surfaced in recent years; many of them are exclusively available in local bookshops, monasteries or private collections.[3]

Since Nangchen was often ruled by monastics and encompassed semi-autonomous religious spheres, local materials are also instructive in terms of political history and economic structures in the kingdom. These previously unexplored compositions, which inform the emergence of a new, "subaltern" narrative of Nangchen's past, were published both in the People's Republic of China, including the minor monastic publishing houses in Nangchen area, and in the course of private and institutionalised enterprises of exiled Tibetans from 1960 onwards. The material currently accessible to me includes some twenty-five works of different genres: *lo rgyus, chos 'byung, gser phreng, rnam thar* and *rgyal rabs* focusing on the region and its lay and monastic rulers; the *gnas yig* of the local power places also contain details about the past of Nangchen. These different works were authored by local lama-historians related to or associated with powerful clans like the Dru ('Bru), Drongpa ('Brong pa) and Tshangsar (Tshangs gsar). In particular, the local scholar Tshangs gsar ba 'Jam dbyangs Blo gros rin chen (d. ca. 1987), author of *'Ba' rom rnam thar,*

3 I was fortunate to be able to collect several publications during fieldwork in Nangchen in 2007 and 2008. I would also like to express my thanks to Prof. Peter Schwieger for sharing his copy of *rGyal rabs ngo sprod* and Bardor Tulku for providing me with a copy of *'Ba' rom rnam thar.*

is often cited as a figure of authority. The Tshangsar clan is said to have been in possession of scriptures that were important for the Barompa ('Ba' rom pa) school, and as such, its members have served as custodians of local history (Puchung 2001: 8).[4]

The above-mentioned compositions repeat or encompass bits and pieces of earlier, identifiable material like *Deb ther dmar po* or *lHo rong chos 'byung*, but also incorporate other details stemming from unverifiable sources. Some of the works contain a large number of irregularities of orthography and grammar. However, there are more serious issues concerning the application of these texts as sources for a historical investigation. Most of them result from the fact that the narratives in question, often by virtue of the characteristics of their genre as such, are aimed at the revival of local (religious) identity rather than the reconstruction of the past through an enumeration of cold facts. Yet as the line between fact and myth becomes blurred, does that automatically exclude a text from serious consideration of its historical value? After all, in the emic understanding, speaking of the past, of place as a container of past events and of local ritual tradition frequently merges into one conceptual sphere. Gillian Tan has recently observed that in Eastern Tibetan narratives, myth and history both emerge as "valid modes of social consciousness" (Tan 2013: 205) and it is therefore possible that they can coexist in a text without necessarily accentuating the dichotomy between fact and fiction.

From an entire list of arguments substantiating the appreciation of the contemporary sources, I would like to begin with a pragmatic justification. As it has already been noted with reference to other Tibetan regions obscure to the Western scholar, for the scarcity of indigenous materials that survived the Maoist period, modern compositions, strongly influenced by oral tradition carried by generations of local knowledge keepers, remain the paramount, if not exclusive, scriptural reference for a reconstruction of the past of regions such as Nangchen.[5]

Already the first glance at our Nangchen corpus will reveal that the material is not entirely ahistorical for different reasons. Thus, local narratives often employ methods known from Central Tibetan historiography, such as periodisation schemes based on or relating to the chronological classification of events in Ütsang (dBus gTsang). This way, local historians also emphasise Nangchen as a decidedly Tibetan kingdom. Regarding adequate contextualisation in the indigenous historical sources or accounting for earlier records, *dGe 'brong lo rgyus* opens with a photographic section featuring not only what

4 For the Barom supremacy in Nangchen, see Turek 2018.

5 Cf. Huber 2003: 678.

is presented as original documents relating to the past of Nangchen, but also "a fragment of an old copy of the reference materials [for the present] chronicle" (*lo rgyus dpyad gzhi'i yig cha dpe rnying khag gcig*) (*dGe 'brong lo rgyus*: 5). More significantly however, as opposed to oral history and "legend" or "myth" (*sgrung gtam*), the narratives are produced by and aimed at a highly literate elite, based on sometimes obscure, but existing sources, and at the same time, they attempt to stay true to "facts".[6] Here, especially Sam van Schaik encourages us to appreciate the competence of the Tibetan historian and his readiness for a critical assessment of available references (van Schaik forthcoming). Our sources also verify the validity of events known from "oral tradition" (*ngag rgyun*) against scripture (*Rin chen sgrom brgya*: 122) or they quote "archival material" (*yig tshags*) to recall specific figures (*Yul shul lo rgyus*: 215). At times, the author will fall back on silence, since "he has not seen a written record" (*yi ge ma mthong*) to refer to, as one compiler stated to explain his inability to elaborate on the specifics of *'u lag*, tax obligations and compulsory transport fees obligatory in the kingdom (*Khams stod lo rgyus*: 87).

The narratives informing this article are presented as accounts of past events, composed for the benefit of the present and future generations. I postulate that we cannot afford to defy them as sources of historical knowledge, ignoring the emic understanding of tradition, of history and of the task of a historian. This is especially relevant when we consider the lack of Tibetan voices on the past of Nangchen.

Nonetheless, it must also be acknowledged that the external accounts of the kingdom can at times be more informative than local narratives. Not only are many of the Chinese, Manchu or Central Tibetan records that are already known to Western scholars doubtlessly valuable as accounts of contemporary witnesses of Nangchen's past, they frequently also contain information we are unlikely to find in the materials published in the People's Republic of China. Balancing the loyalty to their sources and the current constraints of censorship and political sensibilities, contemporary Tibetan historians are often compelled to conceal precarious issues among omissions and innuendos.

The purpose of this paper is therefore not so much to plainly offer criticism of the colonialist approach to the study of dependent polities or to critique the specific primary sources representative of this perspective. Instead, I would like to suggest how the narratives which present Nangchen as a periphery of a larger centre can engage in a meaningful dialogue with local sources in a dynamic negotiation of both local past and identity.

---

6 Cf. Tan's study of the social functions of *sgrung gtam* in modern Kham (Tan 2013) and Schwieger's work on oral history in Eastern Tibet (Schwieger 2002).

Hence the choice of method for this short paper which, I hope, will re-open the topic of Nangchen's past to closer scrutiny. As far as the available Tibetan sources allow, I have extracted several points on taxation in Nangchen in the period between the 17th and 20th centuries, substantiated mostly by examples of larger monastic estates in their manifold political-economic roles as landowners, tributaries of the king and as higher authorities. I then read this data against Central Tibetan accounts, secondary literature presenting some Manchu and Mandarin records and, finally, the rare reports by Western travellers.

In order to understand any pre-modern Tibetan society, we must always take into account the interdependence of the religious, the political and the economic. Many indigenous authors who set out to describe one of these aspects also include information on the remaining two, either directly or between the lines. Therefore, studying Tibetan histories often means discovering new ways in which these three emerge simultaneously. In our case, accounts of the religious elite in Nangchen reveal how doctrinal conversion went hand in hand with fiscal profits and power claims as the kingdom's intermediate geographic position caused its border regions to enter a state of political ambiguity.

2 Taxation in Nangchen

An organised polity first emerged in Nangchen in the mid-13th century with the monastic 'Ba' rom pa rulers with Tangut connections and backed by Goden Khan. At that time, Nangchen constituted a major point on the route from the Tangut capital to the influential monasteries in Central Tibet. After the Mongol subjugation and annihilation of the Western Xia and the fall of the Yuan dynasty, a new corridor leading through the less challenging terrain of southern Kham to the increasingly important Chinese trade and power centres gradually emerged and overshadowed the old route, which seems to have lost most of its importance.[7] These were the geopolitical factors that contributed to Nangchen's gradual loss of significance in the Khampa socio-political landscape. On the inside, Nangchen was afflicted by feuds, which in the early 14th century led to a struggle of succession between the contestants. Consequently, the power over at least the upper sections of the Dzachu basin was split between two competing clans. One of them, the Dru, had received the support

7 Cf. two works by Adshead (1984: 55) and Wang (2011: 58), which discuss the historical development of the passages through Sichuan and especially Derge.

of the Sakya-Mongol alliance and after 1300 became the ruling dynasty of the Nangchen *rgyal po*.

In the first half of the 17th century, like most of the Tibetan world, Nangchen became a Lhasa protectorate. Local sources inform us that in 1639, when Gushri Khan conquered the area, he issued an edict confirming the validity of the previous administrative division of the kingdom (*Khams stod lo rgyus*: 171).[8] In the 1640s, the Fifth Dalai Lama upheld the rights of the *rgyal po* to rule in the monastic and lay estates of Nangchen (*Nang chen rgyal rabs*: 39). Paying taxes to Lhasa was enforced: Shakabpa recounts that in 1648, two representatives of the Fifth Dalai Lama were sent to Nangchen to conduct a census[9] and to fix new tax rates to be paid by the locals. The revenue was to supply local monasteries and pay for their restoration; the remainder was to be deposited in the Central government treasury (*Bod kyi rgyal rabs*: 433). Since a number[10] of Nangchen's monasteries converted to the dGe lugs pa school and received new privileges, a change in the local balance of power and apparently also fiscal relations occurred.

For instance, in 1667/8 the sixteen *grwa tshang* of the newly-converted (in 1652) monastery named Ganden Thubten Gelek Ling (dGa' ldan Thub bstan dge legs gling),[11] located in Zurmang (Zur mang), the largest monastic estate in Nangchen, was registered as an official monastic community of the Central government. The actual/ previous landholder was Zurmang, but the "hat change" (*zhwa sgyur*) made it possible for Ganden not only to collect huge amounts of produce, said to be necessary to sustain its busy ritual schedule, but also to take over the fiscal personnel of the previous proprietor, notably a Karmapa monastery (*Rin chen sgrom brgya*: 121). In his autobiography, the Fifth Dalai Lama recalls that ample amounts of butter, tsampa, tea, salt, etc. prepared for use by the Ganden monks were "strung and stuck together and gradually delivered by the Zurmang steward (*gzhis sdod*)"[12] (Du kU la'i gos bzang: 455 and *Rin*

8 The edict is one of several documents known as *shel bam* and issued for the whole realm or for its specific monasteries by either Gushri Khan, the Ganden Phodrang and later the Qing. See *Khams stod lo rgyus*: 171; *'Ba' rom rnam thar*: 275, 278.

9 Fifty-six books of records were made for the whole of Eastern Tibet, and Shakapba informs us that twenty-six of them were produced in 1914 at the Simla conference as proof of the Tibetans' territorial claims to Kham (*Bod kyi rgyal rabs*: 433, fn. 47).

10 Not more than three or four, which makes a total of all Gelukpa convents in the whole of Nangchen as of today.

11 Newly-converted monasteries were routinely called Ganden (I owe this information to Berthe Jansen).

12 *Rin chen sgrom brgya*: 122 has *gzhi sdod*.

chen sgrom brgya: 122).[13] This generosity (which implies imposing heavy tolls on both nomads and peasants) is emphasised again for a slightly later period as *Rin chen sgrom brgya* quotes from the autobiography of the Seventh Dalai Lama, who admires the richness of ritual offerings made by the Ganden monks and lamas over the course of a year.[14]

The role of the Zurmang *gzhis sdod* is unclear in the passage, as it is debatable whether there was a full transfer of land tenure, and if so, whether it was a lasting agreement.[15] However, in view of later developments of the relationship between Zurmang and the Chamdo-directed Ganden, I argue that this implies Ganden imposing tolls on taxpayers across the whole district, including the estates of its former landlord. The conflicts created by this situation will be elaborated on below.

Local sources suggest that before Nangchen passed into the jurisdiction of the Xining Amban in 1725, the pastoralist population was also taxed by the Kokonor Mongols. The Qoshots calculated taxes on the basis of the number of household animals: horses, yaks and sheep (*'Ba' rom rnam thar*: 275).[16]

2.1 *Local Organisation of Taxes during the Qing Period*

After the taming of the Qoshot princes and the annexation of their territories, the Qing conducted a census of taxpayers in the whole of Qinghai (ibid.: 275), of which we are also informed from reports to emperor Yongzheng issued after the Kokonor rebellion (Wu 1995: 273). Lhasa was banned from collecting taxes and received compensation (Perdue 2005: 247, Wu 1995: 273).

At that time, perhaps because of the distance from the relevant ambanate with its seat in Xining, two imperial representatives were placed in Jyekundo (sKye dgu mdo). They were entitled to collect taxes and *'u lag* from the local population. This is what we learn from early Manchu sources (Wu 1995: 273)[17]

13 [...] *star chags zur mang gzhis sdod kyis rim sprod* (*Du kU la'i gos bzang*: 455). Note that *Rin chen sgrom brgya*: 122 has *kyi instead of kyis.*

14 According to oral tradition quoted in the *Rin chen sgrom brgya*, the Seventh Dalai Lama visited Ganden on his way from Lithang to Central Tibet in 1735. However, we are also told that this could not be confirmed with the latter's biography (*Rin chen sgrom brgya*: 122).

15 I would like to thank both Dr Kalsang Norbu Gurung for his help in dealing with the more ambiguous passages in the local literature, as well as Dr Rudolf Kaschewsky for a brief but insightful discussion of the *gzhis sdod* passage.

16 Also see Wu (1995: 273).

17 Wu's work deals with secret battlefield reports written to Yongzheng emperor in 1723–1724 by the Governor-General of Sichuan and Shanxi, Nian Gengyao, who was in charge of the offensive in the Kokonor area. Several Nangchen officials were said to have been involved in the struggle, and for this reason Nian Gengyao's record is important as one of the rare external witness' accounts of Nangchen's past.

as well as from the French explorer Fernand Grenard, who travelled in the area in 1893–94:

> The fiscal obligations of the inhabitants of this district towards the Chinese government are limited to the payment of a tax of one-eighth of an ounce of silver, say one-third of a rupee, per hearth and per annum, to the maintenance of the two interpreters and their dorghas (sic!) and to the free supply of the animals, straw and fuel which they need for their movements.
>
> GRENARD 1904: 372[18]

We do not know whether this tax was actually implemented, and it was common practice that the Qing did not impose more substantial tolls on the peripheries of the empire, as in the case of neighbouring Golok (mGo log; Yeh 2003: 508).[19] Local sources do not disclose details concerning fiscal obligations to the Qing; the Amban is mentioned mostly in the context of bestowing edicts and insignia upon the Nangchen ruling elite and the realm's monasteries. Other Qing officeholders were likewise engaged in this practice. Thus, in the early 18th century, parallel to the leaders of other Eastern Tibetan regions of Hor and Reb kong, the 18th Nangchen king Dorje Tshewang (rDo rje Tshe dbang; r. 1680–1734)[20] received the hereditary title of *qianhu* (*ching hu*), equivalent to the Tibetan designation of *stong skor* or "chiliarch".[21] Officials subordinate to the *rgyal po* received the lesser ranks of *be hu* or "centurions"[22] (*bai hu/ brgya grangs dpon*) and *be cang* (*be rkyang/ brgya shes dpon*) (*'Ba' rom rnam thar*: 274–75).[23] For the Manchu dynasty, these originally military decimal units were an instrument of exercising nominal power in the fringe areas, while for the Tibetans the titles either confirmed or reorganised the earlier local

18 Rockhill (1891: 191 and elsewhere) also brings up the existence of a small annual levy that he calls "horse tax" as well as transport duties imposed for the benefit of Qing officials usually travelling to and from Xining.

19 To further substantiate this theory, I will quote Grenard (1904: 372) who reports that no imperial garrisons were stationed at Jyekundo.

20 Dates after *Rgyal rabs ngo sprod*: 13.

21 Also referred to as *stong khri'i rgyal po* (*ibid.*: 86).

22 Translation after Tuttle, An Overview of Amdo (Northeastern Tibet) Historical Polities. http://www.thlib.org/about/wiki/An%20Overview%20of%20Amdo%20(Northeastern%20Tibet)%20Historical%20Polities.html?#ixzz4bCOlMz5x., accessed 13.03.2017.

23 For a list of the titles, centres of authority and names of the officials from recent times see *Khams stod lo rgyus*: 86; *'Ba' rom rnam thar*: 275–77 and Sperling (2003: 13–37), who draws on a Chinese survey from 1951.

administration.[24] The decimal system of ranks corresponded with the right to charge duties upon a fixed number of families.[25]

Accordingly, the *qianhu* would receive the levies of 700 households (*Khams stod lo rgyus*: 81).[26] There were different types of taxes in Nangchen; generally speaking, the fees and obligations that had to be paid to the king were divided into the twofold system of *ser khral* and *skya khral*: accordingly, the "monastic" and "lay" taxes (*Rin chen sgrom brgya*: 410–11). Local history informs us that all king's subjects, regardless of their rank in the political hierarchy had to to fulfil both obligations (*Khams stod lo rgyus*: 86). Moreover, both monastic and lay estates had to pay both categories of dues, which is likely to mean that taxpayers were obliged to provide monks to Nangchen's monasteries as they had to provide lay labour force to the king's disposal to fulfil the *skya khral*. The latter also included horse racing and archery contests during festivals taking place at the royal court (*Nang chen rgyal rabs*: 74).[27]

All the local sources expound in great detail on the hierarchy of the *be hu* and *be cang* and even the borders of their respective domains, which at the same time must have been boundaries of fiscal subordination. Generally speaking, land was divided into eighteen "inner" [monastic] districts (*nang sde*) and twenty-five "outer" districts (*phyi sde*). The estates in the *be hu* rank charged duties from approximately 100 households, whereas *be cang* taxed 50 families each.[28] Travellers' impressions of the political organisation as well as fulfilment of the *skya khral* are presented by Ma Ho-t'ien and Albert Tafel. The latter author is cited by Carrasco (1959: 151–52), but the information he provides is vague as he describes land and animal tax as well as *'u lag* owed to the *be hu*, *be cang* and lesser officials as "without fixed rates or a fixed schedule."

24 The king's rights were confirmed (*'Ba' rom rnam thar*: 275). Compare with Weiner (2012: 69).

25 Compare with *Khams stod lo rgyus*: 81.

26 It is uncertain which period this figure pertains to, since it is said that the *rgyal po*'s power was gradually augmented. The number of subjects was approximate, as has also been noted for other Tibetan regions. For example, statistics from 1958 speak of Kyodrak (sKyo brag) monastery in the *be hu* rank—among a total population of 1400 households, the Kyodrak abbot had the service of 350 families at his disposal (*rGyal rabs ngo sprod*: 116).

27 Compare with horse racing as tax duty in Central Tibet (Carrasco 1959: 91).

28 The number of *be hu* and *be cang* vary from source to source. The following are the figures from the time of king Trashi Tshewang Dorje (bKra shis Tshe dbang rdo rje): in the eighteen inner districts—seven *be hu*, twenty-eight *be cang*; in the twenty-five outer districs: four Tibetan divisions (*dpon chen khag bzhi*), i.e. governed from Chamdo, seven districts governed by the Atro (A 'phro) clan and three regions of Gyade (rGya sde; *Khams stod lo rgyus*: 79–80).

2.2 *Monastic Obligations*

Some travellers' reports and oral accounts suggest that the further away from the power centre, located in the vicinity of Sharda (Shar mda'), the more the fiscal and political subordination to the king was nominal (Jackson 2003: 523–24, Grenard 1904: 144, Carrasco 1959: 151–52). This would mean that the submission of *ser khral* and *skya khral* could have merely been an ideal of symbolic value narrated by the local tradition. However, at least one specific monastic obligation towards the king was carried out duly: *sku rim*, ceremonies dedicated to the long life of the *rgyal po*. In fact, there was a multitude of types of *sku rim* service in Nangchen. Some of them were rituals to be carried out uninterruptedly in a small circle or by alternating, individual monks (*Rin chen sgrom brgya*: 568), others were large annual ceremonies which endowed the participant monasteries with great prestige. Even if the costs were paid from the king's treasury (*Nang chen rgyal rabs*: 74), hosting the ritual was compulsory and absolution was possible only by means of official relief from *ser khral* duties. Accordingly, in the 17th century, when the abbot of the Drikhungpa ('Bri khung pa) monastery of Pelme Gön (dPal me dgon) was recognised in the Nangchen royal prince, the monastery was given considerable amounts of land, relieved of both *ser khral* and *skya khral*, and exempted from taking part in the *sku rim* (*Rin chen sgrom brgya*: 410–11).

Another type of monastic obligation known in Nangchen in case of monasteries which possessed little land and few dependants involved monks contributing to regular rituals by means of a duty called *sham thabs kha khral*[29] (*ibid.*: 568–69). Less wealthy monasteries also financed their costly calendar rituals by raising a fund (*thebs rtsa*) through interest from loans paid by local lay patrons (*ibid.*), a practice analogous to some descriptions of Buddhist monastic economy in Sikkim (Miller 1961: 434).

The monasteries engaged in the annual *sku rim* obligation were wealthy, powerful, "privately owned" (*sger btsan*) spheres of special privileges and tax exemptions (*Deb ther smug po*: 80). Their abbots ruled in the high *be hu* rank over the secular and religious matters (*Nang chen rgyal rabs*: 72). According to tradition, they were three or four convents[30] of different sectarian denomination: (1) Labgön (Lab dgon; Gelukpa), (2) Kyodrak (Barompa), (3) Zurmang

29 Goldstein describes *sham thabs khral* as 1. tax collected from monks, 2. duties for monastic work falling on all monks (Goldstein *et al.* 2001: 1093, "*sham thabs kyi khral*"); *kha khral* would mean that it was paid *per capita*.

30 The sources are not consistent on whether the number was three or four; Tshangsarwa even leaves out Zurmang completely and mentions Tshangsar monastery instead. Since Zurmang was the largest estate in the realm, I suppose this is unlikely; on the other hand, the author must have been well informed at least about the *sku rim* duty carried out by

(Zurmangpa = Karmapa), and (4) Tana Gön (rTa rna dgon; Yelpa [Yel pa]) (*Khams stod lo rgyus*: 85).[31] Local sources suggest that their rights to land and to the service of many dependants resulted from their tributary connection to the king, as they alternated in the yearly performance of the *sku rim*: the monastery whose turn arrived, assigned fifteen monks and lamas to recite prayers of their respective tradition and/or to read the complete Kangyur in the presence of the king and his court (*Nang chen rgyal rabs*: 74, *Khams stod lo rgyus*: 85):

> Annually, during the *sku rim* ceremony, the precious Kangyur was completely read aloud for the king and a retinue of his subjects, who would travel to where the ritual was held. The monasteries were obliged to take turns [to carry out the ritual], and when theirs arrived, [the ceremony was performed by] around fifteen lamas and monks. There was a custom [linked to this:] on the way, while travelling, the lamas responsible for *sku rim* would lead the king's mules, laden with his belongings, [while] it was required that the lamas' caravan would be led by the chant master.[32]

Some of these powerful *sku rim* monasteries not only received tax exemptions, but also royal protection against what is presented as false fiscal claims by third parties. Thus, during the reign of last king Trashi Tshewang Dorje (1911–1961)[33] the Barompa monastery of Kyodrak was relieved of "taxes [claimed by way] of interference and false accusations" (*the gtogs snyad 'tshol gyi dpya khral*). The relief was communicated by way of an official document bearing the royal stamp (*Rin chen sgrom brgya*: 299). We can only speculate who the "interfering" party was: the new overlord of Qinghai, the Hui warlord clan of Ma—or the long arm of the Ganden Phodrang, stretching from a Gelukpa monastery located in Nangchen territory and administered from Chamdo. As we are about to see, in the aftermath of the Nyarong (Nyag rong) campaign (1862–1865) during which the Nangchen king was forced to surrender to Nyarong Gönpo Namgyal (mGon po rnam rgyal) and appealed to Lhasa for intervention, the

---

individual ritualists, because it had been in the Tshangsar *sngags pa* lineage for generations (*'Ba' rom rnam thar*: 276; see also *Rgyal rabs ngo sprod*: 302).

31 Note the similarity with the neighbouring Derge, where the king was patron to five monasteries of different schools (*dbu bla khag lnga*) (Hartley 1997). This was important both in terms of legitimising royal power and establishing alliance networks within the realm.

32 *Khams stod lo rgyus*: 85. Also see *Nang chen rgyal rabs*: 75 for other ceremonial duties expected from *sku rim* lamas.

33 The date of his death according to *rGyal rabs ngo sprod*: 16.

Central Tibetan administration imposed fiscal authority in Nangchen at least twice between the 19th and 20th century.[34]

2.3 *"Hat Change" as Means of Lhasa Encroachment*

After the fall of the Manchu dynasty and the domination of the Qinghai area by the Ma clan, changes that befell the political-economic landscape of Nangchen focused on the commercial centre of Jyekundo (Yus hru'u, Yushu), a major point on the Xining-Lhasa trade route. The Nangchen pastoralists were renowned for their prolific wool production, and when Ma Bufang (1903–1975) established his administration in Jyekundo, their main task was overseeing the taxation of wool commerce in this region. Local sources do not relate much about the exploitation of herders during this period; however, elsewhere we learn that Ma's harsh taxation policies forced the locals to drastically increase production (Marshall and Cooke 1997: 168), since they paid in wool and in yak hides. An annual tax in hides was said to have been enforced on monasteries as well. A much-feared Hui garrison stationed in Jyekundo oversaw the collection of levies and went on punitive expeditions if the obligations were not met (Horlemann 2012: 155–57). The Ma administration employed local Tibetan supervisors and tax collectors (*sa 'go*), three of which were active in Nangchen: (1) at Sharda (Shar mda'), (2) at T'ridu (Khri 'du), and (3) at Jyekundo.[35]

The Chinese warlord was not the only foreign power who made fiscal claims on Nangchen. As already indicated above, since the second half of 19th century, in the wake of the Nyarong campaign, many areas of Eastern Tibet including Nangchen became the scene of growing Lhasa encroachment, expressed through ideological and economic pressure.[36] One such instance from the early 20th century is described in the history of the Karmapa monastery of Japa Gön (Ja pa dgon) and its relations with the Gelukpa convent of Kada (Ka mda'), governed from Chamdo:[37]

> In the course of auspicious circumstances, one reincarnate of Kada monastery was reborn as the king's son [and] the noble Japa monastery

34 Compare with Rockhill's report from an earlier period which also points at Central Tibet, adding that the rulers of Derge also coerced "extortionate levies" in parts of Nangchen (Rockhill 1891: 185).

35 According to a Tibetan source cited in Jackson (2003: 621, fn. 552).

36 The famed Rime (Ris med) movement bears many traces of a socio-religious response to the influence the Gelukpa government was increasingly exercising in Kham at that particular time (Gardner 2006).

37 For Kada and its links to the Central Tibetan government as well as its outpost in Chamdo compare *Rin chen sgrom brgya*: 114–15.

offered a portion of [their] wealth [to him?]. Because of this, later, every year, they would make a corresponding record in the tax register, [in the list of expenses paid]. [Regardless of that,] afterwards, the taxes which had to be paid were unending.

[The Japa monks] were also told to change their religious affiliation, and several yellow hats, *mālā*s and Gelukpa capes (*zla gam*) were dispatched [to the monastery].

At that time, Situ Rinpoche was asked if this was appropriate. Then, because the sublime Situ specially wrote to Phakpa Lha of Chamdo, [the Ja pa monastery] did not change their religious affiliation and ever since, the former yearly tax [became] like this: one fourth of each new *khal* was enough.

Rin chen sgrom brgya: 247[38]

In this case, in order to negotiate tax reduction and relief of sectarian pressure, it took an intervention by Situ Rinpoche, a high Karma Kagyüpa cleric (based in Derge) with the Chamdo Phakpa Lha incarnate, the authority responsible for governing Kada as one of the distant outposts of the Central Tibetan administration in Nangchen. This instance of negotiation was successful, although, as we are about to see, the religious, political and economic encroachment was often perceived as not only undesired or oppressive, but also became a source of real conflicts.

2.4 *"Reviving an old custom": Gaden versus Zurmang*

Let us now return to the specific "hat change" described in the beginning of this paper. I argued that the sectarian "renomination" of the minor monastery known to us as Ganden to a Gelukpa institution was followed by a conversion of taxation rights. The Fifth Dalai Lama reports that Ganden collected tax from peasants and nomads in what I understand to be the entire vast estate previously belonging to the convent of Zurmang.[39] In this peculiar case of distor-

38 *ka mda' dgon pa'i sprul sku zhig nang chen rgyal sras su 'khrungs pa la rten 'brel gyi legs skyes su ja pa dgon zhabs nas dkor phud phul ba la brten nas/ de rjes lo ltar re bzhin de 'dra gdos pa'i khral yig la bkod nas 'jal dgos byung ba ma zad/ chos lugs kyang bsgyur dgos pa skad byas nas zhwa dang phreng ser zla gam bcas kha shas shig gnang bskur byas/ de yi tshe si tu rin po che la ci 'os zhus pas/ si tu mchog nas chab mdo'i 'phags pa lha la phyag bris ched bskur mdzad pa brten/ chos lugs ma bsgyur ba dang de nas bzung sngar gyi lo khral de khal gsar res gtsos gsum tshan tsam res chog pa byung/* [...].

39 In the 20th century, dGa' ldan was reported to have 350 monks and three lamas (*Rin chen sgrom brgya*: 122). In contrast, at the time of the last Nangchen king, the Zurmang monastery was said to have owned 450 *khal* of arable land and 440 head of cattle (sheep and goats excluded) and was by far the largest estate in Nangchen (*Yul shul lo rgyus*: 215). To

tion of proportions, the act of endowment in favour of Ganden was a political move. Therefore, whenever the balance of political power later changed, the rights to tax the Zurmang population would become the object of dispute.

It is highly probable that a chance to solve the controversy occurred during the period of the Yongzheng Emperor (1723–1735), when the representative of the Nangchen king was summoned to Chamdo by the Yunnan governor Hao yu-ling (Tib. Ho tA lo yan).[40] Thus, the Qing confirmed the *rgyal po*'s rights to Nangchen territories and granted him the *qianhu* title; lesser titles were bestowed on members of the local elite. At the same time, officials from Lhasa were dispatched to the southwesternmost point of the Zurmang estate at Ashak Dorgön (A shag rdor mgon) to compose "a historical report" (*lo rgyus kyi snyan sgron*) (*'Ba' rom rnam thar*: 274–75). Since Tshangsarwa elsewhere refers to Ashak Dorgön as Ganden Phodrang's ultimate demarcation point in the northeast of Nangchen (*ibid.*: 277), I presume that the governmental investigation in the disputed region of Zurmang was aimed at estimating the boundaries between what was to become Qinghai and Central Tibet.

The hypothesis that in the mid- to late 1720s Lhasa Tibetans and Khampas from Nangchen were engaged in border negotiations is consistent with the account of the Manchu general in charge of the Amdo offensive against the Kokonor revolt, who also reports on the need for a fixed boundary in the Jyekundo area, albeit for strategic reasons: after the Qoshot revolt, since the locals had been loyal to the rebel Danjin, the border between Tibet and Nangchen had to be sealed with guards posted on both sides (Wu 1995: 264–65).

Needless to say, after 1725 both the Central Tibetan state and Nangchen had become incorporated into the Qing empire. Borders were required, since Tibetan territories were not only placed under the jurisdiction of different imperial representatives, but also their local forms of government were assimilated into the Manchu rank system with the aid of varying offices. Most importantly, however, these local authorities were in possession of land entitlements and legal privileges to impose tolls on populations in their respective regions, which therefore required precise definition. As I have already mentioned, many modern histories of Nangchen are very specific about the borders (*sa mtshams*) of areas taxed by members of the kingdom's elite. What is more, one of the *rgyal po* reportedly composed a land record (*sa yig*), where his

illustrate this point, an earlier US government map from the 1860s shows "Sourman" as representative for the entire region of Nangchen, omitting even the locally famous trading center of Jyekundo. See also Trungpa (2010).

40 *'Ba' rom rnam thar*: 274 and *Khams stod lo rgyus*: 85. It is to Dr Liu Kuo-wei that I owe the identification of Ho tA lo yan as the Yunnan governor Hao yu-ling.

whole realm was delineated clearly enough for one of our sources to include a map drawn according to the king's descriptions (*Nang chen rgyal rabs*: 80). Therefore, even if we assume that the notion of a border between Tibet and Nangchen (i.e. Qinghai) appeared no sooner than in the 20th century, local narratives suggest not only that the specific idea of place as a source of identity emerged much earlier; it was even that negotiations and historical-legal analyses took place long before the Sino-Tibetan border struggles of the 1930s.

The work of 18th-century Tibetan historians could well have helped to locate Zur mang or its particular estates on the one or the other side of the Qinghai-Tibet border. However, as time elapsed and Qing control over the empire's peripheries loosened, the controversy between Zurmang and Gaden flared up again. In 1894, Grenard notes during his visit of the Amban representatives in Jyekundo:

> [...] Li had to go to Tao La[41] to settle [...] a difference caused by the Tibetans, subject to Lhasa, who had gone in search of suit in the direction of Surmang and who laid claim to the right to revive an old custom by which the population, who were once themselves subject to Lhasa, were obliged to furnish a thousand yaks for the carriage of the salt from their territory to that of the Debajong.
>
> GRENARD 1904: 173–74

"Reviving an old custom" meant taxing the Zurmang population by Tibetan Central government representatives from what I take to be Ganden, whose administrators based their claim on the "hat change" and the rights once given by the Fifth Dalai Lama. We are not informed how the dispute was settled, but the pattern to call in Chinese authorities to negotiate in the local fiscal conflict between Zurmang and Ganden was repeated in 1932 with much more substantial consequences.

While the 1932 Sino-Tibetan border conflict is a well-established fact, it is less known that the actual fighting broke out as an escalation of the resumed Zurmang-Ganden dispute about the rights to demand tax and *'u lag*. Contemporary local sources issued in the PRC give their accounts of the conflict, but they do so by either providing subtle clues or describing little more than the sides of a military struggle in 1932 between "Tibet"/"Ganden Phodrang"

---

41 The author explains elsewhere that the place to which he refers to as "Tao La" lies 20 miles southeast of Jyekundo (Grenard 1904: 366); this description points at Ganden monastery. See also *ibid.*: 169, 362.

versus "Zurmang"/"the Chinese"/"Xining".[42] *rGyal rabs ngo sprod*, published in exile, goes a step further and states that in 1932 an armed conflict "about the authority of ownership" (*bdag dbang ched*) took place (*rGyal rabs ngo sprod*: 252). Also Tshangsarwa gives us his brief account about Tibetans "planning to seize territories" (*sa khul len rtsis*) (*'Ba' rom rnam thar*: 280), while *dGe 'brong lo rgyus* (85–86) is only little more explicit and mentions "various quarrels" (*rtsod gleng du ma*). It is from Chinese sources such as memoirs of Kuomintang generals that we first learn the details about the background of the struggle. Gao Changzhu, head of the Nationalist government's Mongolian and Tibetan Affairs Commission reports:

> Zurmang of Jyekundo is administered by the Ganden monastery. Ninety years ago [...], the Dalai, as requested by the monastery, appointed a *khenpo* as its supervisor. The *khenpo*, with the powerful Ganden behind him, grew increasingly domineering [...]. In a display of defiance against this evildoer, the inhabitants refused the corvée his monastery assigned them. In retaliation, the Ganden took away forcibly the crops grown in the nearby fields. Since then for over a decade the Ganden would come each year to take possession of the crops as if it owned the land. As the land was in possession of the Dutsi Til monastery [Zur mang bDud rtsi mthil] of the Older Sect and of the Zurmang tribe, the Dutsi Til monks and some of the tribesmen appealed several times to the Jyekundo garrison headquarters and the magistrate for justice. They won the case, but the Ganden [...] took the dispute to the Dalai, who then instructed the *sawang chenpo* (governor-general) of Chamdo to look into the matter. Soon, the representatives of the *sawang chenpo* went into negotiations with the local authorities of Jyekundo, but nothing came out of the talks. [...] Ma Biao declared that as the land over which the dispute had arisen was clearly in our possession, Tibet had nothing to do with its settlement [...] Then Tibet, made unbearably arrogant by its military victory in Xikang, sent a large body of troops to the Jyekundo area in the name of protecting the Ganden [...].
>
> YA 1991: 353–54

42 One source suggests the involvement of Ganden in that it recounts for the battle at Zurmang in the chapter dedicated to Ganden, although no justification for this is given (*Rin chen sgrom brgya*: 122–23). As indicated, this elusive manner of history writing is characteristic of Tibetan works composed in the PRC. Also see *Rin chen sgrom brgya*: 247, *Khams stod lo rgyus*: 209, and *'Ba' rom rnam thar*: 280.

Both the Chinese and local sources are unanimous about the fact that it was Lhasa that launched the offensive. On 24 March, the Tibetans assembled 4,000 troops under the command of Thubten Künkhyen (Thub bstan kun mkhyen)[43] and advanced on both Zurmang Dutsi Thil and its branch monastery, Zurmang Namgyeltse (rNam rgyal rtse) in a surprise attack. The monasteries were severely damaged, but suffered even more harm as they became a battleground in a clash with Qinghai troops in August later that year (Ya 1991: 355). The defence was weak, and the whole Nangchen area fell to the Tibetans by 3 April. It took several months for Qinghai forces to recapture the territories, concluded with their decisive victory at Jyekundo (Ya 1991: 355).[44] For both sides of the struggle, controlling the town was increasingly important in terms of its strategic and commercial potential. Since the early years of the Chinese Republic, in consequence of the tensions between the Sichuan governor and the Ganden Phodrang, trading key goods such as tea from China and transporting Tibetan and Indian commodities to China could only take place via Jyekundo, since the direct route through Sichuan was not in use (Lin 2011: 59).

Among the reported five hundred Qinghai troops were also people from Nangchen. Apparently, soldier duty (*dmag khral*) was also effective under the *be hu* and *be cang*. Jackson relates the account of Dezhung Rinpoche (sDe gzhung rin po che; 1906–1987), an important local reincarnate whose uncle was conscripted to fight for the Qinghai side by the Labda (Lab mda') *be cang* and was killed in battle (Jackson 2003: 610, fn. 395).

As we are curtly informed by our sources, the king "suffered no harm" (*'Ba' rom rnam thar*: 280). After Ma's victory, over a year would pass until truce was finally signed, but in the meantime, the warlord communicated to the Nationalist government of the Chinese Republic at Nanking that he would be extracting even more taxes in Qinghai "in order to protect the border" (Lin 2011: 65). This must have meant more local pressure in Nangchen because of its strategic position in the key fringe areas of Qinghai.

As a result of the 1933 treaty between Qinghai and Tibet, a border on the Drichu ('Bri chu) was drawn (Goldstein 1991: 223)[45]—with Lhasa controlling territories on the West bank of the river and Ma from the East. But how was the boundary drawn in relation to the dispute between the two feuding monasteries? The Ganden monks lost their fiscal rights over Zurmang estate and were

43 See Petech (1973: 109).

44 The victory at Jyekundo and the subsequent counteroffensive into Sichuan became decisive for the Sino-Tibetan border struggles of the 1930s (Ya 1991: 356–58, Lin 2011: 64–65 and Goldstein 1991: 222–23).

45 See also: Goldstein (1991: map 6).

barred from engaging in politics; the entire Nangchen kingdom was returned to the political and economic control of Ma Bufang (Ya 1991: 357). Therefore, we can safely assume that Zurmang was restored to its full land rights from before the 17th century, including the entitlement to tax the population up to and excluding Ashak Dorgön (*'Ba' rom rnam thar*: 277).[46]

3 Concluding Remarks

In pre-modern Tibetan societies, the religious, the political, and the economic often emerged together in various contexts. Therefore, missionary zeal could potentially also be linked to concealed claims of political or monetary nature. Such was the case of fiscal endowment of new Gelukpa monasteries in 17th-century Nangchen, where the earlier balance of sectarian, economic, and political control was altered disproportionately. Taxation rights awarded under such circumstances were largely dependent on external political forces, which in turn contributed to a further destabilisation of local power. As soon as the political climate or alliances with outside powers shifted, the fiscal privileges would become controversial and if not successfully negotiated, as in the case of Japa monastery in relation to Kada Gön, the conflict could escalate further.

Our example of such escalation was the dispute between the Zurmang estate and the Ganden convent. In the 20th century, precisely because of its political background, this local strife transformed into a large-scale issue, which embraced a new local power (Ma Bufang), but also contained a new ideological element: two nation-states of China and Tibet emerging from both sides of Nangchen and inevitably colliding on its territory.

4 Epilogue

The *Nang chen rgyal rabs* narrates how the traditional taxes, *'u lag* and other dues were abolished by the Chinese Communists in the early 1950s. However, as one of the few sources on Nangchen published in exile, the rhetoric of the work dramatically differs from the phraseology of subtle allusions and evasions

46 Ashak Dorgön had been under Lhasa since the 17th century (*'Ba' rom rnam thar*: 274–75). Maps of the region reveal that the 1933 delineation corresponds with the contemporary definition of the provincial TAR-Qinghai border. However, due to the rough terrain and possibly also to the long legacy of border ambiguities, the boundary has remained fluid in spite of the PRC's strict TAR entry policies. I had a first-hand experience of this flexibility while travelling from Zurmang Namgyeltse to the TAR in 2007.

prevalent in publications on recent history issued in the PRC. The *rGyal rabs* presents the total reorganisation of the socio-economic order in dark tones of a prophecy of an impending downfall. In a prophetic vision which appeared to the last king Trashi Tshewang Dorje, the Chinese Communist Party emerges as a cunning, three-headed beast intoxicated with the three poisons of ignorance, greed and hatred. Wearing a fake smile, the beast misuses local people's naiveté with promises of equality and the invalidation of the old economic system in what is described as an act of "trickery and deception" (*Nang chen rgyal rabs*: 52).

References

Primary Sources

'Ba' rom rnam thar

Tshangs gsar blo gros rin chen. 2005. *dPal ldan 'ba' rom bka' brgyud kyi rnam thar chos 'byung mdor bsdus gsal byed sgron me*. Zi ling: mTsho sngon mi rigs dpe skrun khang.

Bod kyi rgyal rabs

Zhwa sgab pa. 1976 edition. *Bod kyi srid don rgyal rabs. An Advanced Political History of Tibet*. Kalimpong: Tsepal Taikhang, 2 vols; vol. I. (also known from English translations: Shakabpa, Tsepon Wangchuk Deden. 1967. *Tibet: A Political History*. New Haven: Yale University Press, and Shakabpa, Tsepon Wangchuk Deden. 2009. *One Hundred Thousand Moons: An Advanced Political History of Tibet*. Leiden: Brill, 2 vols).

Deb gter smug po

'Brong pa rgyal po. 2003. *Bod ljongs mdo khams nang chen spyi dang bye brag gi byung ba brjod pa ldong 'brong pa'i deb gter smug po*. Dharamsala: Amnye Machen Institute.

Dge 'brong lo rgyus

Lho bstan 'dzin nyi ma. 2012. *mDo khams dge 'brong lo rgyus deb ther lci zla'i zegs ma*. Lanzhou: Gan su mi rigs dpe skrun khang.

Du kU la'i gos bzang

Ngag dbang blo bzang rgya mtsho, Fifth Dalai Lama (1617–1682). 1979–1983 edition. *Rgyal dbang lnga pa'i rang rnam du kU la' i gos bzang*. 'Bras spungs: dGa' ldan pho brang. 3 vols; vol. III.

Khams stod lo rgyus
'Jam dbyangs tshul khrims. 1995–1999. *Khams stod kyi lo rgyus thor bsdus su bkod pa gangs phrug bsu ba'i shing rta*. A Brief History of Upper Kham, Eastern Tibet. Zi ling: Kan su'u mi rigs dpe skrun khang, 2 vols; vol. II.

Nang chen rgyal rabs
Karma phrin las. 1965. *Gangs ljongs mdo stod nang chen rgyal rabs dang 'brel ba'i lo rgyus phyogs bsdud ya rabs rna rgyan*. Manuscript of 80 pages scanned for the Tibetan Buddhist Resource Center, W00KG09734.

Rgyal rabs ngo sprod
Ba ri zla ba tshe ring *et al.* (eds). 2005. *Nang chen nyer lnga'i rgyal rabs ngo sprod dang lo rgyus rgyu cha 'dems bsgrigs*. Dharamsala: Nang chen nyer lnga'i mthun tshogs.

Rin chen sgrom brgya
sGa Karma don grub phun tshogs. 1999. *Khams sgom sde nang chen pa'i dgon khag rnams kyi byung ba phyogs bsgrigs rin chen sgrom brgya 'byed pa'i deb ther gser gyi lde mig*. sKye dgu mdo: Nang chen rdzong srid gros rig gnas lo rgyus gzhung don khang.

Yul shul lo rgyus
Yul shul rdzong/ dGon sde'i lo rgyus mdor bsdus. n.d. sKye dgu mdo (?): Yul shul rdzong mi rigs chos lugs don gcod khang.

Secondary Sources

Adshead, S.A.M. 1984. *Province and Politics in Late Imperial China: Viceregal Government in Szechwan, 1898–1911*. London: Curzon Press.

Carrasco, P. 1959. *Land and Polity in Tibet*. Seattle: University of Washington Press.

Causemann, M. 1989. *Dialekt und Erzählungen der Nangchenpas*. Bonn: VGH Wissenschaftsverlag.

Gardner, A.P. 2006. The Twenty-Five Great Sites of Khams: Religious Geography, Revelation, and Nonsectarianism in Nineteenth-Century Eastern Tibet. Ph.D. thesis, University of Michigan.

Goldstein, M.C. 1991. *A History of Modern Tibet, Volume 1: The Demise of the Lamaist State (1913–1951)*. Berkeley: University of California Press.

Goldstein, M.C., T. Shelling and J. Surkhang. 2001. *The New Tibetan-English Dictionary of Modern Tibetan*. Berkeley: University of California Press.

Grenard, F. 1904. *Tibet. The Country and Its Inhabitants*. A.T. de Mattos (transl.), London: Hutchinson and Co.

Gruschke, A. 2004. *The Cultural Monuments of Tibet's Outer Provinces: Kham*. Volume 2: The Qinghai Part of Kham. Bangkok: White Lotus.

Hartley, L.R. 1997. A Socio-Historical Study of the Kingdom of Sde-dge (Derge, Kham) in the Late Nineteenth Century: Ris-med Views of Alliance and Authority. Ph.D. thesis, Indiana University.

Horlemann, B. 2012. Tibetans and Muslims in Northwest China: economic and political aspects of a complex historical relationship. *Asian Highlands Perspectives* 21, 141–86.

Huber, T. 2003. Contributions on the Bon religion in A-mdo: the monastic tradition of Bya-dur dGa'-mal in Shar-khog. *In* A. McKay (ed.) *The History of Tibet*, vol. 2. London: Routledge Curzon, 675–78.

Jackson, D.P. 2003. *A Saint in Seattle: The Life of the Tibetan Mystic Dezhung Rinpoche*. Somerville, MA: Wisdom Publications.

Lin, H.-T. 2011. *Tibet and Nationalist China's Frontier: Intrigues and Ethnopolitics, 1928–49*. Vancouver: University of British Columbia Press.

Marshall, S.D. and S.T. Cooke. 1997. *Tibet Outside the TAR: Control, Exploitation and Assimilation, Development with Chinese Characteristics*. Hong Kong: Alliance for Research in Tibet.

Miller, R.J. 1961. Buddhist monastic economy: the Jisa mechanism. *Comparative Studies in Society and History* 3(4), 427–438.

Perdue, P.C. 2005. *China Marches West: The Qing Conquest of Central Eurasia*. Cambridge: Harvard University Press.

Petech, L. 1973. *Aristocracy and Government in Tibet, 1728–1959*. Rome: Istituto italiano per il Medio ed Estremo Oriente.

Puchung Tsering. 2001. The Early History of the Barom Kagyu School and the Biography of Darma Wangchug. M.A. thesis, University of Oslo.

Rockhill, W.W. 1891. *The Land and the Lamas: Notes of a Journey Through China, Mongolia and Tibet*. New York: The Century Company.

Samuel, G. 2005. *Tantric Revisionings: New Understandings of Tibetan Buddhism and Indian Religion*. Delhi: Motilal Banarsidass Publications.

van Schaik, S. (forthcoming). The advent of the Dharma: religion and rationality in the coming of Buddhism to Tibet. *In* G. Hazod, M. Fermer and C. Jahoda (eds) *The Social and the Religious in the Making of Tibetan Societies*. Vienna: Austrian Academy of Sciences Press.

Schwieger, P. 2002. History as oral tradition: the construction of collective identity in Brag g.yab, Khams. *In* L. Epstein (ed.) *Khams pa Histories: Visions of People, Place and Authority*. PIATS 2000: Tibetan Studies: Proceedings of the Ninth Seminar of the International Association for Tibetan Studies, Leiden 2000. Vol. 4. Leiden: Brill Academic Publishers, 127–154.

Sperling, E. 2003. Introduction. *In 'Brong pa rgyal po. Bod ljongs mdo khams nang chen spyi dang bye brag gi byung ba brjod pa ldong 'brong pa'i deb gter smug po.* Dharamsala: Amnye Machen Institute, 7–37.

Tan, G. 2013. Transforming history and myth: On the mutuality and separation of shared narratives in Eastern Tibet. *The Australian Journal of Anthropology* 24, 193–212.

Trungpa, C. 2010. *Born in Tibet.* Boston: Shambhala Publications.

Turek, M.M. 2013. "In this Body and Life": The Religious and Social Significance of Hermits and Hermitages in Eastern Tibet Today and During Recent History. Ph.D. thesis, Humboldt University.

Turek, M.M. 2018. Contemporary Revival of the Barom Kagyü school in Kham. *In* F. Jagou (ed.) *The Hybridity of Buddhism: Contemporary Encounters between Tibetan, Chinese, and Japanese Tradition.* Paris: Ecole française d'Extrême-Orient (EFEO) Publications.

Wang, X. 2011. *China's Last Imperial Frontier: Late Qing Expansion in Sichuan's Tibetan Borderlands.* Lanham, MD: Lexington Books.

Weiner, B.R. 2012. The Chinese Revolution on the Tibetan Frontier: State Building, National Integration and Socialist Transformation, Zeku (Tsékhok) County, 1953–1958. Ph.D. thesis, Columbia University.

Wu, S. 1995. *Die Eroberung von Qinghai unter Berücksichtigung von Tibet und Khams, 1717–1727: Anhand der Throneingaben des Grossfeldherrn Nian Gengyao.* Wiesbaden: Otto Harrassowitz Verlag.

Ya, H. 1991. *The Biographies of the Dalai Lamas.* Beijing: Foreign Languages Press.

Yeh, E.T. 2003. Tibetan range wars: spatial politics and authority on the grasslands of Amdo. *Development and Change* 34(3), 499–523.

CHAPTER 10

"By Ancient Custom and Engagements": Trade, Taxes and Diplomacy in Ladakh and Western Tibet between the 17th and 20th Centuries

John Bray

1 Introduction

William Moorcroft (1767–1825) was the first Englishman to encounter the rules of Ladakh's historical trading relationship with Western Tibet, and in the most practical of circumstances. In the summer of 1812, he took leave from his official post as an East India Company veterinarian to travel to Lake Mansarowar in disguise as a *gosain* trader/pilgrim (Moorcroft 1816). To his mortification, he was at first forbidden to purchase a sample of the region's famous shawl wool because of an official monopoly restricting its sale to the agents of the king of Ladakh, who in turn would forward the wool to Kashmir. Moorcroft eventually made his purchase, but at a high cost to the seller, who was subsequently imprisoned.[1]

As Moorcroft subsequently confirmed, the shawl wool monopoly had been established "by ancient custom and engagements" between Ladakh and Tibet (Moorcroft and Trebeck 1841, vol. 1: 347). The most important of these "engagements" was the Treaty of Temisgang (gTing mo sgang), which concluded the 1679–1684 Tibet-Ladakh-Mughal war. The treaty in turn was reinforced by an underlying system of local taxes, labour obligations and compulsory purchases of trade goods.

This essay explores the practical workings of this system, with a particular focus on its evolution in the 19th and early 20th centuries as seen through the eyes of British, Indian and—where the sources are available—Tibetan officials. It addresses three main questions:

1 Particulars of a visit paid by Captain Webb employed on a Survey in Kemaon to the Deba or Chief of Ticklakot. British Library, Asia, Pacific and Africa Collections (hereafter "APAC"). Bengal Political Letters. F/4/552/13384. See also Alder (1985: 151), citing the Moorcroft papers in the APAC: F36/57.

 | DOI:10.1163/9789004529465_012

- The first concerns taxation, especially taxation in the form of labour obligations. What role did these obligations play in sustaining the wider economic and therefore diplomatic relationship between Ladakh and Tibet?
- The second concerns the beneficiaries of the system: what kinds of individuals benefited most?
- The third question addresses the perspectives of those who lost out—the kinds of people who might otherwise "escape the historian's net" (cf. Ramble, Schwieger and Travers 2013). What can we learn of their fate, and what strategies of resistance were open to them?

To set the context for these questions, I begin with a review of the political and geographical factors that influenced the Ladakhi kingdom's approach to trade. The following section provides an overview of the changing relationship between Ladakh, Tibet and Kashmir between the 17th and 20th centuries. I then examine the role of trade and taxation within this relationship in some detail, before offering a preliminary set of discussion points and conclusions.

2 Trade, Taxation and Royal Power in the Ladakhi Kingdom

Ladakh (La dwags) has limited natural resources but occupies a strategic position on the main trade routes between Central Asia, Kashmir and the Indian plains. Trade was therefore always central both to the wider Ladakhi economy and to royal power.[2]

Until 1834 Ladakh was an independent Himalayan kingdom with a high degree of continuity in the basic structure of its political and social institutions. The king (*rgyal po*) claimed descent from the old Tibetan monarchy, and stood at the apex of a local hierarchy consisting of a hereditary group of nobles (*sku drag*) as well as a group of regional rulers. Some of the latter likewise styled themselves *rgyal po*, for example in the case of Zangla and Padum in the Zangskar valley. Others were classified as *jo* (chiefs).[3]

In a mid-19th century historical review of the regional economy, the British official Alexander Cunningham (1854: 241) wrote that "the chief source of wealth in Ladák is the carrying trade, or transport of foreign produce from one country to another through its territories". He added that the king was the "chief trader in his own dominions". All his traffic passed duty-free, and he

2 See Grist (1985) and Rizvi (1999) for thoughtful reviews of the historical role of Ladakhi trade drawing on both oral and documentary sources.

3 See Petech (1977: 153–63) for a succinct review of government and administration under the monarchy.

therefore realised between forty and fifty thousand rupees a year from trade: this amounted to almost half his total revenue (*ibid.*: 271). The other sources of income included customs duties and house taxes.

If the carrying trade was Ladakh's chief source of wealth, it follows that the region's single most important economic resource was the human labour needed to carry goods and drive pack animals. Corvée transport labour—known as *'u lag* in Tibetan and *begar* in Urdu and Persian—was therefore always one of the most important forms of taxation in Ladakh as it was in Tibet.[4] The king, the *sku drag* and the monasteries were all entitled to allocations of *'u lag* and as well as taxation in kind.

Cunningham (*ibid.*: 272) gives an example of taxation in kind when he notes that:

> [The king] was supplied with corn and butter, wood and grass, for four months in the year, by Nubra for two months by Rukchu; and for four months by Tangtse. Certain villages also supplied the royal table with apricots, apples, and grapes.

It seems to have been common practice for kings to issue edicts exempting successful royal servants from taxes and other obligations in return for services rendered, and from these one can get a flavour of the sheer complexity of the system. For example, in 1777 King Tshe dbang rnam rgyal, r. 1753–1782) issued an edict exempting the Zangskar village elder Ngag dbang rgya mtsho from taxes (Schuh 2008: 229–33). These included war service, transport of grain, delivery of roasted grain, compulsory purchases, rounding up donkeys, carrying loads and delivering beer.

On a similar note, an undated tax register from the village of Sabu near Leh gives a detailed description of the tax hierarchy there. According to a summary of the register prepared by A.H. Francke, the lowest class of tax-payer—known as *'bab mi*—had to fulfil as many as thirty-five distinct kinds of service.[5]

4 See Petech (1977: 158–60) for a summary of the tax system. For earlier studies of corvée transport labour in Ladakh, see Grist (1994) and Bray (2008). Grist (1994: 272) anticipated the theme of this essay with her observation that *begar* "acted as one of the means of exchange between neighbouring states, and provided a mechanism by which they implicitly recognised each other's legitimacy and status". I gratefully acknowledge the inspiration of her pioneering work on this subject.

5 Tax register from Sa-bu (Ladakh). "Bonds and Contracts". Nachlass A.H. Francke. NL 256/91. Universitätsbibliothek Leipzig. Francke's notes were based on a document collected by the Ladakhi historian Joseph Gergan (Yo seb dge rgan). I have so far been unable to trace the original text.

Significantly, many of these related to transport including: providing sacks for transport; providing transport to Hor (Turkestan?) and Mon yul (probably Kulu); providing grass and wood for the Lhasa traders; and providing assistance in "crossing the pass".

The most fundamental form of trade consisted of the traditional bartering arrangements involving the villages in the region's valleys who exchanged agricultural produce—primarily grain—for salt and wool from the pastoral regions of eastern Ladakh and Ruthog (Ru thog, also anglicised as "Rudok") in what is now Western Tibet.[6] Many of these exchanges took place in regional fairs. For example, in 1851 Cunningham's colleague Henry Strachey described the "Changdus" fair which took place in the village of Shey, five or six miles from Leh, every August and September.[7] He wrote that the traffic of the fair varied from fifty to 100 tents of Changpa nomads, primarily from Ruthog, each bringing from 100 to 500 sheep, amounting to a total of between 20,000 to 30,000 animals. Each of the sheep carried saddle bags laden with salt and wool.

The barter trade was vital for the inhabitants of Ruthog because their region produced scarcely any grain. The same was true of the Tibetan regions of Guge (Gu ge) and Puhrang (Pu hrang) further to the east where similar exchanges took place with Bhotia traders from Garhwal and Kumaon on the southern side of the Himalayas.[8] For the inhabitants of all these regions, trade made the difference between bare subsistence and—if all went well—a modest prosperity. As far as the king of Ladakh was concerned, trade provided the economic resources that made it possible to support his court and exercise his role as a patron of local Buddhist monasteries.

The most lucrative trade was in *pashm*, the fine wool that was made into Kashmiri "pashmina" shawls. *Pashm* was produced from the underhair of a species of highland goat that flourished in Ruthog and Tibetan Changthang. As will be seen, the trade in this item was originally a royal monopoly, conducted through a small group of Khartsongpa (*mkhar tshong pa*—"court traders", also known as "state traders" in the British sources). Almost all Khartsongpa were Muslims, resident in Ladakh but of Kashmiri or Argon (mixed race) descent. The family and commercial networks of these Muslim trading families extended across Tibet to Lhasa, where they formed the core of the

6 See Figure 10.3. See van Spengen (2000: 96–128) for a concise but wide-ranging review of the geohistory of Tibetan trade in the 19th and 20th centuries.

7 Letter from Captain Henry Strachey to H.M. Elliot. 6 July 1851. National Archives of India. Foreign Department, Pol. A. Hereafter cited as "NAI. Strachey 1851". I am grateful to Rigzin Chodon for visiting the archives on my behalf.

8 On the Bhotia trade networks see Brown (1984, 1991–1992, 1992–1993). I hope to explore these parallels in greater detail in future research.

Kha che ("Kashmiri") Muslim trading community, as well as north to Yarkand and Khotan.

The second key long-distance trade item was brick tea, which originated in Sichuan and, as will be seen below, was the most important item carried by official Tibetan government trade missions.[9] Other items included Kashmiri saffron, Ladakhi and Balti dried apricots, Ladakhi and Tibetan borax, as well as *charas* (cannabis) from Yarkand and a multitude of other goods, including musk, sugar candy, otter skins, and a variety of textiles, spices and medicines.[10]

3 The Changing Relationship between Ladakh, Tibet and Kashmir between the 17th and 20th Centuries

For the period until the end of the 17th century, it is anachronistic to write of "Ladakh" and "Western Tibet" as though they were separate entities. The entire region belonged to the threefold dominion of Ngari Korsum (mNga' ris skor gsum) established in the 10th century AD by sKyid lde nyi ma mgon, a descendant of the old Tibetan kings.[11] Over subsequent centuries, the frontiers of local kingdoms and sub-kingdoms expanded and contracted according to the fortunes of individual rulers. At times the authority of the kings of Ladakh scarcely extended beyond the Indus valley around Leh. By contrast, in the 1630s King Seng ge rnam rgyal (r. 1616–1642) conquered Guge and Purang, thus extending his control over the whole of the original Ngari Korsum.

In any case, the frontiers of these kingdoms were never demarcated in the manner of a modern political boundary. The wider region shared a broad cultural unity and was exposed to the same religious currents, for example the Second Diffusion of Buddhism (*phyi dar*) from the 10th century onwards. At the same time, it was connected through a broad pattern of regional trade networks, such as the barter of grain for salt and wool between Ladakh and Ruthog described above, as well as marriage alliances between ruling families.

3.1 *The Tibet-Ladakh-Mughal War and the Treaty of Temisgang*

The 1679–1684 Tibet-Ladakh-Mughal war therefore represents a decisive shift in the regional power structure although, as will be seen, there were significant economic continuities. The eventual outcome was that Ladakh's eastern border

9 On the Sichuan connection, see Booz (2011a,b).

10 For representative lists of items, see Cunningham (1854: 241–44) and—in still greater detail—Davies (1862: clxxxvii ff.).

11 The term "mNga' ris" is nowadays applied solely to what is now Western Tibet, not including Ladakh, but this is a relatively recent usage.

FIGURE 10.1 The castle in Basgo, the king of Ladakh's headquarters in the 1679–1684 war, as seen at the turn of the 19th and 20th centuries
MORAVIAN CHURCH HOUSE, LONDON
Note: I thank Lorraine Parsons, Moravian Church House archivist, for permission to use the photographs in figures 10.1 and 10.2.

with Tibet was fixed more or less where it is now, and the Temisgang peace treaty established the ground rules of Ladakh's trade relationship with the territories ruled by the Ganden Phodrang (dGa' ldan pho brang) from then on.

The war should be seen in the context of the expansion of Ganden Phodrang power in the second half of the 17th century, and attempts by the Gelukpa (dGe lugs pa) to establish primacy over other Buddhist schools—in this case notably the Drukpa ('Brug pa).[12] In earlier decades, supported by Mongol military force, the Ganden Phodrang had consolidated its authority over Central Tibet before turning its attention to Kham and Bhutan. Now it was the turn of Western Tibet.

In 1679 a Tibetan army led by the Mongol general Ganden Tshewang (dGa' ldan tshe dbang) invaded Western Tibet and rapidly beat the Ladakhi forces back to the royal citadel of Basgo (Ba sgo) to the west of Leh (see Figure 10.1). King Delek Namgyal (bDe legs rnam rgyal) of Ladakh eventually appealed to Ibrahim Khan, the Mughal governor of Kashmir. In 1683 combined Mughal

12 For the background and political context of the war see: Ahmad (1968), Halkias (2009), Nawang Jinpa (2015), Petech (1947, 1977: 71–80), and Schuh (1983). For the wider context of Ganden Phodrang expansion see Sperling (2003) and Schwieger (2011). For relations between Tibet and Bhutan in the 17th and 18th centuries see Ardussi (1999).

and Ladakhi forces recaptured Leh and forced the Tibetans to retreat as far as Tashigang (bKra shis sgang), which lies just inside the present Tibetan border.

The 1684 Treaty of Temisgang, which was brokered through the good offices of the Sixth Drukchen Mipham Wangpo ('Brug chen Mi 'pham dbang po), was therefore designed to reconcile the interests of all three warring parties: the Ganden Phodrang, Ladakh and Mughal Kashmir. The text as it has come down to us is not a formal diplomatic document accompanied by seals and signatures, but rather a section in the *La dwags rgyal rabs*, the royal chronicle of Ladakh, which itself is a composite document.[13] The wording is often obscure on points of detail, but the main outlines are clear.

The treaty begins by evoking the memory of sKyi lde nyi ma mgon and then observes that Tibet is a Buddhist country whereas Kashmir is non-Buddhist: it is therefore not appropriate for Ladakh and Tibet to be hostile to one another, or for Ladakh to call up foreign armies. The specific provisions—the first three of which will be discussed in greater detail below—include:

- Shawl wool from Ngari Korsum would be sold only to Kashmir via Ladakh.
- The Zhungtsong (*gZhung tshong*), the Tibetan government's trade mission, would carry 200 loads of tea to Ladakh each year.
- Ladakh would send a Lopchak (*Lo phyag*)[14] mission carrying a prescribed set of gifts to Lhasa every three years. The Lopchak would be allocated 200 animal loads.
- The Lhasa government would annexe Ruthog, Guge and other parts of what is now Western Tibet (except for a small enclave at Menser [Men ser], near Mount Kailash), ostensibly in order to finance the lighting of sacred lamps during the annual Mönlam (sMon lam) festival in Lhasa.

As the 19th and 20th century sources demonstrate, it was understood that the transport offered to the Lopchak and Zhungtsong missions would come from corvée labour.

3.2 *Ladakh's Incorporation into Jammu and Kashmir*

In 1834 Ladakh was invaded by the Dogra general Zorawar Singh, who was in the service of Raja Gulab Singh of Jammu. The invasion led to the demise of the Ladakhi kingdom as an independent entity and to its formal incorporation into a South Asian polity rather than a Central Asian one. However, once again,

13 On the different versions, see Francke (1926: 1–15), Petech (1977: 1–2). On the treaty itself see Francke (1926: 42–43, 115–18), Petech (1977: 76–80) and Ahmad (1968: 352–57).

14 In this case, out of deference to my many friends in Leh, I favour the Ladakhi phonetic version—"Lopchak"—rather than the Central Tibetan "Lochak".

there was a high degree of continuity in economic matters, including in tax and corvée labour practices.

In 1841, having consolidated Dogra authority in Ladakh, Zorawar Singh invaded Western Tibet with a view to controlling the main sources of shawl wool (Datta 1970, 1975). However, his army was weakened by the bitter winter cold and defeated in battle near Purang. Zorawar himself was killed. In the 1842 "Letters of Agreement" that concluded the war, Tibet and Ladakh agreed to continue the same trading arrangements as before, with specific reference to corvée labour:

> The annual envoy [Lopchak] from Ladakh to Lhasa will not be stopped by Shri Maharajah. Trade between Ladakh and Tibet will continue as usual. Tibetan government traders coming into Ladakh will receive free transport and accommodations as before, and the Ladakh envoy will, in turn, receive the same facilities in Lhasa.
>
> SHAKABPA 1984: 327[15]

In 1846 the British installed Gulab Singh as the first Maharaja of the combined princely state of Jammu and Kashmir. Again, the Dogra regime adapted many of the economic practices of the former Ladakhi kingdom. As noted above, Cunningham (1854: 271) had described the Ladakhi king as the "chief trader in his own dominions". Three pages further on (*ibid.*: 274), he uses precisely the same words to refer to Gulab Singh. The Maharaja did not visit Ladakh in person but assigned the supervision of his commercial activities to Basti Ram, the *thanadar* (local commander) of Ladakh, who had been one of Zorawar's chief lieutenants. Basti Ram was also allowed to trade on his own account and, according to a contemporary British source, "there can be little doubt that he has made an undue use of his opportunities" (Davies 1862: 60).

In 1853 Basti Ram signed a further trade agreement with Tibet (Shakabpa 1984: 328). It seems that this followed a dispute with an official Tibetan government trader—presumably representing the Zhungtsong—who complained that he had not received his due allocation of horses needed to transport his cargo of tea. The agreement provided that Tibetan government traders would be provided with horses as well as "kitchen boys and grooms" as in the past.

15 Shakabpa says that he consulted copies of the letters in the office of the Kashag in Lhasa. I only have access to the translation of the letters in the English version of his book which refer to "Maharaja Gulab Singh of Kashmir". This may be a gloss by the translator because Gulab Singh did not hold this title until four years later.

The Dogras likewise continued the old practice of seeking tax payments in both labour and kind. For example, in June 1855 the Moravian missionaries A.W. Heyde and E. Pagell (1984: 125) travelled up the Indus valley to Leh and regularly encountered Ladakhis accompanying horses, donkeys and cattle loaded with salt from Ruthog which they were obliged to transport to Kashmir as a form of corvée labour tax for Gulab Singh. Similarly, in July 1867 Heyde reported that—unusually—he had encountered a group of well over a hundred men and women near the village of Sakti.[16] These people had come together from some 20 villages to carry wood to Leh as a form of taxation. Heyde was glad of the opportunity to preach to an unusually large gathering.

Although these tax and labour obligations had their roots in the old Ladakhi kingdom, it seems that the Dogra regime enforced them particularly harshly. One outcome was that large numbers of Ladakhis fled to British India. On their first visit to Ladakh in 1855, Heyde and Pagell (1860: 126) travelled from Lahul via Zangskar to the Indus valley. They passed through three villages in Zangskar that had been abandoned for this reason, while only two of the 20 houses in the village of Hanupatta (on the path to Lamayuru) were occupied. The houses were mostly in good condition, but the surrounding fields lay waste.

3.3 *British Interests in Kashmir, Ladakh and Western Tibet*

The British installed Gulab Singh as Maharaja of Jammu and Kashmir in the hope that the state would serve as a buffer on the northern frontiers of India without requiring them to manage its internal administration. At first, they therefore had little interest in the details of Kashmir's internal relationship with Ladakh. However, they always insisted that, since the Government of India was the paramount power, it should retain responsibility for Kashmir's external relations, including with Tibet.

In 1846 the Government of India sent Alexander Cunningham (1854: 13–15) and Patrick Alexander Vans Agnew on an expedition to define the boundary between Ladakh and Tibet. In 1847 a further mission consisting of Cunningham, Henry Strachey and Thomas Thomson visited the region. All three men were assiduous in collecting information on Ladakh, including on trading practices. However, they were unable to make contact with officials in Western Tibet, and the boundary question remained open.

16 Reisebericht Heyde Ladakh Zanskar 1867. R. 15. U. a. 2 Nr 11. Archiv der Brüder-Unität (Moravian Church), Herrnhut. I am grateful to Bernd Düring and Frank Seeliger for sharing their transcription of this source. On corvée labour continuities under the Dogras see also Bray (2008).

FIGURE 10.2 British Trade Agent Jai Chand's camp en route to Tibet
MORAVIAN CHURCH HOUSE, LONDON

In 1867 the Government of India sent a British official to spend the summer months in Leh, primarily so that he could monitor political developments in Chinese Turkestan.[17] Three years later, the Government of India signed a commercial treaty with the Maharaja providing for the appointment of a British Joint Commissioner who—together with the Kashmir government's *wazir* (governor) of Ladakh—would share responsibility for the administration of the trade routes running through Ladakh. From then on, successive British Joint Commissioners spent the summer months in Ladakh and from there monitored developments in Turkestan and—to a lesser extent—Tibet.

The Government of India had a second, somewhat greater interest in Western Tibet on account of the annual trade expeditions conducted by Bhotias from Garhwal and Kumaon. According to Hugh Richardson (1945: 77), some 12,000 British subjects including 2,400 traders, from various hill communities, visited the region each year. As in Ladakh, they exchanged grain and

17 See Bray (2015).

other Indian goods for salt and—more particularly—wool which became a major source of supply for wool mills in Cawnpore (Kanpur).

The 1904 Lhasa Convention provided for a trade mart "to which all British and Thibetan subjects shall have free right of access" at Gartok in Western Tibet as well as at Gyantse and Yatung.[18] From 1905 onwards, successive British Trade Agents undertook annual summer tours to Western Tibet to look after the interests of British Indian traders.[19] The first holder of the post was Thakur Jai Chand who came from one of the leading families of Lahul.[20] Unlike in Gyantse, all subsequent holders of the post were Indians rather than British expatriate officials, although officers from the Indian Civil Service (ICS) and Indian Political Service (IPS) made occasional supplementary visits to the region.

3.4 *Political Administration in Western Tibet*

The most senior officials with whom British representatives had to deal were the two Garpöns (*sgar dpon*) who were appointed by the Lhasa government to serve terms of three to four years. The Garpöns spent the summer months in Gartok (sGar thog, sGar dbyar sa) and the winter in Gargunsa (sGar dgun sa) further to the west. Gartok was the site of an annual fair involving traders from Ladakh, Kumaon and Garhwal as well as the surrounding nomadic regions.

Western Tibet was further divided into districts or *rdzong* ("castle", often anglicised as "Jong"), each administered by a Dzongpön (*rdzong dpon*, often anglicised as "Jongpen"). The Dzongpön closest to Ladakh was based at Ruthog, only two to three days from the Indian border. When ICS officer E.B. Wakefield visited Ruthog in 1929, he found that the resident Dzongpön was Mondo (sMon grong), one of the four Tibetan boys from Lhasa who had studied at Rugby School in England during the First World War.[21] Wakefield explained that Mondo—and presumably his counterparts elsewhere—had had to make extensive gifts in Lhasa in order to secure his appointment. He hoped to recoup this investment through the profits made through his service in Western Tibet: these included surplus tax income after the official dues had been paid to the Tibetan government as well as the profits from trade. For example:

18 Convention between Great Britain and Thibet (1904). Downloaded from www.tibetjustice.org, 8 June 2014.

19 For a broad review of the British Trade Agents' activities in Western Tibet between 1904 and 1947, see McKay (1997: 158–65).

20 See Figure 10.2. On Thakur Jai Chand's ancestry, see Francke (1926: 195–206).

21 Narrative of the personal experiences of Mr E.B. Wakefield, I.C.S., in Western Tibet 1929. APAC. L/P&S/12/4163.

FIGURE 10.3 Ruthog Dzong
WAKEFIELD 1961
Note: I am grateful to Sir Humphry Wakefield for permission to use this photograph.

> Every year he buys sheep at one rupee each from one section of his subjects and sells them to another at six rupees each. When he buys anything, he pays in rupees at the rate of 2 ½ tankas to the rupee, the buying and selling price in every case being fixed in tankas. No method by which money can be extracted from impoverished subjects has not been practised by this avaricious Jongpen. To me, however, he was charming.[22]

In addition to the resident Garpöns and Dzongpöns, the people of Ngari also had to deal with two other sets of tax collector. These were the Serpön (*gser dpon*—"gold lord") who was responsible for collecting taxes from the region's gold producers, and the leader of the Zhungtsong mission to Ladakh. As will be seen, both of these benefited from corvée transport labour, and made forced sales of tea as a form of taxation, as well as trading on their own accounts.[23]

4 Themes and Issues: How the System Worked in Practice

Sources for the economic history of Ladakh in the 17th and 18th century are still relatively thin. However, a clearer picture begins to emerge from the reports of British travellers and officials from the early 19th century onwards. In this section I discuss a selection of the most important themes.

4.1 *The Shawl Wool Trade*[24]

The 1684 Treaty of Temisgang's provisions on shawl wool come immediately after the preface, and the order of priority may reflect the importance of the issue to all three parties to the treaty.[25] The key points are:

- The goat's wool (*ral*) of Ngari Korsum[26] must not be sold to any other country than Kashmir.

---

22 *Ibid.*

23 For further studies of taxation in Ruthog, see also Levine (in this volume) and Korpon Lobsang Khenrap (2000: 36–39).

24 For an authoritative overview of the history of the Ladakh shawl wool trade in its political as well as commercial aspects see Rizvi (1999: 50–68).

25 Francke's edition of the Tibetan text is in Francke (1926: 42–43). His translation appears in Francke (1926: 116–17). Ahmad (1968: 352–56) offers a revised translation.

26 This evidently refers to all three parts of Ngari Korsum, i.e. Ladakh and Zangskar as well as what is now Western Tibet.

- The price is specified at two silver rupees[27] for 80 *nyag*[28] of wool, or one rupee for 40 *nyag* according to an alternative version of the *La dwags rgyal rabs*.
- It should not be said of the wool of Chang[thang] that it contains soil, stone or moisture.
- Only the [Ladakh] court merchants (Khartsongpa) are to be admitted to Ruthog.
- Four Kashmiri merchants will reside at Spituk (dPe thub) and conduct the trade with the Kashmiris of Kashmir.

The first point to note is the division of labour—and therefore of profit—between Ladakh and Kashmir. The treaty specifies that the Ladakh Khartsongpa and no one else should trade with Tibet. Many of these Khartsongpa were in fact Kashmiri, or of Kashmiri origin, but they were accountable to the king of Ladakh and not to Kashmir. The distinction is clear from Moorcroft's account of his visit to Western Tibet in 1812. He reports that he met a "Cashmírian" called Ahmed Khan Kazalbash who was a *wakil* (agent) of the king of Ladakh, and he briefed him on the main points of the treaty arrangements between Ladakh and Tibet (Moorcroft 1816: 452–54). A few pages later, Moorcroft (1816: 458) muses that he had supposed that the Kashmiris—here referring to the Kashmiris of the Valley—might have traded with Tibet direct. Learning that they did not, he was at first "disposed to blame them for want of enterprise". He now understood that the treaty gave them no choice.

Further details come from Henry Strachey who visited Ladakh as part of the unsuccessful boundary demarcation mission in 1847 and 1848. In 1848, there were "25 licensed traders from Ladak to Nari, only 6 of whom were Tibetans and the rest Kashmiri or Argon".[29] In order to participate in the shawl wool trade, they had to apply for official passports on condition of doing a certain portion of trade for the Dogra government.[30] This meant that they had to "take advances in bad money and small articles of merchandize charged at double or treble their market value". As long as they made repayments that were two or three times the value of the original advances, they were at liberty to conduct private trade on their own account.

The person to whom they had to apply was Basti Ram, the *thanadar* of Ladakh. In a broad review of India's trade prospects with Central Asia, Davies

---

27 *rin dngul*—"price-silver" translated by Francke as "rupees".

28 A *nyag* is equivalent to 4.25 ounces according to Das (1902: 474).

29 NAI. Strachey 1851: 563. See footnote 7 above for the full reference. "Nari" refers to Ngari, but now in the narrow sense of "Western Tibet", not including Ladakh. By "Tibetans", Strachey probably means "Buddhist Ladakhis".

30 NAI. Strachey 1851: 561.

(1862: ccxxxv) describes this official as the "greatest speculator in Ladakh", and explains how he worked the system to his own advantage:

> Instead of cash he pays the Changthan [Byang thang] traders for the annual purchase of shawl-wool, tea, etc., for the Maharaja's Government in goods belonging to himself, at his own prices, and receives the articles when imported, in a manner best conducive to his own interests—for instance he does not give them the usual allowance for the inferior stuff (coarse hair, etc., which has to be cleaned out of the wool received).

The result was that about half the estimated 600 maunds of shawl wool imported each year counted as the Maharaja's share, while the other half went to the official traders (Davies 1862: cxxxi, cxxxvi).

In view of the potential for market fluctuations, one might imagine that it would be hazardous to rely on a rate of exchange—2 rupees for 80 *nyag* of *pashm*—that had been fixed by the 1684 treaty. According to Strachey, the traders had found their own way of dealing with this:

> … the Kashmiris [i.e. the official traders from Ladakh] have introduced an improved Nyaga of their own, a quarter heavier than the Tibetan standard whilst the dzong of Nari moreover for its own benefit collects a good deal of the Lena [shawl wool] by forced contribution from the peasantry.[31]

The trade was all the more profitable because, as Strachey explains, the official Ladakh traders benefitted from free carriage—i.e. corvée labour—on either side of the border:

> This system is rendered possible or profitable to the merchants by the barbarism of the Nari Changpa [mNga' ris byang pa] who allow themselves to be cheated to any extent, and of the Nari Government which assists in defrauding its own subjects and especially by the gratuitous carriage of all the merchandize through a journey of 300 miles by the forced labour of the peasantry of both territories. It is commonly reckoned that one rupee of merchandize or money exported from Le will bring back six from Gar [Gartok], of which extortionate profit the Dogra government of course appropriates the lion's share.[32]

31 NAI. Strachey 1851: 562.

32 *Ibid.*: 561.

In this system, sellers of the shawl wool had little recourse. However, one possibility, as noted by the 1684 treaty itself, was to adulterate the product so that it contained "soil, stone or moisture". Shrewd as he was, Moorcroft had been alert to this possibility and, in his account of his own purchase, noted that:

> The morning was hot, a circumstance in our favour, as the sellers of wool are in the habit of wetting it, under an idea, as they pretend, of its twisting the closer, but more probably to make it weigh heavier.
>
> MOORCROFT 1816: 459

According to Strachey, the sellers were prepared to consider even more drastic forms of adulteration:

> … the Naripa [mNga' ris pa] defend themselves by debasing the quality of the down, mixing it with hair, dirt, dead dogs [sic], and other such frauds …[33]

The other possibility was to break the terms of the Kashmir/Ladakh monopoly and to sell the shawl wool to other traders who were prepared to pay higher prices. Despite the best efforts of the Ladakhis, this did happen. Moorcroft's purchase is one example: in his case the seller was a Tibetan official. A few years later, according to Moorcroft's companion George Trebeck, the Ladakhi authorities intercepted an attempt by Gaddi shepherds from Kulu who had tried to smuggle shawl wool via Spiti (Moorcroft and Trebeck 1841, Vol 2: 63–66). Similarly, Gerard (1841: 115–16), who visited Kinnaur in 1830, reports that Kinnauris had previously smuggled shawl wool across the border in small quantities of two or three pounds per person, but that the trade had now grown enormously in response to British demand.

After the defeat of Zorawar Singh's invasion of Tibet in 1841 the British official J.D. Cunningham wrote to the Tibetan commander Kalon Surkhang hoping to ensure that there would now be no obstacle in the export of shawl wool by this route (Datta 1997: 60). However, he responded in similar terms to Moorcroft's interlocutors to the effect that it was not the practice of the rulers of Tibet to interfere with any old custom, and the Ladakhis retained their monopoly. In 1846 the British again attempted to persuade the Tibetans to end the monopoly, again without success (*ibid.*). Nevertheless, in the early 1860s, Davies (1862: 30) reported that "a good deal of shawl wool is brought by different paths on sheep" to the wool market in Rampur (Bashahr) and from there

33 *Ibid.*: 562.

to Punjab. By this time, it was clear that the old Kashmir/Ladakh monopoly on shawl wool had been decisively undermined.

The system of providing corvée labour to official Ladakhi and Tibetan traders was also soon to be challenged, but proved more durable. In 1871 Frederic Drew, an Englishman serving as the Kashmir government's *wazir* in Ladakh, abolished the system whereby Ladakhi taxpayers had to provide corvée transport labour to official traders without payment. However, according to British Joint Commissioner J.E.T. Aitchison (1874: 360), the Kashmiri authorities reinstated the old system the following year as a concession to Tibetan officials from Ruthog and Gartok. It seems that Tibetan peasants were now no longer willing to sell wool at non-market prices. The Kashmir government therefore reinstated corvée transport labour on their own side of the border, in the hope of persuading Tibetan officials to support them in their attempts to make forced purchases of wool in Ngari.

By the end of the 19th century, according to British Joint Commissioner R.L. Kennion it seems that the Argon "State traders" from Ladakh had lost the "ancient privilege of having their goods free" in Ruthog district although they had to pay no other taxes.[34] Meanwhile, a new set of questions had arisen concerning the administration of corvée transport labour for the Lopchak and Zhungtsong missions.

4.2 *Corvée Labour for the Lopchak Mission and Zhungtsong Missions*

Ostensibly, the main purpose of the *Lopchak* mission was to carry a prescribed set of ceremonial gifts to Lhasa, thus symbolically expressing Ladakh's deferential relationship with the Tibetan government.[35] At the same time, the mission was highly lucrative for its participants. Ladakh's exports to Lhasa via the Lopchak included Kashmiri saffron, Ladakhi and Balti apricots, and cloth from the Indian plains. On the Lhasa to Leh route the single most important trade item was Chinese tea, and Ramsay (1890: 20) reports that the head of the Zhungtsong was popularly known in Ladakh as the "Chaba" or "tea man" (*ja pa*).

According to information provided by the Indian pundit Nain Singh in the early 1870s, a tea brick that sold for seven shillings in Lhasa would fetch twelve shillings in Ladakh (Trotter 1877: 104). In addition, both the Zhungtsong and the Lopchak were entitled to corvée transport along the entire four-month journey

---

34 R.L. Kennion to Resident in Kashmir, 8 November 1899. Reprinted in Chohan (1984: 253–58).

35 On the political and ceremonial aspects of the Lopchak see: Bray (1990, 2018) and Bray and Gonkatsang (2009, 2010).

from Lhasa to Ladakh and back. Arguably, it was these transport privileges—even more than the price differences between Leh and Lhasa—that made the two missions commercially profitable.

Strachey (1851: 557) was characteristically forthright in his account of the Zhungtsong's transport arrangements:

> They get cattle, porters, saddle horses, tents or houses lodging, wood and water all the way between Lhassa to Le and back, taken from the peasantry without payment, indeed with further extortions of money on the pretext of articles not duly furnished.

Transport labour was not the end of it:

> ... at Le they get free lodgings, taken by force from any person who has a convenient house for the purpose.[36]

Strachey reported that the Lopchak's mode of proceeding was similar but commented that the head of the Lopchak "does more mischief to his neighbour's territory than to his own, having a much longer run in Nari [Ngari] than in Ladak". He added that:

> Both the Lhassa Tsongspon and the Le Lopchak are remunerated by driving a private trade of their own in conjunction with that of their governments and are all equally exempt from the payment of its expenses in transit.[37]

On a similar note, British Joint Commissioner R.B. Shaw argued in the 1873 Ladakh Trade Report, that the trade between Lhasa and Ladakh was "more or less a fictitious one" (Aitchison 1874: 386). By that, he did not mean that the trade was imaginary, but rather than it could scarcely bear the costs associated with a four months' journey across mountainous territory without the artificial subsidies provided by corvée labour:

> Thus, to the price of the tea drunk by the Kashmiris, and of the dried apricots and saffron consumed by the people of Lhassa, there has to be added the unpaid labour of a long line of Tibetan peasants leading a

36 NAI. Strachey (1851: 557).

37 *Ibid.*: 557.

miserable existence along the upper reaches of the Sanpu [gTsang po] and the Indus.

Whatever Strachey and Shaw may have thought about the inequities of corvée labour, the Lopchak and the Zhungtsong were at first of limited interest to the Government of India. However, they came under closer scrutiny in 1889 when British Joint Commissioner Henry Ramsay for the first time made a detailed examination of the historical antecedents and current workings of the Lopchak. Ramsay (1890: 85) noted that the post of Lopchak leader "carried with it certain commercial advantages of a very lucrative description". The financial arrangements were that the leader received a cash advance of Rs 9,000 from the Kashmir government with which to buy goods to take to Lhasa. On his return, he had to give the government Chinese tea to a total value of Rs 18,000. However, Ramsay suggested that:

> He probably gives tea to half or three quarters of that value, and divides the difference between himself and the State Accountants, who give him a receipt for 18,000 rupees worth of tea. The Mission is therefore, notwithstanding the exaction of free transport, a probable source of pecuniary loss to the Kashmir State.
>
> RAMSAY 1890: 85

In his official report, Ramsay argued that the Lopchak constituted a form of tribute on the part of Kashmir/Ladakh and was incompatible with the Government of India's status as the paramount power. It should therefore be abolished.[38]

Ramsay's recommendations were never taken up, perhaps in part because he quarrelled with his superior, the British Resident in Kashmir, and was therefore transferred to another post. However, his successor R.L. Kennion returned to the matter in 1899 and conducted a series of investigations as to who was and who was not entitled to corvée labour.[39] From Kennion's account, it emerged that the Lopchak and the Zhungtsong were now entitled to 260 baggage animals on either side of the Ladakh/Tibet border. They were not the only ones. For example, Hemis monastery was entitled to sixty baggage animals and five

38 Again, see Bray (1990, 2018) and Bray and Gonkatsang (2009.) My main source for Ramsay's enquiries is: China and Kashmir. Existing Relations between Ladak and Lhasa. APAC. L/P&S/7/57.

39 R.L. Kennion to the Resident in Kashmir, 8 November 1899. APAC. L/P&S/7 125. Letter No. 891.

riding ponies when accompanying the Lopchak. Tashi Lhunpo monastery was entitled to 50 baggage animals and seven riding ponies at intervals of ten to fifteen years. The two Garpöns were entitled to 30 baggage animals and two riding ponies each year. However, by now the only private individual entitled to transport was a Muslim merchant, Haji Nasr Shah, who was entitled to ten baggage animals on annual visits to Gartok and back.[40]

Kennion was in favour of abolishing the entire corvée labour system but realised that—particularly with regard to Tibet—there were wider diplomatic considerations. As I discussed in an earlier paper (Bray 2008: 59–61), the eventual outcome under the terms of the 1908 Ladakh Land Revenue Settlement was that the British and Kashmir governments agreed that it was as yet impractical to abolish corvée transport labour altogether. However, the porters would be paid for their services, and the Kashmir government would pay for the transport costs incurred by the Lopchak and the Zhungtsong. All other visitors from Tibet would be required to pay for transport.

This was not quite the end of the matter. In 1919 a fresh dispute arose after the Garpöns and the Ruthog Dzongpön sent their traders to Ladakh to secure grain, flour and other goods.[41] When they arrived, they found that the Kashmir government had forbidden the export of these items because of a shortage and, furthermore, they were unable to secure the free transport animals to which they believed that they were entitled. This dispute led to a three-way exchange of letters between the Tibetan, Kashmiri and British Indian governments. The outcome was that the Kashmir government explained that the ban on grain exports was a temporary measure which would soon be lifted. The Zhungtsong mission would continue to benefit from transport at no cost to itself but other traders would not enjoy this privilege.

As a later incident shows, the leader of the Zhungtsong continued to feel a sense of entitlement to fill his quota of trade goods, regardless of whether they were readily available on the market in Leh. In June 1927 the British Trade Agent visited Tashigang and found 11 Ladakhi traders who reported that an agent of the Zhungtsong had forced them to sell some three maunds of apricots at the rate of six seers per rupee: this was even below the price prevailing in Baltistan, the source of the best quality apricots.[42] In a written reply, the Zhungtsong agent stated he had been unable to fulfil his usual demand, and

40 In a separate report, Kennion noted with regard to the "state traders" that "the ancient privilege of having their goods carried free has for some years been withdrawn". See Kennion to Resident in Kashmir, 8 November 1899. Reproduced in Chohan (1984: 253–58).

41 The correspondence on this affair is in APAC R/2 (1066/57A).

42 Copy of a Letter No 22/A. Dated 22nd July 1927 from the British Trade Agent, Western Tibet to the Superintendent, Hill States, Simla. APAC. L/P&S/12/4163.

that the Wazir and Tehsildar of Ladakh had allowed him "to purchase apricots from Ladakhi traders at Leh and in its vicinity and also at Tashigang to meet my requirements forcibly". In his report the British Trade Agent commented that he was not in a position to contradict this claim, but if the Wazir wished to make such concessions he should do so within his own jurisdiction.

It seems that Lopchak mission likewise abused its privileges on the Tibetan side of the border. An official memorandum issued by the Lhasa government in 1915 noted that both the Lopchak and the Serzhung (gSer zhung, presumably the tax/trade mission led by the Serpön) had exceeded their transport quotas the previous year, and this must not continue:

> Those concerned have been issued orders to the effect that apart from providing the horses and pack mules as officially sanctioned in accordance with the law, they must refrain from coveting, robbing and aggressively harassing locals.[43]

Despite such frictions, regular Lopchak missions to Lhasa continued until 1946 and benefited from corvée labour transport to the last.

4.3 *Forced Purchases and Sales of Trade Goods in Western Tibet*

Meanwhile, the reports of the British Trade Agents were full of complaints concerning oppressive trade practices on the part of government officials in Western Tibet, especially the forced sale of tea. This practice was known as *spus gyur*, rendered phonetically as "pujjar" in British records. The term *spus gyur* means literally "to change quality" and was introduced by the Tibetan government as a means of getting rid of old stocks of tea before they deteriorated.[44]

An account by Blo bzang phun tshogs (1998), whose father was appointed Serpön in the late 19th century, offers an official view of the system.[45] The leader of the Zhungtsong was allocated 280 loads of quality tea for compulsory sale, along with 260 pack mules plus 16 horses. The Serpön was allotted 220 boxes of tea and 150 pack mules as well as 16 horses. At that time, the market rate was Rs 20 per tea brick, and they were permitted to charge Rs 25 per brick for a cash purchase, or Rs 30 if they had to sell the tea on credit and collect the

43 Library of Tibetan Works and Archives, Dharamsala. Document 1061_LTWA_272. I am very grateful to the late Tsering D. Gonkatsang for locating and translating this document.

44 I am grateful to Christoph Cüppers for his explanation of the etymology of *spus gyur*/pujjar. E-mail communication, 12 May 2014.

45 I am grateful to Tashi Tsering of the Amnye Machen Institute for sharing this source, and to Tsering D. Gonkatsang for translating it.

FIGURE 10.4 Nomads in Western Tibet, *c.*1905. Note the packages of tea encased in leather beside the tents. The tea had been left for sale by the official Tibetan government trader
SHERRING 1906: 319

money later.[46] Both officials had to submit detailed accounts of their tea sales to the Lhasa government's treasury but were also permitted to conduct private trade on the side.

The Garpöns and the Dzongpöns also participated in the pujjar system and, according to 20th century British accounts, the mark-up could be much higher. Perhaps with a touch of exaggeration, Wakefield reports of Mondo, the Old Rugbeian Dzongpön of Ruthog, that:

> When he came from Lhasa to take up his appointment at Rudok he brought with him 300 mule loads of tea, for which, of course he had free transport. This was sold at ten times its proper value to his poorer subjects and at twenty times its value to the richer ones.[47]

46 During this period British Indian silver rupees were in wide circulation in Tibet alongside Tibetan currency.

47 Narrative of the personal experiences of Mr E.B. Wakefield, I.C.S., in Western Tibet 1929. APAC. L/P&S/12/4163. See also Figure 10.4.

The practice of inflicting compulsory pujjar sales could affect Ladakhi traders as well as Tibetan subjects. For example, in October 1926 the British Trade Agent reported a complaint from Nono Dawa Shah, a leading Ladakhi trader.[48] He had been trading in tea on his own account and had engaged two nomads to carry his tea to Ruthog for sale. When they reached Ruthog, they were "molested, beaten and arrested" by the agent of the Zhungtsong who had not completed his own sales of tea in the district and was not prepared to accept any competition. The agent concluded by expressing the view that the Government of India should again press Lhasa to curb the power of the Zhungtsong or "the hope of expansion of British trade in this part would be a dream".

In the Trade Agents' view, the problem was not simply that Tibetan government traders were competing with British Indian subjects to sell the same kinds of goods, such as tea. Worse still, Tibetan traders would have no more funds to pay for Indian imports once they had paid for the officials' tea at extortionate prices.[49] The Trade Agents therefore repeatedly argued that the Government of India should press Lhasa to abolish the pujjar system altogether.

The Lhasa government never went that far but in 1939 it did issue an official order intended to curb the worst excesses.[50] The Zhungtsong and Serpön were allowed to demand pujjar "only according to old customs". They were not allowed to sell at more than the old rates, nor could they make private sales or charge interest. Similarly, government officials "cannot take riding ponies and free service, etc., from the subjects unless they are in possession of Government orders with seal on them", and they were forbidden to requisition more animals than were provided for in the official documents.

4.4 *"Tax Flight" from Tibet*

Given the difficulties of obtaining official remediation, many Tibetan peasants chose to flee from their home regions in order to escape their tax and labour obligations. This was a matter of serious concern in a society where human labour was the most valuable economic resource and labour obligations the most important form of taxation.[51] From a humanitarian point of view, fugitive peasants might be considered to be economic refugees. From a Tibetan official perspective, they were absconders evading their legitimate tax and labour obligations.

---

48 Copy of a letter No. 35/A, dated the 27th October 1926, from the British Trade agent, Gartok, Western Tibet, to the Superintendent, Hill States, Simla. APAC. L/P&S/12/4163.

49 From Major R.R. Burnett, Political Agent Punjab Hill States to Secretary to the Hon'ble Resident for the Punjab States, Simla 21st April 1939. APAC. L/P&S/12/4164.

50 Translation of Lhasa Government order regarding pujjar tea given to Tibetan subjects by the Tibetan officials. L/P&S/12/4164.

51 Cf. Bischoff (2013) and Mullard (2013).

A report from Ch. Pala Ram, the British Trade Agent in 1925, recounts the kind of incident that could lead to a local exodus.[52] It seems that, in addition to fixed taxes, the Dzongpön of Ruthog had "extorted a large number of goats and sheep, yaks and horses from his Zamindars [land holders][53] without paying for them". The zamindars subsequently failed to settle their annual accounts for "Begar, etc." (i.e. labour obligations). The Garpöns therefore summoned them to Ruthog for a court hearing. When the Garpöns arrived, they ordered that seven of the zamindar leaders should be arrested, whereupon the Dzongpön took matters into his own hands and shot two of them. The Garpöns left without resolving the dispute. Some days later, the Dzongpön's servants shot two more zamindars. The Trade Agent concludes his report with the observation that "almost all fear stricken Zamindars have left Rudok Ilaqah [district], which resembles a desert now".[54]

Some of these fugitives may well have returned to Ruthog once the immediate crisis had blown over. However, as Wakefield reported in 1929, there was "little doubt that the population of Western Tibet has decreased greatly in the course of the last hundred years" and outgoing officials returning to Lhasa were required to account for the number of subjects in their areas of responsibility before handing over their posts to their successors.[55] The emigration or—in the Tibetans' view—tax evasion of peasants fleeing across the border was therefore a recurrent problem in relations between Tibet and British India and, more specifically, between Western Tibet and Ladakh.

An early example of what appears to be a reference to tax exiles comes in the Tibetan version of the 1842 agreement with Ladakh, which contains the phrase: "If any of our subjects stray into your country, they should not be protected" (Shakabpa 1984: 328). Later on, in 1917, the Tibetans' seizure of a Ladakhi called Lhagyal (lHa rgyal) near the border between Tibet and Ladakh led to a protracted dispute between Tibet and the governments of Kashmir and India.[56] Lhagyal had been seized at Dokpo Karpo, a pasture area near the Panggong

---

52 Copy of a letter No. 17 A, dated the 12th August 1925 from the British Trade Agent, Gartok, Western Tibet, to the Superintendent, Hill States, Simla. APAC.L/P&S/12/4163.

53 *Zamindar* is an Indian term meaning "land holder". Indian officials applied the same term to Ladakhi householders, who had a specific set of tax obligations, in the 1908 Ladakh Land Settlement. See Bray (2008: 60–61).

54 *Ibid.* In August 1927 the Trade Agent reported that the Dzongpön had been put on trial in Lhasa, although the outcome was not yet known. See: Copy of a letter dated the 22nd of July from the British Trade Agent, Western Tibet to the Superintendent, Hill States. Simla. L/P&S/12/4163.

55 Narrative of the personal experiences of Mr E.B. Wakefield, I.C.S., in Western Tibet 1929. APAC. L/P&S/12/4163.

56 For a discussion of the Lhagyal affair, see Bray (1995: 260–64). The main source is: APAC. R/2 (1066/57A).

(sPang gong) lake which straddles the border, and the first question—which was never resolved—was whether this was in Kashmir or Tibetan territory. The second question concerned Lhagyal's tax obligations. Earlier he had married a Tibetan woman and had accumulated a substantial fortune of thirty yaks, two ponies and a large flock of sheep and goats in Ding-med near Ruthog. Later he had returned to Ladakh, together with his animals, and the Tibetans argued that in doing so he had evaded his tax obligations in Ruthog.

Under pressure from the Government of India, the Tibetans eventually agreed to release Lhagyal. However, as Richardson (1945: 124) records, they felt they should be rewarded for this concession, and continued to press for the return of Tibetan subjects from Ladakh. They were told that "this could only be considered where some offence was alleged". Local Tibetan officials were dissatisfied with this explanation and in the 1930s went so far as to make armed raids into the Rupshu region of Ladakh to force their subjects to return to Tibet.

5 Discussion: Reciprocity, Wealth and Resistance

In the view of Luciano Petech (1977: 79) the 1684 Treaty of Temisgang—the most important of Moorcroft's "ancient engagements"—reduced Ladakh to the status of a "third-rank state". There is of course no doubt that the annexation of Ruthog, Guge and Purang was a severe blow to the prestige of the Ladakhi monarchy, and the economic implications included the loss of access to the Western Tibetan gold fields.[57] However, with regard to the shawl wool trade, the most striking point is not so much what Ladakh lost as what it preserved. The treaty secured Ladakh's essential economic interests and, in this crucial respect, was by no means as disadvantageous as Petech implies.

Indeed, as British 19th-century sources show, the Ladakh court traders—the Khartsongpa—enjoyed the special privileges of being able to purchase shawl wool at non-market prices as well as the benefits of corvée transport labour. Far from being outsiders in Western Tibet, they were treated as members of a high-status elite. Their privileges provided a major source of income to the king of Ladakh in his capacity as the "chief trader" as well as to the Khartsongpa themselves. Still greater profits accrued in Kashmir.[58] The people who gained least were the primary producers, the nomads of Western Tibet.

57 The economics of the Western Tibetan gold fields is a topic that deserves further research: how important were they first to the Ladakhi kingdom and, after 1684, to the Ganden Phodrang?

58 For an analysis of the economics of shawl trade imports to Kashmir see Rizvi (1999: 50–68).

A similar set of points applies to the Lopchak and Zhungtsong missions. Both within their own territories and across their respective borders, the people who managed these missions were treated as members of an elite who—as of right—could demand both accommodation and transport. Corvée labour provided the essential ingredient that made both missions highly profitable. The fact that this came at a high social cost was obvious enough at the time. For example, the Bengali pundit Sarat Chandra Das, who witnessed the arrival of the Lopchak in Gyantse in 1881, reports that:

> As the mission passed by, we heard the people remark that all this splendour and ostentation was at the expense of the Government of Lhasa, and to the ruin of the poor people of Tibet.
>
> DAS 2001 [1904]: 57

This analysis serves to answer the first question posed in the introduction to this essay: corvée labour helped fund a system that provided reciprocal benefits to both the Ladakhi court and the Ganden Phodrang. It therefore played a vital role in underpinning their diplomatic relationship. The answer to the second question is likewise clear. The "ancient engagements" benefitted the Ladakhi court and the Ganden Phodrang at an institutional level. More than that, they provided a source of profit to individual state officials and traders who were able to make use of corvée labour and forced sales for their own enrichment. As for the "losers", these were the farmers and nomads who had to provide the labour and buy and sell at non-market prices in both Ladakh and Tibet.

From a 21st-century perspective, making use of an official position for personal gain might be seen as a form of corruption and therefore an abuse of power.[59] This analysis does not quite hold in pre-20th century Ladakh or Tibet. Making use of an official position for private gain was not in itself an abuse of the system. Rather it was more accurate to say that it *was* the system.[60]

Nevertheless, it is significant that the Lhasa government felt it necessary to redefine the Lopchak mission's corvée labour entitlements in 1915, and to limit the quantities of tea sold under the pujjar system in 1939. These interventions imply that there was a notion of acceptable limits, and that demands

59 Transparency International, the leading anti-corruption NGO, defines corruption as "the abuse of entrusted position for private gain". See www.transparency.org.

60 British Trade Agents were by no means immune from the temptation to engage in trade alongside their official positions, but in their case this was definitely seen as an abuse of power. For example, Thakur Hayat Singh was dismissed for this offence in 1928. See: An enquiry into the conduct of previous Agents and their staff since the retirement of R.S. Devi Das. L/P&S/12/4163. See also McKay 1997: 160–62.

beyond these limits were illegitimate. The problem was that Western Tibet was far from the main seat of power in Lhasa and, for that matter, of no more than peripheral interest to the Government of India. It was all too easy for abuses to continue undetected and unaddressed.

In these circumstances the farmers and nomads at the bottom of the hierarchy had few choices. They could resort to forms of passive resistance such as dampening or adulterating shawl wool to increase its weight at the point of sale. Otherwise, the only realistic option was flight.

References

Archival Sources

Archiv der Brüder-Unität (Moravian Church), Herrnhut.

Reisebericht Heyde Ladakh Zanskar 1867. R. 15. U. a. 2 Nr 11.

British Library. Asia, Pacific and Africa Collections (APAC).

F/4/552/13384. Bengal Political Letters. Particulars of a visit paid by Captain Webb employed on a Survey in Kemaon to the Deba or Chief of Ticklakot.

L/P&S/7/57. China and Kashmir. Existing Relations between Ladak and Lhasa. L/P&S/7 125. Letter No. 891.

L/P&S/12/4163. Diaries of British Trade Agent, Gartok, 1930–1938.

L/P&S/12/4164. Diaries of British Trade Agent Gartok, 1938–1940.

R/2 (1066/57A). The Lhagyal affair.

National Archives of India, Delhi.

Foreign Department, Pol. A. 6 July 1851. Letter from Captain Henry Strachey to H.M. Elliot.

Library of Tibetan Works and Archives, Dharamsala.

Document 1061_LTWA_272. La-dwags sa-spyod pa'i lo-phyag dang, he-mdzod, gser-gzhung sogs kyi rta-khal sdod-bsgrigs (bsgrub-thad bstsal-ba'i) bkod-rgya. Online version available at: https://dtab.crossasia.org/4251.

Universitätsbibliothek Leipzig.

Nachlass A.H. Francke. "Bonds and Contracts". NL 256/91. Tax register from Sa-bu (Ladakh).

Primary Published Sources

Aitchison, J.E.T. 1874. *Handbook of the Trade Products of Leh.* Calcutta: Wyman and Co.

Cunningham, A. 1854. *Ladák, Physical, Statistical and Historical with Notices of the Surrounding Countries.* London: W.H. Allen.

Das, S.C. 1902. *A Tibetan English Dictionary.* Calcutta: Bengal Secretariat.

Das, S.C. 2001 [1904]. *Journey to Lhasa and Central Tibet.* Reprint ed. Delhi: Classics India Publications.

Davies, R.H. 1862. *Report on Trade and Resources of the Countries on the North-Western Boundary of British India.* Lahore: Government Press.

Francke, A.H. 1926. *Antiquities of Indian Tibet. Vol. 2.* Calcutta: Archaeological Survey of India.

Gerard, A. 1841. *An Account of Koonawur in the Himalaya.* London: James Madden.

Heyde, A.W. and E. Pagell. 1984. Auszug aus dem Tagebuch der Brüder Heyde und Pagell vom 24. Juni bis 4. August 1855. *Unitas Fratrum* 16, 122–39.

Heyde, A.W. and E. Pagell. 1860. *Reisebericht der zum Zweck eine Mission unter den Mongolen ausgesandten Brüder Pagell und Heyde.* Gnadau: Verlag der Buchhandlung der evangelischen Brüderunität bei C.H. Pemsel.

Blo bzang pun tshogs. 1998. sTod mnga' ris skor gsum de snga gser dpon dang gzhung tshog zhes pa gtong srol gi lo rgyus skor. *In Bod kyi rig gnas lo rgyus dpyad gzhi'i rgyu cha bdams bsgrigs.* Beijing: Mi rigs dpe skrun khang, 178–188.

Moorcroft, W. 1816. A journey to lake Mánasróvara in U'n-dés, a province of little Tibet. *Asiatick Researches* 12, 381–456.

Moorcroft, W. and T. George. 1841. *Travels in the Himalayan Provinces of Hindustan and the Panjab, in Ladakh and Kashmir, in Peshawar, Kabul, Kunduz and Bokhara.* Ed. H.H. Wilson. 2 vols. London: John Murray.

Ramsay, H. 1890. *Western Tibet: a Practical Dictionary of the Language and Customs of the Districts Included in the Ladák Wazarat.* Lahore: W. Ball.

Richardson, H.E. 1945. *Tibetan Precis.* Calcutta: Government of India Press. Reprinted in: H.E. Richardson. 1998. *High Peaks, Pure Earth. Collected Writings on Tibetan History and Culture.* Ed. Michael Aris. London: Serindia, 519–666.

Sherring, C. 1906. *Western Tibet and the British Borderland.* London: Edward Arnold.

Schuh, D. 2008. *Herrscherurkunden und Privaturkunden aus Westtibet (Ladakh).* Monumenta Tibetica Historica. Abteilung III. Band 11. Halle: International Institute for Tibetan and Buddhist Studies.

Trotter, H. 1877. Account of the pundit's journey in Great Tibet from Leh in Ladákh to Lhása and his return to India viâ Assam. *Journal of the Royal Geographical Society* 47, 86–136.

Wakefield, E.B. 1961. A journey to Western Tibet, 1929. *Alpine Journal* 66(302), 118–33.

Secondary Sources

Ahmad, Z. 1968. New light on the Tibet-Ladakh-Mughal war of 1679–1684. *East and West* 18, 340–61.

Alder, G. 1985. *Beyond Bokhara. The Life of William Moorcroft, Asian Explorer and Pioneer Veterinary Surgeon 1767–1825*. London: Century Publishing.

Ardussi, J. 1999. The rapprochement between Bhutan and Tibet under the enlightened rule of sDe-srid XIII Shes-rab-dbang-phyug (r. 1744–63). *Journal of Bhutan Studies* 1, 64–83.

Bischoff, J. 2013. Right there but still unnoticed: information on dGa' ldan pho brang *mi ser* from archival material published in German(y). *In* C. Ramble, P. Schwieger and A. Travers (eds) *Tibetans who Escaped the Historian's Net*. Kathmandu: Vajra Books, 9–26).

Booz, P. 2011a. Tea, Trade and Transport in the Sino-Tibetan Borderlands. D.Phil. thesis, Faculty of Oriental Studies, Oxford University.

Booz, P. 2011b. Fear of Indian tea and the failure of British India to break the Chinese tea monopoly in Tibet. *In* A. McKay and A. Balikci-Denjongpa (eds) *Buddhist Himalaya: Studies in Religion, History and Culture. Vol.1 Tibet and the Himalaya*. Gangtok: Namgyal Institute of Tibetology, 277–90.

Bray, J. 1990. The Lapchak mission from Leh to Lhasa in British Indian foreign policy. *The Tibet Journal* 15(4), 75–96.

Bray, J. 1995. Kashmir, Ladakh and Western Tibet. Episodes in frontier diplomacy during British rule in India. *In* H. Osmaston and P. Denwood (eds) *Recent Research on Ladakh 4 & 5*. London: School of Oriental and African Studies, 255–70.

Bray, J. 2008. Corvée transport labour in 19th and early 20th century Ladakh: a study in continuity and change. *In* M. van Beek and F. Pirie (eds) *Modern Ladakh*. Leiden: Brill, 43–66.

Bray, J. 2015. Dr Henry Cayley in Ladakh: medicine, trade and diplomacy on India's Northern frontier. *In* C. Ramble and U. Roesler (eds) *Tibetan and Himalayan Healing. An Anthology for Anthony Aris*. Kathmandu: Vajra Books, 81–96.

Bray, J. 2018. Ladakh's Lopchak missions to Lhasa: gift exchange, diplomatic ritual, and the politics of ambiguity. *In* J. Bischoff and A. Travers (eds) *Commerce and Communities: Social Status and the Exchange of Goods in Tibetan Societies*, Berlin: EB-Verlag, 43–90.

Bray, J. and T.D. Gonkatsang. 2009. Three 19th century documents from Tibet and the *lo phyag* mission from Leh to Lhasa. *In* J. Bray and E. de Rossi Filibeck (eds) *Mountains, Monasteries and Mosques. Recent Research on Ladakh and the Western Himalaya*. Supplement No. 2 to *Rivista degli Studi Orientali* 80 (New Series). Pisa and Rome: Sapienza, Università di Roma, Dipartimento di Studi Orientali, 97–116.

Bray, J. and T.D. Gonkatsang 2010. A letter from the Dalai Lama. *Ladakh Studies* 26, 24–30.

Brown, C.W. 1984. *The Goat is Mine, the Load is Yours. Morphogenesis of "Bhotiya-Shauka", U.P. India.* Lund: Lund Studies in Social Anthropology.

Brown, C.W. 1991–1992. What we call "Bhotias" are in reality not Bhotiyas. *In* M.P. Joshi, A.C. Fanger and C.W. Brown (eds) *Himalaya: Past and Present.* Vol. II. Almora: Shree Almora Book Depot, 147–72.

Brown, C.W. 1992–1993. Salt, barley, pashmina and tincal—contexts of being Bhotiya in Traill's Kumaon. *In* M.P. Joshi, A.C. Fanger and C.W. Brown (eds) *Himalaya: Past and Present.* Vol. III. Almora: Shree Almora Book Depot, 215–258.

Chohan, A.S. 1984. *Historical Study of Society and Culture in Dardistan and Ladakh.* New Delhi: Atlantic Publishers.

Datta, C.L. 1970. Significance of the shawl-wool trade in Western Himalayan politics. *Bengal Past and Present* 89, 16–28.

Datta, C.L. 1975. *Ladakh and Western Himalayan Politics 1819–1848.* New Delhi: Munshiram Manoharlal.

Datta, C.L. 1997. *The Raj and the Simla Hill States.* Jalandhar: ABS Publications.

Grist, N. 1985. Ladakh, a trading state. *In* P. Kaplanian and C. Dendaletche (eds) *Ladakh Himalaya Occidental. Ethnologie, Écologie. Recherches Récentes sur le Ladakh.* Pau: Centre pyrénéen de biologie et anthropologie des montagnes, 91–102.

Grist, N. 1994. The use of obligatory labour for porterage in pre-independence Ladakh. *In* P. Kværne (ed.) *Tibetan Studies. Proceedings of the 6th Seminar of the International Association of Tibetan Studies.* Oslo: Institute for Comparative Research in Human Culture, 264–74.

Halkias, G.T. 2009. Until the feathers of the winged black raven turn white: sources for the Tibet-Bashahr treaty of 1679. *In* J. Bray and E. de Rossi Filibeck (eds) *Mountains, Monasteries and Mosques. Recent Research on Ladakh and the Western Himalaya.* Supplement No. 2 to *Rivista degli Studi Orientali* 80 (New Series). Pisa and Rome: Sapienza, Università di Roma, Dipartimento di Studi Orientali, 61–86.

Korpon Lobsang Khenrap. 2000. Ru thog District before the Chinese occupation (1900–1958): a preliminary study of its cultural history. *The Tibet Journal* 25 (4), 33–77.

McKay, A. 1997. *Tibet and the British Raj.* London: Curzon.

Mullard, S. 2013. Recapturing runaways, or administration through contract: the 1830 covenant (*Gan rgya*) on Kotapa tax exiles and Sikkimese border regions. *In* C. Ramble, P. Schwieger and A. Travers (eds) *Tibetans who Escaped the Historian's Net.* Kathmandu: Vajra Books, 180–207.

Nawang Jinpa. 2015. Why did Tibet and Ladakh clash in the 17th century? Rethinking the background to the 'Mongol War' in Ngari (1679–1684). *The Tibet Journal* 40 (2), 113–150.

Petech, L. 1947. The Tibetan-Ladakhi-Moghul war of 1681–83. *Indian Historical Quarterly* 23, 169–99.

Petech, L. 1977. *The Kingdom of Ladakh (c.950–1842 A.D.)*. Rome: Istituto Italiano Per Il Medio Ed Estremo Oriente.

Ramble, C., P. Schwieger and A. Travers (eds). 2013. *Tibetans who Escaped the Historian's Net*. Kathmandu: Vajra Books.

Rizvi, J. 1999. *Trans-Himalayan Caravans. Merchant Princes and Peasant Traders in Ladakh*. New Delhi: Oxford University Press.

Schuh, D. 1983. Zu den Hintergrunden der Parteinahme Ladakh's für Bhutan im Krieg gegen Lhasa. *In* R. Sander and D. Kantowsky (eds) *Recent Research on Ladakh*. Munich: Weltforum Verlag, 37–50.

Schwieger, P. 2011. The long arm of the Fifth Dalai Lama: influence and power of the Fifth Dalai Lama in Southeast Tibet. *In* A. McKay and A. Balikci-Denjongpa (eds) *Buddhist Himalaya: Studies in Religion, History and Culture* Vol. 1. Gangtok: Namgyal Institute of Tibetology, 239–57.

Shakabpa, Tsepon Wangchuk Deden. 1984. *Tibet. A Political History*. New York: Potala Publications.

van Spengen, W. 2000. *Tibetan Border Worlds. A Geohistorical Analysis of Trade and Traders*. London and New York: Kegan Paul.

Sperling, E. 2003. Tibet's foreign relations during the epoch of the Fifth Dalai Lama. *In* F. Pommaret (ed.) *Lhasa in the Seventeenth Century*. Leiden: Brill, 119–32.

CHAPTER 11

Taxes and Corvées in the Manorial and Monastic Estates of Zangskar (Western Himalayas)

Isabelle Riaboff

The following pages set out to discuss some data bearing upon the economic organisation of Zangskar.[1] More precisely, the purpose of this paper is to present the taxes and corvées, or obligatory chores, for which Zangskari households are liable. In other words, neither volunteer services and gifts (such as donations, alms, and so forth) nor relationships based on exchange (i.e. barter, trade, reciprocal or paid work) will be taken into account. Moreover, the various duties fulfilled for the whole village will not be examined. Among compulsory taxes and corvées, I will only consider those imposed on the villagers to the advantage of their lords, whether lay or religious.

This paper draws on the findings of twenty-two months of fieldwork conducted for my Ph.D. research into Zangskar's monarchic structures and monastic authorities (Riaboff 1997). As regards the villagers' relationship with the monasteries, the paper describes the situation as I found it in the 1990s. The villagers' labour obligations to the local monarchy ceased to apply after 1950.

1 The Economic Protagonists

1.1 *The Households*

In Zangskar, the basic economic unit is the household, which systematically lives from farming. There are three categories of household, depending on who owns the fields.

1 This paper was originally presented at the Eighth Seminar of the International Association for Tibetan Studies (IATS) held at Bloomington (US) in 1998. I conducted my research as an affiliated member of the Laboratoire d'ethnologie et de sociologie comparative (Nanterre University-CNRS), thanks to a research grant from the French ministère de l'enseignement supérieur et de la recherche. I also received financial support from the Société d'ethnologie (through the Eugène Fleischmann award, 1997) and from the Fonds Louis Dumont d'aide à la recherche en anthropologie sociale (1998). I am grateful to John Bray for encouraging me to publish the paper after all these years, and for copy-editing the text.

 | DOI:10.1163/9789004529465_013

- In the first category, a household owns its entire holding. Its members are freeholders. They are called *rang 'bad pa*, that is "those who farm on their own"; or *hril po*, "whole entire"; or else, referring to the cadastre, *par shog pa*, "those [who hold a] printed paper".[2] This status, which is widespread among the Zangskari farmers, may be surprising for Tibetologists, given that, to the best of my knowledge, it does not have an equivalent in Central Tibet.[3]
- In the second category, part of the household's land belongs to a lord (either lay or religious). The householders are then tenant farmers: they are called *khral pa*, "those liable for *khral*".
- In the third category, the household does not own any fields. Its members work as servants on the lords' domanial lands. By contrast with tenured land, the domanial lands are distinguished by the fact that their yields go entirely to the lord. These farm servants, of whom there are very few, are called *chun pa*, possibly meaning "those who are under control"; their tasks include manuring, ploughing, sowing, irrigating. In return for their daily services, the *chun pa* receive tax-free grants of land (*chun zhing*) for their own use.[4]

In all these cases, the fields cultivated by a Zangskari household form an undivided holding, called *zhing khang*, "fields and house". The main part of the holding is cultivated by the members of the so-called "big house" (*khang chen*), that is to say the eldest son with his wife and children. Concurrently, a few fields of the *zhing khang* are allotted to the parents who may have retired to the "small house" (*khang chung*) with their unmarried sons and daughters.

It is worth highlighting that, economically speaking, households are understood as equivalent to each other. Regardless of their respective sizes, they are considered as the basis of assessment for tax and labour obligations, and they all function as village actors.[5]

1.2 *The King of Zangla*

From the 15th to the 19th centuries, Zangskar was divided into two kingdoms (*mnga' 'og*). These were the kingdom of Padum, by far the larger, and the

---

2 In the village of Zangla, all the *rang 'bad pa* houses seem to be the original properties: none of them is descended from a split in a former household, at least not within living memory.

3 The closest Central Tibetan equivalent would probably be the non-noble *sger pa*, "private owners". While the majority of *sger pa* were aristocrats, there were some who were ranked as commoners.

4 Although little is known about those who worked on the demesne lands in the Tibetan cultural area, we can assert that the *khol po* of Derge (Carrasco 1959: 145–46) and the "tied *dud chung*" of Salu (Goldstein 1968: 112–13, 122) were similar in status to the Zangskari *chun pa*.

5 At the village level, big and small houses are dissociated: a big house has more extensive rights than a small house, but in return it faces heavier duties.

kingdom of Zangla, confined to the north-east. Once Zangskar was conquered by the Dogras in the 1830s, the king of Padum was deposed. However, Zangla's king, who had been most obliging towards the occupying army, remained on his throne. His lineage continued to govern until 1950, when his estate was broken up in accordance with the Jammu and Kashmir agrarian reforms.[6] It should therefore be noted that the monarchic system of Zangla that I shall now describe vanished seven decades ago.

Before 1950, only four villages constituted the so-called "kingdom of Zangla", namely Tsazar, Pishu, Pidmo and Zangla itself. In other words, the inhabitants of these four settlements without any exception recognised the authority of the Zangla king. However, this unanimous allegiance did not imply that all the lands of the kingdom were royal lands. As a matter of fact, within the limits of his kingdom, the king of Zangla owned only approximately 50 per cent of the fields.

1.3 *The Monastic Authorities*

Zangskar has eight monasteries, founded between the 11th and the 18th centuries. At present, Karcha monastery is the main one, in terms of both wealth and the number of monks: the Karcha community has almost a hundred members. In addition to these monasteries, there are also eight nunneries.

Each Zangskari village is affiliated to a monastery. This affiliation finds expression in two rules. On the one hand, if a boy of the village takes religious vows, he will inevitably join the monastery in question. On the other hand, the monastery appoints one monk in the village to perform Buddhist rituals, whether collective or private.[7] In Zangskar, contrary to the situation in Central Ladakh, villages that are affiliated to the same monastery are always contiguous with one another: their territorial unity is designated as the *dgon pa'i mnga' 'og*, literally "under the power of the monastery". Of course, all monastic territories are not equally extensive. Karcha monastery's is the largest and comprises about thirty villages.

By contrast with the *dgon pa'i mnga' 'og*, the monastic landed properties (all spared by the agrarian reform) are not necessarily consolidated into the same areas. Thus, the lands of Karcha monastery are scattered all over Zangskar in numerous villages, whether these are affiliated to Karcha or not. To put it another way, it is possible that Karcha may own no fields in a village that is affiliated with it: it is even possible that other monasteries may own some

6 Act No XVII of 2007 [1950 CE], known as the Big Landed Estates Abolition Act.

7 The appointed monk is referred to as *mchod gnas*.

fields in these same villages.[8] This state of affairs stems from the fact that these lands were granted to the monastery by various donors over the centuries.

Since 1779, Ngari Rinpoche (mNga' ris Rin po che) has been the "owner" (*bdag po*) of the Karcha monastery.[9] As such, he personally possesses most of Karcha's fields, administered in his name by the *bla brang*'s staff. As for the remaining fields, they were offered to the monastic community by the 18th Bakula Rinpoche (1860–1917), who was a native of Zangskar. They are managed by three monks called the "mana stewards" (*mana'i gnyer pa*).[10]

2 The Supply of Goods and Labour

In Zangskar, the Tibetan terms *lag 'don* (payments in kind) and *rkang 'gro* (corvée duties) are not in use, although these expressions are well known in Central Ladakh. In Zangskari, *khral* is the word commonly used, and refers to both categories of tax. In spite of this terminological fusion, I shall organise the following pages in two parts in order to make my analysis as clear as possible. I shall first present the taxes in kind before focussing on the corvée obligations.

2.1 *The Payment of Taxes in Kind*

Liability for taxes applies only to the tenant farmers (*khral pa*).[11] This is presumably why the Tibetan *khral pa* is usually translated as "taxpayer", even though the term *khral* also embraces compulsory service.

In Zangskar, taxes are usually paid in grain, and on average equate to up to a third of the yield. We may therefore speak of sharecropping. However, the English expression "sharecropping" should not mislead us: the amount of grain paid per Zangskari tenure (*khral zhing*), which is fixed once and for all, is not proportionate to the annual crop. Furthermore, no matter what is actually planted, the grain in which the tax is paid has to be barley.

8 This is the case in the village of Karcha itself, where Bardan monastery has some land.

9 In Tibet, the monasteries that—like Karcha—belonged to powerful reincarnate masters were said to be "private" (*sger dgon*), by contrast with those owned by the Tibetan State (the *gzhung dgon*).

10 The mana is a unit of measure of Indian origin, and corresponds to 0.57 litre.

11 As a matter of fact, the Zangskari monasteries also receive a little grain from villagers who do not farm monastic fields. This grain is the annual "interest" (*skyed*) paid for the loan of a silver coin. Therefore, in my view, it cannot be considered as a tax strictly speaking, even if its payment is understood as an unquestionable duty (people invariably claim that such loans cannot be cancelled).

In actual fact, instead of being brought to the lords, many of the land taxes are disbursed on the lords' behalf to support secular or religious events. These allotted taxes are paid in flour instead of grain.[12] Thus, in Zangla, several taxes imposed on specific royal fields used to be assigned to numerous village festivals, notably the celebrations of *tshes bcu chen mo* and *bcu gsum mchod pa*, archery (*mda' rtsed*), the whitewashing of the religious buildings (*sku dkar*), the *dge rtsa* ritual and the collective readings of religious scriptures, such as the *bKa' 'gyur* and *Yum*. Some tenant households were entitled to receive one additional irrigation turn after every two turns (this is called *phyed ka*, or "half [regulation]"). In compensation for this irrigation privilege, the *phyed ka* beneficiaries needed to contribute half a portion more of butter and flour than any other house on the occasion of gatherings for religious readings.

An additional quantity of flour owed to the king of Zangla was sent directly to Karcha monastery. Some of it was used to prepare a soup served to the community during *smon lam chen mo*, and some was shared out among the monks. For example, at the *dgu gtor* festival about one hundred *khal*[13] of flour was distributed this way.

As for the Karcha monastic community, it receives almost as much in allotted taxes as in ordinary taxes. The latter amounts to 171 *khal* of grain per annum (collected from forty-six tenant farms). The near total of this grain is divided among the monks. The distribution occurred in two stages: at the *dgu gtor* festival each monk receives one *khal* of grain, and half a *khal* at the *dge rtsa* celebration.

The allotted taxes amount to a total of 145 *khal* of flour. The liturgical celebrations that benefit from these taxes are eight in number. For each of these celebrations, one or two fields are concerned, sometimes more than two. However that may be, the tax imposed on each of these fields is unvarying: it amounts to 6 *khal* of flour. This flour, called *tshags* ("provision"), is distributed to each of the monks at the rate of one *bre* per monk.

By contrast with the dues collected on the fields owned by the monastic community, none of the taxes paid on a *bla brang* holding (that is: on one of Ngari Rinpoche's holdings) is ever dedicated to one particular event. This means that the yearly amount of grain (about 500 *khal*) owed to the lama is entirely stored within the *bla brang*. Later on, some of this grain (about a fifth) is shared out: every monk receives one *khal* as "wages" (*phog*). Some 70 more

12 Note that Toni Huber (1997: 248) speaks of "purpose-designed taxes" to describe a similar arrangement at the Tibetan pilgrimage site of Tsari (Tsa ri).

13 The *khal* is a volumetric measure equal to twenty *bre*, and corresponds to roughly 10 kg of grain.

khal is transferred to the community as a whole (the so-called *gzhung*). This grain is referred to as the "barley put aside" (*bkar 'jug nas*). In the past, this was the grain lent to needy villagers. Nowadays, the "barley put aside" is consumed by the monks when they all work together. Last, but not least, the remainder of the grain (about two thirds of the total) is kept in the *bla brang* and used to feed guests, donors and the workers received within the monastery.

2.2 *The Provision of Corvée Services*

Until 1950, the king's trading expeditions required several men who had to be away from home for weeks at a time. This porterage corvée (*'u lag*) involved all the big houses of the king's tenant farmers (*khral pa*). The corvée was discharged for two years in succession by farmers living in Zangla village, and then for the next two years by farmers residing in Pishu, Pidmo or Tsazar. Within Zangla, the requisition of the porters was based on a rotation (*tshir*) from one tenant farm to the next.

Unlike the corvée duties incumbent upon the king's tenantry as a whole, some corvées were fulfilled exclusively by the tenant households that farmed specific royal fields, that were otherwise free of taxes in kind. These corvées all benefited the monks who visited the village of Zangla. Some (called *khral rdig*, "tax furniture") consisted of ensuring a comfortable reception for the monks when they came to the village to collect alms. Another corvée, which still applies, consists of bringing drinking water to the officiating monks appointed to Zangla during the winter. Like the payers of the allotted taxes, the farmers liable for these special corvées were entitled to the *phyed ka* irrigation privilege. Another corvée of a similar type remains alive: the members of the tenant household who cultivate the so-called *chu zhing*, "water field", continue to fulfil their former corvée, which consists of bringing drinking water during the winter to the officiating monks assigned to Zangla. In exchange, they still benefit from the *phyed ka* irrigation privilege.

Besides, a number of tasks had to be performed by the king's subjects, regardless of whether they were tenant farmers or freeholders. Over and above their economic status, the big houses of the kingdom (except for the *chun pa* households) had to take turns to provide a daily worker, known as the *gsol dpon*) who was responsible for bringing water and wood into the palace kitchen. Each year the houses of the kingdom also had to provide the king with a load of wood for each plough-animal (*rmo glang*) in their possession. This was called the "wood of the *dzo*" (*mdzo shing*). Moreover, once a year, wild fodder (*ri rtswa*) had to be collected for the palace: it was gathered on the mountainside by members of all the small houses of the kingdom and then carried to the royal cowsheds by members of all the big houses. The same division of tasks applied to the harvest gathered on the royal domanial lands. The farm servants of the palace (the *chun pa*) were too few to complete all the work, so each big house sent a worker to help with the reaping, while one person per small house had to carry the sheaves to the threshing floor. Finally, the king's subjects were again requisitioned at haymaking time: under the supervision of the *chun pa*, big houses' workers cut the alfalfa, while the small houses' workers bundled it. This full day work was specifically called *zhabs las* or "service".

The corvées from which Karcha monastery benefits at the present time are very similar to those that the former kings of Zangla used to receive. First of all, the *bla brang*'s *chun pa* are compelled to carry out porterage. This happens twice a year, when a large number of monks spend a few days away from the monastery for the celebration of major rituals, at Sani (in the springtime) and at Padum (in the autumn). The Karcha *chun pa* are then responsible for carrying the necessary carpets, kitchen utensils and ritual paraphernalia. Additionally, at the time of two other events celebrated outside of the monastery, the dignitaries involved need horses: they are provided with these mounts, which are considered as *rta 'ul* (literally "horse porterage"), by the big houses of the villages concerned, regardless of their farm status.

From all the villages under Karcha's religious authority, each big house has to supply one wood load per year (as for the small houses, they provide wood as they wish).[14]

The haymaking on the *bla brang*'s domanial lands does not need the participation of all the affiliated households. Consequently, the eight villages nearest to Karcha divide into two groups: every two years, the big houses belonging to each of these groups are responsible for cutting the alfalfa for a full day. This work, which is understood as a tribute paid to Ngari Rinpoche, is again called *zhabs las*, "service".

3 Conclusion

Put side by side, the former palace of Zangla and the present-day Karcha monastery lead us to draw some concluding remarks regarding Zangskari economic organisation.

Landed property ownership and exploitation constitute the cornerstone of the circulation of goods and labour. Not only do the lords (whether lay or religious) benefit from taxes and corvées from their tenantry, but further there are

14 In any Zangskari village, uncultivated land, where wood grows, is a collective possession. Therefore, the supply of wood is a corvée duty rather than a tax in kind.

no taxes other than land taxes. That being the case, beyond land property, local political and religious allegiances also require a number of corvées. Therein, the Zangskari situation proves enlightening, insofar as a great number of peasants are freeholders (unlike the Tibetan peasants). This feature makes it easy to identify the corvées that bear no relation to the farming of someone else's lands. In the past, such were the corvées fulfilled for the king by all the subjects of Zangla kingdom (apart from the king's *chun pa*). Nowadays, the provision of horses, loads of wood and workers to the monks of Karcha or to Ngari Rinpoche's *bla brang* is still supported by those who are religiously affiliated to Karcha monastery.

References

Carrasco, P. 1959. *Land and Polity in Tibet.* Seattle/London: University of Washington Press.

Goldstein, M.C. 1968. An Anthropological Study of the Tibetan Political System. Ph.D thesis. University of Washington.

Huber, T. 1997. Ritual and politics in Eastern Himalaya: the staging of processions at Tsa-ri. *In* S. Karmay and P. Sagant (eds) *Les habitants du Toit du Monde. Etudes réunies en hommage à Alexander W. Macdonald.* Paris: Société d'ethnologie, 221–60.

Riaboff, I. 1997. Le Roi et le Moine. Figures et principes du pouvoir et de sa légitimation au Zanskar (Himalaya occidental). Ph.D. thesis, Paris x-Nanterre University.

CHAPTER 12

The Fiscal Status of Buddhist and Bönpo Institutions in Mustang (Nepal): A Historical Overview

Charles Ramble

1 Introduction

According to a much-cited statistic, the main beneficiary of land taxes in early 20th century Tibet was the clergy, which accounted for 42 per cent of revenue received. Next was the government, with 37 per cent, and finally the aristocracy, who received just half of the monasteries' share at 21 per cent (Carrasco 1959: 86). While these figures may have contributed to a general impression that religious institutions were on the receiving end of the Tibetan fiscal system, it is important to remember that by no means all monasteries and clerical estates (*bla brang*) were its beneficiaries. As Peter Schwieger (in this volume) points out, many monasteries, including those of the Gelukpa (dGe lugs pa) school, were themselves liable for taxes, and these payments were further increased by the Thirteenth Dalai Lama as a means of enhancing the resources of the Tibetan army.

If we still know very little about the fiscal situation of religious institutions in the Tibet of the Ganden Phodrang period, we know even less about the taxation of monasteries and nunneries in the Himalayan regions of adjacent countries. In Nepal, which was a Hindu kingdom until 2008, there was certainly no state support for the structures of Tibetan Buddhism, but although the caste-based antipathy of certain political regimes to Tibetans in general and Tibetan clerics in particular did at times result in prejudicial treatment,[1] Buddhist institutions generally benefited from some of the fiscal advantages extended to religious bodies in the country.

1 In his excellent article "Social mobility in the Newar caste system", Colin Rosser examines the long-term social consequences of the Rana government's hostility to a Tibetan lama who was briefly influential among Buddhists in the Kathmandu Valley (Rosser 1966).

 | DOI:10.1163/9789004529465_014

In spite of a few landmark studies of the subject,[2] a great deal of research remains to be done on the history of taxation in Nepal in general. Part of the reason for the complexity of the situation is that both the Shah rulers who unified Nepal and their Rana successors perpetuated the local fiscal policies of the previously independent states that made up the nation, and that when modifications were subsequently introduced, they were rarely extended to the entirety of the country. The only way to advance our knowledge of this important but rather neglected field of study is through the comparative examination of a multiplicity of case studies, and the present article aims to contribute to such a hypothetical project by presenting some of the sparse data that are available for the taxation of Buddhist and Bönpo institutions in Mustang. The period on which I wish to focus covers the late 19th and early 20th centuries, but the antecedents to certain fiscal regimes will be traced back to the 17th century (and possibly much earlier), while the curious local survival of one obsolete category of tax will be followed into the 1990s, several decades after its official abolition. The particular area with which we are concerned here is the southern part of Mustang known as Baragaon, and the community of Geling that stands between the territories of Baragaon and North Mustang, also known as Upper Lo (see Map 12.1).

A few words may be said here about what is meant by "Buddhist and Bönpo institutions". These are essentially of two sorts: first, establishments of celibate monks and nuns, and secondly, households or clusters of hereditary lamas, sometimes referred to as "householder-priests". The latter may be either priestly families living in communities consisting principally of a lay population, or else they may comprise entire villages of families belonging to the priestly social stratum. There will be little to say about the fiscal circumstances of institutions in the first category, since the only sources available to me are from the archive of one long-abandoned Nyingmapa (rNying ma pa) convent, although these documents do shed some light on the tax liabilities of other monasteries and convents in the vicinity.

We are better served by sources concerning householder-priests. Broadly speaking, the society of Mustang is stratified along a number of "castes" or "ranks" (*brgyud pa*), in accordance with a model that is found in many parts of the Tibetan world, although some of the terminology (including this use of the term *brgyud pa*) may be specific to Mustang. The highest rank is occupied by the aristocracy (*sras po, sras mo*); below these are the priests (*bla mchod*), followed by commoners (*phal pa*), who are subdivided into at least two subsidiary

2 The single most important contribution to the field remains Mahesh Chandra Regmi's *Land Tenure and Taxation in Nepal* (Regmi 1978a).

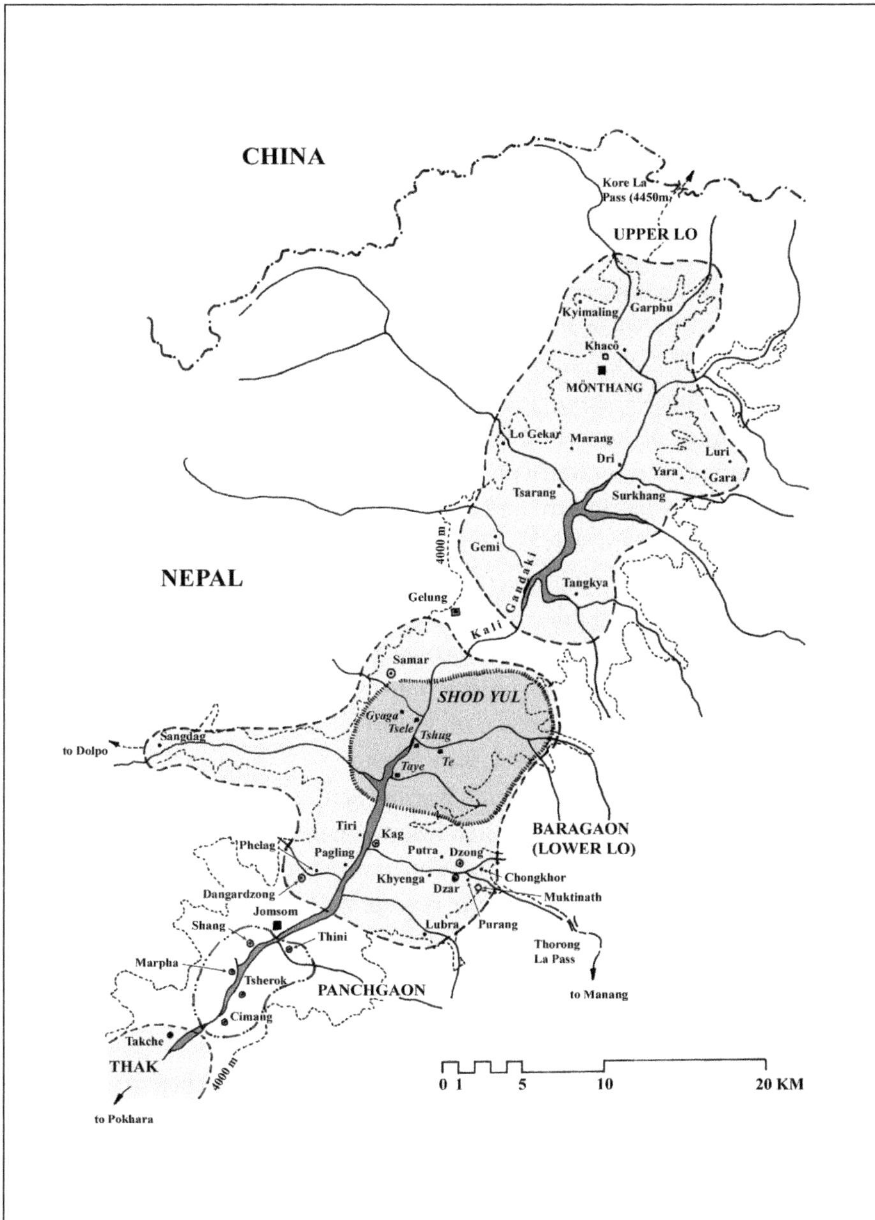

MAP 12.1 Map of Mustang District, showing the enclaves of Upper Lo, Baragaon, Panchgaon, and Thak. The broken lines highlight the "core" areas of the enclaves, and do not correspond to the boundaries of their much more extensive territories.
DRAWING BY NIELS GUTSCHOW

strata, and finally different categories of artisans (*dman rigs*). Traditionally, the lowest ranks were made up of Nepali-speaking occupational caste groups. The aristocracy and the artisans tend to be endogamous, whereas the marital boundaries between priests and commoners are more porous. The hierarchical ordering of these ranks is objectivised in a number of ways, including seating order at gatherings, dress-codes, and differential bridewealth payments in inter-rank marriages. There is also a fiscal manifestation of social status. Artisans do not pay land-taxes within certain mixed-rank villages because they have no land; aristocrats in the same settlements are also exempt from these and other taxes, not because they have no land but as an aristocratic privilege. The extension of these exemptions in the mid-19th century caused widespread resentment and protest among the commoner majority (Ramble 2014). While the fiscal position of most ranks seems to have been reasonably stable, the bracket occupied by hereditary priests was more variable, and whatever privileges they enjoyed frequently had to be negotiated and defended. A further factor in this fluctuation was the difference in the political and social environments of the three examples considered here. The first of these is a small hamlet—just two households—on an area straddling the territorial boundary of two commoner settlements. The second is a free-standing village of Bönpo lamas, and the third is a single priestly household that was established in the mid-19th century in the northern community of Geling. Householder-priests do not represent a large proportion of Mustang's population, but there are other examples besides these—three priestly settlements and several individual households—about whose tax liabilities we currently have no information, and the picture presented here is therefore a very incomplete one that we can only hope will be filled out with future research.

2 Sources

The documents on which this article is based were photographed in the course of several research projects undertaken in Mustang. The first of these was the *Nepal-German Project on High Mountain Archaeology* (NGPHMA), which extended from 1992 to 1996 and was directed by Dieter Schuh, with financing from the German Research Council (DFG). Documents from this project that are cited here are published in a series of collections with the general title *Tibetan Sources for a Social History of Mustang*, abbreviated here as *Tibetan Sources* (see bibliography for details). Items in this series bear the prefix HMA. Documents photographed within the framework of the Franco-German project the *Social History of Tibetan Societies, 17th to 20th Centuries* (SHTS), which ran from 2011 to 2016, have the prefix SH.[3] The archive of Geling was photographed in the course of a collaboration between SHTS and the DFG-funded project *The Mustang Archives: Analysis of Handwritten Documents via the Ethnographic Study of Papermaking Traditions in Nepal*, directed by Agnieszka Helman-Ważny (2015–2019). Documents photographed in the course of this collaboration have the prefix MA.

3 The Taxation of Monasteries and Convents

In the 19th and early 20th centuries, there were three monasteries (*chos sde*) and five nunneries in Baragaon. Two of the former were (and still are) located in the villages of Dzar and Dzong in the Muktinath Valley, and the third is in Kag, at the confluence of the Kali Gandaki river and the Dzong Chu, which runs westwards from Muktinath (see Map 12.1). Two of the convents, Gar and Tshultrim, are located respectively near Muktinath and Dzar, and the other three are north of Kag in the territories of Tiri, Taye and Tshug. It is thanks to certain documents in the archive of Gönpa Gang, which stands on the territory of Tshug, that we know something about the fiscal status of these establishments. A document from 1904, issued by "the lord and subjects of Lower Lo", gives notice of the imminent visit of the government tax collector and presents a summary of the anticipated payments:

> As in the past, the three monasteries are [together] liable to pay 100 rupees. Fifty rupees should be paid collectively by Dzar monastery, Dzong monastery, Gar convent and Tshultrim convent; and Kag monastery shall pay 50 rupees together with Tiri convent, Taye convent and Gönpa Gang convent. In accordance with past obligations, and as it is clearly set out in the government document (Nep. *pharid patra*) as well as above, Gönpa Gang shall pay 10 rupees....[4]

3 The project was jointly funded by the German Research Foundation (Deutsche Forschungsgemeinschaft, DFG) and the French National Research Agency (Agence nationale de la recherche, ANR). Work on the publications *Tibetan Sources 2* and *Tibetan Sources 3* was carried out in the framework of this project. Documents from the archives of Geling and of Lubrak, which have not yet been published in book form, may be found on the website of the project, www.tibetanhistory.net.

4 *chos sde dgo gsuṃ la dngul brgya phogs pa la / dngul lnga bcu / rdzar chos sde rdzong chos sde / dgar dgon / tshul dgon dang / skag chos sde dngul lnga bcu byang dgos la / sting ris dgon / stang yed dgon / dgon pa dgang gsuṃs the dgos nas / dgon ba gang la phogs tho sngon khyun star dngul bcu' 'byung pa'i pha rag dang / slar phyisu (phyis su) yang sde stard gong bsal star dngul bcu byang dgos ...* (*Tibetan Sources 3*: HMA/KCh/01, p. 21).

The precise designation of the tax in question is a matter that will be discussed in more detail below. The two monasteries of the Muktinath Valley, Dzar and Dzong, formed a unit with two convents: Gar Gönpa, which recruited nuns from the villages of Dzong, Putrak, Purang and the priestly community of Chongkhor, near which it is located; and Tshultrim Gönpa, located in Dzar, which is the "mother convent" (*ma dgon*) of the nuns who serve at the Buddhist temples of Muktinath itself. Kag monastery was grouped with three nunneries to the north of it: Tiri, Taye, and Gönpa Gang itself. It is likely that each of the nunneries in this group paid an annual tax of 10 rupees, and that the monastery paid 20 rupees. How the 50-rupee liability of the other group was distributed across the two monasteries and two convents that comprised it is not specified.

The convent of Gönpa Gang had been founded in 1684 by a certain Künzang Longyang (Kun bzang klong yangs, 1644–1698),[5] and it recruited nuns from five settlements in an enclave in Baragaon known as the Shöyul (Shod yul), though Taye, one of the five villages, broke away from the community probably around the late 18th century following the establishment of its own nunnery. The annual tax liability of 10 rupees was therefore shared equally among the nuns from the remaining four communities, Tshug, Te, Gyaga and Tsele,[6] though the record is rather sparse concerning the recruitment of nuns from the last two of these settlements.

In addition to this annual fiscal obligation, Gönpa Gang was required to make an occasional payment of another kind of tax, and this category will be discussed below.

The conventions followed in the transliterated passages are as follows: [±2S]: roughly the specified number of syllables missing; =: missing letter or stack; {abc}: material that were better omitted for a more intelligible reading; Z: *che rtags*; ^: *tsha rtags*, a small diagonal stroke used as an abbreviation for various letters, but most frequently *tsha*. The Tibetan text of the excerpts is unedited unless stated otherwise, though emended versions of all the documents cited here may be found in the corresponding publications. Contracted forms (*bskungs yig*) are represented as closely as possible as they appear in the text, followed by a full-length form in brackets.

5 A brief account of Künzang Longyang's life, based on his autobiography, is given in Harrison *et al.* 2018: 101–16. The proper name of Gönpa Gang is actually Künzang Chöling (Kun bzang chos gling), though the former designation appears frequently in documents, and has now completely replaced the official name in everyday usage. Gönpa Gang (dGon pa sgang) means "convent ridge" and, strictly speaking, denotes the hill on which the building stands. This hill was the site of an earlier community of nuns even before Künzang Chöling was built; see *Tibetan Sources 3*: 5–6).

6 The names of villages that appear in documents with a variety of spellings will be given only in roughly phonetic form.

4 The Lamas of Tshognam

The convent suffered a major crisis in 1903 when the nuns of Te abandoned Gönpa Gang to set up a new community on their own territory, under the tutelage of a lama named Ösal Dorje ('Od gsal rdo rje). Ösal Dorje was a native of Tshognam (Tshogs rnams), a little settlement of just two households, of which the lower house stands on the territory of Tshug and the upper one on the neighbouring village of Te. He had been born in Lower Tshognam, but had left following a dispute, and moved to the upper part of the hamlet, on Te's territory (*Tibetan Sources 3*: 16–17). Ösal Dorje's mother was from a Nyingmapa priestly lineage named the Clan of the Kings of Sikkim ('Bras ljongs rgyal po'i rgyud pa), that had settled in Tshug at some unknown time and founded (or rather occupied) a temple called Sang-ngak Chöling (gSang sngags chos gling). Ösal Dorje's cousin, Tshewang Bumpa (Tshe dbang 'bum pa), was the heir of this temple, but its actual ownership was called into question in the course of an incident that occurred in or shortly before 1892. Like most hereditary lamas, Tshewang Bumpa was also a trader, and maintained that his ownership of the temple exempted him from paying transit duties when passing through the territory of the King of Lo on his way to Tibet. The king sent him a stiffly-worded letter contesting the claim, and insisted that the temple actually belonged to the crown since it had been restored by an earlier queen, Nordzin Wangmo (Nor 'dzin dbang mo), prior to its occupation by Tshewang Bumpa's ancestors (*Tibetan Sources 2*: HMA/LTshognam/Tib/10, pp. 64–66).

This episode occurred during a period of discontent against the payment of tariffs (*khur chang*) imposed on traders travelling through Lo. In 1863 the Government of Nepal had demanded that traders pay the customs office in Dana, in the very south of Mustang, revenues that had until then been paid to the King of Lo. However, the latter refused to accept the withdrawal of these traditional taxes, and there appears to have been a period when traders from the Shöyul were paying double tariffs. In 1900 the Shöyul petitioned the government to intervene, but it was not until 1910 that an official order (*rukka*) was issued expressly forbidding the King of Lo to levy *khur chang* duties.[7]

In the event, although the king denied that Tshewang Bumpa's family owned the temple, he nevertheless granted the lama and his family exemption from trade tariffs on the grounds of their priestly status and religious deeds. The letter warns against unspecified improper activities that might in the future result in the forfeit of these privileges. Although the nature of these activities is

7 For a more detailed account of these events, see Ramble 2008: 64–66.

not detailed, they probably refer to an attempt by the priests to make an illicit profit by including the animals of tax-liable traders in their own caravans.

The priestly rank of the family had important consequences for their status in the village itself. This privileged status was questioned in the course of a conflict with the rest of the village that occurred in 1910. The nature of the challenge is not recorded, but the document that was drawn up to mark the reconciliation of the two parties confirms these privileges, and anchors them in historical precedent. At an earlier occasion, the text states, when a local lord was building his mansion, he requisitioned labour from the surrounding villages. A woman of the priestly house was ordered to take part, but the family maintained that, in view of their rank, they were exempt from corvée duties, and the lord of Baragaon, Khamsum, accepted their argument. The document goes on to confirm the family's entitlement to the provision of firewood by the community, and concludes with the assurance that "their customary exemption both from taxes and from the obligation to perform communal labour for the community shall be maintained, and this shall not be changed as long as the world-age and the sun endure" (*Tibetan Sources 2*: HMA/LTshognam/Tib/17, p. 87).

The declaration that the family was exempt from tax (*khral med*) is actually rather misleading, since it implies that it paid nothing to the government. In fact this is not the case, and here again we are the beneficiaries of the dispute that required a written exposition of the state of affairs. The background to this story provides some important insights into the status of hereditary lamas in the region, but since the events concerned a dispute between two branches of the family over three generations, the following diagram (Figure 12.1) may serve as a reminder of the relations between the protagonists.[8]

Lama Ösal Dorje (in the second generation), whom we have encountered above, grew up in a dependency of his cousin's household that had been allocated to his mother, Phurpa Angmo (Phur pa dbang mo), until her death. However, he subsequently maintained that he had the right to inherit the dependency and to pass it on to his son Namkha (Nam mkha'). Namkha's cousin, Tshewang Angyal (Tshe dbang dbang rgyal), contested this claim and set out his version of the story (which, on the basis of comparison with other documents, seems to be the correct one). Tshewang Angyal insisted that the temple had the status of a religious cooperative (*guṭhi*), and that the dependency that had been allocated to his aunt was an inalienable part of it. "We [the main family] paid all the tenancy costs to His Majesty's Government relating to the fields, the house and the occupants as well as the *gha sti rtsu rman*

8 An extended version of this genealogy, covering seven generations, in provided in *Tibetan Sources 3*: 4.

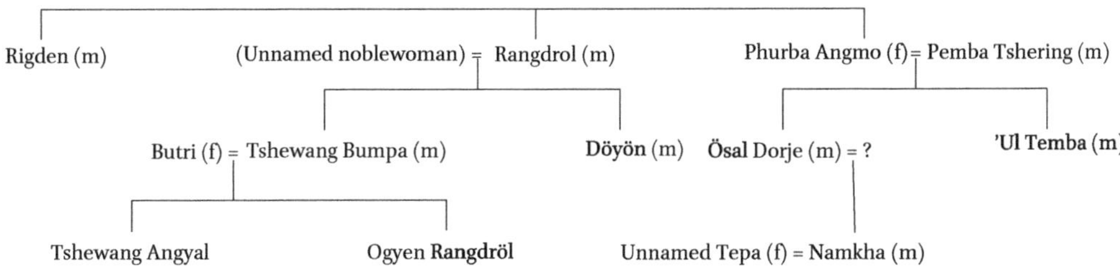

FIGURE 12.1 Three generations of the priestly Clan of the Kings of Sikkim, reconstructed from documents from Tshognam

liability for a religious cooperative". The phrase *gha sti rtsu rman* is discussed below. He later adds that "for the past six or seven generations we have had to make payments for a religious cooperative to his Majesty's government, and I have been being paying [this] rent to the village" (*Tibetan Sources 2*: HMA/LTshognam/Tib/27, p. 120). While there is an extensive literature about *guṭhi* in Nepal, and particularly among the Newars of the Kathmandu Valley,[9] to the best of my knowledge the status of the category in Buddhist highland areas has not yet been the subject of any research, and we must make do with the few documents available to us.

At this point we may make a brief digression from the development of the family quarrel to try to identify the category of government taxes that Tshewang Angyal and Gönpa Gang convent were paying. Tshewang Angyal refers to the payments that his family had been making as *gyal Zzhabs*[10] *rinoe'i* (*rin po che'i*) *rti ro dang sgo krid la phogs pa'i gha sti rtsu rman*, and later as *sgo kris sti ro* (*ibid.*: 119, lines 5, 9). While *sgo khrid* and *sgo kris* clearly represent the Nepali *guṭhi*, *gha sti rtsu man* and *sti ro* are worth our attention. *sTi ro* is the Nepali term *tiro*, which Turner defines as "payment; fare; rent". *Gha sti rtsu man* appears in variant forms in two documents from Tshug, where it is apparently something separate from the annual 10-rupee payment that the convent of Gönpa Gang was required to make:

> A document concerning the obligation to pay the *rtsu ma ṇi* [tax]. Regarding the arrival of the person who collects the *rtsu ma ṇi* of the great nation for a period of one year ...[11]

---

9 See, for example, Regmi 1976: 629–843; Toffin 2007: 289–315 and *passim*.

10 As noted above, the capital Z that prefixes certain terms in the transliteration of documents stands for the honorific *che rtags* symbol, resembling the Tibetan number 7.

11 *rtsu ma ṇi byang dgos kyi ra shi bkrad don la / don skres 'di lo——1 brgyal khab chen po'i rtsu sma ṇi bdu mi sleb sten dkor* ... (*Tibetan Sources 3*: HMA/KCh/01, lines 1–2).

> Regarding the fiscal liability of our convent, Gönpa Gang: it is a convent for which we must collectively pay varieties of taxes including this *gha rdi* [and] *tsu ma ṇi.*[12]
>
> We nuns of the four communities have been collectively responsible for whatever [dues] there may be, such as *bhis thun, tsu ma ṇi* and *gha sdi.*[13]

In the light of the document from 1910 cited above—probably also written by Tshewang Angyal—in which the family are described as "exempt from taxation" (*khral med*), it may be significant that in this 1912 petition he seems to be assiduously avoiding the use of the term "tax"; the *guṭhi* payments are described either as *tiro*—payment, or rent—or by their particular names. This is in contrast to the documents from Gönpa Gang convent, cited above, in which the *gha rdi tsu ma ṇi* is explicitly described as a category of tax (*phral rig* < *khral rigs*).

Elsewhere I have suggested that *tsu ma ṇi/rtsu rman*, etc.

> probably stands for the word *cumān*(*i*), "kissing", and *gha sti/gha sdi* for *gaddi*, "throne". Until further information is available, we may conclude tentatively that these are all categories of taxes or other payments on religious estates that were considered at least partly to be symbolic gestures of loyalty or subservience to the Nepalese Crown.
>
> *Tibetan Sources 3*: 152

"Further information" has indeed since become available, making it necessary to revise this suggestion. A document of 1906 from the archive of Geling, a large village situated immediately to the north of Baragaon, opens with a resolution about the course of action the community should take "if a sealed document from the royal palace should arrive this year requiring us to pay *'gu ru bdu pa* and *tshu sma ni*, those two …".[14]

---

12 *nged dgon gang gis dgon pa la phral babs——brgyal Zzhab porien (rin po che'i) /gha rdi tsu ma ṇi 'di sogs gis / phral rig rnyaṃ la byang dgos pa'i dgon pa yin* (*Tibetan Sources 3*: HMA/KCh/37, p. 146, lines 14–15).

13 *bhis thun tsu ma ṇi / gha sdi sogs gang byung skyang / ngos yul khags bzhi yis byo mo snyaṃ la 'khur dgos …* (*Tibetan Sources 3*: HMA/KCh/37, p. 152, lines 16–17). The Nepali term to which *bhis thun* corresponds is not clear, but may be connected to *beṭh*, "Rent for land paid in kind" (Turner 1931).

14 *'di lo 'gu ru bdu pa dang tshu sma ni gnyis phe ri a ṇa byang dgos gsung pa'i rgyal khang phyags rtaṃ slebs na …* (MA/Geling/080, lines 3–4).

While the meaning of *phe ri a ṇa* immediately after the two above-mentioned terms in the resolution is not certain, it is clear at least that *'gu ru bdu* and *tshu sma ni* refer to two types of taxes that the people of Geling feared might be imposed on them. A clue to the identity of these taxes and also that of the *ga sdi* mentioned earlier may be the detail that they are levied by the royal palace. According to Regmi, there was a category of taxes known as Raja-Anka, which were "meant exclusively for the use of the royal palace", and these "included the Gadimubarak, levied on the occasion of a royal coronation, the Goddhuwa, levied during the marriage of the eldest royal princess, the Chumawan, levied during the sacred thread investiture ceremony of the Crown Prince, and the Godan, which was meant to be used to finance gifts of cows on special occasions such as funeral ceremonies of members of the royal family" (Regmi 1976: 856, 858, 864).[15]

The terms *ga dhi/ga sdi, cu man/tshu man* and *gu ru bdu pa* almost certainly refer respectively to the Gadimubarak, the Chumawan and the Goddhuwa taxes. Just how the amounts in question were determined throughout the country was somewhat arbitrary, as the particular examples cited by Regmi suggest. If the sums demanded of Gönpa Gang and other religious institutions were relatively modest, this is likely to have been because of a special concession for monasteries and convents, but they were certainly not specific to religious foundations, as the document from Geling makes clear.[16]

Let us return now to the family quarrel. Even if it is true that, as Tshewang Angyal claimed, the main household (*grong pa*)[17] had been paying all local and national dues on the dependency inherited by his cousin Namkha and his uncle (Namkha's father) Ösal Dorje, there were other payments to the village for which the occupants of the dependency were personally responsible: taxes on the fields that Ösal Dorje had acquired as private property. As the natural son of the sister of the lama who occupied the household, he inherited no land

15 The glossary of an unpublished work by the late Madhav Lal Karmacharya lists the term *cumāuni*, which is defined as "tax paid for the sacred thread ceremony of a monarch" (Karmacharya n.d.: 68).

16 An attempt to impose the Chumawan on Geling had already been made in 1903, but the village succeeded in securing an exemption, and even a reduction in their existing tax payments, since it was able to demonstrate convincingly that its fiscal burden was already intolerable (MA/Geling/Tib/133).

17 In other publications I have generally translated the term *grong pa* as "estate", since it denotes not just a dwelling and a family but an associated area of agricultural land as well as a set of civic rights and responsibilities, and to this extent corresponds to the Western Tibetan *khang chen*. However, since the term "estate" is primarily used in the present volume to translate the Tibetan *gzhis ka*, I have rendered *grong pa* as "household" in order to avoid confusion.

but managed to purchase numerous fields over the course of his life. Between 1886 and 1888, he was involved in a protracted legal dispute with the village in defence of his claim that he should be exempt from these taxes. As the conclusion of a lengthy document in which he itemises all the expenses he had incurred over the duration of the case, he observes that:

> After returning sixteen years' worth of taxes to the people of Tshug, paying it at the rate of the government tax, in grain, according to village custom, the matter was just about settled.[18]

Unfortunately, we do not know whether the taxes in question were for the local community or for the government. We may tentatively conclude, however, that they were in the latter category: grain taxes within villages are generally referred to as *sa 'gro*, rather than *khral*; and furthermore, the fields of the main household were presumably exempt from this category of taxes because of its *guṭhi* status, and it may be that Ösal Dorje had been claiming similar exemption for his own fields on the grounds that he was part of the household.

The fiscal status of the dependency became a major issue again in the following generation, when Ösal Dorje's son, Namkha, brought a legal claim that he was entitled to inherit it. The claim was at first successful, and his cousin Tshewang Angyal, the head of the main household, was even imprisoned for a while, but the court's decision was subsequently overturned, resulting in a dramatic reversal of Namkha's fortunes. Tshewang Angyal and his supporters forcibly evicted Namkha and his family from the house and set a new lock on the door. But—according to Namkha's testimony—the measures taken by Tshewang Angyal and his family did not stop there:

> As a result of the machinations [of Tshewang Angyal and his family], and through no fault of our own, the people of Tshug have taken us out of the "internal tax" (*nang khral*) category and placed us in the "external tax" (*phyi khral*) class. [Tshewang Angyal] is planning to remain in the internal category, but this should not be allowed. Whether our two households are in the "internal" or the "external" class—we have always been in the internal tax category—but now because of him, we have been placed in the external tax group, while he is in the internal category. If I am indeed not his inferior in any respect, on the basis of the court's investigation,

18 *tshug yul pa la / lo ngo bcu drug gi phral klog nas zhing thog yul srol gis zhung phral ltar sbyang nas thags mchod rtsam byung /* (*Tibetan Sources 2*: HMA/UTshognam/Tib/14, pp. 173, 175, lines 42–44).

> since the two of us have always both been in the internal tax category, so now, too, whether it is a matter of being in the "external" or the "internal" class, may the law decide that we are in the same bracket.[19]

The law decided against Namkha, and he and his family moved to the neighbouring village of Te, where his father already had a number of patrons.

For the present, we have no documents that might shed light on what the terms "internal tax" (*nang khral*) and "external tax" (*phyi khral*) might have signified in Mustang in the early 20th century. It is at least clear from the context that the latter was a disadvantageous category. Since we know that the main household was classified as a *guṭhi* and probably paid only the dues for which a religious institution was liable to the government, it is probably safe to conclude that *nang khral* referred only to taxes paid to the community of Tshug itself. This would be broadly consistent with the meaning of the term in Central Tibet during the period of the Ganden Phodrang, where *nang khral* denoted goods and services (*lag don* and *rkang 'gro*) paid to or performed for one's immediate lord, whether monastic or private/aristocratic, while *phyi khral* referred to those destined to the Central Government.[20]

5 The Lamas of the Shari Pungita Clan

In addition to the household in Upper Tshognam that had been occupied by Lama Ösal Dorje, Te had another priestly household on its territory, in an area called Baza. This house had been abandoned after the death of its last occupant, and in 1893 the community of Te invited a family from a priestly lineage to take up residence here. The lama in question, actually a physician (*am chi*) who had probably been trained in Nubri, was the natural son of a headman of Dzar, in the Muktinath Valley, who belonged to a lineage called Shari Pungita (Sha ri dPon rgyud pa). Leaving his eldest and youngest sons in the family home

---

19 *da cha khoo'i* (*kho bo'i*) *byus ngan byas rkyen ngos skyon med la tshugs yul pas nang phral nas phyir ston / khoo* (*kho bo*) *nang 'dad rtsis byas mi phyogs cing / ngos gnyis phyi nang gang byas kyang sngon nas da* {*da*} *bar nang phral la dus yod pa la / da cha khoo* (*kho bo*) *dbang gi ngos phyi phral dang khoo* (*kho bo*) *nang la cugs dugs na / nged gnyis las don gang byas kyang khong las nga zhen pa mdi dugs na / dgongs bka' khrim nas bzhibs dpyad snang nas ngos gnyis sngon nas da bar nang phral gcig pa yod pas da cha yang phyi nang gang byas kyang bka' khrim nas phral rigs gcig pa la bcugs nas snang thabs mkhyeeen* (*mkhen mkhyen mkhyen*) / (*Tibetan Sources 2*: HMA/UTshognam/Tib/33, pp. 247–48).

20 For more on the categories *nang khral* and *phyi khral*, see the articles by Peter Schwieger and Kalsang Norbu Gurung in this volume.

near Muktinath, Amchi Tshewang (Tshe dbang) accepted the Tepas' invitation and settled in Baza with his wife and their middle son, Namgyal (rNam rgyal). According to the agreement that was drawn up, the family would pay an annual rent of one *se khal* (a local term for *gyang bo*, about 46 litres) of barley for the fields that were attached to their household and for irrigation rights, but would be exempt from all taxes.[21] The terms of their tenancy, then, seem to have been much the same as those on which the priestly family of Lower Tshognam, and presumably that of Upper Tshognam too (though we have no documentation to confirm this) occupied their respective households.

6 Lubrak: The Changing Fiscal Fortunes of a Priestly Community

The next case I would like to consider here is a small Bönpo village, Lubrak (Klu brag), situated in a valley south of and parallel to the Muktinath Valley. The village, a community of hereditary Bönpo lamas, has been the subject of numerous studies,[22] and since our concern here is with the history of its fiscal status it will be sufficient to offer a very general outline of the relevant features of its history and institutions by way of an introduction.

The main importance of Lubrak for the Bön religion lies in the fact that it was founded by a member of the well-known Yangal (Ya ngal) lineage in the early 13th century, and remained a stronghold of the clan until its last member died in the late 19th century (see above). The Yangal household was preserved intact by another family, and the clan itself continues to flourish in several villages in Dolpo. The village at present comprises ten households (*grong pa*), some of which are divided into subsidiary households (designated by different terms according to their status).

Lubrak stands on the southern side of the Pandak River (see Map 12.1), but the original settlement was located in a cave complex in cliffs on the north side. The inhabitants were speakers of a non-Tibetan language—they are referred to as "demons" (*srin po*) in the pious narratives—and the historic "founding" of Lubrak by the Yangal clan actually entailed the establishment, in an existing settlement, of a Bönpo household and temple that later became a magnet for other Bönpo priests from the north, who founded their own residential temples at the site.

---

21 A brief account of this family is given in Ramble 2008: 162–68. The document in question is published in *Tibetan Sources 2*: HMA/UTshognam/Tib/37.

22 For example Ramble 1984.

The Pandak River was, at certain periods in history, a territorial boundary marker between shifting political configurations to the north and south. Although the later literary tradition and oral accounts—which may well have reinforced each other—have it that the original Yangal foundation was south of the river, it is far from certain that this is actually so. In fact, the existence of a plastered and whitewashed wall inside one of the caves suggests that there was once a temple on the northern side. (Other caves in the complex are used to this day for retreats by the lamas and outsiders.) In any event, either the founding lama or one of his descendants decided to establish a residential temple on the south bank. This land used to lie on the territory of a polity called Thini. Modern Thini is a small settlement that has been eclipsed by its former satellite, Jomsom, which is now the administrative centre of Mustang District. In the past, however, it was the centre of a polity that subsumed several other communities in the area, including Marpha, Cimang and Syang, among others. Until the end of the 17th century, the subordinate status of these satellites was expressed in the form of taxes that they had to pay in kind and in labour.

The main source for our knowledge of the history of these settlements at this early period is a document, known as a *'bem chag*, that exists in different versions in Marpha, Cimang and Thini itself. It is actually a compilation of accounts, some apparently written and others oral, relating to events from different periods. Regarding the taxation of the satellites, we are told about Marpha that

> For the people of Marpha to plough the fields of King Thangmigcen [of Thini], ten young men shall come bringing their own oxen and bringing their own ploughs, yokes and implements, and ten women shall come to do the weeding. Ten young men shall come for the harvest time.[23]

The same text further claims that the two villages of Phelag and Dangkardzong had to pay Thini nine large baskets of meat annually, while the settlement of Sangdak, near Dolpo, provided eight buck goats in their second year (Ramble and Vinding 1987: 32). The text also has an intriguing passage about Lubrak:

> Previously, the village of Lubrak did not exist. The Bönpo Lama Yangtön came from Dolpo and asked the headman of [Thini]... to give him a piece

23 *mar pa'i rgyal pos sdong rmig spyan kyis zhing mod be la rang gi glang rang gi khyer de rang gis thongs pa dang nya shing rang gi ca la rang khyer de khyogs tong cu yong gyu yin / yur ma yur pa'i bu me cu 'ong gyu yin / ton thag byed pa'i dus gsu khyogs tong cu 'ong gyu yin no /* (Old Thini *'bem chag*, cited in Ramble and Vinding 1987: 32, fn. 103).

> of land. The headman ... gave him the land of Lubrak. The Bönpo lama Yangtön settled there.
>
> *ibid.*: 18

In fact the founder of Lubrak did not come from Dolpo, but one of his nephews did go there to found a settlement, and the Yangal clan, as stated above, is widely associated with Dolpo. It is therefore not clear whether the lama in the *'bem chag* is actually the founder himself, whose provenance is erroneously given as Dolpo because of this association, or a later figure who came to ask for land on behalf of the clan. Whatever the case, Thini agreed to the lama's request, and gave Lubrak the land. In contrast with the relatively onerous taxes demanded of its other satellites, Thini's fiscal demands on Lubrak were extremely light:

> "We won't demand any taxes—just come", they said. "Give us 3 *zo ba* (4.6 litres) of *buboli* (*bu bo li*) berries from Thini's Latak Hill". [Lubrak] also gave three bundles (?) of birch bark and a small basket of wild chives.[24]

The items specified in this document are all natural products that grow in abundance in the forest that Thini had given Lubrak, and apart from the symbolic weight this would have lent them, their provision would have represented no hardship at all.[25] What exactly Lubrak had to pay Thini varies slightly across some of the *'bem chag*—in the Cimang version, for example, the birch bark is replaced by two measures of barley—but the point is the same: that Lubrak's status as a priestly community exempted it from the burdensome requirements demanded by Thini of its other dependencies.

While the items that Lubrak was required to pay were too insignificant in material terms to qualify as *khral*, their symbolic importance as an expression of political allegiance should not be underestimated. Thini's eastern boundary

---

24 *Phral phri yang mi za shogs bsung pas / gsum pa'i ga la tags la lo re re la bu bo li zo ba sum rnang gsungs so / stags pa'i lags 'drus ka les gsum dang dzum bu bags dang gang snang ngo /* (*ibid.*: 31, fn. 103).

25 The pronunciation of the word *buboli* varies from village to village, and the spelling is inconsistent in the different versions of the *'bem chag*. The bright-red berries, which are slightly smaller than a cherry and may be eaten fresh or dried, are from the tall shrub *Malus baccata*, which is actually a variety of apple. I am indebted to Monika Kriechbaum for this identification. *Dzimbu* (*'dzim bu*) may refer to either of two species of chives, *Allium przewalskianum* and *A. hypsistum*, that are widely used in cooking throughout Nepal. The bark of the Himalayan birch (*Betula utilis*) has numerous domestic uses, for example in forming one of the layers of flat mud roofs and for wrapping butter, as well as certain ritual functions.

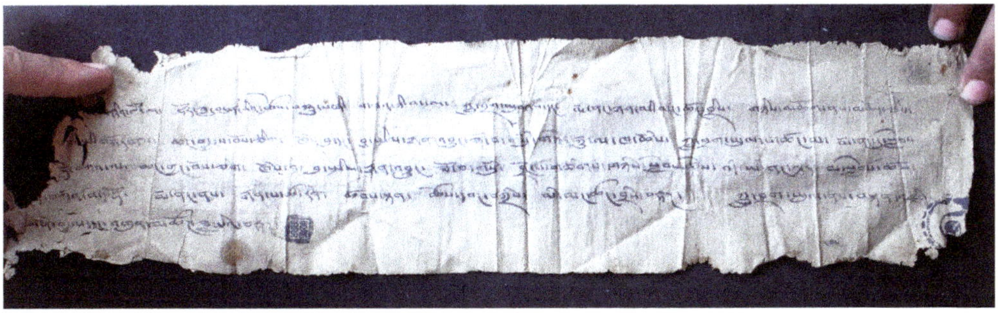

FIGURE 12.2 Undated document to Lubrak from Manang, probably mid-18th century
MA/LUBRAK/TIB/61

is marked by a high pass called the Meso Kanto, which crosses the watershed between the Kali Gandaki Valley to the west and the Marsyangdi to the east. Thini's eastern neighbour is Manang, also known as Nyeshang. The nature of the relationship between the two polities is not clear. In some versions of the *'bem chag* it is Manang that makes symbolic payments of commodities to Thini as a gesture of fealty, while other versions reverse the direction. Interestingly, the only documentary evidence we have from Lubrak itself concerning this tribute to its landlord makes it clear that the landlord in question was not Thini but Manang. The text of this—unfortunately undated—document runs as follows:

> [Lubrak] shall give 1 *gyang bo* of *chang*,[26] and 3 *zo ba* (4.6 litres) of either wild peaches or *buboli* (*bu spil*) berries, whichever one. [If] all the people of Lubrak come to Manang the settlement will be authorised (*sde bka'*), and if just one or two households [come with the] 1 *gyang bo* of *chang*, and 3 *zo ba* of either peaches or *buboli* berries, it will be the same [i.e. the settlement will be authorised]. But if they do not come, there will be no settlement authorisation.[27]

26 A *gyang bo* is a volumetric measure for dry goods corresponding to 30 *zo ba* (45.9 litres). A *gyang bo* of chang therefore denotes the quantity of beer that can be made from that volume of barley or wheat.

27 *klu brag yul pa dang / sma nang rgan mi mang tshang bris / gnyis mchog nas mchod rtsis* [±3S] *bskor la / chang brgyangs bos cig / khaṃs bu dang / bu spil rgan 'byung zo ba gsuṃ gter rgyu la kha chaṃs / klu brag yul pa tshang ma / sma nang du slebs /* [±2S] *sde bka' la / chang gyang bos cig / khaṃs bu / bu spil rgan 'byung zo ba gsuṃ / drong pa gcigs gnyis slebs tshes / 'di yi nang ltar / ma slebs tshes* [*sde?*] *bka' med sdo /* (MA/Lubrak/Tib/61; see Figure 12.2).

The tribute may have been symbolic, but it was nevertheless essential: failure to pay it would have been construed as a gesture of disloyalty for which Lubrak's priestly inhabitants would have forfeited their right to occupy the land.

We do not know when Lubrak ceased to pay this tribute to Manang or Thini, but at a certain point the community came unambiguously under the political authority of the dukes of the Muktinath Valley immediately to the north. During the Gorkha unification of Nepal, the *de facto* rule of this aristocratic coterie was formalised in an edict, issued in 1788 and confirmed in 1790, which gave them jurisdiction not only over Baragaon but also Manang:

> [We] issued, be it recalled, a [*lāl*]*mohar* in the past [lit. yesterday] to the effect that you should enjoy the *birtto* [of] Bahragāũ (Baragaon), Nar, and Manaṅ (Manang) along with the *jāgāt* of Kak, which you have enjoyed since olden times.
>
> PANT AND PIERCE 1989: 21

If Lubrak was indeed within the orbit of Manang immediately beforehand, as the previous document suggests, this is likely to have been the moment when it came under the direct rule of the dukes of Baragaon.

7 The Loss of Priestly Tax Privileges

There are no local records that would enable us to know whether Lubrak continued to enjoy exemption from all but symbolic tax payments in the period after the unification and the early Rana era (which began in 1846). We know that by 1872, at least, the village was paying government taxes of some sort. In a will that she drew up in that year, a certain Chöndze Nyishar (Chos mdzad nyi shar), the last surviving member of the Yangal line that had founded the village, mentions her anxiety about finding an heir to her household who would be able to honour the obligation to pay *bzhes khral*, a term that invariably denotes taxes paid to the state (Ramble 2020). There is evidence to suggest that the amount the village was paying was suddenly increased in or around 1885. In 1857, the power traditionally enjoyed by Baragaon's hereditary rulers was curbed as a consequence of a policy introduced by the Rana regime. According to this scheme, known as *ijāra*, the right to collect revenues in certain parts of the country was auctioned off to the highest bidder. The successful bidder was often an outsider who had no connection with local cultural sensibilities and was concerned only to ensure as substantial as possible a return on his investment (Regmi 1978b: 81–83). This was demonstrated in Baragaon in 1863, six years after the implementation of the *ijāra* system. The violation of the traditional relationship between the rulers and subjects, especially with respect to unreasonably high demands in terms of goods and services, prompted a coordinated protest by all the communities of Baragaon in which the Rana Central Government had to intervene. The individuals who are singled out for criticism in the protest were actually a group of local aristocrats who were not the traditional rulers, but it is not certain whether these were the contractors themselves or merely the local representatives of an outsider (Ramble 2014).

From the mid-1880s onwards, two previously unseen categories of taxes make their appearance. One of these is the "Great Grain Tax" (*'bru khral chen mo*). This was apparently an annual levy, since two of the receipts are for consecutive years, 1905 and 1906. The components of this tax and the amounts are broadly similar in each case. In 1906, for example, Lubrak paid:

> Three *'bo khal* (61.2 litres) of wheat, 3 rupees for the national Dasain festival, 1 *'bo khal* (30.6 litres) of rice, 1 *zo ba* (1.53 litres) of salt, 1 rupee for *rgyab cha*, 1.5 rupees in lieu of a young goat, and 0.75 rupees as the cash equivalent of a quantity of butter equal in weight to 1 *zo ba* of barley.[28]

The other payment that appears at around that time is the Great Government Tax (*gzhung khral chen mo*). This levy was actually meant to be a grain tax. From 1916, the receipts are no longer in Tibetan but in Nepali. There are eight of these altogether, spanning the period from 1916 to 1956.[29] Out of seven of the receipts (in the earliest one the relevant information is missing due to damage), the tax is referred to as *sirto*, which Regmi defines as "tribute payable by a few categories of feudatory states to the government" (Regmi 1978a: 865). In the two others, it is referred to as *serma*, "tax on unmeasured Pakho holdings in the hill districts and Kathmandu Valley" (*ibid.*: 865), while *pakho*, in turn, is defined as "unirrigated land in the hill districts and Kathmandu Valley on which only maize, millet, ghaiya [a variety of rice] and other dry crops can be grown" (*ibid.*: 863).

Thus Lubrak's new land tax was assessed not on the basis of seed capacity or crop yields,[30] but according to some other system. It is likely that the government had determined a global figure that Baragaon had to pay, and that

28 MA/Lubrak/Tib/62; the meaning of the term *rgyab cha* is unclear.

29 The documents in question are SH/Lubrak/Nep/01, 02, 05–10; for the text and translations, see https://www.tibetanhistory.net/documents/mustang/lubrak-nepali.

30 This being said, actual grain yields do seem to have been taken into consideration in certain circumstances. In 1917, for example, after a particularly poor harvest, the village received a rebate of 6.25 rupees.

it was left up to the local rulers to decide how this burden was to be distributed across the eighteen communities that comprised it. Baragaon was divided into eight counties (*tsho*), with the larger villages (such as Te) being rated as a single county, and smaller communities as fractions ranging in size from one quarter to three quarters, and villages paid taxes in conformity with this rating. Lubrak had to pay 31.25 rupees, and since it was assessed as a quarter-county, the tax liability for a full county would have been 125 rupees, and therefore for Baragaon as a whole 1,000 rupees.[31]

The distribution of Baragaon's new tax burden on the basis of counties and sub-counties meant that any traditional tax-concessions Lubrak may have enjoyed were suddenly removed. Whatever the taxes were that Lubrak had to pay from the 1880s on, we know that they were without precedent, since the document in which the villagers registered their protest states that the taxes had been imposed "even though there had been no such custom in the past". When these taxes were first announced, the lamas flatly refused to pay, arguing that the measure contravened a time-honoured tradition. But the authorities insisted: they presented the village with a bill for 50 rupees in arrears, and declared that, in the event of failure to cooperate they would send bailiffs to confiscate property to the value of the unpaid taxes from a randomly-chosen house. The Lubrakpas, in turn, stiffened their resistance and resolved among themselves that if the bailiffs did descend on someone's house, the owners would be compensated for their losses from the village fund (Ramble 2013: 242).

But there was clearly little point in resisting, and in the absence of any apparent support from the rest of Baragaon, Lubrak had no choice but to accept its fiscal demotion to the status of a commoner village.

31 Thanks to a document from Geling we know that this figure is commensurate with what other communities in region were paying at the time. Until 1904, Geling's annual tax payment to the government was so high—300 rupees—that nine out of twenty-three of the village's households had been abandoned, and the others were heavily in debt. The incumbent headman, Taklha (sTag lha) (about whom more will be said below), argued that Geling should pay the same rate as in Tsharka (Dolpo) and Lo, where each household paid an annual tax of 3.20 rupees and the headman paid double. The appeal was successful, and the taxes for the community as a whole were reduced to 48.28 rupees, a figure that corresponds almost exactly to what we would expect for fourteen estates, if the fiscal liability of one of them (that of the headman) were doubled (MA/Geling/Tib/133).

8 Fiscal Concessions for a New Priestly Household in Geling

About the time that the *ijāra* system came into operation, one member of the community was singled out for special fiscal concessions precisely because of his priestly lineage. The private chaplains of the Kings of Lo belonged to a family named Drangsong (Drang srong), whose original seat is said to have been the small settlement named Jaragang (Bya ra sgang) a short distance to the west of Mönthang (sMon thang), the capital city of Lo.[32] One of the clans in Lubrak is named Jaragang, and claims to be a branch of the same clan. Around the middle of the 19th century, the King of Lo arranged for a young man of the family, named Shilok (Shi log), to marry an heiress from Geling and to act as his private chaplain. The Jaragang/Drangsong family in Lo Monthang continued to provide chaplains until the 1950s or 1960s, so if the king thought it necessary to turn to an outsider, we can only surmise that there had been a temporary problem—such as the premature death of a serving chaplain. The edict contains the following passage:

> Since Drangsong Shilok, the holder of a Bönpo lineage from Lubrak, is to come here as the husband of Palzang (dPal bzang) [who dwells] at the main entrance of Geling, in our dominion, and will now be the royal chaplain of Lo, he shall be sent up here. No taxes whatsoever—such as transportation duty, making beer for the community (*chug rlum*), constabulary duty, milling grain for the community (*dras khal*), gathering community firewood (*si shing*) or acting as long-distance or short-distance messenger—shall be imposed on [the household of his future wife] Palzang of Geling.[33]

32 The actual family name is Awa ('A pha), but the lineage is more widely known either by the name of its provenance, Jaragang, or its priestly function: the term *drang srong* is the Bönpo equivalent of the Buddhist *dge slong*, a fully-ordained monk, but in the present case is presumably derived from its more general meaning as "sage".

33 *§ glo po bsrid 'dzin dpal bgyis gzim chung pho brang nas rang bzhabs su khod pa'i dger lung rgyas 'go'i dpal bzang la za zla klu brag bon gyud 'dzin pa'i bdrang srong shi log sleb 'dug par / de da lta glo bsrid 'dzin che mo'i dbu lha gsol par dgos 'dug pas / yar brdzong dgos dang / dger lung dpal bzang mo la 'u lag / chug rlum̩ / do ram̩ / bras khal / si shing / ri lag / thug lag / gang yang bskal mi mchog pa'i dpal kyi gzim chung pho brang nas bsrid 'dzin nas lung pa'i khral 'og bdu 'chud pa'i tham̩ ka / (seal of the community of Geling)* / (MA/Geling/Tib/127; see Figure 12.3). The meanings of the local terms *chug rlum*, *dras khal* and *si shing* were determined in the course of inquiries made in Geling.

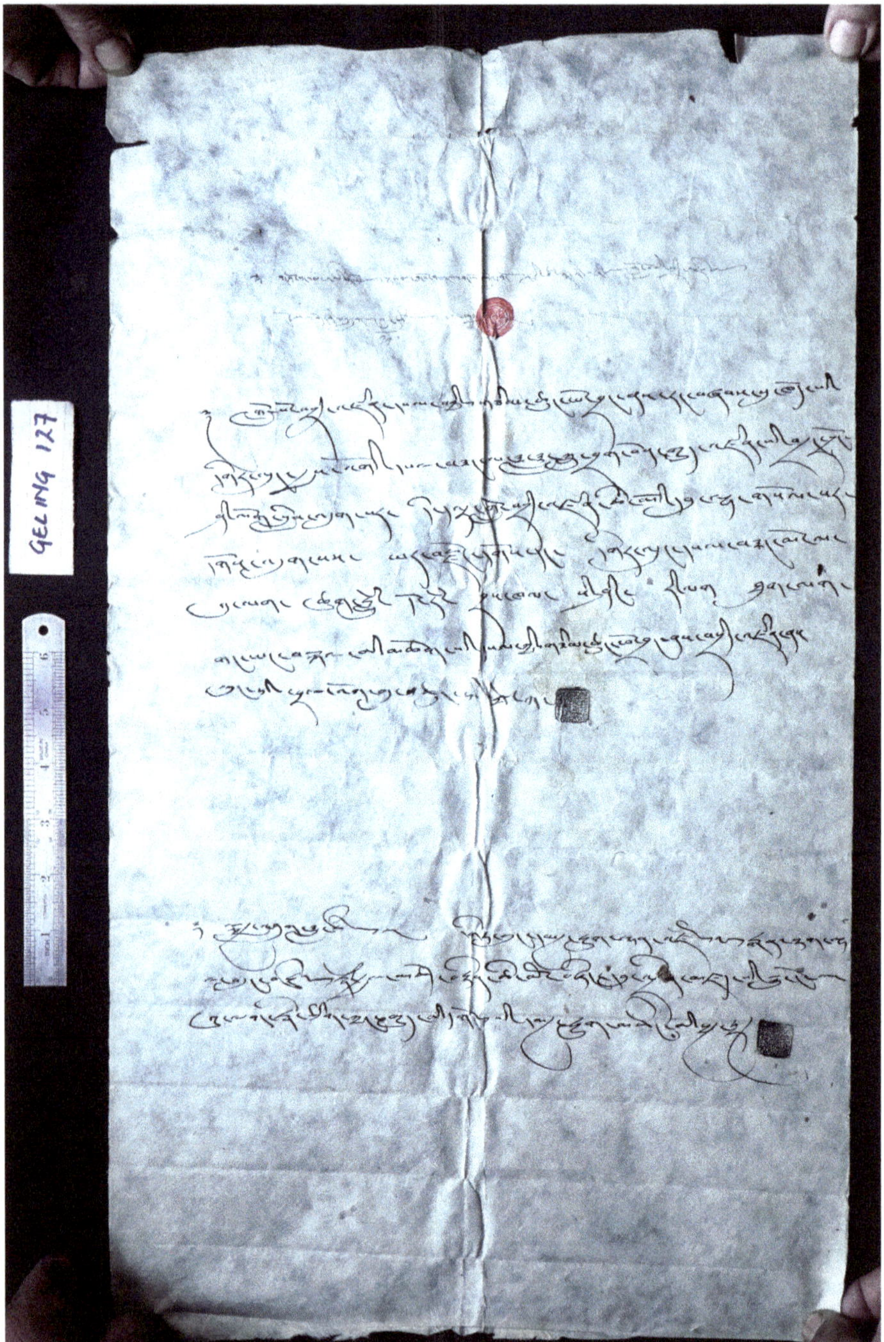

FIGURE 12.3 Copy of document from mid-19th century confirming tax exemption for a priestly family in Geling, Mustang
MA/GELING/TIB/127

The document is a copy that was made in 1964. It bears the seal of the community of Geling, and is preceded by a sealed certification by the King of Lo. Unfortunately, the date that the original would have borne is omitted, but Shilok is likely to have been invited from Lubrak around 1860. To this day, the house into which he married enjoys significant tax exemptions. The excerpt cited above makes no mention of the continuation of the concessions after Shilok's lifetime, and the privileges that the family enjoys now may derive at least in part from the time of Shilok's son, Taklha. Below the passage cited here is the text of another document, dated 1880, that concerns the construction of a new stupa. The entry specifies that Taklha and his heirs (*gdung 'dzin*) should not be liable for any communal labour (*'u lag*). The wording is ambiguous, since it may mean either that Taklha and his sons are exempt from the particular task of helping to build the stupa, or else that he and *all* his descendants should be exempted from such chores in perpetuity. In fact it seems more likely that the 1880 addition was merely an extension of the status accorded to Shilok's household, because Taklha was awarded tax-free privileges in his own right less than a decade later. From 1885 to 1888 he served as the headman of the community—one of several stints—and achieved such benefits for the common good that the villagers decided to reward him for his services with a gift of cash and grain. However, when he declined these, apparently letting it be known that he considered his contribution to be worth more than that, the villagers granted him and his family exemption from a number of onerous duties for three generations (MA/Geling/Tib/099). It may be this arrangement that has been perpetuated—for a further three generations—to the present day. From his time the status of headman came to be a hereditary one, and the incumbency alternates between two households inhabited by Taklha's descendants. The privileged status the family enjoys now may be the result of a dual legacy: first, the exemptions granted to Shilok, the founder of the line, in recognition of his priestly function, and secondly those that were won by his son Taklha for services to the community.[34]

34 As mentioned above, in 1904, Taklha managed to negotiate a significant reduction in the crippling taxes that the village had to pay—to less than a sixth of the former figure—and this can only have served to cement his position as a community treasure (MA/Geling/Tib/133).

9 The Afterlife of the Great Government Tax in Lubrak

The so-called "Great Government Tax" was not of course a tax like a *guṭhi* payment that was specifically intended for religious institutions. Its significance in the present context lies precisely in the fact that its imposition across Baragaon contributed to the erosion of the special fiscal status that Lubrak had enjoyed since its foundation. If Lubrak objected to it so strenuously, that is no doubt as much because of the implications for its social standing in the enclave as out of material considerations. Still, at 31.25 rupees per annum, the demand would have amounted to over 3 rupees per household, which was by no means a negligible sum at that time.

As a community of householder-lamas, Lubrak has a ritual cycle comprising some twenty ceremonies that are performed over the course of the year in the village temple. Each ceremony is perpetuated by its own endowment fund, known as *sbyor 'jags*. Put simply, contributions for a new ceremony are collected from donors from inside and outside the community, and distributed among the lamas. The lamas use this cash as capital in their trading ventures. They must give goods (flour, grain, oil and so forth) to the value of 10 per cent per annum of this capital for the performance of the ceremony, and any profit they make above that figure they are entitled to keep for themselves. Since the capital is never returned to the investor, it is understood that the latter will receive annual merit corresponding to the value of this interest in perpetuity, either for him- or herself or for a designated beneficiary.

In all the archives of Mustang and Dolpo I have had an opportunity to examine, the term *sbyor 'jags* refers almost without exception to an endowment for a religious ceremony. There is only one case of which I am aware in which the term denotes a fund that was to be used not for spiritual but for social benefit, and that case concerns the Great Government Tax in Lubrak.

In 1947, five of the wealthiest lamas in the village decided to set up an endowment fund that would generate exactly enough interest each year to cover the cost of the annual tax. The text of the document runs as follows:

> Document concerning the government tax. Friday, the 13th day of the 12th month in a Fire-Pig Year. As the principal for the Great Government Tax of Lubrak, Lama Angyal has given 100 rupees; Rabgye has given 100 rupees; Tsomchogkyab has given 50 rupees; Tshering Tenzin has given 50 rupees; Pema Angdü has given 15 rupees. They have given this as an endowment. This makes a total of 315 rupees. The government tax should be paid on the basis of an exact calculation of the interest. The government tax must be paid every year from the hands of the stewards. These stewards must hold office for two years per pair, and they should settle

FIGURE 12.4 Agreement to create an endowment with which to pay the annual government tax of Lubrak
SH/LUBRAK/TIB/036

> the accounts on the 24th day of the 11th month. One should not say about this matter "I skidded on the meadow and was snagged in the forest". It has been decided that it should be paid without a shortfall of even one peanut, and the document is ratified by being passed from hand to hand among the members of the community of Lubrak. It has been decided that the two stewards shall receive a fee of 6 *ṭam* (3 rupees) at the end of two years. The people who convey the taxes shall take it in turns to go [as arranged during] the meeting.[35]

Had she been alive, the above-mentioned Yangal nun Chöndze Nyishar, who had fretted in her will about whether her heir would be able to pay the government

35 The unedited text of the document is as follows: *me mo phags lo zla 12 ba tshe 13 res za 6 nyin [1S] [klu] brag yul gi zhung phral che mo gyu bstan la / bla ma dbang rgyal gi dngul—100 rab rgyad db= [1S] nas dngul—100 / rtsoṃgs (rtso mchogs) kyab nas dngul—50 / tshe ring bsten^in nas dngul—50 / padma dbang [=dud] nas dngul—15 / 'di byar phyog snang ba yin / dom par / dngul 315 / suṃ rgya dang bco snga / kyed nas sas rtsi nas zhung phral sbyang gos yin / 'di snyer ba gnyis phyags nas / lo rim zhin zhung phral byang gos yin / los ngos gnyis gnyis snyer pa gnyis 'dzin zhing/ zla ba 11 tshe 24 rtsi krad gyu mchod / 'di la spang la brad song dang nag la thog song zer sa med/ ba ṭaṃ 1 cig kyang chad med bdu byang gyu mchod pa klu brags yul pa spyi la kor rtags / snyer pa gnyis la los ngos gnyis nas ṭaṃ drug drug bla cha ter rgyu mchod pa yin / {1S} phral kyal mi dzoṃ pa'i kas nas gro rgyu yin kris (kra shis) dpal par dzaṃ rling rgyan bdu byon* / (SH/Lubrak/Tib/036; see Figure 12.4).

tax, would surely have been happy to see that the greatest share of this endowment came from her own household: Lama Angyal and Pema Angdü were respectively the grandson and great-grandson of the young man whom she had chosen as her heir.

The operation of this fund differed in certain significant respects from those associated with religious ceremonies. To begin with, the fund was not distributed across the community to anyone who wished for an injection of capital. It was used by the stewards themselves, who held this responsibility for two years before passing it on to their successors according to a strictly-observed household-based roster. Ten per cent of the total would have yielded 31.50 rupees, which would have left a balance of 25 paise minus 4 paise for a government stamp that the Nepali receipts record as having been paid. The remaining 21 paise would not have been enough to generate the 6 rupees that the two stewards were paid at the end of their two-year term of office, and we may assume that their stipend was taken from the village fund to recompense them for managing the investment on behalf of the community.

The last receipt for the Great Government Tax in Lubrak's archives is dated 1956, and it is likely that the category was abolished altogether as part of the tax reforms that were being undertaken in Nepal at that time. It is therefore no small surprise to find that the fund was still being maintained in much the same way more than three decades later. In the Lubrak archive there are two documents containing short entries for each year in which the stewardship of the fund rotated. The date of the first occasion is given as 1968, and the last as 1992. Since the form of all the entries is very similar, we may take just the first as an example before discussing the significance of the series.

> Saturday, the 25th day of the 11th month in the male Earth-Monkey Year. The purpose of writing this loan document is as follows. Regarding the Great Government Tax of Lubrak, the two borrowers Tshewang Trashi and Tenzin, who live in Lubrak, have taken a loan of exactly 315 rupees. It has been decided that, from next year on, they should each year pay a sum calculated on the basis of 10 to 100. Tshewang Trashi willingly sets his thumbprint in confirmation; Tenzin willingly sets his thumbprint in confirmation. After three years have passed, they shall receive a fee of 5 *ṭam* each. The total will be 10 *ṭam* [5 rupees].[36]

36 The unedited text of the document is as follows: *sa pho spres lo tshesl* (*zla tshes*) *nyin 11 25 o / brtam zug yi gi 'bri don la / don rtsa klu 'brags yul gi bzhung 'bral che mo 'di / klu 'brags yul nang la 'dod mi a sa mi tshe dbang bkra shis dang brten 'dzin gnyis la dngul 315 gsuṃ cos lnga thaṃ pa bun yod bzhin / gsang lo kyed rgya la cu kur tsi nis lo ltar 'byang rgyul chod pa*

This entry, like all the others in the series, differs from the original text of 1947 in a number of respects. First, the two fund managers are no longer referred as "stewards" (*gnyer pa*), but as *a sa mi*, a Nepali term—*asāmi*—meaning "borrower" or "debtor". Likewise, the document itself is referred to as a *brtam zug*, reproducing the Nepali *tamsuk* or *tamasuk*, a receipt for a loan. The total endowment of 315 rupees is not described as *sbyor 'jags* but simply as *bun*, a loan or a debt. The period of incumbency of the two managers has been increased from two to three years—something that is reflected in the intervals between the entries—while the sum with which they are recompensed has been raised from 3 rupees to 5 rupees each.

Setting up the endowment fund to pay the government tax in 1947 was clearly a charitable act, motivated by a civic-minded concern for the less well-off households in Lubrak. Since the donors were not expecting to recover any interest on the original capital, there was no material benefit in it for them. That the scheme should have been formulated in terms of an endowment for a religious ceremony is consistent with the underlying principle of investing capital to alleviate the sufferings of others and to accrue intangible benefits for oneself—in this case, perhaps social prestige rather than merit in a more conventional sense.

The 1964 reformulation of the scheme marks a sort of secularisation of the endowment. Since the Great Government Tax had been abolished, the very rationale for the fund—to ease the tax burden on less well-off villagers—had evaporated. The endowment had effectively been transformed into a means of raising cash for the village fund, and its inevitable obsolescence—it was abandoned soon after 1992—arose from the fact that it had been created in order to generate precisely 31.25 rupees per annum, a sum that did not vary for over sixty years. Contributions to endowments for religious ceremonies are made in cash, but the interest is paid in the same quantities of commodities—grain, butter and so forth—that the cash would have purchased at the time the endowment was originally made. Thus an endowment of a few rupees made in the 19th century (and there were many) continues to generate substantial amounts of comestibles as the basis for calendrical rituals. In contrast, by 1992 the cash interest on the endowment of 312 rupees that had been made in 1947 was not worth the trouble of maintaining the fund.

---

yin don 'di la mi 'rgyur pa tshes dbang bkra shis slo bseṃ rang thags rtags / the 'ung stags / bstan 'dzin slo bseṃs rang thad gi the 'ung rtags / lo gsuṃ gsong nas bla bya ṭaṃ phyed lnga lnga kred rgyu yin / sdom ṭaṃ [*d*]*gu yin* / (SH/Lubrak/Tib/017).

10 Conclusion

The scope of the present article has been constrained primarily by the documents it has been possible to obtain in the course of field research. The relative sparseness of sources that might tell us more about the changing fiscal obligations of Buddhist and Bönpo religious establishments means that our understanding of this situation is still very limited. This is particularly the case with monasteries and convents, for which we currently have information from just one archive. Nevertheless, on the evidence of a few documents contained in this collection, we know that all the Buddhist establishments in Baragaon had fiscal obligations to the national government, at least during the Rana period; that they were organised into clusters with equal tax liabilities, and that this tax burden was shared among their component establishments according to their economic capacity. We also know that these monasteries and convents were not exempt from the irregular taxes—those in the Raja-Ankha category—that were levied on certain occasions for the benefit of Nepal's royal family.

While there remain considerable lacunae in our knowledge of the fiscal status of Buddhist and Bönpo householder-priests in Mustang, we have a wide enough range of sources at our disposal to be able to make certain general observations. As we might expect, the tax liabilities of such priests were inversely proportional to the esteem in which they were held by the fiscal authorities. The lamas of Lower Tshognam (in Tshug), Baza (in Te) and Geling were all exempted from paying taxes by the village communities on whose territory they lived. In the case of Lower Tshognam, these privileges were not extended to the household inhabited by Lama Ösal Dorje and his son Namkha, partly because this was a dependency of the main household and perhaps partly also because these lamas did not have the priestly "bone"—the patrilineal transmission—that defined the Clan of the Kings of Sikkim. The status of the main household was also recognised by the King of Lo, who exempted the lamas of Tshognam from tariffs that he would have been entitled to exact.

The community of Lubrak seems to have originated in much the same way as these more northerly examples: as a priestly family establishing itself on the territory of a large community, and being exempted from taxes by the ruling authority, in this case Thini. The status was maintained even after the founding family had been joined by others, and the settlement had grown into a small village; it was even recognised by a more distant principality, Manang, that had an important political presence in this part of Mustang at some point. Lubrak's fiscal privileges may have been preserved when it came within the immediate jurisdiction of the Muktinath Valley, under the authority of the Gorkha rulers of Nepal, in the late 18th century, but they were removed soon after the implementation of the contractual *ijāra* system in the second half of the 19th century: the contractor, the *ijārdar*, was not only a Hindu operating within a regime that had little respect for Tibetan religions and their institutions, but had certainly paid handsomely for the position he held and would have wanted to make the most of any opportunity to maximise his investment.

Perhaps the most interesting aspect of one of the national taxes Lubrak had to pay, the *sirto rakam* or Great Government Tax (*gzhung khral chen mo*), amounting to an annual levy of 31.25 rupees, was the way in which it came to be reconceived by the community. A group of lamas assumed responsibility for the payment by creating an endowment fund (*sbyor 'jags*), the interest from which would amount to precisely the sum required. While this was on the one hand an act of civic-mindedness that would certainly have helped poorer households, it might also be understood as a way of recasting an imposition that had deprived the village of an important emblem of its priestly rank—exemption from taxes. Treating this tax like one of the many other endowments the village managed in order to perpetuate its annual cycle of rituals was tantamount to declaring that even if they had to pay this sum, they regarded it not as a demeaning tax but as a part of their time-honoured priestly function.

References

Carrasco, P. 1959. *Land and Polity in Tibet*. Seattle: University of Washington Press.

Harrison, J., C. Luczanits and C. Ramble, in collaboration with Nyima Drandul. 2018. *A Blessing for the Land: The Art and Architecture and History of Künzang Chöling Convent, Mustang, Nepal*. Kathmandu: Vajra Books.

Karmacharya, M.K. N.d. *Mustang Documents in the Nepali Language (1667–1975 AD)*.

Pant, M.R. and P.H. Pierce. 1989. *Administrative Documents of the Shah Dynasty Concerning Mustang and Its Periphery (1789–1844 AD)*. Bonn: VGH Wissenschaftsverlag.

Ramble, C. 1984. The Lamas of Lubra: Tibetan Bonpo Householder Priests in Western Nepal. D.Phil. thesis, University of Oxford.

Ramble, C. 2008. *The Navel of the Demoness: Tibetan Buddhism and Civil Religion in Highland Nepal*. New York: Oxford University Press.

Ramble, C. 2020. Longing for retirement: the will of Chos mdzad nyi shar, the last Ya ngal. *In* J. Bischoff, P. Maurer and C. Ramble (eds) *On a Day of a Month of the Fire Bird Year: Festschrift for Peter Schwieger on the Occasion of his 65th Birthday*. Lumbini: Lumbini International Research Institute, 635–49.

Ramble, C. 2013. Hidden Himalayan transcripts: strategies of social opposition in Mustang (Nepal), 19th–20th centuries. *In* C. Ramble, P. Schwieger and A. Travers (eds) *Tibetans who Escaped the Historian's Net: Studies in the Social History of Tibetan-speaking Regions*. Kathmandu: Vajra Books, 231–51.

Ramble, C. 2014. The contractor, the duke, the prime minister and the villagers: exploitation and resistance in nineteenth-century rural Nepal. *In* T. Lewis and B.M. Owens (eds) *Sucāruvādadeśika: A Festschrift Honoring Professor Theodore Riccardi*. Kathmandu: Himal Books.

Ramble, C. and M. Vinding. 1987. The *'Bem-chag* village record and the early history of Mustang District. *Kailash* 13(1–2), 5–48.

Regmi, M.C. 1976. *Landownership in Nepal*. Berkeley: University of California Press.

Regmi, M.C. 1978a. *Land Tenure and Taxation in Nepal* (second edition). Kathmandu: Ratna Pustak Bhandar.

Regmi, M.C. 1978b. *Thatched Huts and Stucco Palaces: Peasants and Landlords in Nineteenth-Century Nepal*. New Delhi: Vikas.

Rosser, C. 1966. Social mobility in the Newar caste system. *In* C. von Fürer-Haimendorf (ed.) *Caste and Kin in Nepal, India and Ceylon: Anthropological Studies in Hindu-Buddhist Contact Zones*. New York: Asia Publishing House, 68–139.

Toffin, G. 2007. *Newar Society: City, Village and Periphery*. Kathmandu: Social Science Baha/Himal Books.

Turner, R.L. 1931. *A Comparative and Etymological Dictionary of the Nepali Language*. London: Routledge and Kegan Paul.

Tibetan Sources 2

Ramble, C., in collaboration with Nyima Drandul. 2016. *Tibetan Sources for a Social History of Mustang, Nepal. Volume 2: the Archives of the Tantric Lamas of Tshognam*. Andiast: International Institute for Tibetan and Buddhist Studies.

Tibetan Sources 3

Ramble, C., in collaboration with Nyima Drandul. 2019. *Tibetan Sources for a Social History of Mustang, Nepal. Volume 3: the Archive of Künzang Chöling Convent*. Andiast: International Institute for Tibetan and Buddhist Studies.

Index

Figures in bold: definition of the term to be found in the lexicon at the end of Saadet Arslan's chapter.
Terms followed by *: other occurrences are too numerous to be included.